D0082060

At the Point of Production

At the Point of Production

THE LOCAL HISTORY OF THE I.W.W.

Edited by
JOSEPH R. CONLIN

CONTRIBUTIONS IN LABOR HISTORY, NUMBER 10

GP

GREENWOOD PRESS
Westport, Connecticut • *London, England*

Library of Congress Cataloging in Publication Data
Main entry under title:

At the point of production.

   (Contributions in labor history ; no. 10
ISSN 0146-3608)
   Bibliography: p.
   Includes index.
   1.   Industrial Workers of the World--History--Case
studies.   2.   Strikes and lockouts--United States--
History--Case studies.   I.   Conlin, Joseph Robert.
II.   Series.
HD8055.I4A86   331.88'6'09   80-1708
ISBN 0-313-22046-8 (lib. bdg.)

Copyright © 1981 by Joseph R. Conlin

All rights reserved. No portion of this book may be
reproduced, by any process or technique, without the
express written consent of the publisher.

Library of Congress Catalog Card Number: 80-1708
ISBN: 0-313-22046-8
ISSN: 0146-3608

First published in 1981

Greenwood Press
A division of Congressional Information Service, Inc.
88 Post Road West, Westport, Connecticut 06881

Printed in the United States of America

10 9 8 7 6 5 4 3 2 1

CONTENTS

PART THREE

THE I.W.W. AFTER THE FALL

PART FOUR

BIBLIOGRAPHY

PREFACE

This book will be most useful for readers having some familiarity with the subject, the Industrial Workers of the World. It is a collection of specialized studies of the I.W.W., published with the purpose of stimulating further research into the local history of the Wobblies. If the contributors and I are lucky, the reader whose eye has just been caught by the I.W.W. will return here. In the meantime, there are many proper histories of the subject to which the new student may turn. Discussed in some detail in the historiographical introduction below, they are Paul F. Brissenden's classic, *The I.W.W.: A Study of American Syndicalism* (1919); Fred Thompson's "official history," *The I.W.W.: Its First Seventy Years* (with Patrick Murfin, 1975); Joyce Kornbluh's diverting as well as informative *Rebel Voices: An I.W.W. Anthology* (1964); Philip S. Foner's thorough *The I.W.W., 1905-1917* (1965); Patrick Renshaw's popular *The Wobblies: The Story of American Syndicalism* (1967); and the regnant standard history, Melvyn Dubofsky's *We Shall Be All* (1969).

Because this book is intended for scholars and students already familiar with the rudiments of I.W.W. history, I have dispensed with a narrative account of Wobbly doings that might otherwise appear here. However, another convention of prefaces—acknowledgments—cannot be omitted so easily. The editor is grateful to the contributors for their helpful cooperation in assembling the volume and, most of all, to a noncontributor who has in a way donated his assistance to every effort in the writing of Wobbly history since he did his own account in 1955. Fred Thompson is well known to every historian interested in the I.W.W., whether in his voluble and hospitable person or through his voluminous letters in response to, no doubt, often stupid questions. Thompson was instrumental in transferring the I.W.W.'s records to the Labor History Archives at Wayne State University in Detroit. He and the files in his head, however, remain the single greatest repository of Wobbly lore and interpretation from which he graciously draws for the benefit of every investigator who approaches him. He is not so gentle a critic as he is generous an advisor. His running commentary on historians of the I.W.W. in the pages of the *Industrial Worker* comprises an astute analysis of I.W.W. historiography that, if indulgent in the interests of research into the I.W.W., is often scathing and, if you are the object of comment, chastising.

But scathing or pleased, Fred Thompson never ceases to be open to the next question. "Fellow worker" or no, he is remarkable. His comments during the preparation of this book were only the most recent of his assistances to the editor; and the volume, for what he thinks it is worth, is dedicated to him.

At the Point of Production

INTRODUCTION

JOSEPH R. CONLIN

In graduate school in 1962, fishing about for a dissertation topic, I suggested to a number of cronies and advisors that I might venture a reinterpretive study of the Industrial Workers of the World. If not quite rich, the sources looked adequate; I had some ideas about how to use them; and, best of all, in graduate school jargon, "nothing had been done" on the subject since 1919. That was a geological epoch by the tempo of revisionism that measures the pace of historical writing in the United States. As a group, rather oddly, historians show little appreciation for their predecessors. The "need" to redo a book comes under discussion the week it is published. Implicitly, there is no such thing as a classic. There is something self-serving in this attitude, some makework job justification that one is more likely to associate with assistants to assistants. But there is also a principle of some merit here: the historian's frame of reference has as much to do with the history he produces as do the materials he works with; a history tells as much about the milieu in which it was written, as about the period of its topic. Conversely, in order to appreciate a history fully, it is necessary to know about that milieu.

Such a concept is the premise of this introduction, which is a survey of the histories and the historians of the I.W.W. It also relates to my bright idea of the early 1960s in that, despite the force of the revisionist temper among my colleagues, I was almost unanimously advised to scrap the project. There was such a thing as a classic, after all. Nothing *could be done* on the subject of the Wobblies beyond what had already been done in 1919, Paul F. Brissenden's *The I. W. W.: A Study of American Syndicalism*.

This advice was incorrect. The present volume, which, after some reflection, calls for *more* research into the history of the I.W.W., is being published almost twenty years after the counsel to forget the Wobblies was given with a minor flood of books and essays about the I.W.W. intervening. At the time I began my own researches, at least Joyce Kornbluh, Philip S. Foner, Patrick Renshaw, Robert Tyler, and Melvyn Dubofsky would seem to have had histories of the I.W.W. in preparation, and the total number of historians who have since contributed to the Wobbly bibliography fills a good many pages at the end of this volume. If not every item in the literature can be called "essential," the quality of the whole is remarkably good. There is far less junk in the pile than there is in the bins of other boom themes in history-book publishing of the 1960s and 1970s. There were (and are) things to be learned about the I.W.W.

But the significance of that consensus of a leading graduate school of history in the early 1960s is not in that it happened to be off the mark. The significance, it seems to me, after reading *A Study of American Syndicalism* for the purposes of the present volume, is that its testimonial to Brissenden's achievement was entirely warranted. An economist actually, Brissenden succeeded in writing a comprehensive, "definitive" history of a phenomenon that was, at the time the book was published, still "news." Not only news, the I.W.W. was in 1919 in the midst of the warmest controversies of the day: labor unrest, revolutionary challenge to the established order, and the rights of dissenters in American society.

The great strikes of 1919 were seething when Brissenden published his *Study*. It was the year of the founding of the American Communist parties. The Palmer Raids held national attention. Indeed, Brissenden wrote and proofed the book during the time of the federal government's raids on the I.W.W., the hysterical reign of lynch law against the Wobblies, and the infamous Espionage and Sedition Act trials. And yet, for all of that, Brissenden composed a dispassionate, "objective" analysis of his subject. Of course, this is what "social scientists" are supposed to do. But one needs to search very little to realize how rarely the ideal is attained, no further back than to the 1960s and early 1970s, when American intellectuals trundled fish-eyed and feverish behind every crusader's banner unfurled on the local quad, in order to appreciate Brissenden's dispassion. The spirit of 1919 was no less agitated than that of the age of the New Left and counterculture. But where, with the far vaster academic community of the 1960s, is the calm contemporary history of those latter movements?

A major reason for Brissenden's accomplishment lies in an aspect of his scholarship with which more recent labor historians are most likely to take exception. He was an "institutional" labor historian, of the order of John Rogers Commons and Selig Perlman, although not immediately associated with them. To say that a certain work of labor history is "institutional" means many things. Among them, it means in this case that Brissenden conceptualized the I.W.W. as an institutional structure created in response to an institutional weakness in a basically functioning society. The particulars of industrial and capitalist evolution in the late nineteenth century had caused a maladjustment in the economic position of labor that existing devices, including the more-or-less-established unions of the American Federation, were unable to accommodate. The I.W.W. was an attempt to do so, and whatever else such abstraction of a social phenomenon meant, it meant to the institutionalist like Brissenden that it was to be scrutinized under a cool light away from the tremblors and flames.

Such institutional history is essentially conservative, and Brissenden personally did not look forward to the day when the I.W.W. would establish its industrial democracy. But simply by virtue of being dispassionate amidst the furor of the era, Brissenden could appear to be sympathetic to the I.W.W., something that has been appreciated by Wobbly readers of his book from Big Bill Haywood to Fred Thompson. There is nothing like victimization to keen up gratitude for a square deal, and Brissenden insisted on treating the movement as a legitimate, institutional force while more than a few of his scholarly colleagues were calling for blood. Viewing the I.W.W. in institutional terms also enabled Brissenden to foresee the development of successful legatees of the I.W.W., the nonrevolutionary industrial unions of the Congress of Industrial Organizations, which writers with hindsight have in fact put in the Wobblies' debt.

Of course, Brissenden's kind of history if incomplete. It does not satisfy the sort of questions labor historians ask today. The vantage of the institutionalist is from the top and center and particularly from the inside. *An* institution has *a* character, ideology, and set of policies. Because *it* evolves and interacts with other institutions, Brissenden graphs systematically and thoroughly the ideologies that "resulted" in the founding convention of 1905 and, with equal attention to detail, brick by brick, the organizations that either merged to form the I.W.W. or foreshadowed it in one policy or another. The early chapters of his book treat methodically each "contributor" to the new institution. With the character of the organization clearly defined, the book moves on to trace structural changes, development of policy, interaction with other institutions—all in terms, however, of the I.W.W.'s central office and official pronouncements.

It is a very tidy kind of history. Its narrative is seamless but also compartmentalized, easily outlined and divisible into brief sections headed by accurate subtitles and little roman numerals. Its sources are "documents" in the strictest sense of the term: manifestos, charters, constitutions, resolutions, executive orders, minutes of meetings, and the reflections and "findings" of other intersecting institutions: committees, commissions, the media, agencies. It is interesting to note that "Father Hagerty's Wheel of Fortune," a grandiose scheme of organization adopted at the founding convention when the number of committed Wobblies scarcely exceeded 1,000, holds a particular fascination for Brissenden. The "Wheel" was

ridiculed in its own time. It never had much to do with the realities of
I.W.W. development. It was, in fact, modified to the point of abandon-
ment from the start. But it figures prominently in Brissenden's disquisitions
and is reproduced in the volume in a foldout. It was eminently "institutional."

But people figure in this sort of history only when they are leaders, the
writers of the documents, or the occasions of them. Labor is "labor," not
laboring people. The members of the I.W.W., the actual Wobblies, appear
only as aggregate numbers attesting the significance or insignificance of an
institution or the effectiveness of a strike. The notion that historical force is
exerted in a noninstitutional way, outside the meeting hall or editorial
room, is foreign to this methodology.

For all these inadequacies, it bears reemphasis that Brissenden's clear-
cut reconstruction of the I.W.W. origins and evolution provide an unim-
provable outline for understanding the history of the union. In his *Decline
of the I.W.W.* (1932), John S. Gambs picked up the Wobbly narrative
where Brissenden left it and adopted the methodology and organization of
the *Study* without modification. The historians of the 1960s, while introducing many other elements to I.W.W. history, had first to come to terms
with the original definitions and categories. Brissenden could not know
what themes would be peculiarly interesting to later decades, but he knew
what a fundamental was. No one could (or can) study the I.W.W. without
closely examining his book. That cannot necessarily be said to the historian
who is addressing a problem previously treated by Commons and his
associates.

Brissenden was an indefatigable researcher faced with a manageable
body of sources. If his view of what made for a "document" was traditional, he ransacked every one of those within his purview. Only some of
the Wobbly files seized by the justice department in 1917 escaped his
scrutiny. Because these were destroyed during the 1920s, it was perfectly
reasonable for scholars familiar with the situation (and committed to
Brissenden's definition of a document) to consider the subject closed, even
in the 1960s.

There is a more general explanation of why, after Brissenden's book, the
I.W.W. was struck from the historians' list of "things to be done." Historical interest in labor and radical subjects generally flagged in the 1920s, as
did the nation's. When the historians' concern with such matters revived
during the Great Depression, other seemingly more pertinent organizations
and movements had their eye. Today, it is common lecture-hall wisdom to
point out that the images of the Roaring Twenties, Coolidge Prosperity,
and smug satisfaction with the established order tell about only a small
part of American society during the 1920s. Labor and social historians

especially have contributed to a history of the precrash decade that is not so affluent and flapperish as the pictures drawn by imperfect memories and the popular media. But the section of the population that did lead a life and share in values approximated by the vision of a complacent 1920s, the urban middle classes, included the academic community.

The Genteel Tradition, in retreat in letters by the 1920s, was still solidly ensconced in the universities, as it had been during the 1910s, and would remain, despite a misleading political drift, through the 1930s and 1940s. The professoriat was drawn almost to the man from comfortable and decidedly unalienated "old stock" for whom the profession was a traditional monopoly. Such a community of scholars could be attracted to "social" themes when, as in the Progressive Era and depression decade, the spirit of the age drifted in that direction. But when the middle classes lost interest in a declining labor movement and an inconspicuous, virtually underground radical movement, so did the historians among them.

Not much labor history was written during the 1920s. Even the small presses of the anticapitalist parties neglected "American topics." The Communists looked abroad for inspiration. The Socialists had not yet accepted the fact that their history was already just heritage. As for the Wobblies, reflection on their own past was too painful. Their history—all of it recent—was a series of traumas and setbacks, not the sort of thing on which an individual or an organization is likely to dwell.

The only book of the 1920s that needs historiographical notice is *Bill Haywood's Book: The Autobiography of William D. Haywood*, published shortly after his death in Moscow in 1927. The book was an object of controversy from the beginning. Recrimination, rather, for the essence of the squabble was not the writ but the person of the author. Despite near silence in his last years, Haywood's person still hung heavily on the mind of the American Left. For the Wobblies, there was no doubt about the meaning of Haywood's defection to the Soviet Union. It had been a major setback, a mortal blow to their morale, because it had been Haywood who had devised and been chief exponent of the strategy of legal acquiescence in the government's prosecutions of the union. Moreover, Haywood had been the outside world's personification of the I.W.W. by the time of the world war.

However, as the lines between proworkers' state Communists and disillusioned anti-Communist leftists hardened during the 1920s, with the I.W.W. bitterly within the second camp, the word circulated among the anti-Communists that Big Bill had himself soured on the Soviet way and was detained in Moscow against his will. This rumor meant that he was no longer a traitor at all but another victim of the Bolshevik conspiracy. The Communists scoffed at such tales and pointed to the fact that Haywood was still active in the Comintern-sponsored International Labor Defense and appeared regularly at official Red functions. Like other exiles in Russia, Haywood was to them a symbol of capitalist oppression and a witness to the revolutionary centrality of the Soviet Union.

About one thing alone there is no doubt: whichever side he was on during his last years, Haywood was not a happy warrior. He was homesick—he manifested that to many visitors. He was chronically ill with diabetes and other afflictions. Whatever he had expected when he went to Russia, there was nothing for him to do once the shouting was over and the building begun, except to be hung out as platform bunting at ceremonials. In terms of evidence for where his sympathies lay, the Communists have what little there is of it. There is no documentation to support the anti-Communists' claim that he had turned against sovietism or that, as some variations had it, he had written a recantation and scathing denunciation of the Russians in his book, which functionaries in Moscow and at the New York offices of International Publishers expurgated before publication, effectively transforming *Bill Haywood's Book* into a novel.

It is not difficult to understand that the Wobblies should have looked in Haywood's book for a signal from "the old Big Bill" that they had been right—communism was a snare. They wanted to reclaim the one who had headed their movement during its best days. As for the other anti-Communists who denounced the book as spurious—Socialists, liberals, and rightist Red baiters alike—they were willing to take their corroboration where they could find it, and Haywood was and has remained an attractive figure despite his malefactions. He is one of those characters who are claimed by all sides. (The most preposterous claim is surely Ben Gitlow's in *The Whole of Their Lives*; Gitlow made Haywood a flag-waving patriot.)

But the sum of what the anti-Communists supported their contention with was the dearth of information about Haywood's Russian years in his book and that it was eminently plausible that Haywood should have found mature soviet communism stifling, even intolerable. A lack of hard evidence has never discouraged believers. It is more interesting, perhaps, that the line has been perpetuated by many historians, well into the 1970s. They also have written off *Bill Haywood's Book* as largely ghostwritten or thoroughly renovated.

The frequent repetition of this judgment has always been a little mystifying to me. Many who have tacked it on to a footnote have simply been copying papers, an ancient historical method. But to make the statement is also to accept one side in a controversy as gospel and repetition as corroboration, a not-so-acceptable technique (if equally ancient). The durability of the line, without much questioning, must reflect the longevity of bitterness toward the Communist party in the American intellectual community, an especially powerful emotion among anti-Communist leftists, a workable description of most historians of the Wobblies. So deeply have they rued the consequences of American Communist party policies and actions for the democratic radical tradition in the United States that they have developed a "taint" reflex: everything touched by the party is necessarily corrupted.

The most interesting side of the tradition from an historiographical point of view is that virtually every historian who has maintained it has drawn from *Bill Haywood's Book* as sole source in other parts of his work. The taint seems to extend only to those statements in Haywood's autobiography that contradict congenial themes.

It could hardly be otherwise—that historians should draw on *Bill Haywood's Book*—unless Haywood is to become an historical figure on the order of Father Hagerty, drifting willy-nilly from obscurity to the center of events, and then fading away again. Haywood's book is not in fact the only source of information about his career. He read an autobiographical sketch into the proceedings of the Industrial Relations Commission, another at the sedition trial in Chicago, and he often regaled latter-day associates with tales of Silver City and the Western Federation that they subsequently wrote down. But the point is that the stuff of *Bill Haywood's Book* accords neatly with these other relations. The style of the book is the same as Haywood's earlier writings: straightforward, measured, unstyled. There is no evidence in either syntax or content to imply that the published autobiography was not Haywood's work.

Finally, the taint argument is perplexing in that Haywood's book can in no manner be construed as a tract that might serve Communist purposes, at least not a very good one. All but the tail of it is about Haywood's life before 1919 when the American Communist parties were founded and Big Bill's career was effectively over. And the story does not lead internally and inexorably toward the moment when Haywood, after a lifetime searching for same, stands agog in the presence of V. I. Lenin. Haywood gets himself there all right, but the preceding narrative is random and nonsequential. It is far from "scientific" in the preferred Communist mode of the day. It is not even linear. The book is not soviet-justifying; it is self-justifying, as autobiographies have been known to be. It is a frequently unsatisfying document, another trait of the genre, and the omission of Haywood's Russian years is suspicious, although explainable in a number of ways. It was the work of a tired, ill, and unhappy man, prematurely old and useless, looking back on better days. And, heaven knows, there are editors! But the reasons for writing it off as fiction are found in the predilections of the historians who do so and nowhere in the text or other reliable source.

In the 1930s and 1940s, American historians were once again drawn to questions of labor and radicalism. However, as in the 1960s, the intellectual imagination of the era was intensely involved in the problems of the day, affixed by what was "relevant." The Wobblies were not. Although the discontent engendered by economic collapse led to new I.W.W. initiatives and actions, it was the Communist party that was now the center of leftist protest, and, in the labor movement, it was the CIO's industrial organizing campaign first within and then outside the American Federation. The I.W.W. was a sideshow or less, an unfrequented little popcorn stand in a corner of the grounds.

Even the Communist writers no longer felt the need to cozen groups like the Wobblies with disquisitions relating them to "the party." Until the Popular Front period, they were inclined to emphasize the glories of soviet success as their justification and not the CPUSA's indigenous roots. When they did trace the American background of the party's history, the Communists wrote in the manner of the Augustinian historians of the Middle Ages. Groups like the Wobblies and the Socialist party and so on, like the Mosaic dispensation, were "good things" in their time as part of the plan to prepare the way for the full gospel. But, with the promulgation of that faith, they were obsolete or even, when they persisted in obstructing palpably ordained historical evolution, damnable.

This conceptualization of the Wobblies characterized Communist ideological, historical, and personal writings during the Red Decade and for some time thereafter. The Wobblies figured in them only incidentally. (The Socialist party was a far more formidable infidelity.) But James P. Cannon, albeit himself no longer a CPUSA member in good standing at the time, wrote a thorough analysis of the I.W.W. in this vein in 1955, entitled, in fact, "The Great Anticipation."

Only in later years, when old Communist war-horses like Elizabeth Gurley Flynn wrote their memoirs, did this half-interested view of the I.W.W. undergo a change. Flynn and others (including non-Communists like Ralph Chaplin) mused on the I.W.W. with a great deal of nostalgia. There is a flavor of the "good old days" in the recollections that were written in the late 1940s and 1950s, a taste of the "when we were young and gay" that would have been impossible in the passionate 1930s. If not the real thing, the I.W.W. was bold, unafraid, heroic, aggressive, and ready to take on the bosses and strike a blow whatever the odds and counsel of common sense and Marxist science.

In part, this good-natured appreciation of the revolutionism of their youth was due to the superannuation of former activists at the time they wrote out their recollections. In part, it was because by the late 1940s there was not much "present" that might have preoccupied the American Left. But the new twist also reflected how even participants in the Wobbly struggles were affected by the creative literature of the intervening years.

If historians and social scientists lost interest in the I.W.W., the writers of fiction never did. If not quite a central theme in American letters, the

I.W.W. was featured regularly in novels, plays, and poetry of the 1920s and 1930s, some of which were widely read and influential. It would not be excessive to say that the novelists, singers, and poets kept the popular memory of the Wobblies alive. Brissenden's book was still on the library shelves and known to historians. But when a scholar found cause to mention the Wobblies in the 1940s (or even later)—in a few throwaway lines in a textbook, for instance—he was as likely to misidentify them as "the *International* Workers of the World," a curious grammatical redundancy as well as a rather simple factual error. The historians were not only failing to read Brissenden, they were not taking a very good look at his title page.

It would be a task beyond the scope of this essay to compile a complete list of novels, plays, and poems that mentioned the I.W.W. during these years. The organization suddenly appears at least as a symbol or point of reference in the most unlikely minor creations. John Dos Passos's *1919* (1930) is a novel of importance in which the I.W.W. figures significantly. Eugene O'Neill's *Hairy Ape* (1921) comes to mind as the most significant drama. And the use made of old Wobbly songs (and retrospectives like *I Dreamed I Saw Joe Hill Last Night*) on C.I.O. organizing drives illustrates the Wobbly presence in quasipopular music.

In these and in the host of lesser-known works in which the I.W.W. figures, the message is much the same: the I.W.W. was once a hope for the wretchedly oppressed, a way to fight in a far-off, less complicated time for the weak and forgotten in society and for the alienated and misunderstood. Every element of nostalgia appears to be there: times were simpler then; *we* —for these fictional accounts of the I.W.W. are generally sympathetic— had more vitality than we do now; the end was tragic, the attempt of the oppressed for justice beaten down by the ruling powers. James Jones summed it up in his influential novel of 1951, *From Here to Eternity*, when he has an old-timer telling a young companion struggling personally like himself to stay off the skids: "You don't remember the Wobblies, you were too young or not even born yet. There has never been anything like them before or since. They called themselves materialist-economists, but what they really were was a religion. They were workstiffs and bindlebums like you and me, but they were welded together by a vision we don't possess." So does Wallace Stegner in writing a rather different kind of book, a fictionalized biography of Wobbly martyr Joe Hill. "The I.W.W. was a fighting faith," Stegner wrote, introducing *The Preacher and the Slave* in 1950: "No thoroughly adequate history of the I.W.W. exists. The standard histories are factual and doctrinal summaries, valuable for the record of the I.W.W.'s organization and activities . . . but lacking in the kind of poetic understanding which should invest any history of a militant church."

In such hands (although Stegner was decidedly unsympathetic to the Hill legend), a "militant church" is what the I.W.W. became. In a way, the writers were merely carrying on a literary conceit that began contemporaneously with the I.W.W. (and, with different objects of admiration, dates back to Byron at Missolonghi), the fascination with the vitality of those on the bottom. Mable Dodge and other fashionable literati had introduced Big Bill Haywood and other Wobblies into their Fifth Avenue salons, and writers of the 1910s had also put a romanticized I.W.W. into their books and poems.

Nor was the romantic image of the Wobblies ever entirely inappropriate, a fantasy projected on a different reality. Haywood and the others accepted the invitations readily enough. Beginning no later than 1908, the Wobblies were vividly conscious of their romantic aspect and took easily to self-dramatization. In 1908, for the decidedly unromantic purpose of purging the little union of Daniel DeLeon, a group of Portland and Washington state Wobblies trekked to the national convention in Chicago via freight train. They funded their journey by staging programs of sarcastic songs and playlets—most of them parodies of the Salvation Army—at rest stops on their way, and by selling a little leaflet containing the sardonic lyrics they sang, the predecessor of the famous "Little Red Songbook." In the "free speech fights" that began in Missoula, Montana, and Spokane, Washington, the following year, the I.W.W. devised a number of theatrical tactics for defeating their unimaginative foes and winning attention: packing the jails, reading the Declaration of Independence from interdicted soapboxes, roaring out songs loudly through the night from the prisons of the West Coast towns that had taken them on.

Although such antics hardly appealed to everyone, the Wobblies developed a hang-the-consequences sense of humor about their "revolution" when it was still going on that—if it touched on self-righteousness—was also a vital force. Contemporary sociologist Carlton Parker and others noticed that the Wobblies considered their defiance of conventions as an index of their radicalism. It also caught the eye of journalists and others who saw the "eccentricity" as a manifestation of human vitality.

These were western Wobblies, a group comprised largely of casual workers in the woods, sawmills, construction camps, and agricultural regions of the extractive and still-developing West. This workforce was male, usually unattached to family or place, footloose and adventurous. To the settled population among whom they moved they were vaguely dangerous and unequivocally "undesirable" hoboes and bums. To themselves, however, and to observers inclined to be looking for such a symbol, they were the last frontiersmen. Although they did not have the use of the word, these western Wobblies and their literary celebrators defined them as "alienated," a trait calculated to serve the I.W.W.'s posterity in the literature of later decades.

The easternWobblies were also rather out of the ordinary for a labor union. In the East, the I.W.W. was the medium or at least the focal point of immigrant discontent and ethnic solidarity, again the union of the excluded and despised. However briefly, the I.W.W. succeeded in forging an alliance of these alienated peoples, and the I.W.W. knew how to make the most of its material and the appetite of the news media for the unusual and colorful. In Lawrence, Massachusetts, in 1912, the union organized an exodus of workers' children from the city. It was economically a shrewd device in that it relieved badly strained strike funds. In addition, the Wobblies made it clear that they feared for the safety of the children given the proved irresponsibility of police and soldiers. Even without the ready cooperation in the drama of the authorities—the police attacked the first parade of mostly women and children at the depot—the tableau of hundreds of sad marchers, forced to separate by employer avarice, was brilliantly calculated to attract sympathy to the strikers' cause.

The most explicitly theatrical project of the Wobblies was the "Paterson Pageant," a huge panoply acted out by actual strikers at Madison Square Garden in 1913. Partially endowed by Mable Dodge and other wealthy sympathizers, and produced by the ebullient John Reed, the pageant was seen by the Wobbly leadership as a blunder even before it was actually staged. It distracted the strikers (and the leadership) from their real business "at the point of production," dissipated resources, and led to bickering and resentment among leaders and rank and file. The pageant was a turning point in the I.W.W.'s attitude toward dramatic gesture. Along with the official repudiation a short time later of the free speech fight tactic, the I.W.W. turned to more proper union activity. But it was the memory of the fights and the pageant that lived on for the writers who, during the next generation, almost alone remembered the I.W.W. If the Wobblies had planned for nothing but a posterity, they could not have done better than what, with the collaboration of their enemies, they did. The movement was spontaneously colorful. Its brutal treatment at the hands of mobs and government provided the martyrs. And, in 1917 and 1918, the cause was lost in an apocalypse.

This wealth of lore was collected in 1964 in *Rebel Voices: An I.W.W. Anthology*. The author, Joyce Kornbluh, assembled I.W.W. writings, graphics, songs, and poetry into a handsomely produced full quarto volume that was the first widely distributed book on the I.W.W. since Brissenden's *Study*. Kornbluh was not concerned primarily with the dry-as-dust matters of ideology, component organizations, and factionalization that had engrossed Brissenden so. It was the legacy, particularly the cultural legacy, of the remarkable movement that chiefly interested her. The emphasis is heavily on the more vivacious western Wobblies, six of ten chapters devoted to that group compared to two on eastern strikes and four dealing with general matters. Carl Keller, secretary-treasurer of the I.W.W. at the time, chided Kornbluh's "Big Volume of I.W.W. Literature" for taking seriously such artifacts as "hobo hieroglyphics," a code of esoteric symbols to be written on water tanks and gateposts that Keller called "a publicity gimmick of the 'Hobo King' never taken seriously by even the youngest kid on the road, to say nothing of "Wobblies."

But *Rebel Voices* was more than a pleasant retrospective on Wobbly folklore. The author had been a labor-union activist in Detroit. She appreciated the humdrum workaday toil that necessarily underlay the Wobblies' color in a way that was lost on the novelists and poets. So, although relying heavily on Brissenden and Gambs, *Rebel Voices* includes serious analyses of ideology, policy, structure, and tactics, as well as the cartoons and quips. Kornbluh took the union seriously as an expression of working-class discontent and not merely as a fount of verse. She pointed to the I.W.W.'s legacy to the Congress of Industrial Organizations and, in certain tactics, to the Civil Rights Movement of the 1960s. In this, *Rebel Voices* was the first book in the thoroughgoing revision of I.W.W. history in that decade.

Before considering the further historiography of the 1960s, however, it is necessary to return briefly to a small book published in 1955 which, if not widely known, was also a guide to the historians of the 1960s. *The I.W.W.: Its First Fifty Years* was an official publication of the I.W.W. which, in good "We have no leaders" Wobbly style, listed Fred Thompson only as its "compiler."

Thompson was a lifelong Wobbly. Born in Canada in 1900, he joined the OBU (the One Big Union, the Canadian I.W.W. in effect) at the age of twenty. When he went to work in Washington state in 1922, he transferred to the American organization and, about a year later, was arrested in Marysville, California, and convicted of violating the state's Criminal Syndicalism Law. He spent four years in jail and resumed organizing for the I.W.W. when he was released.

In the 1940s, Thompson was the secretary of the Cleveland Metal and Machinery Workers Industrial Union, the I.W.W.'s last effective bargaining jurisdiction. This personal experience of a functioning, effective union local as late as the Eisenhower era is imprinted on Thompson's work. It is not merely the work-in-progress optimism of his book's title, *Its First Fifty Years*. Thompson alluded throughout the book, and in his running commentaries on I.W.W. history in the Wobbly weekly (now monthly) *Industrial Worker*, to the I.W.W.'s ongoing relevance to workers' needs. He was not oblivious to the I.W.W.'s heritage of bombast and color, but he did not emphasize it, preferring to chart the I.W.W.'s tangible bread-and-butter successes, and, when he looked at the historical writings of others, he liked best the approaches that saw the I.W.W. as "a rational response to the industrial situation, and not the bugaboo that myths and journalists have made it."

While of minor value to students of the I.W.W. today because of the many more exhaustive books that have succeeded it, *Its First Fifty Years* is still unique in that Thompson neither ended with 1919 nor, chronologically speaking, devoted disproportionate attention to the eleven years of the fifty during which the I.W.W. was a significant force in American society. (A little more than half of the book is devoted to the years before the wartime persecutions but, given the overall salience of background, ideology, and the settlements of the early factional disputes, it is not excessive.) As a result, the book remains a first source for Wobbly history in the 1920s and 1930s and a good reminder that if minor, the I.W.W. continued to regard itself as a fighting union.

None of the union's subsequent historians took Thompson's cue. Patrick Renshaw sums up the I.W.W.'s latter-day history. Robert Tyler's sectional account tails off in the early 1920s. Philip S. Foner's volume on the I.W.W. terminates with 1917 (although, as volume four of his general American labor history, it may be considered a chapter of a work still in progress). Melvyn Dubofsky's *We Shall Be All* ends with the rapid disintegration of the I.W.W. after 1924. The author's *Bread and Roses Too* treats only the I.W.W.'s prewar period.

Thompson did not revise his text when, in 1976, the book was reissued as "*Its First Seventy Years.*" A chapter by Patrick Murfin on the two subsequent decades related Wobbly work as an "educational organization," especially among students, and mentions that the union actually served as bargaining agent in some marginal small businesses, mainly around Chicago.

The book required no retooling. It is as much document as history—Thompson had participated in many of the events he chronicled—and it is a remarkably "candid account" and no bubbly "history of the lodge." Unlike autobiographies and official histories generally, *Its First Fifty Years* is frank and incisive in dealing with I.W.W. failures (if not with *the* failure). An introduction to the second edition notes that in conversation Thompson is fond of quoting the French communard Lissagary to the effect that to omit what is embarrassing is like giving sailors a chart that leaves out the shoals. More striking, Thompson does not fall back on the "easy excuse" of repression as the explanation of every aspect of the I.W.W.'s demise.

Needless to say, Thompson's book was not widely circulated. The credit for reaching a broad readership with a reminder of the union's place in American history was Kornbluh's and that of a popular account of 1967, Patrick Renshaw's *The Wobblies: The Story of American Syndicalism*. Renshaw was a journalist for the English *Oxford Times* at the time the book was published. He had the journalist's eye for "the story" and this characterized his book. *The Wobblies* followed the high points of I.W.W. history, the dramatic strikes and free speech fights, the martyrs, the great trials. Renshaw did not add appreciably to the reinterpretation of the I.W.W. then under way except, perhaps, by an international perspective that included new information about English Wobblies.

The book was faulted for a number of factual errors. These were numerous and sometimes "simple," but also mostly minor, not distorting the composition of Renshaw's picture: crediting Vincent St. John with the cross-country trek of "the bummery," for example; placing Haywood at the 1908 convention; attributing Big Bill with an extra daughter; incorrectly dating quotations; and so on. It was in the telling of the tale that *The Wobblies* was concerned, and in this and the book's wide circulation was its chief contribution.

Renshaw also introduced the theme, fully developed only later, that the I.W.W. was not a crusading "hang-the-consequences" antiwar organization as has generally been assumed, an assumption which, because of the growing movement against the war in Vietnam in the 1960s, partly accounted for the revival of interest in the I.W.W. It would be difficult to find a history of the World War I period that defends the Wobbly trials, of course. But most accounts focus on the government's role in the affair, as indeed the initiative was Washington's. The trouble with this approach from the perspective of I.W.W. history is that it treats the Wobblies as entirely passive, objects merely acted on, and—oddly enough—the essence of the government's case as a given: the I.W.W. was opposed to the war and had a right to be. In citing, albeit skipping lightly over, several of Bill Haywood's attempts to accommodate the wartime hysteria, Renshaw opened the question of the I.W.W.'s attitude toward the war.

The narrative history of the I.W.W. was filled out more thoroughly for the Wobblies of the Pacific Northwest by Robert Tyler's *Rebels of the Woods* (1968). Tyler, a poet as well as a professional historian, appreciated the romantic dimension of the I.W.W. The Northwest was the region that produced "the bummery" and the technique of the free speech fight. But he did not sacrifice the firm, factual grounding of his subject for the sake of anecdote. It was also in the Northwest that the I.W.W. survived longest as a force to be reckoned with in labor relations, and it was the successful strike among loggers in 1917 that not only alarmed the federal government into pursuing the sedition trials, but led as well to Washington's most direct and thoroughgoing attack on a labor union of any period, the Spruce Division of the United States Army and the Loyal Legion of Loggers and Lumbermen, a government-sponsored cartel aimed at the I.W.W. down to the parody of its alliterative initials. Tyler's book is a thorough and reliable narrative of the I.W.W. in its most important venue.

The first comprehensive, interpretive history of the Wobblies since Brissenden was actually published several years before these two books, in 1965. Philip S. Foner's *The I.W.W., 1905-1917* was the fourth volume in

Foner's monumental *History of the Labor Movement in the United States*, itself an explicit effort to provide an alternative to the great Commons project.

Like all of his many books—no contemporary historian was so productive as Foner: he published several books on various subjects every year of his career—*The I. W. W.* is doggedly comprehensive and detailed. For example, Foner closely narrates the events of about a dozen of the Wobbly free speech fights, whereas every other account, including Melvyn Dubofsky's more voluminous *We Shall Be All*, centers on three or four.

Foner's books are also immediately identifiable as his from just a paragraph or two of text. He is a Marxist historian, to his critics a woefully simplistic one whose conception of class conflict is crude and mechanical. The bosses in his labor histories are simply villainous, so driven as "members of the employing class" as to be stereotypes. Their motive is profit alone. They are capable of subtlety and dissembling but not of submitting to impulses contradicting their economic interests. In their conflict with their workers, the employers are sometimes shrewd, especially in the arts of cooptation, but they submit to working-class demands only when forced to capitulate before superior power.

Working-class ferment is a constant in Foner's historiography. The almost exclusive interest of his long and prolific career has been revolution, rebellion, and resistance. His workers often are misguided by "false consciousness," fooled by capitalist deception, and betrayed by False Dmitris (especially reformist politicians and class-collaborationist trade union leaders). But the workers too are impelled by the force of class interest and involved in a more or less perpetual and explicit state of struggle with their overseers. In the end, because their struggle is inevitable and their historical role ordained, they can be thwarted only by repression of the most brutal kind.

Foner is not given to abstract speculation. He is an empiricist. He stakes his arguments on the evidence that he marshals in boggling quantities and presents them—fact one, fact two—like an aggressive lawyer. The breadth of his research has been acknowledged by his most scathing critics who, however, accuse him of evading or ignoring outright the contradictory data, distracting attention from them by starting hares in another direction, and pursuing those relentlessly to the ground. Foner has written, in fact, several close examinations of courtroom trials, and his defenses are in the style of: my client's dog bit this man only because it was kicked; there is no proof my client's dog bit this man; my client does not own a dog.

There is the shadow of the propagandist in Foner's histories and he makes no claims to detachment. He is a frank partisan of the oppressed in struggles between classes, races, colonists and colonizers, "progressive" thinkers and reactionary ones. This has provided a convenient excuse to ignore him to ostensibly "objective" historians who need "to see both sides of the question." The consequence has been far less recognition than simply the bulk of his work would seem to merit. While never Red-baited to the point of the academic shunning that was the lot of Communist party theoretician and historian Herbert Aptheker, Foner has been identified as peddling a Communist party "line" similar to Aptheker's, and he has been ignored, sometimes superciliously, on that basis.

The identification of Foner's history with old-fashioned CPUSA writ and policy owes less to his partisanship of the underdog (a sentiment shared by many of his critics) than to the fact that Foner extends taking sides to squabbles among radicals and labor-union strategists, unfailingly ending up on behalf of that argument which, injecting the party into it, would represent its position precisely. History lives for Foner. The struggle is perpetual, ongoing, and even static. There is a curious lack of historical process in his history in that every controversy endures, no matter how topical it seems. It remains to be settled, like the guilt or innocence of the Haymarket anarchists or Joe Hill. This quality informs his book on the I.W.W.

The I.W.W. appealed to Foner. The union was in many ways the perfect subject for him. It was the medium during its brief career for one seemingly hopeless, enervated, "unorganizable" group of workers after another: waiters, busboys, menial service workers, racially divided workers in the southern pineys, harvest hands, destitute immigrant factory workers, individualistic timber beasts, black longshoremen whose chaotic work place was made more difficult by the onus of race they bore. But the I.W.W. proved they could and did fight, bluntly frank about their revolutionary goal. Foner was no romantic, at least in the first connotation of the word. He preferred to examine closely the I.W.W.'s ideology, structure, polity, and praxis to dwelling on gay anecdotes.

Published soon after a full-length study titled *The Policies and Practices of the American Federation of Labor*, volume three in Foner's opus, *The I.W.W.* provided its author with further opportunity to examine (and excoriate) the deleterious consequences of the AFL's domination of the organized labor movement in America. Indeed, the systematic and devastating critique of the federation's structure and ideology, which the founders of the I.W.W. had compiled in the years before 1905, included the essentials of every subsequent attack on the AFL, Foner's included.

The I.W.W. was also a congenial subject for Foner because of the enemies the Wobblies made. The union fell afoul of the "reformist" wing of the Socialist Party of America, another bugbear in Foner's chronicles. And finally, few organizations in American history of any stripe have experienced repression so cynical as did the I.W.W. In addition to some of its tactics, which Foner criticizes, the I.W.W. is seriously faulted in this book only on its hard and fast commitment to "dual unionism," an issue on which it split bitterly from the Communists in the early 1920s. Foner's *The I.W.W.*, however, concludes with the dispersion of the union in the wake of World War I so that, except for allusions, he did not take up that controversy in the book.

The I.W.W. is not marred by Foner's commitment to justifying the conceits of the Communist party. One must dig for the links and "buzz words": making quite too much of Wobbly enthusiasm for the Russian revolution of 1905; emphasizing the European intellectual ("syndicalist") contribution to the I.W.W.'s "revolutionary industrial unionism" and the I.W.W.'s connections with the French *Confédération Générale du Travail* and, by extension, the international movement of the workers; downplaying the depth of the bitterness between the Wobblies and William Z. Foster's Syndicalist League of North America; and so on.

In the context of the whole, they are not important. In many ways, perhaps because of Foner's appreciation of the Wobblies' commitment to struggle, *The I.W.W.* is the best because it is the most positive volume in the incomplete *History of the Labor Movement.* The most important of its contributions to I.W.W. historiography is that Foner took the Wobblies seriously as a labor union. To Brissenden, the I.W.W. was too much an "institution" to be quite conveyed in workaday union form. To the numerous writers of the world war period, the I.W.W. was either a dangerous threat to the national community or, from the other side of the hysteria, an innocent victim, a persecuted waif around which to flock. In the literary tradition that congealed in the 1920s and 1930s, the I.W.W. became that colorful assemblage of singing vagabonds, endearing and inspiring but by no means having much to do with the world of pension funds, dues books, and the clack of typewriters on triplicate forms. Joyce Kornbluh appreciated the unionist essence of the I.W.W. but was chiefly interested in its lore. It was Foner's *The I.W.W.* that focused attention on what, after all, the I.W.W. considered itself.

Less salutary was Foner's emphasis on repression, a theme common in his writings. Of course, it would be a neat trick to tell the story of the I.W.W. without the repression. But to dwell on the martyrs and the debacle that did in the I.W.W. is to detract or at least to distract from the Wobblies' importance as a functioning and, at the time of the American intervention in the war, an apparently successful union. To focus on the I.W.W. as the victim of the government is almost to cast them as extras, just standing around upstage, important only because of what was done to them.

This was one of the images of the Wobblies I wanted to correct in *Bread and Roses Too*, published in 1969, a sequence of essays, each focusing on a problem of I.W.W. historiography. Several of my points coincided with Dubofsky's findings in *We Shall Be All*, albeit with differing emphases and modes of presentation. One that did not and the least successful of my "revisions" was the plea that those who wished to understand the I.W.W.

should drop the term "syndicalism" in referring to it on the grounds that the word was loaded with European connotations and even, to American ears, a vaguely sinister sound. The book pointed out that the I.W.W. disliked the term and that their "revolutionary industrial unionism" or "industrialism" not only had distinctively different origins than those of the syndicalists, but differed from the European ideology in several important particulars, particulars that were quite the essence of the I.W.W.'s history.

It was a futile little campaign, perhaps because it turned out to be the semantic exercise more than I thought. If syndicalism is defined very broadly as meaning the union is the agency of revolution and will become the postrevolutionary governing body, then syndicalist the Wobblies were. My purpose was to point attention toward the peculiarly American origins and character of the I.W.W., and this Melvyn Dubofsky did far more thoroughly and effectively while retaining a latitudinarian definition of the troublesome term.

Two themes of *Bread and Roses Too* that have fared better in the historiography were its emphasis on the nonviolence of the I.W.W. in both theory and practice and the neutral stance that the Haywood I.W.W. tried to maintain on the war issue. It is a reflection on the roles of singing vagabonds and victims in which the Wobblies had been cast that these two rather obvious points could be displayed as proudly as Little Jack Horner's plum. The I.W.W.'s actual culpability of wheatfield fires and sawmill wreckings had become unimportant because of the government's greater offenses. The I.W.W.'s attitude toward the war did not matter because the organization had the right to its position, and the crux of the thing was the government's cavalier disregard for liberal principles. The effect of both lines of contemplation was, like romanticization, to "de-unionize" the I.W.W., to draw attention away from the fact that the I.W.W. was first and foremost a workers' organization.

The Wobbly leadership warned against violence because violence provided authorities a pretext to break strikes, which were what counted. The I.W.W. tried to soft-pedal the war issue not only because the leadership knew the union was impotent in the matter and, again, because Haywood did not want to invite government repression, but because there was more pertinent business at hand at the point of production. The drift of *Bread and Roses Too*, with the "*Too*" modifying the "*Roses*," was to play down even the I.W.W.'s "revolutionary" aspect, not because the union was not sincerely committed to the idea of a postcapitalist commonwealth, but because it was a hardheaded labor union first of all, a fact attended to by neither romanticizers, sympathizers with victims, nor searchers for revolutionary heritage. It is not difficult to conceive of an I.W.W. uninterrupted by the disaster of the war evolving into something very much like what the CIO turned out to be.

Certainly the I.W.W.'s great spokesman, William D. Haywood, showed signs of moving in that direction, a theme of *Big Bill Haywood and the Radical Union Movement*, also published in 1969. Haywood was primarily a union leader, even more than a little of what is referred to pejoratively as a union bureaucrat. This image is not congenial to many because Big Bill was "larger than life" during his career (a *persona* he knew how to exploit), and he remained, despite the disgrace of his flight to the Soviet Union, a hero. Indeed, *Big Bill Haywood and the Radical Union Movement* was taken to task by a reviewer in a scholarly journal because it did not make a proper hero of the man. But there you are. Haywood was not Olympian stuff but a lifelong union administrator who found his flourishing charge of 1916 threatened with a persecution he hoped against hope it could ride out and in this purpose he was willing to make decidedly unheroic concessions. If it is not demonstrable that Haywood's residence in the Soviet Union was either endorsement of bolshevism or a disillusioning experience, it can be said that it was an accident.

The I.W.W. remains an institution of heroes and martyrs despite the deromanticizing effects of the books of the late 1960s and intensive studies of the sort collected below. And the individual Wobbly who has received the most attention is not Haywood but songwriter Joe Hill. He "never died." A martyr even before he was executed in Utah for first-degree murder in 1915, Hill's songs and his epitaph—"Don't Mourn, Organize!" —were adopted by the CIO in the 1930s and 1940s. In 1980, as part of the commemoration of its eightieth anniversary, the I.W.W. sponsored a demand for his full pardon.

Hill is not a hero to everyone. In an essay in *The New Republic* in 1948 and a novel published two years later, *The Preacher and the Slave*, Wallace Stegner depicted him as no labor organizer at all but an ordinary working stiff who "was probably guilty of the crime the State of Utah executed him for," a crime without any social connotations. Stegner's opinion, however, coming at a time of a general offensive against organized labor, provoked a passionate defense of Hill as a genuine hero and victim.

The most systematic defense of Hill was published in 1965. In *The Case of Joe Hill*, Philip S. Foner examined every aspect of the case in minute detail, naturally as an advocate. He took on Stegner as well as the prosecution, although more the novelist's motive than his argument, pointing out that a year before the *New Republic* article, Stegner had written in the *Pacific Spectator*, "It might be possible, if one wished to do it, to whittle the figure of Joe Hill down to the stature of a migrant yegg."

Stegner did just that and Foner riposted with the I.W.W.'s insistence (for which there is no evidence) that Hill was an organizer for the union who was framed by the government of Utah, state mining interests, and the Mormon church for reasons of class. Hill had not murdered the grocer and his son, for which he was ostensibly convicted and executed.

In 1969, a less strident but more comprehensive study was published by Gibbs M. Smith called simply *Joe Hill*. Without returning to Stegner's view of Hill's inconsequence (for Smith was as much interested in the legend and historical impact of Hill as in the particulars of the case), he concluded that Hill's guilt or innocence "is no more certain today than it was in 1915." Smith did not accept the arguments for Hill's positive innocence in the crime, but he agreed with Hill's defense, the I.W.W., and Foner that the prosecution's case was full of holes. Smith concluded that there is "considerable reason to believe that Hill was denied justice in the courts of Utah," that the "reasonable doubt" in the case was certainly more than sufficient to have warranted acquittal.

The reason for the miscarriage, however, was neither conspiracy nor a class action. On the contrary, Smith stated, much of the blame rested on Hill's "naive faith in the abstract concept of justice" and Hill's and the I.W.W.'s errors in arguing the case. This is putting a good face on it. Given the evidence and irregardless of Hill's many tactical blunders, the verdict was an absurd one. On the other hand, there is no evidence that the State of Utah knew anything about Hill's I.W.W. connections at the time he was arrested (which seem to have been very nebulous) or for some period of his incarceration. It was the I.W.W. that injected a class import into the trial in which issue, unlike in the Haymarket of Haywood-Steunenberg or Sacco-Vanzetti cases, the prosecution never fully obliged them. The Joe Hill case looks to be more a case of shabby police work and a subsequent cover-up than a battle in the class war.

But there is no gainsaying its importance in the Wobbly legend that, in many ways, reached its zenith in the late 1960s and early 1970s. Swedish filmmaker Bo Wilderberg directed a film on Hill, and other Wobbly topics were dramatized on television. Historiographically, the zenith of the "Wobbly boom" was the publication in 1969 of Melvyn Dubofsky's *We Shall Be All*, a massive and masterful history of the union that combined sympathy for its subject with a disinterested purpose of understanding the Wobbly phenomenon. A few years before *We Shall Be All*, Dubofsky had published an influential essay in *Labor History* on the peculiar character and origins of working-class radicalism in the western states, specifically of the Western Federation of Miners. This line of thought was the preface to the I.W.W. history because Dubofsky identified the I.W.W. as very much a contribution of the Western Federation's long-standing effort to organize all workers in the West.

With this "native" context as a background, *We Shall Be All* for the first time successfully integrated I.W.W. history into the larger story of the

Progressive Era. The book gave the I.W.W. its proper recognition and an appropriate monument. Oddly, because Dubofsky's vision of the I.W.W. was realistic and restrained, the book coincided with—and partly stimulated —a new, popular romanticization of the Wobblies. The New Left of the late 1960s and early 1970s was attracted by the songs and hi-jinks of the Wobblies but, in addition, had their own conception of the union's revolutionary militance. Parts of the American New Left and, somewhat later, New Left-like movements in Europe, especially Italy, built up an image of the I.W.W. centered on the fact that *it acted*.

As always in these historical reconstructions, there was a germ of truth in the idea that the I.W.W. was at its heart a "simply-do-*something*" organi- zation. The Wobblies rarely shrunk from a confrontation (although it is interesting to note the I.W.W. "called" far fewer strikes and protests than were thrust upon them). What was missing in the New Left appreciation of the I.W.W.—although certainly not from *We Shall Be All*—was the I.W.W. actions were always based on and related to a set of principles, or, when they were not, the Wobblies regretted and repudiated them.

There is a further irony in the idea of children of American affluence or the Italian university elite imagining themselves reincarnations of Nebraska bindle-stiffs and Massachusetts broadcloth weavers. Nevertheless, the ghosts of Wobblies were called on to testify for aimless thrashings-about such as those spirits, were they able to speak, would have sneered at through carious teeth as "scissor-bill." The I.W.W. was not always successful in avoiding involvement in actions that led nowhere but to their own gratifica- tion. But it strived in that direction, and its significance lies in the fact that it mostly was a working-class movement with mostly hardheaded, concrete objects in view.

The major historiographical consequence of *We Shall Be All* is to close the general subject of the I.W.W. for a while, just as Brissenden's book did in 1919. Where there was one general history of the union for almost half a century, there are now five with a few other books shading the category. Until Dubofsky's book, there was no adequate one. With it there is a definitive reference standard.

However, the situation is somewhat different from what it was in the wake of the publication of Brissenden's *Study*. Then, there was a consensus on how labor history was to be written, and Brissenden had thoroughly examined all the sources that could then be so defined. Now, with new sources regularly uncovered, more by virtue of new approaches and method- ologies than attic discoveries, the thrust of Wobbly historiography must be in the direction of specialized inquiries based on new methodology (quan- titative analysis, for instance) and especially intensive studies of local Wobbly action based on sources that the general historian needs necessarily pass over lightly.

It is clear that the further historians move from Brissenden's conception of the I.W.W. as an institution, mechanically motivated and controlled by an ideology and a central policymaking administration, the more they will realize that there is much more to be learned about the Wobblies. The immediate effect of "little" episodes involving the Wobblies will be, collectively, to bewilder. What Brissenden and Dubofsky made coherent will become confusing and irreconcilable. Even the few studies collected in this book depict "many I.W.W.'s," impossible to rationalize from the perspectives of a labor union or a revolutionary group or an ideology.

This has been the effect of the "new social history" in general and will continue to be, given the somewhat historicist character of the method. So I must conclude where I began, with the profession's fondness for revisionism which will not abate regardless of whether it ought to do or not. The rewriting of specific paragraphs of the standard, from a more intimate understanding or from a different frame of reference, is the order of the day. The articles in this book are offered as examples of what "needs to be done."

Centro di Studi Americani, Rome

PART ONE

THE I.W.W. IN THE INDUSTRIAL CITIES

WOMEN, WOBBLIES, AND WORKERS' RIGHTS: THE 1912 TEXTILE STRIKE IN LITTLE FALLS, NEW YORK

ROBERT E. SNYDER*

The Little Falls textile strike lasted for nearly three months, from October 9, 1912, until January 4, 1913. During this period, 664 workers braved inclement weather and entrenched local interests to strike against the Phoenix and Gilbert Knitting Mills, and another 659 workers were indirectly affected by work stoppages and layoffs. During this bitterly fought dispute, these employees lost an aggregate of 68,379 days of work.[1] The Little Falls textile strike, coming as it did between the spectacular strikes led by the Industrial Workers of the World (I.W.W.) at Lawrence, Massachusetts, and Paterson, New Jersey, has been neglected by labor historians. An overview of the crosscurrents involved at Little Falls suggests that a discussion of the strike can make contributions to our knowledge of several matters: I.W.W. strike activities, Socialist participation in working-class radicalism, and immigrant disenchantment and disillusionment. What the textile dispute can tell us of women workers and strike leaders may be most significant of all, for an estimated 70 percent of the strikers were female laborers. While these inarticulate Polish, Slavic, Austrian, and Italian women may have seen their actions only as a protest over a reduction in wages, the movement for protective labor legislation for women was actually the backdrop to the Little Falls textile strike.[2]

At the request of the New York State Federation of Labor in 1911, Assemblyman Edward D. Jackson of Buffalo responded to demands that had been heard in Albany's legislative halls for at least a decade by introducing a bill designed to reduce the hours of labor of women and minors in

---

*Portions of this chapter have been previously published in Robert E. Snyder, "Women, Wobblies, and Workers' Rights: The 1912 Textile Strike in Little Falls, New York," *New York History* 60 (January 1979): 29-57. Reprinted by permission of *New York History*.

factories to fifty-four per week. While New Hampshire had passed the first hour law applicable to women in 1847, New York had not come around to protective hour legislation for female workers until 1886. Although revision of the sixty-hour law was badly needed and long overdue, battle lines over the Jackson bill formed early and firmly at the hearings held before the Committee on Labor and Industries.[3]

Knitting mills from the Mohawk and Hudson valleys joined the canning factories of central and western New York in hiring the ablest lawyers, retired judges, and former legislators in opposing the Jackson bill. Attorney Thomas D. Watkins of Utica, representing knitting mills with a capitalization of over $35,000,000, presented the most formidable opposition, skillfully arguing that the measure would cripple the textile industry by reducing output and would handicap native manufacturers in competition with factories of other states. The representative of New York Mills, which also owned factories in the South, provided substance to the charges, indicating that the concerns he spoke for would have to move knitting operations to Georgia, where workers were allowed to labor sixty-six hours a week.

Proponents of the Jackson bill relied on various civic, educational, and labor groups to argue their case. John Golden, president of the International Textile Workers, spoke on behalf of the bill, arguing that since the sixty-hour law had been enacted, textile operators had speeded up machinery and intensified the strain on workers. Among the formidable array of groups supporting the Jackson measure were the New York Child Labor Committee and the Consumer's League of New York City, represented by Frances Perkins, a future New York State Industrial Commissioner under Governor Franklin D. Roosevelt and secretary of labor during the New Deal.[4]

The campaign to improve the working conditions of female labor through protective legislation received considerable assistance from the tragic Triangle Shirtwaist Factory fire. In the aftermath of the Triangle disaster, which claimed the lives of 145 Jewish and Italian immigrant women in a New York City sweatshop in March of 1911, several aroused civic groups, led by the Women's Trade Union League, induced the New York State legislature to establish a Factory Investigating Commission (FIC). Originally appointed to examine safety and health standards, the FIC utilized its broad power to hold public hearings, compel the attendance of witnesses, and take testimony to conduct a far-reaching probe of the way manufacturing was conducted in the Empire State.[5]

Through public hearings scheduled around the state, dedicated public servants, such as State Senator Robert F. Wagner and Assemblyman Alfred E. Smith, were able to expose the wide-ranging abuses that muckraking journalists had been clamoring about. The FIC focused considerable attention on the use of women workers and the conditions under which they labored. In a special report prepared for the legislature, Violet Pike, a Vassar College graduate and FIC investigator, revealed the adverse physical and mental effects on women of long hours, continuous standing, and over-crowded conditions among other injurious situations. The Pike report forcefully announced:

Modern industry has been developed chiefly by men for men. . . . Unlimited speed and unlimited production is the manufacturer's dream, but modern machine production is taking no account of the strain upon women workers of long hours at monotonous and nerve-racking tasks in destroying their health, and thus lowering the efficiency of future generations.[6]

During the four-year course of its investigations, the FIC visited Little Falls. The city, which the I.W.W. would derisively refer to as "the city of Little Faults," is situated on the Mohawk River in central New York. Described by a mid-nineteenth-century editor as "the Lowell of the Empire State," Little Falls had a variety of industrial and transportation assets. The presence of cheap and abundant water power attracted industries ranging from leather, felt shoes, cotton yarn, batting, shirtwaist, and hosiery to paper, lumber, meat packing, metal polishing, dairy equipment, and knitting machines. While the city advertised itself as having the largest bicycle and hammer works in the world, textiles became the linchpin of the local economy after the first knitting mill was organized by a group of local entrepreneurs in 1872.[7]

On its tour of Little Falls in August of 1912, the FIC found some of the most abominable working and living conditions in the entire state. The FIC uncovered mills employing children as young as five years of age and pro-prietors circumventing the scrutiny of busy state inspectors by having the children take their work assignments out of the factories to the confines of their homes. The FIC inspected factories whose utterly wretched working conditions were exceeded in repulsiveness only by the fact that the manu-facturer turned out to be a member of the local board of health. When the commission turned to local living conditions, State Senator Wagner and Chief Counsel Abram I. Elkus requested the appearance of M. Helen Schloss, the local tuberculosis nurse, and personally conducted the ques-tioning. Miss Schloss, who would later play a prominent role in the textile strike, informed investigators in the most graphic terms of unsanitary con-ditions among the foreign population. Her testimony revealed such out-rageous situations that Mary E. Dreier, the president of the Women's Trade Union League appointed to the FIC by the governor, recommended that a digest of recent legislation should be printed in several languages and con-spicuously posted throughout Little Falls to apprise inarticulate workers of their rights and to deter unscrupulous proprietors from abusing them.[8]

In his annual message to the New York State legislature, Governor John
A. Dix called for a reduction in the hours worked by women and children.
Embracing the belief that a sixty-hour work week, frequently under adverse
conditions in sweatshops and factories, was detrimental to the health of
women and, hence, to future generations of Americans born to them,
Governor Dix advised the legislators that it was "the duty of the State to
protect its women workers against those who would unduly profit by their
labor." After considerable wrangling the legislature passed the Jackson
fifty-four-hour bill. Besides reducing from sixty to fifty-four the hours that
women could legally work, the law closed other loopholes by further
stipulating that women could not be employed for more than ten hours in
any one day nor before six o'clock in the morning or after nine o'clock at
night.[9]

While the fifty-four-hour law addressed itself to certain areas of exploitation, it totally skirted the volatile issue of wages and thereby created
the same kind of situation which had only recently precipitated textile
strikes in the Massachusetts communities of New Bedford, Clinton, and
Lawrence. If factory owners in New York State should react to the reduction
of hours as their Massachusetts brethren had—by cutting wages a propor-
tional amount—then labor struggles like those at Lawrence appeared inevitable.[10] When the fifty-four-hour law went into effect on October 1, 1912,
candy manufacturers immediately instituted a test case to determine the
law's constitutionality, and workers receiving reductions in pay staged
walkouts at scattered locations around the state. After testing the willingness
of workers to strike, employers settled most disputes by adjusting wages.
The longest and most violent reaction to the fifty-four-hour law occurred
at the Phoenix and Gilbert Knitting Mills in Little Falls.[11]

Upon receiving short pay envelopes, workers began spontaneously and
peacefully walking out—first, eighty workers from the Phoenix Mill and
then, a week later, seventy-six employees of the Gilbert Mill. Unlike Lawrence, there was no sabotage of machinery, breaking of windows, or other
acts of violence. With each passing day smaller numbers joined the strikers
until the number out of work and those who continued to cross the picket
lines were about equal. Virtually all of the strikers were immigrants who
had arrived in Little Falls within the past few years, largely from Italy,
Poland, Hungary, and Austria, and who still spoke only in their native
tongues. Newspaper dispatches indicated that at least two out of every three
strikers were women.[12]

These immigrants came to Little Falls to share in the city's considerable
industrial development. In the period from 1904 to 1909, Little Falls registered
the third largest gain in the value of manufactured goods in the entire state.
The value of products produced by fifty-five manufacturing establishments
climbed by 89 percent, from less than $4.5 million to nearly $8.5 million

annually. This dramatic rise was principally the result of increased production of hosiery, knit goods (underwear and sweaters), and leather.[13]
Each of these industries had several entry levels open to unskilled labor and
required only short periods of on-the-job instruction.[14]

During this period of growth, mill management kept unions out and
wages low. In 1912, there were only twelve labor unions in Little Falls
covering 6 percent of the total labor force. The only workers within the
textile industry covered by union representation were the Jack Spinners,
seventy-five in number, who comprised 23 percent of the union membership
in Little Falls and received day rates of $2.60 for a sixty-hour week. While
this day rate compared favorably with the $2.13 received by spinners in
Cohoes and the $2.29 received in Hudson, the vast majority of textile
workers received considerably lower wages.[15] Out of 800 male day workers,
the weekly wages of nearly 49 percent amounted to $9.00 or less. Only 23
percent exceeded $12.00 per week. Out of 900 female workers, the weekly
wage of nearly 49 percent amounted to $7.50 or less. Only 21 percent
exceeded $10.00 per week, and 30 percent did not exceed $6.00 per week.[16]

The strikers repeatedly asserted that these wages were inadequate to
support either themselves, their families, or loved ones still in Europe. But
local interests saw matters differently. "The question of whether wages paid
were starvation or not, did not, and cannot enter into the merits of the case,"
the *Little Falls Journal and Courier* contended. "The employer fixed the
wages that he was willing to pay, and the men were at liberty to accept the
employment or not. . . . There were no extraordinary conditions, no disturbances, no suffering, no distress, so far as anyone here knew."[17]

The labor discontent immediately attracted the attention of Socialists in the
city of Schenectady, some fifty-five miles east of Little Falls on the Mohawk
River.[18] Led by the Reverend George R. Lunn, mayor of Schenectady, the
Socialists hoped to organize the strikers into an orderly and effective labor
force and persuade other textile workers into joining them. The Socialists
insisted on addressing the strikers at Clinton Park, a grassy piece of land
located directly across from the textile mills. But the Little Falls city charter
provided local authorities with several ordinances for exercising extraordinary control over what went on within the community. One provision
of the city charter required all persons to obtain a permit in order to hold a
street meeting, while another forbade more than twenty people from con-
gregating on the streets. "We will have no speaking by anyone in front of
the mills where the strike is in progress or in that vicinity," Herkimer
County Sheriff James W. Moon indicated. "Socialist speeches at this time
would tend to 'rioting' among the strikers, a thing we intend to prevent if
we have to call out every regiment of the national guard in the state."[19]

Although neither regulation had been judicially enforced before, especially in this the year of the Bull Moose campaign, the strikers and their

Socialist sympathizers were arrested for disturbing the peace and blocking traffic whenever they attempted to speak in Clinton Park, but others, most notably William Sulzer and Martin W. Glynn, Democratic candidates for governor and lieutenant-governor respectively, were not. Through his vigorous enforcement of law and order, Police Chief James "Dusty" Long revealed the kind of society which the city fathers had fostered and were interested in controlling. "We have a strike on our hands and a foreign element to deal with. We have in the past kept them in subjugation and we mean to continue to hold them where they belong." Chief Long declared. "We will not allow any one to attempt publicly to stir up a feeling which might cause serious trouble to this city, county, and state. . . . The city may have these local quarrels, but I will at all times object to butters-in."[20]

Several newspapers of considerable editorial influence in the Mohawk Valley criticized Little Falls for the suppression of free speech and the double standard that was being applied. "Had it been the mayor of Utica or of Albany who came to Little Falls to speak to the strikers we question whether the police would have been so prompt. Had the speaker urged the men to return to work we doubt whether the obstruction of traffic would have caused so much police indignation," the *Syracuse Post Standard* declared. "By their course the authorities of Little Falls give rise to the suspicion that the Socialist has not the same right of free speech that belongs to the Republican or Democrat in their city; and that in the enforcement of the law there is a spirit of favoritism in the direction of the employers whose men are out."[21]

To break the grip which entrenched local interests exerted over the inarticulate and unskilled workers, the Schenectady Socialists relied on tactics which the Wobblies, the popular nickname of the I.W.W., had utilized in several struggles around the country: Insist on free speech rights, submit to arrest, overcrowd the penal facilities, demand separate jury trials, clog administrative machinery, and burden the taxpayers with excessive costs. Responding to Lunn's call for 5,000 protesters, hundreds of Socialists, Wobblies, and other labor sympathizers from nearby towns flocked into Little Falls.

Local officials soon found themselves in a difficult position. Protesters taken prisoner had to be either released on bail or incarcerated in a nearby town because the Little Falls jail was totally inadequate for retaining and segregating male and female prisoners. The state prison commission had already condemned the Little Falls bullpen, and the town fathers were engaged in litigation to avoid making recommended improvements. Governor John A. Dix also reprimanded Little Falls officials for the vigorous and frequent arrest of free speech advocates. "Your attention is invited to the fact that the Constitution of the State of New York guarantees the right of free speech and the right of people peacefully to assemble and discuss public questions,"

Governor Dix cautioned Mayor Frank Shall and Herkimer County Sheriff James W. Moon. "The people of the State of New York wish to see that these rights are not unnecessarily curtailed, but are respected in spirit as well as in letter, within your jurisdiction."[22]

The strikers took advantage of every opportunity to secure the right to free speech. On October 21, the Socialist state ticket joined other speakers in Clinton Park and provided four consecutive hours of oratory without any interference from local officials. George Lunn discussed the right of all Americans to organize and strike without fear of retribution. "Let your enemies use violence if they will—which I hope will never be the case—but do not ever use violence yourselves. You have right on your side. You can unite as one mighty army of workers and thus secure the wages to enable you to live peaceably." Speakers like Mrs. Carrie W. Allen of Syracuse, the Socialist party candidate for secretary of state, encouraged the strikers to develop the same kind of class consciousness in fighting for their rights that industrialists had exhibited in exploiting them.[23]

Having established the right to assemble and speak in Clinton Park, the Schenectady Socialists deferred to such Wobbly hands as George Lehney of Chicago, Matilda Rabinowitz of Bridgeport, and Benjamin Legere of Lawrence; they took over the task of organizing the strikers and inculcating the doctrine of solidarity. Following I.W.W. advice, the strikers established a strike committee whose membership was drawn from each plant and nationality involved. The committee placed before mill management three basic demands: sixty hours' pay for fifty-four hours of work; a 10-percent additional increase in wages; and no discrimination against the workers for strike participation. The strikers proceeded to delegate responsibility for matters regarding money, publicity, and relief to appropriate committees, conduct daily parades through town, and introduce mass picketing techniques. At a mass meeting on October 24, the strikers voted to affiliate with the I.W.W., and from the Chicago headquarters Vincent St. John promptly dispatched an I.W.W. charter to Local No. 801—the National Industrial Union of Textile Workers of Little Falls.[24]

A confrontation between strikers and police erupted into violence on October 30 when pickets marching around in circles in front of a mill entrance failed to clear a path across the sidewalks for workers to enter. As Chief Long and his deputies clashed with the strikers, special police and patrolmen mounted on horses closed in on the largely unarmed pickets with their clubs. During the riot, a local police officer was shot in the leg, a special policeman furnished by the Humphrey Detective Agency of Albany was stabbed several times, and numerous strikers were savagely beaten, some into unconsciousness.[25]

From the mill entrance where the conflict began, the police pursued the strikers across the Mohawk River to the side of town where most of the immigrants lived and descended on strike headquarters at Slovak Hall. After throwing women off the steps and breaking down the doors of Slovak Hall, the police broke the instruments of the Slovak Society Band, smashed the I.W.W.'s charter, and confiscated several cases of beer and liquor. The police proceeded to round up throughout the city additional people who had no connection with the riot other than having supported the strikers in one way or another in the past. At day's end, the police had arrested the entire strike committee and other influential supporters.

The strike committee issued a handbill accusing Little Falls authorities of deliberately inciting the riot. "It was the most brutal, cold blooded act ever done in these parts," the handbill declared. "Nothing under heaven can ever justify it, and the soul of the degenerate brute who started it will shrivel in hell long, long before the workers will ever forget this day." The vested interests of the community—mill management, merchants, local politicians, the clergy, and other concerned residents—countered by holding a massive town meeting which came out with a complete and enthusiastic endorsement of the actions taken by Little Falls authorities. The mood was most cogently expressed in an editorial by the *Little Falls Journal and Courier*:

A Godless, lawless group of self-appointed 'leaders' have come to our peaceful home city and by playing upon the ignorance and prejudices of a certain portion of our mill workers . . . have influenced the passions and aroused the excitabilities of a quick-tempered people, who are not too well informed concerning American institutions. . . . Inflammatory speech has been indulged in, parades with the red flag of anarchy and rebellion against constituted authority have been held, the police and other city officials have been held up to ridicule and derision. . . . The wonder is that the lawless were permitted to go as far as they were allowed to go, and then when the break came the politicians held themselves under such restraint. . . . The Industrial Workers of the World should not be permitted to have a place in this, or any other American city. Its teachings are disloyal, its leaders are dangerous characters, and its influence cannot be anything but harmful and dangerous. If the Little Falls exhibit is a fair sample of the whole organization, it should have the attention of the National government, and be thoroughly and effectively suppressed.[26]

Foremost among the women activists arrested by Little Falls authorities was M. Helen Schloss, the local consumption inspector. Schloss's personal and professional activities in Little Falls bring into focus, more sharply than any other individual involved in the strike, the social, economic, and political antagonisms at work. M. Helen Schloss had been brought to Little Falls earlier in 1912 by the Fortnightly Club, a social society comprised of prominent women. The club met every two weeks at the residence of a well-to-do patron to hear members and invited guests present papers and lead discussions on vital issues of the day. Besides providing the women with a sense of cultural fulfillment in an otherwise barren atmosphere, the topics considered by the club actually involved members in various civic projects. At a meeting in January of 1912, for instance, a paper on "Women in Public Life" was followed by a discussion of the Consumer's League. The women of the Fortnightly Club subsequently prevailed upon local merchants to carry only goods marked by the league's little white label, because such products, they felt, were manufactured under sanitary conditions and not in sweatshops. Club members never seemed to associate sweatshop conditions with their husbands' factories or with Little Falls, only with goods manufactured elsewhere.[27]

The campaign which occupied the attention of the Fortnightly Club most extensively, and actually led them to bring M. Helen Schloss to Little Falls, was the issue of tuberculosis. In Little Falls the disease had accounted for at least sixteen deaths every year for the previous twenty years. In conjunction with a statewide campaign geared toward achieving "No Uncared Tuberculosis In New York State In 1915," the city of Little Falls launched in January of 1911 its own campaign against consumption. Over 1,850 residents attended the initial lectures of a week-long educational program on consumption, its extent, spread, care, and prevention. The devastating effect was graphically portrayed to the people in a pictorial display. A black pin for every death caused by tuberculosis was stuck in a large map of the city to show how many deaths and the approximate residence of each contagion. Some 339 pins were placed on the map to represent the toll taken during the past two decades. For the next several years, the most prominent sign displayed in Little Falls would be the double red cross of the international campaign against consumption.[28]

The Fortnightly Club managed and directed the sale of Red Cross Christmas Seals in Little Falls. By encouraging communities to make schools the focal point of local distribution efforts, the state charities aid association hoped to interest and educate thousands of schoolchildren in the antituberculosis movement.[29] The Fortnightly Club kicked off the campaign by selling seals at auction. Local industry indicated what it could actually accomplish. The first one-cent Red Cross Charities Seal was sold to the H. P. Snyder Manufacturing Company for $110. Little Falls businessmen proceeded to offer prizes to the schools dispensing the most seals, and purchased the seals so vigorously that a second lot of 50,000 stamps had to be ordered.[30] Through Fortnightly Club management, Little Falls achieved the distinction of selling more seals per student population than any other city in the state.[31]

A year after Little Falls had launched its crusade against consumption, the Fortnightly Club announced it had engaged M. Helen Schloss as visiting tuberculosis nurse. The club considered her eminently qualified for the position, citing in its orginal press release that she had been district nurse in Malone, New York, for the past year, and prior to that a settlement-house worker. Indeed, through her training as a nurse and settlement-house worker, Helen Schloss had become a medical inspector for the New York City Department of Health. Her investigations into social conditions on New York City's lower east side brought her within the Socialist fold. She subsequently participated in the shirtwaist strike of female labor in New York City in 1910, and several times demonstrated on behalf of shop girls. Exactly how much Little Falls knew about Schloss's political leanings and labor activities is not known, except that when illness raised the possibility of her not coming to Little Falls, the secretary of the Fortnightly Club traveled to New York City, prevailed upon her to retain the $25-a-week position, and extended the date beyond which the post was to be filled.[32]

Upon arriving in Little Falls in May of 1912 to organize the campaign against tuberculosis, Schloss met with the Fortnightly Club at a business meeting held, ironically, in the residence of J. Judson Gilbert, owner of the Gilbert Knitting Mill. Once Schloss had outlined the preliminary steps her experience had indicated must be undertaken, the Fortnightly Club plunged into the task at hand, appointing committees for the location of a clinic office, staff physicians, publicity, relief, and child welfare. The local newspaper advised residents: "The work which these public spirited ladies are undertaking is one that affects the welfare of the whole city and therefore should meet with hearty cooperation."[33] As the spirit of coming together against a common enemy trickled down the social ladder, a Social Service Club was formed by the younger women of Little Falls to augment the work of the older, more established women. The Social Service Club immediately located and leased a room conveniently situated over a drugstore, and undertook to furnish and maintain the free clinic, which would be Schloss's headquarters through the proceeds of a food sale and other fund-raising activities.[34]

For the next several months, Schloss occupied herself with implementing and administering the tuberculosis campaign. She would provide the Fortnightly Club each month with a report detailing her house calls and homes fumigated, mills visited and leaflets distributed, clinic sessions and patients treated. "A good many people hate to know that they are afflicted with tuberculosis and try to deny the facts to themselves," Schloss said on one occasion, "but the germ knows no other law and it must do its deadly work, unless radical action is taken in order to combat the disease." She advised tenement owners to clean, renovate, and fumigate their dwellings for the welfare of the entire community. "The Board of Health may be able to do all in its power to clean up and to try and safeguard public health, but not until citizens all help in this work can we hope for success. Property owners ought to help, and not until all the bad tenements are improved, not until we build some decent homes for the people to live in, will we be able to accomplish any kind of work. It is a public affair," she concluded, "and no one can lay the blame on any one person or group of people."[35]

To reach as many foreign-born residents as possible, Helen Schloss took her message into the mills. The basic facts every person should know about the disease were printed in Slavic, Polish, Hungarian, German, Italian, and English on what were called "don't cards." The cards advised people not to spit, not to share eating utensils, and not to do several other things in order to prevent and contain the disease. At one mill alone over 600 cards were distributed. The mill hands were most receptive to the information, and many applied to the clinic for examination.[36]

As Schloss proceeded from the educational phase of the campaign to direct action, local authorities revealed an unwillingness to move from discussing surface measures to actually expunging root causes. The harder Schloss pressed officials to condemn, repair, or fumigate houses, clean workshops and mills, and enforce antispitting laws, the more strained relations became. "If we are to leave the question of bad tenements and congestion in the air, we had better also leave the tuberculosis problem unresolved. The money spent on such a campaign will be wasted and perhaps if it were put to other purposes it would bring in quicker returns," Schloss complained. "To do anything effective we must get down to the very root of the evil. It is within the power of the local authorities to do these things, and as good businessmen I hope they will recognize the need of new tenements and gradually make Little Falls a model town."[37]

To overcome government and civic inaction, Schloss secured the names of factory and tenement owners, sent them notices requesting redress, and published the names and conditions of those refusing. When Schloss directly confronted those individuals responsible for congested and un-sanitary conditions, her appeals were rejected on the grounds that the people affected were "simply wops and ginnies. They don't count." Stung by the harshness of this attitude, Schloss revolted against local authorities. "They are more than 'wops' and 'ginnies' to me. They are human beings with hearts, souls, and thoughts, just as you have, and I mean to fight and work for them." On October 17, Schloss resigned her position as tuber-culosis visiting nurse. Her five months of work had brought her into such close contact with the downtrodden that their cause was now hers. "The manufacturers have brought on the strike themselves by cutting down the wages almost to the starvation point," she bitterly declared. "I know the life of these people, as perhaps no one else in town will ever know, and I feel that as a nurse and a social worker, it is my duty to sympathize with these poor strikers."[38]

Schloss threw herself into strike activities with a vengeance. She operated the soup kitchen that sustained the strikers during the dispute, and she led many of the strikers' parades and demonstrations. For these efforts she experienced the full wrath of local officials. Several times law enforcement officials roughed her up. On the day of the riot, a police dragnet tracked her down in the post office, and she was placed under arrest along with the other strike leaders, even though she had not been anywhere near the scene of the melee. In an attempt to put her away indefinitely, Little Falls had three doctors examine her sanity. Luckily for Schloss and the strikers she was able to secure release on bail, and eventually her case was dismissed. "The result of the whole thing is that I am a revolutionist. I hate the sight of Little Falls, but I mean to fight until I have cleaned those miserable tenements up," Schloss announced. "There is one thing I shall do, and that is to put Little Falls on the map and let people know of conditions that exist here."[39]

Besides operating the soup kitchen and clinic, and leading parades and demonstrations, Schloss joined Matilda Rabinowitz and others in traveling around the greater Northeast speaking on behalf of the strike cause.[40] Among the outside sympathizers these dedicated women activists were able to attract to the side of the Little Falls strikers was Helen Keller. Most people probably know of Helen Keller as the deaf and blind girl who triumphed over her disabilities to become a noted author, educator, and source of inspiration to all mankind.[41] Less well known, however, is Helen Keller the radical—member of the Socialist party, defender of the I.W.W., and champion of the working class in its struggle against industrial exploitation.[42]

Miss Keller credited her appointment in 1906 to the Massachusetts Commission on the Blind with providing the initial radicalizing influence in her life. The commission took her step by step into the industrial world—"a world of misery and degradation, of blindness and crookedness, and sin, a world struggling against the elements, against the unknown, against itself." Through her investigations as a commission member into the causes of blindness she discovered "too much of it was traceable to wrong industrial conditions, often caused by the selfishness and greed of employers. And the social evil contributed its share. I found that poverty drove women to the life of shame that ended in blindness." Helen's walks with Anne Sullivan, her companion and teacher, through industrial slums affirmed her belief that "our worst enemies are ignorance, poverty, and the unconscious cruelty of our commercial society."[43]

Her displeasure with existing industrial conditions quickened and deepened as she sampled the Socialist literature of the day. She read Marx, Engels, and Kautsky, subscribed to German bimonthly Socialist periodicals printed in braille, and asked visitors to read to her selections from the *National Socialist* and the *International Socialist Review*. In 1909, Miss Keller joined the Socialist party in Massachusetts and became an honorary member of many Socialist locals throughout the country. She confronted immediately and forcefully any and all charges that she was being used and exploited. She firmly said: "I am no worshiper of cloth of any color, but I love the red flag and what it symbolizes to me and other Socialists."[44]

But she became impatient with the pace and procedures of the Socialist party. Claiming that the party moved so slowly "it is sinking in the political bog," and feeling it was "impossible for a party to keep its revolutionary character as long as it occupies a place under the government and seeks office under it," she became an "Industrialist," a term sometimes applied to the I.W.W. She attributed the I.W.W. strike at Lawrence with providing her the inspiration to become a Wobbly. "I discovered that the true idea of the I.W.W. is not only to better conditions, to get them for all people, but to get them at once."[45]

From her home in Wrentham, Massachusetts, Miss Keller penned an inspirational letter to the strikers at Little Falls. Describing the strikers as "brave girls . . . starving so courageously to bring about the emancipation of the workers," Miss Keller declared, "their cause is my cause. If they are denied a living wage, I also am defamed. While they are industrial slaves I cannot be free. . . . I cannot enjoy the good things of life which come to me if they are hindered and neglected." Miss Keller asked John Macy, the husband of her teacher and companion, to deliver the letter and a contribution of $87, which represented the proceeds recently received from writing sentiments for Christmas cards. "Surely the things that the workers demand are not unreasonable," Miss Keller said. "It cannot be unreasonable to ask of society a fair chance for all. It cannot be unreasonable to demand the protection of women and little children and an honest wage for all who give their time and energy to industrial occupations."

John Macy read the letter to the strikers during a regular meeting at Slovak Hall. It was impressed upon those gathered that she had overcome afflictions more severe than the strikers themselves faced. Calling her contribution "not a dole of charity, but a token of love," Big Bill Haywood proudly proclaimed during his stay in Little Falls, "She sees what philosophers, politicians, and priests cannot see; have never seen. She reads unerringly the destiny of labor." Both the radical and establishment presses widely publicized the emotional metaphor of a deaf and blind girl helping those handicapped in other ways.[46]

Just as Little Falls officials could not crush the strikers, so the dissidents could not overcome mill management. Ignoring the daily picketing, mass meetings, and calls for a general strike, skilled labor continued to work. Native American laborers refused to join the foreigners in this dispute because mill management in the past had used immigrants to break their strikes. Many of the present strikers had helped management to break a spinners' strike only two years earlier.[47]

Just as divisive to the strike cause as the conflict between American and foreign-born labor was the fighting between the Industrial Workers of the World and the American Federation of Labor (AF of L) for the allegiance of textile workers. Shortly after the I.W.W. became involved in the dispute, C. A. Miles, an organizer for the AF of L from Auburn, arrived in Little

Falls and immediately set out to undercut I.W.W. efforts at every turn. Miles joined the politicians, mill management, and clergy in painting a picture of the I.W.W. as a godless and anarchistic organization. He repeatedly claimed that no industry could come up with a settlement satisfactory to the I.W.W., and supported the clergy's contentions that the I.W.W. was turning immigrants into a "menace rather than a safeguard of society." Miles established a temporary organization of textile workers which he claimed netted an initial organization of fifty-two from among the strikers. While mill management refused to meet with any representatives of the I.W.W., Miles conferred at will with the owners and repeatedly announced that a settlement had been reached.[48]

But the strikers persevered. In their most dramatic action, they sent their children away. Since October 18, the Women's Committee of the Schenectady Socialists had been making preparations for transporting the children to homes in Schenectady and Amsterdam. On December 17, some eighteen children, the first group of a planned fifty children, left Little Falls. Authorities provided the strikers with more publicity than they could have ever hoped for through a constant barrage of harassment. The paraders were ordered off the sidewalk and into the road. When this failed to provoke disorder, the marchers were ordered off the road and back onto the sidewalk. Placards and singing were prohibited. Even at the railroad depot, truant officers demanded legal documents from parents authorizing the exodus, a contingency the strikers had prepared for in advance from experience at Lawrence. The strikers challenged officials right back by sending some of the children to Pittsfield, Massachusetts, so as to force legal authorities to prove the contention that such an exodus violated interstate commerce laws.[49]

The Little Falls strike became so protracted that on December 24 the New York State Department of Labor finally ordered an official probe. At hearings held in Little Falls, the strikers indicated to state inspectors through interpreters that the wage issue, and that alone, caused the dispute and sustained it. Although the strikers also complained about police brutality, the bribing of mill bosses in saloons in order to get jobs and daily work, life in substandard housing, and work at long hours without breaks, it was the cutback in wages that pushed them below the subsistence level and forced them to fight back. Mill management vigorously denied the charges of workers suffering economic privations and asserted that the strike would have been settled long ago if it had not been for the intervention and provocations of the I.W.W. Police Chief Long contended that the city had always been a peaceful place to live and work.[50]

State mediators completed their investigation by visiting the foreign section of town and inspecting tenements that were so squalid the *New York Times* likened them to "rabbit warrens." The state examiners inspected tenements that were poorly lighted, ventilated, and heated, and in which bathrooms were entirely absent. Tenements not served by the Board of Health wagon commonly dumped human and animal wastes in and around the buildings, providing the south side with an unimaginably foul odor and unsanitary condition. Although families of the foreigners were not large—those of more than four children being unusual—overcrowded conditions were the rule and family privacy was unknown. Despite these highly adverse conditions, state inspectors considered the people to be of good moral character—doctors having recorded only two illegitimate births among them during an eighteen-month period of time.[51]

After conferring with mill management and labor officials in Albany, the state mediators conveyed to the strikers a settlement signed and submitted by the Phoenix and Gilbert Knitting Mills, and providing:

1. employers would not discriminate against individual strikers;
2. all employees would be reinstated as soon as production warranted;
3. workers would receive sixty hours of pay for fifty-four hours of work;
4. piece-work rates would be adjusted to compensate for the reduction of time caused by the fifty-hour law.

On January 2, 1913, the strikers gathered at a mass meeting presided over by Matilda Rabinowitz.

The proposal was read to the various nationalities by interpreters—the most notable being Carlo Tresca—and chief state mediator W. C. Rogers tried to answer any questions raised. To the sound of thunderous applause and shouting, Fred Moore stepped on stage to address the gathering. "Whatever action the strikers may take today, the fact remains that when they go back into the mills, the industrial struggle with their employers is again renewed. All we can hope to do today is that a temporary truce and settlement be made," the Los Angeles attorney declared. "It is for you to determine whether you as individuals are willing to give your bodies, your homes, and your lives to the making of cotton and woolen cloth for a certain wage scale." The strikers voted unanimously to accept the settlement, agreed to return to work beginning January 6, 1913, and concluded the meeting with a hearty singing of the Marseillaise.[52]

What, then, can be said of the Little Falls textile strike? In his annual message to the common council, Mayor Shall continued to articulate the town fathers' interpretation that immigrant mill hands had been exploited, and the city victimized, by "outside sources, fakirs, fanatics, and those who profit by industrial disturbances." While condemning outside elements for aggravating, misrepresenting, and protracting the situation, Mayor Shall recommended that the city approach the evils attendant upon overcrowding and industrial disorders by better educating and assimilating foreign residents. The mayor declared:

With an understanding of our customs and better modes of living, and with an appreciation by them of the fact that their interests are ours, and that we with whom they live are their friends and well wishers, rather than those outsiders, who would exploit and mislead them for their own gain, both of which would come to them with a knowledge of language and customs, there would be less likelihood of a repetition of our recent troubles.

The town fathers paid only lip service, however, to educating the immigrants and rehabilitating their environment.[53]

Once the strikers had agreed to a settlement, Helen Schloss left Little Falls, feeling that her involvement had engendered so much hostility with local officials that she would not be able to function effectively there in the future. The Fortnightly Club continued the free tuberculosis clinic under the direction of another nurse and instituted a child welfare station for the summer months. Helen Schloss had indicated that sick babies coming under her observation were suffering in general from malnutrition. Mothers, not nursing their babies because of work responsibilities or health problems, were feeding their children condensed milk diluted with water or tea mixed with sugar. Schloss consequently recommended that an all-purpose day nursery be provided for the entire city. The Fortnightly Club's response was a milk station on the south side, where children could be examined by physicians, mothers instructed in proper child care, and clean, iced milk distributed free of charge. In the course of a two-week period, over 175 quarts of milk were provided to needy youngsters. The milk station was, however, a seasonal operation contingent on volunteers and private contributions, and when these sources dried up so did the needed service.[54]

The City of Little Falls instituted a clean-up week. Residents were asked to clean their yards, alleys, cellars, and attics to eliminate insects and control disease. "The time has now arrived to urge those who are inclined to be slothful and negligent," the *Little Falls Journal and Courier* declared, "to wake up and place their surroundings in as sanitary condition as possible before the warm weather permits the flies and other insects to increase and multiply to spread the germs of typhoid and disease broadcasts." The Phoenix Mill built four houses for workers, a loan association was started to provide the foreign population with opportunities for acquiring their own property, and a retired industrialist built a church on the south side. Considering the deplorable condition and deep-seated problems of the foreign section, these efforts were shamefully inadequate; the town's fathers were motivated more by self-preservation than social improvement. Instead of launching the far-reaching reforms that local conditions demanded, Little Falls did everything possible to remain a city of physical proximity and social distance.[55]

The radical press hailed the strike as "another victory for the One Big

Union" and, indeed, in certain respects it was. The workers received wage increases ranging from 5 to 16 percent, and the strike caused New York State to launch an investigation into conditions in the city. Even more significantly, the Wobblies had withstood "the Iron Heel," and had overcome considerable ethnic differences among the strikers to teach the meaning of solidarity. Within months of the settlement, however, the I.W.W. had to dissipate considerable time, money, and energy in a futile defense of fourteen strike activists arrested in the aftermath of the riot and imprisoned by Herkimer County authorities. Benjamin S. Legere and Phillipo Boccini received the most severe penalties—one year each in Auburn prison. With leaders in jail or proselytizing elsewhere, the I.W.W. local in Little Falls fell into disarray. Although the AF of L remained, it was of a more conservative ideology than the I.W.W. and was interested primarily in skilled workers.[56]

In this situation the working women of Little Falls had to look to the legislature and the courts for protection and advancement. In upholding the constitutionality of the fifty-four-hour law, the New York State Supreme Court held out considerable hope for the future. Justice Abel Blackmar delivered a strongly worded decision affirming the right of the state to enact laws for the general welfare of all people, notwithstanding the constitutional guarantee of individual liberty. "The development of the industrial life of the Nation, the pressure of women and children entering the industrial field in competition with men physically better qualified for the struggle, has compelled them to submit to conditions and terms which it cannot be presumed they would freely choose," Justice Blackmar declared. "Their liberty to contract to sell their labor may be but another name for involuntary service created by existing industrial conditions. A law, which restrains the liberty to contract, may tend to emancipate them by enabling them to act as they choose, and not as competitive conditions compel." For the next several years, various civic and labor groups in New York State pushed hard for remedial factory legislation.[57]

NOTES

1. State of New York, *New York Labor Review* 15 (March 1913), 3, 13.

2. The Little Falls textile strike of 1912-1913 is mentioned in Philip S. Foner, *The Industrial Workers of the World 1905-1917* (New York: International Publishers, 1965), pp. 351-52, and Julian F. Jaffe, *Crusade Against Radicalism* (Port Washington: Kennikat Press, 1972), pp. 27-28. Phillips Russell, "The Strike at Little Falls," *International Socialist Review* 13 (December 1912), 453-60, and William D. Haywood, "On The Picket Line At Little Falls," *International Socialist Review* 13 (January 1913), 519-23, constitute somewhat longer treatments, including some provocative photographs, reported from the strike scene and the strikers' perspective. Among unpublished sources an excellent overview is presented by Schuyler

Van Horn, "The Little Falls Textile Strike of 1912," Independent Study Project, Hobart College, Geneva, New York, May 12, 1968.

3. United States Department of Labor (USDL), Women's Bureau, Bulletin No. 66-1, Clara M. Beyer, *History of Labor Legislation For Women In Three States* (Washington, 1919), pp. 80-82; USDL, Women's Bureau, Bulletin No. 66-2, Florence Smith, *Chronological Development of Labor Legislation For Women In The United States* (Washington, 1929), pp. 141, 207-11; USDL, Women's Bureau, Bulletin No. 115, Eleanor Nelson, *Women At Work* (Washington, 1933), pp. 27-28; Elizabeth Brandeis, "Women's Hour Legislation," in John R. Commons, *History of Labor In The United States, 1896-1932* (New York: MacMillan Company, 1935), 3: 478-79.

4. *Utica Observer*, February 15, 1911, p. 5; *Little Falls Journal and Courier*, February 21, 1911, p. 3; *New York Times*, February 18, 1911, p. 12; *Journal of The Assembly of the State of New York At Their One Hundred and Thirty-Fourth Session* (Albany: J. B. Lyon Company, 1911), 1: 139, 536; 2: 1266, 1308, 1389, 1452, 1539-40, 1649-50; *Journal of the Senate of the State of New York At Their One Hundred and Thirty-Fourth Session* (Albany: J. B. Lyon Company, 1911), 1: 819; 2: 1377.

5. Thomas J. Kerr IV, "New York Investigating Commission and the Progressives" (Ph.D. diss., Syracuse University, 1965); Abram I. Elkus, "Social Investigation and Social Legislation," *Annals of the American Academy of Political and Social Science* 48 (July 1913), 54-65; Abram I. Elkus, "New York's New Labor Legislation," *Survey* 30 (June 21, 1913), 399-400; Leo Stein, *The Triangle Fire* (Philadelphia: Lippincott, 1962). The *Little Falls Journal and Courier*, March 28, 1911, simply reported the Triangle disaster without additional comment on local conditions.

6. Violet Pike, "Women Workers In Factories In New York State," in State of New York, *Preliminary Report of the Factory Investigating Commission* (Albany: Argus Company, 1912), 1: 294-95.

7. Informative overviews of the history and development of Little Falls, Herkimer County, and the Mohawk Valley can be found in: City of Little Falls, *Centennial Review—Development of Little Falls, 1811-1911* (Little Falls: The Art Press, 1911), pp. 8-10, 19-33, 53-61; City of Little Falls, *Little Falls Sesqui-Centennial, 1911-1961* (n.p.: n.p., 1961), *passim*; Nelson Green, ed., *History of the Mohawk Valley: Gateway To The West 1614-1925* (Chicago: S. J. Clarke Publishing Company, 1925), 2: 1481-1504, 1759-1777, 4: 825-29; George Hardin, ed., *History of Herkimer County New York* (Syracuse: D. Mason and Company, 1893), pp. 242-301.

8. *Utica Observer*, August 13, 1912, p. 11, and August 12, 1912, p. 8; *Utica Daily Press*, August 13, 1912, p. 3, and August 12, 1912, p. 1; *Little Falls Journal and Courier*, August 13, 1912, p. 3.

9. *Journals of the Assembly and Senate of the State of New York At Their One Hundred and Thirty-Fifth Session* (Albany: The Argus Company, 1912), 1-2: *passim*; State of New York, *Laws of the State of New York Passed At The One Hundred and Thirty-Fifth Session of the Legislature* (Albany: J. B. Lyon Company, 1912), 2: 1102-5; *New York Times*, March 30, 1912, p. 2, and October 1, 1912, p. 12. For a comparative analysis of the labor laws in various states regarding women see: Josephine Goldmark, "Legislative Gains For Women in 1912," *Survey* 28 (April 13, 1912), 95-96; Josephine Goldmark, "Labor Laws For Women," *Survey* 29 (January

25, 1913), 552-55; Florence Kelley, "Limiting Women's Working Hours," *Survey* 25 (January 21, 1911), 651-52; "Women's Work," *American Labor Legislation Review* 2 (October 1912), 495-501.

10. *New York Times*, September 29, 1912, 1, p. 5; Josephine Goldmark, "The New York 54-Hour Law," *Survey* 29 (December 14, 1912), 332-33; "Shorter Hours In New York Factories," *Survey* 29 (October 12, 1912), 51-52.

11. *Little Falls Journal and Courier*, October 8, 1912, p. 3; *New York Call*, November 12, 1912, p. 3; *Solidarity*, October 19, 1912, p. 3.

12. State of New York, Reports of the Board of Mediation and Arbitration and Bureau of Labor Statistics, "The Little Falls Textile Workers Dispute," *New York Labor Bulletin* 15 (March 1913), *passim*. The Little Falls strike should be comparatively analyzed with Lawrence by consulting the excellent study of the Massachusetts dispute provided in Melvyn Dubofsky, *We Shall Be All* (New York: Quadrangle Books, 1969), pp. 227-62.

13. The value of products manufactured in Little Falls was as follows: 1899, $4,070,596; 1904, $4,471,080; 1909, $8,460,408. Only Plattsburgh (196.9%) and Olean (113.9%) registered larger relative gains in the period 1904-1909, and these increases were largely the result of establishing a new industry and reopening an idle one. USDC, Bureau of the Census, *Thirteenth Census of the United States: 1910, Abstract With Supplement For New York State* (Washington, 1913), p. 702.

14. State of New York, Department of Labor, "Conditions Of Entrance and Advancement In Individual Industries," in *Twenty-Sixth Annual Report of the Bureau of Labor Statistics For The Year Ended September 30, 1908* (Albany: State Department of Labor, 1909), pp. 125-41.

15. State of New York, Department of Labor, *New York Labor Bulletin*, 57 (January, 1914), 25-26; State of New York, Department of Labor, *Annual Report of the Bureau of Labor Statistics: 1912* (Albany: State Department of Labor, 1913), pp. 128-29, 482.

16. The wages paid to the textile workers were actually lower than these statistics suggest because the state investigators analyzing the data did not have the time under strike conditions to separate the wages of superintendents, foremen, machinists, and other skilled workers from the overall payrolls. State of New York, "The Little Falls Textile Workers Dispute," pp. 32-44.

17. *Little Falls Journal and Courier*, October 22, 1912, p. 2.

18. Kenneth E. Hendrickson, Jr., "George R. Lunn And The Socialist Era In Schenectady, 1909-1916," *New York History* 47 (January 1966), 22-40; Larry Hart, "Lunn Was Prominent In City's Socialist Era," *Schenectady Gazette*, March 12, 1975, p. 33.

19. *New York Call*, October 17, 1912, p. 1, October 18, 1912, pp. 1, 2, and October 19, 1912, p. 1; *Utica Daily Press*, October 15, 1912, p. 14, October 16, 1912, p. 12, and October 17, 1912, p. 12; Schenectady *Citizen*, October 18, 1912, p. 1, and January 10, 1913, p. 1; *Little Falls Journal and Courier*, October 22, 1912, p. 2; "The Constitution And The Police," *Survey* 29 (October 22, 1912), 93-94.

20. *Utica Daily Press*, October 16, 1912, p. 12. Similar statements by Herkimer County Sheriff James W. Moon in the *New York Call*, October 19, 1912, p. 1, and Mayor Frank Shall in *Little Falls Journal and Courier*, October 22, 1912, p. 2. In the decade 1900-1910, the population of Little Falls increased 18.2%, from 10,381 to

12,272 people. This increase of 1,891 people was accounted for almost exclusively by an influx of immigrants. While the native-born population declined during the decade from 81.5% of the total population to 67.6%, the foreign-born percentage increased from 18.4% to 31.9%. USDI, Census Office, *Eleventh Census of the United States, Population: 1890* (Washington, 1892), 1, pt. 1, 447, 564; USDI, Census Office, *Twelfth Census of the United States, Population: 1900* (Washington, 1901), 1, pt. 1, 630; USDC, Bureau of the Census, *Thirteenth Census of the United States, Population: 1910* (Washington, 1913), 3, 208, 245.

21. *Syracuse Post Standard*, October 17, 1912, p. 4, and October 19, 1912, p. 4.

22. For the dispute with the State Prison Commission, see *Little Falls Journal and Courier*, April 2, 1912, p. 2, April 9, 1912, p. 2, May 14, 1912, p. 3, and June 18, 1912, p. 3. For the comment of Governor Dix, consult State of New York, *Public Papers of Governor John A. Dix: 1912* (Albany: J. B. Lyon Company, 1913), pp. 429-30.

23. *Utica Daily Press*, October 22, 1912, pp. 5, 9; *New York Call*, October 21, 1912, pp. 1, 6, and October 22, 1912, p. 1; *Schenectady Gazette*, October 19, 1912, p. 1, and October 21, 1912, p. 1; *New York Times*, October 21, 1912, p. 5; *Syracuse Post Standard*, October 21, 1912, p. 1.

24. *Utica Daily Press*, October 24, 1912, p. 4, October 25, 1912, p. 9, and October 30, 1912, p. 7; *Schenectady Gazette*, October 24, 1912, p. 1; *New York Call*, October 24, 1912, p. 1.

25. *Utica Daily Press*, October 31, 1912, p. 4, and November 1, 1912, p. 12; *Little Falls Journal and Courier*, November 5, 1912, p. 3.

26. Handbill proclamation dated October 30, 1912, in the possession of the Little Falls City Historian, City Hall, Little Falls, New York; Haywood, "On The Picket Line," pp. 520-22; *Schenectady Citizen*, November 1, 1912, pp. 1, 6; *Utica Daily Press*, November 4, 1912, p. 14, November 5, 1912, p. 4, and November 7, 1912, p. 3; *Little Falls Journal and Courier*, November 5, 1912, p. 2.

27. *Little Falls Journal and Courier*, January 2, 1912, p. 3.

28. *Little Falls Journal and Courier*, January 10, 1911, p. 2, and January 17, 1911, p. 2.

29. *Little Falls Journal and Courier*, November 14, 1911, p. 2.

30. *Little Falls Journal and Courier*, December 5, 1911, p. 3.

31. Little Falls outdistanced runner-up Tarrytown 65.2 seals per pupil to 34.3, selling overall 90,476 seals. *Little Falls Journal and Courier*, April 16, 1912, p. 3.

32. *Little Falls Journal and Courier*, January 30, 1912, p. 3, and May 14, 1912, p. 3; *Utica Daily Press*, October 19, 1912, pp. 1, 7; *Utica Saturday Globe*, December 28, 1912, p. 12.

33. *Little Falls Journal and Courier*, May 21, 1912, p. 3.

34. *Little Falls Journal and Courier*, June 4, 1912, p. 3, and June 18, 1912, p. 3.

35. *Little Falls Journal and Courier*, September 10, 1912, p. 2.

36. *Little Falls Journal and Courier*, October 8, 1912, p. 3.

37. *Little Falls Journal and Courier*, August 27, 1912, p. 1, and May 28, 1912, p. 2.

38. *Utica Saturday Globe*, December 28, 1912; *Utica Daily Press*, November 2, 1912, p. 18; *Little Falls Journal and Courier*, November 26, 1912, p. 3; *Albany Times Union*, November 21, 1912, p. 8.

39. *Utica Daily Press*, October 19, 1912, pp. 1, 7, October 18, 1912, p. 14,

December 10, 1912, p. 12, and January 9, 1913, p. 10; *Utica Saturday Globe*, December 28, 1912, p. 12; *Rochester Democrat and Chronicle*, December 9, 1912, p. 14; *New York Tribune*, January 8, 1913, p. 7.

40. Female strike leaders, like M. Helen Schloss and Matilda Rabinowitz, made speaking appearances and solicited funds in Albany, Utica, Rochester, Buffalo, Detroit, and Minneapolis among other cities. It is difficult to secure a complete picture of their activities, however, because of inadequate press coverage and uneven reporting. Local correspondents commonly dwelled on the speaker's physical characteristics and recent participation in Little Falls. Only infrequently would the coverage quote parts of a speech and delve into the speaker's background and involvement in the labor movement. See, for example, coverage of a Schloss speech in *Rochester Democrat and Chronicle*, December 9, 1912, p. 14. June Sochen, *Movers and Shakers* (New York: Quadrangle, 1973) provides a scholarly treatment of twentieth-century American women thinkers and activists.

41. *Helen Keller* (New York: American Foundation For The Blind, 1960); *National Cyclopedia of American Biography* (New York: James T. White & Company, 1916), 15, 177.

42. Consult the excellent introduction, speeches, articles, and letters provided in Philip S. Foner, ed., *Helen Keller: Her Socialist Years* (New York: International Publishers, 1967).

43. Foner, *Helen Keller*, pp. 7-10, 29-30; Helen Keller, *Out Of The Dark* (Garden City: Doubleday, Doran & Company, 1930), pp. 9-11, 160-61, 185-87; Helen Keller, *Midstream: My Later Life* (Garden City: Doubleday, Doran & Company, 1929), pp. 86-88, 330-32; Van Wyck Brooks, *Helen Keller: Sketch for a Portrait* (New York: E. P. Dutton & Company, 1956), pp. 90-92.

44. Foner, *Helen Keller*, pp. 10-14, 21-26; Keller, *Out Of The Dark*, pp. 18-29; Brooks, *Helen Keller*, pp. 48-49.

45. Foner, *Helen Keller*, pp. 14-15, 82-85, 91-97; Brooks, *Helen Keller*, pp. 86-89.

46. Haywood, "On The Picket Line," pp. 518-20; Schenectady *Citizen*, November 29, 1912, p. 2; *Industrial Worker*, December 5, 1912, p. 4; *New York Call*, November 21, 1912, p. 1. Keller's letter to the Little Falls strikers has been conveniently reprinted in Foner, *Helen Keller*, p. 37; Keller, *Out Of The Dark*, pp. 34-35.

47. *Utica Daily Press*, October 25, 1912, p. 9; *Little Falls Journal and Courier*, October 29, 1912, p. 3; *Syracuse Post Standard*, October 24, 1912, p. 2; *Schenectady Gazette*, October 24, 1912, p. 1. A cogent appraisal of I.W.W. and AFL commonalities and differences is provided by Joseph Conlin, *Bread and Roses Too* (Westport: Greenwood Press, 1969), pp. 2-4, 13-21.

48. *Little Falls Journal and Courier*, November 19, 1912, p. 3, November 26, 1912, p. 3, December 3, 1912, and December 31, 1912, p. 3; *Utica Daily Press*, December 23, 1912, p. 8; *Solidarity*, November 23, 1912, p. 2.

49. *Schenectady Gazette*, October 19, 1912, p. 1, December 18, 1912, p. 1, and December 20, 1912, p. 1; *Utica Daily Press*, October 22, 1915, p. 5, and December 17, 1912, p. 14; *Solidarity*, December 21, 1912, p. 1, and December 28, 1912, p. 1; *Industrial Worker*, December 26, 1912, p. 1; *New York Call*, December 20, 1912, p. 2, and December 23, 1912, p. 2; *New York Times*, December 18, 1912, p. 11.

50. See, for example, *Little Falls Journal and Courier*, December 31, 1912, p. 2; *Utica Daily Press*, December 23, 1912, p. 8, December 28, 1912, p. 5, and December

31, 1912, pp. 5, 6; *New York Call*, December 28, 1912, p. 1; *New York Times*, December 28, 1912, p. 2; *Solidarity*, January 4, 1913, p. 1.

51. State of New York, "The Little Falls Textile Workers Dispute," 50-57. For Little Falls criticizing the state report as incomplete and biased consult *Little Falls Journal and Courier*, March 13, 1913, p. 2.

52. *Utica Daily Press*, January 2, 1913, p. 12, and January 3, 1913, p. 7; *Utica Observer*, January 3, 1913, p. 3; *Little Falls Journal and Courier*, January 7, 1913, p. 2; *Syracuse Post Standard*, January 3, 1913, p. 1; *Schenectady Gazette*, January 3, 1913, p. 1; *New York Call*, January 3, 1913, p. 2; *Solidarity*, January 11, 1913, p. 1; *Albany Times Union*, January 2, 1913, p. 1.

53. *Little Falls Journal and Courier*, January 14, 1913, p. 3.

54. *Little Falls Journal and Courier*, July 29, 1913, p. 3, and September 9, 1913, p. 2; *Utica Daily Press*, August 14, 1912, p. 10, and November 2, 1912, p. 18.

55. Van Horn, "The Little Falls Textile Strike of 1912," pp. 3, 42-43, 47; *Little Falls Journal and Courier*, April 22, 1913, p. 3.

56. "State Investigation of Little Falls Strike," *Survey* 29 (January 4, 1913), 414; "Two Reports On the Little Falls Strike," *Survey* 29 (March 29, 1913), 899; *New York Times*, March 20, 1913, p. 6; *Utica Daily Press*, March 20, 1913, p. 6; *Herkimer Citizen*, March 25, 1913, p. 4; Phillips Russell, "The Fourteen in Jail," *International Socialist Review* 12 (February 1913), 598-99; (Charles E. Kerr), "Will Prosecute Mill Owners," *International Socialist Review* 13 (March 1913), 670; J. S. Biscay, "Liberty Or The Penitentiary?" *International Socialist Review* 13 (April 1913), 750-54.

57. State of New York, *The Miscellaneous Reports of the State of New York* (Albany: J. B. Lyon Company, 1913), 79, 140-49; *New York Times*, January 11, 1913, p. 13, and January 13, 1913, p. 10; *Utica Daily Press*, January 13, 1913, p. 4; "Women And Their Hours Of Labor," *Chatauquan* 67 (September 1912), 14-15.

THE I.W.W. AND THE AKRON RUBBER STRIKE OF 1913

ROY T. WORTMAN

"Of course there is no need to jettison a fundamental commitment to social change. Equally dangerous, however, is a commitment to political judgments that have been surpassed by history."   —Stanley Arnowitz

"Akron remains, to this day, the supreme mistake of the I.W.W.," declared the *One Big Union Monthly* in 1920. "Never in the history of the I.W.W. has a strike that opened with such alluring prospects led to such a crushing disillusionment."[1] The supreme mistake was Akron's rubber strike in 1913.

Akron's industrial development in the early twentieth century took place at top speed.[2] In addition to incentives offered by the city to the rubber industry, an extra resource was present in the form of a readily available labor pool. Seventy percent of this pool were native-born Americans who were "internal migrants" hailing from rural Ohio, West Virginia, and Pennsylvania; an immigrant workforce from central and eastern Europe, lured to the United States by promotional agents' glowing pictures of wealth, comprised the remainder.[3] This polyglot labor pool satiated the burgeoning industry's demand for employees, and by 1913 eight corporations—Goodrich, Firestone, Goodyear, Star, Swinehart, Buckeye, Miller, and Diamond—were the main employers in Akron.

"We really were a big family," said Harvey Firestone as he looked back to 1902, when he had twelve employees.[4] A paternalistic sense of community marked his early years in the industry, a community that would, by 1913, become fragmented and torn by strife. By 1913, however, Firestone's 1,800 employees were subject to industrial regimentation and discipline, the cult of efficiency, and the diminution of individual status. As "family" transmogrified into corporation, the once-familiar bond between employer and employee was lost. "I don't even know the names of my foremen," Firestone lamented. "It used to be different."⁵ *India Rubber World*, the industry's trade journal, noted a similar problem: production efficiency and accelerated growth made the industry a depersonalized one in which foremen were removed from the problems and grievances of wage earners.⁶ And, on the other side, the I.W.W. noted the shift in Akron's development from community to impersonal industry when Wobblies noted that "Akron has become a city of furnished rooms," with a turnover of eight hundred workers moving in and out of the city monthly.⁷

Workers attempted to better their situation through organization. In 1906, five hundred rubber workers organized a union but it was short-lived: the union's office was burglarized, its records stolen, and union members lost their jobs in the rubber industry.⁸ Yet as of 1913 Akron's chamber of commerce was still blind to a problem between labor and management and smugly asserted that the "oppression of labor is so uncommon as to be almost unknown" and declared that rubber factories had modern, fire-proof buildings with ample sanitation, ventilation, and light.⁹ Workers in Akron and State Senator William Green of Coshocton, a trade unionist and vociferous opponent of labor radicalism, disagreed with the assessment offered by the chamber of commerce. Green argued that the rubber industry, coddled by protective tariffs from the government, made "enormous profits from the American people." In a populistic vein, he added, "Notwithstanding the favors extended to them by the people's government, these corporations have assumed an autocratic and arrogant attitude, refusing to meet with employees to hear grievances and to settle differences."¹⁰ Green specified such grievances as the Taylor speed-up system, which granted employees bonuses if they produced more than their fellow workers. Proponents of Taylorism, the new gospel of efficiency in Progressive life, maintained that speed-up rewarded employee initiative and efficiency. Yet rubber workers countered that Taylorism, the gospel of the "world of the factory," forced them to work faster, causing exertion and injuries to health.¹¹ Moreover, the length of the workday was contested by workers. With the exception of Goodyear's eight-hour shifts in its tire-building department, hours for male workers in the industry ran between ten to eleven for day work and thirteen for night work. Women employees worked a fifty-four-hour week. Rubber workers complained that they would be discharged if they voiced their problems to management.

These findings came from the Green Committee, appointed in February 1913 to investigate the background causes of the strike. The committee documented many of the workers' fears that complaints would lead to reprisals by management, and noted the rubber industry's general inability to deal with employee problems that led to worker discontent in the factories.

Related to this issue was the workers' fear of the blacklist system. The

Green Committee found no conclusive evidence that a list formally existed but noted that each company's employment department maintained "a minute description" of each worker which, in essence, constituted a surveillance dossier. Workers reacted adversely to the system and with good reason: "They seemed to regard the minute description of them taken upon the employment card as an unfair and humiliating espionage." Management argued that these measures were needed to protect the industry from workers with bad backgrounds, but rubber workers saw it as a de facto blacklist. The committee found that prior to the strike rubber industry wages were comparable to other industries, but that was not the real issue. At issue was the piecework system, the corollary of Taylorism, which made for wide disparities in wages in some cases.[12]

These complaints, coupled with unsanitary conditions and wage cuts in 1912, led to worker frustration and resentment,[13] a situation that was ripe for the I.W.W. The Wobbly campaign began in the summer of 1912 when organizer Elizabeth Gurley Flynn spoke in Akron, urging organization from "cellar to roof."[14] "What was done in the Lawrence textile mills," she declared, "may be done in the Akron rubber shops."[15] Six months later the I.W.W. in Akron burgeoned into an angry, albeit awkward, union. Organization was rationalized as a means of countering the corporate structure. Wobbly organizer Walter Knox considered Akron's rubber industries as a huge trust that demanded the counterorganization of workers into a "labor trust." The I.W.W. seized the moment.

Thus, in 1912, I.W.W. organizers from Cleveland established Akron's Rubber Workers' Industrial Union No. 470. They attempted to maintain secrecy because of an effective labor spy organization that had six years earlier destroyed an embryonic union group.[16] At first the Wobblies managed to recruit only a few members. Then an innovation at Firestone's works sent workers running to the I.W.W. New machines were introduced that enabled workers to produce more tires, but a new, reduced pay scale also was introduced.

On February 11, 1913, protesting Firestone's policy, a group of twenty-five tire finishers walked off the job. Three hundred other Firestone workers followed.[17] Firestone refused to negotiate with the workers and instead gave notice that "all tire makers and . . . finishers who leave the building . . . and who do not return for work this afternoon, we will consider as having given up their positions. . . ."[18] The announcement did not halt the spread of the strike. Other departments in the Firestone plant and then other companies in Akron quickly joined in. Governor James Cox ordered the State Board of Arbitration to visit Akron and attempt a settlement, but the companies refused the board's services.[19] With the possibility of arbitration rejected by the rubber companies, angry, unorganized workers went to the I.W.W.

Events moved so rapidly that the strike came as a surprise even to the Wobblies. Prior to the strike, the I.W.W. was weak in Akron and Cleveland, and local issues were neglected in favor of the famous Wobbly strike in Paterson, New Jersey, then in full swing. Seeing the possibility of a new radical stronghold in Ohio, however, allies from the Socialist party were soon supporting Wobbly efforts to capture the organization of the Akron strike. Socialists also urged public support for a nonviolent struggle.[20]

On February 13, an I.W.W. strike committee representing the rubber workers announced that it would post pickets and intercept men going to work on the morning shift.[21] As organizational strength grew, and as the momentum of the strike increased, I.W.W. veterans from other strikes and and free speech struggles throughout the United States converged on Akron.[22] Arturo Giovanitti, one of the leading Italian-language Wobbly spokesmen, noted the climate of the city when he stated that "Akron is shaken. . . . All creeds, colors, and flags are represented in the strike." Yet there was a calmness about the strikers that prompted the *Beacon Journal*, a Progressive party newspaper, to note that "not a single address was made which in any way could be calculated to inspire hatred or violence."[23] A nonviolent stance was maintained, consistent with Wobbly policy in other strikes.

Membership in the Akron I.W.W. local quickly swelled to more than 2,000. With glee a Wobbly wrote: "Haven't seen a cop since I have been here . . . and everybody says it's the most peaceful strike ever heard of. All hail the rebel proletaire! Hurrah for the strike! Less booze for the bosses! More bread for the workers!"[24] By the strike's fourth day over 12,000 workers were staying home. Strikers maintained their peaceful ways, but Akron's mayor, Frank W. Rockwell, telegraphed Governor Cox: "Situation here alarming. . . . Local authorities will be unable to cope with it if it breaks loose. Request two companies ONG [Ohio National Guard] with more available."[25] Rockwell knew from Ohio's adjutant general that guard units from Cleveland, Youngstown, and Warren were within a one-hour railroad trip of the strike.[26] Yet Governor Cox did not jump into the situation. He refused Rockwell's request for troops and offered instead the State Board of Arbitration "to establish amicable relations" in Akron. The offer was refused by the rubber industry.[27]

Despite its rejection, the board attempted to use moral suasion on the parties in the strike. One member of the board, D. H. Sullivan, a former miners' organizer with a reputation for being fair-minded, met with Akron's police chief, who told him that no trouble was expected.[28] On February 17, with I.W.W. membership now estimated at 6,000, board members met with organizers George Speed and Walter Glover, who assured arbitrators that strikers would "remain quiet." "We believe your assurances," replied the board, and "we find you a good natured crowd, not intent on violence."

Such assurances were borne out by speeches made earlier in the day by Speed and Glover:

It is not the laboring classes who resort to violence and rioting. . . . It is the so-called upper classes, the capitalists, who resort to such means; they have robbed the working man and all their wealth was gained by violent, unscrupulous means. What chances has an honest man in such an age? . . .

No, use no violence, boys; show the bosses that the laboring men have the brains to stand together and organize; show them that you do not depend on violent methods to gain your purpose and you are sure to win out in this strike.[29]

By February 18, the I.W.W. claimed 12,000 members out of a total of 20,000 rubber workers.[30] The situation was still peaceful and the sheriff saw no reason to act.[31] Wobblies could thus far claim control of the situation, and they paraded triumphantly with an eighteen-piece marching band followed by strikers holding signs reading, "We are the I.W.W.," and "Thirteen Hours Killed Father." From an exuberant atmosphere heady with momentary triumph, the I.W.W., after consulting with strikers, presented a list of grievances. The forty-two grievances touched on three areas: all employees fired because of strike participation had to be rehired; work schedules were to be an eight-hour day and a six-day week; and attention was to be given to wage increases. But despite the enthusiasm and élan, the I.W.W. had already passed its zenith. In the third week of the strike, fewer and fewer strike badges could be seen in the street. Cold weather reduced the number of pickets, and workers returned to the job. Ben Williams, Wobbly editor of *Solidarity*, had high hopes for a sustained strike, but his aspirations never materialized.[32]

When the I.W.W. strike committee called for 5,000 pickets at the Goodrich plant on February 25, only 200 showed up, met by as many police officers and deputies. The temper of the strike now changed; police, for the first time, arrested one of the strike leaders, Frank Midney, for allegedly "promoting disorder."[33]

By this time a schism had developed between workers who wanted compromise with management and the more militant strike position espoused by the I.W.W. A spokesman for workers stated that the I.W.W. alienated the strikers. Perhaps Wobbly unwillingness to make concessions disturbed some workers. On that same day, William D. Haywood visited Akron in an effort to bolster sagging morale by urging unity and nonviolence. Significantly, Haywood recognized that the strike was lagging, and thus he looked to future tactics rather than to the present condition of the strike. "If the boss starves you back to work then you . . . win this strike on the inside of the factory. Don't use the speeding-up, but the slowing-down process."[34] Despite this attempt to regroup the strike force, the rubber workers continued to lose interest in the issue. By March 3, even while the

Green Committee probed the causes and grievances of the strike, workers were returning to the factories in large numbers. The emergency period was over. Mayor Rockwell, who had earlier feared the potential of the strike, now relaxed and allowed saloons to reopen.[35]

For workers, getting back to the job was more important than the goals of the I.W.W. Haywood no doubt recognized this when he spoke again in Akron on March 6. "Do not depend on the Senate Probe committee to help you," he said to an audience of 1,000. "Get out on the picket line . . . I know how anxious you are to get back to work. You are like an old horse which has been on a treadmill. It doesn't know what to do. But hold out a little longer. Don't give in." Haywood's appeal fell on deaf ears as Wobblies signed up only thirty-seven members that day. Nearly everybody had returned to their jobs.[36]

On the evening of March 7, as the strike peaked, the first serious clash occurred between police and strikers. The disorders were repeated on March 8 when, against city orders, 350 strikers picketed the Goodrich plant. To disperse the illegal picketers, sheriff's deputies charged the crowd and made seven arrests. The use of force was significant: it indicated the strong desire of those in authority to destroy the strike and showed as well their contempt for Governor Cox's conciliatory position, which insisted on the preservation of free assembly and speech.[37] Two Socialist city councilmen protested police interference, but the remainder of the council defeated their resolution.[38] When police-striker confrontation over picketing flared up again on March 11, the sheriff warned against gatherings of three or more people on streets: in short, the right to picket was denied. By now police had a new ally when prominent residents of Akron formed the Citizens Welfare Association, a deputized vigilante group led by the Reverend George P. Atwater, "Bible in one hand and a wagon spoke in the other." This mobile force of well-to-do vigilantes, with sixty automobiles at its disposal, feared the radicalism of the I.W.W. as disruptive to the hegemony of Akron's ruling classes and forced forty to fifty Wobblies to leave the city, thus contributing to the breakup of the local union.[39] Governor Cox was asked by strikers to stop this "mob of the rich," but this time Cox had lost interest in harmony and conciliation. He refused to act.[40]

In addition to worker desertion and resistance from the Citizens Welfare Association, the Wobblies also faced opposition from the more conservative AFL, as the strike lost the support of Akron's Central Labor Union (CLU).[41] Cal Wyatt, AFL organizer who had competed with the I.W.W. for membership at earlier strikes in Little Falls, New York, and Lawrence, Massachusetts, now tried to take over the Akron strike. Under his aegis a rubber workers' local was formally organized, and its AFL members wore small American flags in contrast to the red-ribbon strike badges of the I.W.W.[42] Wyatt tried to influence public opinion against the I.W.W. by raising the issue of "radicalism." Indeed, when the Green Committee entered Akron, Wyatt stated, "I do not see how these I.W.W. people can be very anxious for such an investigation . . . as up to this time they have been stating that they cared nothing for government, and they were not expected to favor having the legislature take up this matter."[43] Wyatt's efforts at AFL organization, however, were not successful. Momentum for worker organization was destroyed with the strike, and the AFL rubber workers' local had a "poorly attended" meeting. Wobblies estimated AFL membership at about 100.[44] Nonetheless, Wyatt succeeded in convincing the CLU to withdraw its support of the strike.[45] Ironically, the anti-Wobbly AFL did not endear itself to manufacturers. Goodrich and Goodyear declined negotiation even with the conservative CLU.[46]

By the third week in March, three-quarters of the striking rubber workers had returned to work. Rubber companies refused to hire Wobbly activists for fear of sabotage. The I.W.W. organization suffered another blow when the rented meeting hall closed its doors on the grounds that the place needed plastering. Moreover, Wobblies claimed that Roman Catholic priests duped their foreign-born congregants by stating that the strike was already over. On top of this, public attention was diverted to another, more pressing problem: a sudden, massive flood. By March 25, 1913, the strike came to a halt and did not flare up again.[47]

A postmortem reveals a variety of factors that caused the strike's failure and, with that failure, also the demise of the I.W.W. in Akron. The strike was spontaneous, while industry was established and well prepared with funds and law enforcement allies. Akron's chamber of commerce, rubber manufacturers, police, and two of the city's three newspapers posed formidable opposition to the I.W.W.[48] Management, reluctant to accept the State Board of Arbitration's services, vitiated whatever bargaining power the I.W.W. might have had. A minor irritant was contributed by strife between two I.W.W. organizers who had personal differrences.[49] Moreover, as the strike's demise was reviewed, another factor was alleged—the use of provocateurs who worked to instigate police action against the I.W.W. Industrial espionage was not unique to Akron. It was, as federal investigators asserted, a nationwide trend used by segments of industry to infiltrate and destroy union organization. What Selig Perlman said of the Lawrence strike applied to Akron: "Hand in hand with the system of blacklisting goes a system of espionage."[50]

This was borne out when, shortly after the strike, J. W. Reid, an employee of Diamond Rubber Company, admitted that he was an operative for the corporation's auxiliary company, an industrial police group. At the same time, Reid served as the I.W.W.'s secretary-treasurer in Akron and helped keep Local No. 470 alive. Reid admitted that some officials of the local acted as industrial spies who sabotaged strike efforts. For instance, I.W.W. membership rolls were taken by industrial spies from union headquarters to the Portage Hotel, where stenographers recorded the names of union members. Another time, Reid, told to abscond with the union's treasury, had qualms of conscience and confessed all in a public affidavit.[51] It was no small wonder, then, that management and other opponents of the I.W.W. in Akron knew in advance the moves the union would make. Industrial spies were the intelligence network for the rubber industry, and law enforcement officers and the Citizens Welfare Association were its janissaries who received ample thanks: after the strike the industry trade journal reported that F. C. Shaw, vice-president of Goodrich, sent a gift of $2,000 to Akron's police department "as a slight token of . . . appreciation for services rendered, not so much to ourselves as to the city generally."[52]

More the the point, the Akron rubber workers were usually ignorant of or indifferent to I.W.W. ideology; the union offered an escape valve for immediate frustrations and tensions, but that was as far as the I.W.W. reached. The overwhelming majority of strikers who joined the I.W.W. during the strike did so without any real knowledge of Wobbly doctrine. One worker epitomized this sentiment when he told the Green Committee that he signed up with the Wobblies without even reading its constitution. The worker simply believed that the I.W.W. would secure better working conditions.[53] The I.W.W., as it looked back on its failure in Akron, attributed defeat to the strikers themselves. "The American striker," noted an I.W.W. writer, "is unschooled . . . in picketing and unamenable to the mass enthusiasms which mean so much to the success of the strike. The American temperament is too phlegmatically individualistic."[54] In short, the issue in Akron was the creation of union organization to respond to local and immediate issues in the rubber factories. The Akron strike magnified the difficulties of union organization and bargaining in an environment that lacked a tradition of worker solidarity.

The I.W.W.'s last stand in Akron consisted of a letter both angry and sarcastic from Frank Dawson, Wobbly publicity director, to Mayor Rockwell:

This day is April Fool's day. That is why I write to the man who holding the highest municipal office, has proven himself the biggest ass since the poor animal died, that Jesus rode into Jerusalem on. I have adhered to the motto, "Appropriateness is the first of virtues."[55]

Aside from his obvious frustration, Dawson's letter also revealed a misreading of the rubber industry's workers. Not only were many of them too "individualistic," as the I.W.W. observed, but many were deeply rooted as well to traditional values that enabled them to accept, stoically, life on this earth devoid of the quest for the radical and visionary long-range goals of the I.W.W. The Akron rubber workers' apparent radicalism in 1913 seemed more a consequence of specific grievances against the rubber industry than a radical alienation from deeply rooted values. That, even more than the vigilantes and police, destroyed the Wobbly effort at organization in Akron. Mayor Rockwell refused, after the end of the strike, to grant the Wobblies a permit for street meetings;[56] Akron's I.W.W. remained dormant until prodded and harassed by the federal government during the Great War.

Yet, the Wobblies were not a failure in Akron. Despite their apparent defeat, achievements were gained by the rubber workers. Between 1914 and 1920 rubber workers, without union support, gained the eight-hour day, voluntary factory sanitary regulations, and "the big money" from lucrative war contracts. With the exception of Goodyear's "Industrial Republic," a company union, Akron rubber workers remained unorganized until the advent of the New Deal.[57] Though rubber workers secured the eight-hour day and higher wages, the fact remained that without unionization the rubber companies refused to respond to the problems caused by industrial poisoning from lead, analine coal-tar, benzol, naphtha, carbon disulphide, and phenol poisoning.[58]

The I.W.W. impulse was, in a limited vein, successful over twenty years after the strike. Industrial union democracy came to partial fruition in the 1930s through the CIO and the modest success of the Wobblies themselves; for in the 1930s the Wobblies—or at least a rebellious faction of the Wobblies—*did* succeed in organizing within the I.W.W. fold as Metal and Machinery Workers Industrial Union No. 440 and made gains in Cleveland's metal-fabricating shops. Yet, for every gain there was a loss: in making collective bargaining a reality for the I.W.W. in Ohio in the 1930s, and in signing contracts with the employer class, No. 440, by virtue of its tactics (which tried to synthesize long-range revolutionary goals with pragmatic job unionism), was forced to disaffiliate from the I.W.W.[59] The "rebel proletaire" of the rubber strike had, by the 1930s, come a long way via a circuitous route. But the 1930s were long removed from the rubber strike of 1913, which was short-lived. Almost four months after the end of the strike, Akron's feeble local made a plea for direct action and the inevitability of the historical process:

If you dam up the river of progress, at your peril and cost let it be.
That river will seaward without you; Twill break down your dam and be free.
And we heed not thy pitiful barriers That you in its way have downcast;
For your efforts but add to the torrent Whose flood must o'erwhelm you at
    last.[60]

But the dam did not break, not did the apocalypse occur. For in the 1930s New Deal NRA codes, the Wagner Act, and organized labor eventually secured many of the specific demands of the Wobblies, but in the process the I.W.W. program was stripped of its radical implications.

NOTES

1. "The Story of the I.W.W.," *One Big Union Monthly* 2 (April 1920), 46 (reprinted New York, 1968).

2. Harold S. Roberts, *The Rubber Workers: Labor Organization and Collective Bargaining in the Rubber Industry* (New York, 1944), p. 8.

3. *Solidarity*, March 1, 8, 1913; letter from Paul Sebestyen to Roy T. Wortman. Sebestyen was a Hungarian I.W.W. organizer in Ohio.

4. Harvey S. Firestone, *Men and Rubber: The Story of Business* (New York, 1926), p. 13.

5. Alfred Leif, *The Firestone Story* (New York, 1951), pp. 67-70.

6. *India Rubber World*, 57 (April 1913), 365-66.

7. *Solidarity*, March 8, 1913.

8. Selig Perlman and Philip Taft, *Labor Movements*, in John R. Commons, ed., *History of Labor in the United States, 1896-1932* (New York, 1935), 4, p. 277.

9. *India Rubber World*, 57 (March 1, 1913), 301-2.

10. Senate Resolution No. 29, in Ohio, Eightieth General Assembly, Senate, *Journal* (1913), 103, p. 247. Green's resolution to investigate the strike and to subpoena witnesses for testimony was adopted in the state senate by a vote of 30 to 3. Green (1870-1952) served as secretary-treasurer of the United Mine Workers, 1912-1924, and became president of the AFL in 1924.

11. "Majority and Minority Reports of the Senate Select Committee appointed to investigate causes and circumstances of the strike of employees of the Akron Rubber Industries," in ibid., appendix, pp. 207-8. Hereafter cited as the Green Committee Report.

12. Ibid., pp. 208-9, 211.

13. *Akron Beacon Journal*, February 13, 1913. For an individual case of a wage cut, and for complaints on unsanitary conditions, see O. S. Miller's testimony to the Green Committee, *Akron Beacon Journal*, March 5, 1913. Discontent over the piecework system is best seen in the testimony of A. E. Mapes and Elizabeth Bryan, ibid., March 10, 1913.

14. *Solidarity*, August 17, 1912.

15. Ibid., February 8, 1913.

16. "The Story of the I.W.W.," 44.

17. *Akron Beacon Journal*, February 12, 13, 1913; *Solidarity*, February 22, 1913.

18. *Akron Beacon Journal*, February 13, 1913.

19. Green Committee Report, p. 207; *Solidarity*, February 22, 1913; *Akron Beacon Journal*, February 15, 1913.

20. "The Story of the I.W.W.," 44-45.

21. *Solidarity*, February 22, 1913; *Akron Beacon Journal*, February 13, 1913.

22. Letter from Paul Sebestyen to Roy T. Wortman.

23. *India Rubber World*, 47 (March 1, 1913), 301; *Akron Beacon Journal*, February 13, 1913.

24. *Solidarity*, February 12, 1913.

25. *Akron Beacon Journal*, February 15, 1913.

26. Ibid.

27. *Akron Beacon Journal*, February 15, 1913; *Solidarity*, March 1, 1913; Green Committee Report, p. 207.

28. *Akron Beacon Journal*, February 17, 1913.

29. Ibid.

30. Ibid., February 18, 1913.

31. Ibid., February 19, 1913.

32. *Solidarity*, March 1, 1913.

33. *Akron Beacon Journal*, February 26, 1913.

34. Leslie H. Marcy, "800 Percent and the Akron Strike," *International Socialist Review*, 13 (April 1913), 723.

35. *Akron Beacon Journal*, March 3, 1913.

36. Ibid., March 6, 1913.

37. Ibid., March 7, 8, 1913; Marcy, "800 Percent," 724.

38. *Akron Beacon Journal*, March 11, 1913.

39. Ibid., March 12, 13, 1913; *India Rubber World*, 47 (April 1, 1913), 365; *Solidarity*, March 22, 1913; Hugh Allen, *The House of Goodyear: Fifty Years of Men and Rubber* (Akron, 1949), p. 172.

40. *Akron Beacon Journal*, March 13, 1913.

41. Ibid., March 15, 1913.

42. Ibid., March 1, 1913.

43. Ibid., February 26, 1913.

44. Ibid., February 25, 1913; *Industrial Worker*, March 6, 1913.

45. Ibid., February 20, 1913; March 15, 1913.

46. Ibid., March 20, 1913.

47. *India Rubber World*, 47 (April 1, 1913), 366; *Akron Beacon Journal*, March 22, 25, 1913; *Industrial Worker*, April 3, 1913.

48. Letter from Paul Sebestyen to Roy T. Wortman.

49. "The Story of the I.W.W.," 46.

50. Selig Perlman, "Preliminary Report on an Investigation of the Relations between Labor and Capital in the Textile Industry of New England," (1914), United States Industrial Relations Commission, unpublished report, Wisconsin Historical Society; Daniel O'Reagan, "Memoranda and Reports on Field Investigation of Private Detective Agencies, May 17, 1914," in USIRC, unpublished reports, National Archives and Records Service, Record Group 174, contains recommendations for curbing professional strikebreaking agencies; letter from Paul Sebestyen to Roy T. Wortman; for an illustrative document giving methods of operation in Ohio, see *United Mine Workers' Journal*, 25 (April 1, 1915).

51. *Solidarity*, January 17, 1914; "The Story of the I.W.W.," 46.

52. *India Rubber World*, 47 (June 1, 1913), 480.

53. *Akron Beacon Journal*, March 10, 1913.

54. "The Story of the I.W.W.," 45.

55. *Akron Beacon Journal*, April 1, 1913.

56. *Akron Beacon Journal*, May 27, 1913.

57. Howard and Ralph Wolf, *Rubber: A Story of Glory and Greed* (New York, 1936), p. 507.

58. Alice Hamilton, "Industrial Poisons Used in the Rubber Industry," U.S. Bureau of Labor Statistics, *Bulletin* No. 179 (October 1915), p. 9; Rey Vincent Luce, "Analine Poisoning in the Rubber Industry of Akron, Ohio," in ibid., appendix pp. 57-58; Rey Vincent Luce and Alice Hamilton, "Industrial Analine Poisoning in the United States," U.S. Bureau of Labor Statistics, *Monthly Review*, 2 (June 1916), pp. 1-12; and Emery R. Hayhurst, *A Survey of Industrial Health—Hazards and Occupational Diseases in Ohio* (Columbus, 1915), pp. 206-29.

59. Roy T. Wortman, "The Resurgence of the I.W.W. in Cleveland," *Northwest Ohio Quarterly*, 47 (Winter 1974-1975), 20-29.

60. *Solidarity*, July 12, 1913.

PATERSON: IMMIGRANT STRIKERS AND THE WAR OF 1913

JAMES D. OSBORNE

In the last third of the nineteenth century, Paterson, New Jersey, became the world's leading center of silk manufacturing. Although an old industrial site, its workshops famous for cotton textiles, ironwork, and locomotives, Paterson was still a small town at the time of the Civil War. But with the coming of the silk looms in the 1860s, the city boomed and was soon solely dependent upon this one industry.[1] Economic prosperity was accompanied by rapid population growth. From a mere 19,000 inhabitants in 1860, the city's population swelled to more than 105,000 by the turn of the century.[2]

Many of Paterson's newcomers were immigrants, flocking to the "Lyons of America" from declining silk centers in the English Midlands; Lyons and St. Etienne; Krefeld in Germany; and Lombardy and Piedmont. All of these districts supplied Paterson with large numbers of skilled silk hands. However, the workforce also brought with it a work ethic and traditions often at variance with the demands of Paterson's ambitious mill owners. William Strange, a leading manufacturer, described the gulf that separated immigrant workers from their new employers. "Manufacturers will not put on these immigrants who are swarming hither," he asserted during a trade lull in the early 1880s. "They are generally a bad set, a very bad set. They are so tainted with a communistic spirit that we prefer to have nothing to do with them."[3]

Immigrant silk workers had fled household- or workshop-based industries. Many had fought a long rearguard action against the mechanization and factory organization of their trade in Europe. Most brought to Paterson's mills combative traditions of independence and fierce resistance to attacks upon customary work habits. Strange complained, "They do not recognize the laws of the trade, when brought to bear upon their labor; but seem to be impressed with the idea that their employers are in duty bound to accede to their demands, however unjust."[4] It was their unwillingness to recognize "the laws of the trade" of a new order of society that shaped the pattern of social and industrial relations in late-nineteenth-century Paterson.

Silk manufacture in the New World was forged upon technological superiority over European rivals. Mechanized production based in the factory was the distinctive mode of production in Paterson. This world of work contrasted sharply with European forms of silk manufacture. An English visitor to Paterson in 1883 remarked:

There are differences between the methods of manufacture adopted in the States and those in vogue here. Anyone who has visited Macclesfield, Leeds, Congleton and Coventry would see many evidences of much of the work being done at the house of the operative. In Paterson and Connecticut, where the silk industry is also carried on, all the work is done at the mill. This work at home is carried on by hand looms, while at the American mills steam power is used in every instance.[5]

In Britain, France, and Germany silk was a predominantly artisan and handicraft industry. It was based upon homework and primitive forms of production until late in the nineteenth century. Nowhere in Europe was the industry a pioneer of mechanized, factory production. Everywhere it lagged behind other textiles in adapting to the new modes of industrial society. In America factory organization and mechanized looms were taken up from the outset, for only by this means could cheaper European labor costs be offset by high productivity in the United States.[6]

An important consequence of the concentration upon mechanized production in America was the altered relationship of the weaver to his labor. If the self-governing, semiindependent weaver of Europe was a mythical idea, fast disappearing on that continent where a semblance of him existed, few immigrant weavers were prepared for the rigors of mechanized factory work. American industry required the weaver to be a machine-minder, the tedium of his task abating only when the loom or the silk proved inadequate. The pace of work was now dictated by loom, not operator, and the weaver was little more than an appendage to the machine. As a result, struggles at the point of production and over the means of production were a constant feature of Paterson's principal industry.

Throughout the last third of the nineteenth century, industrial disruption wracked the Paterson silk industry. Many disputes shared a common source: the determination of Paterson mill owners to impose a new work ethic complementary to factory labor upon an immigrant labor force notoriously wayward in work habits and opposed to the disciplined rigor of factory toil. Harsh disciplinary codes governed workers in the mill. Most mill owners' work rules included the provision that "any employee damaging or walking from loom to loom or any part of the shop during working hours will be dismissed immediately. . . ."[7] Fining employees was another device for curbing irregular work habits. In the 1880s an English weaver, writing home to Macclesfield, complained of the "enormous fines" imposed in Paterson "for the most trifling defects in weaving."[8] Blue Mondays, beer drinking in the mill, thefts of silk, and the sabotaging of machinery were symptomatic of the work heritage of immigrant hands, and all formed part of workers' resistance to the will of their new masters.[9] But as often as not this contest between mill owner and mill hand resulted in industrial stoppages, particularly if the point of issue was the introduction of new mill technologies.

Scarcely a year passed without strikes disrupting the local economy. And to the end of the nineteenth century, the silk masters were unable to impose their will upon mill hands. Time after time immigrant strikers received support from Paterson's middle class, politicians, and city authorities. Herbert Gutman's examination of the trial and imprisonment of radical J. P. McDonnell indicates the barriers local manufacturers confronted.[10] McDonnell's case was not exceptional. Paterson's mill workers, typical of immigrants to industrial society, did not form stable trade unions to combat their employers. Instead, spontaneous walkouts, disorder, and violence formed their stock response at times of crisis. They discovered at least tacit approval of their aims in the social and political structure of the industrial city.

Paterson mill owners could hardly expect to command general and uniform support for their campaigns against mill hands. Most, like their workers, were newcomers to the city. Their factories almost overnight had transformed the social and economic complexion of the social and political supremacy. On the contrary, the workers had the city behind them.[11] The political weight of workingmen induced successive mayors and aldermen to rebuke the demands of mill owners for a peremptory suppression of strike disorders. Processions of strikers to city hall directed politicians' loyalties. Police officers were equally hamstrung or had their roots in Paterson's working-class neighborhoods and strong sympathies with workingmen. The influence of city government upon the police department proved a further channel of restraint. Only in exceptional instances did police intrude in industrial disputes. Thus, Paterson's mill hands were relatively unimpeded when they attacked mill property and strikebreakers.

Mass processions might burn effigies of a hated manufacturer, picket and "serenade" his mill, intimidate "loyal" operatives, and receive general support for their actions.[12] Credit supplied by sympathetic store owners and saloon keepers, verbal support from the pulpit, free legal advice—all these combined to legitimize disorderly strikes. In 1878, strikebreakers brought into the city from Fall River, Massachusetts, were successfully turned back by a strike committee. Their employer has been unable to find

a boardinghouse in Paterson that would offer them accommodation.[13]
Mill owner Strange observed the far-reaching effect of this community
pressure during industrial upheavals: "If a man tried to work he was called
a 'scab' and that clung to him all his life. His wife could not venture on the
streets without being pointed out, and the children were afraid for their
lives."[14]

Paterson, at least during periods of industrial strife, appeared to conform
to Samuel Hays's characterization of the nineteenth-century industrial city
as a place in which the "business classes were greatly outnumbered."[15]
Local manufacturers felt this to be the case:

Paterson has become so accustomed to having her peaceful or orderly work-people
hounded through the streets, driven from their work, and abused and assaulted
even in their own homes, that citizens look on with comparative indifference, while
the police make only the most feeble attempts to curb the riotous elements.

They recognized their problem to be intimately linked to the social and
political structure of the city:

The police are tied up by politics, the tradesmen fear a boycott by the large working
class, the newspapers vie with each other in trimming sail to curry favor with the
same element, the saloons open wide their doors to the beer-drinking mob by which
they live, and they and the brewers go on their bail-bond when any of the wild-eyed
Anarchists, Socialists and others of the heterogeneous masses, who are foremost in
all the strikes, go a step too far and get themselves before the courts.[16]

The 1913 strike appeared to be entirely out of character with past disputes.
The mill owners controlled the city. Police, city government, and the local
judiciary combined to back local manufacturers against strikers. Almost
2,000 mill hands were arrested, picket lines broken up, and workers' processions dispersed. Even strike headquarters were closed down.[17] It was a
distinctly new development in the industrial relations of the city.

The I.W.W. obviously plays a part in any explanation of the novel "War
of 1913." If nothing else, the organization provided opponents with a
convenient scapegoat that was widely despised and feared. However, too
much can be and has been made of the Wobblies' role in the strike. If
individuals were important as leaders, their main role was as coordinators
and publicists. They attracted attention, brought the strike before a national
audience, and for a time seemed near prompting federal intervention and a
favorable settlement, as in the Lawrence strike of 1912.

Over the day-to-day functioning of the strike, however, the Wobblies'
hold was less secure. I.W.W. ideology encouraged workers to manage their
own affairs. In Paterson, there was hardly a choice in the matter. Deeply
entrenched strike traditions would have made it difficult for any outsiders

to dominate events. The bulk of the Paterson workforce was traditionally unorganized. "Almost virgin material" was Elizabeth Gurley Flynn's description, "easily brought forth and easily stimulated to aggressive activity."[18]

Less gratifying to Wobbly leaders, local workers took quite as naturally to violence and disorder. Violence became a hallmark of the dispute. I.W.W. organizers argued that the most violent action they had taken was to counsel: "Fold Our Arms and Refuse to Work." But the strikers' behavior mocked this sentiment. On the streets they acted on their own initiative. Familiar crowds gathered to "serenade." Strikebreakers were beaten, their houses stoned and even dynamited. Attempts were made to bomb mills. More common was the smashing of factory windows and the singling out of mill foremen and supervisors for assault.[19] Flynn noted the limited value of inflammatory suggestion: "Physical violence is dramatic. . . . it's especially dramatic when you talk about it and don't resort to it."[20] Both she and Big Bill Haywood were experienced campaigners at the time of the Paterson strike, too experienced to seriously consider violent resistance. The actions of striking mill workers must have troubled them, for excessive violence would sacrifice Wobbly control of the strike, and their reaction was to deny the incidents or to blame them on the police. "We have never counseled the workers to use any violence," a local activist honestly protested. Another was forced to admit that "at times our people were very hostile . . . and we had a great deal of trouble to hold them in check."[21] On the face of it, the strikers of 1913 acted quite within the traditional industrial patterns of the city.

The central incident of the war was the death of Valentino Modestino, a metal worker who lived in Paterson's Riverside section. Although this Italian was made a celebrated martyr by the Wobbly strike leaders, his murder reflects the extent to which strike disorders were independent of I.W.W. control. Valentino lived close to the city's largest dye house, a notorious trouble spot throughout the strike. He worked in a nearby file works and was neither a striker nor a member of the I.W.W., but his friends and neighbors were. Because his home was located near an important center for pickets, he "used to invite one or two of the strikers in at a time to have a cup of coffee or a bite of lunch." A few yards from Valentino's home was a saloon, the natural meeting place for dye mill pickets. Tensions between police and pickets were high, exacerbated by the presence of private guards patrolling the dye house. A few days prior to Valentino's shooting, "a riot took place. . . . There had been stoops blown off houses, and bombs had been exploded in the rear of houses where people were sleeping, and the glass of the windows shattered and thrown upon the beds of children and wives." The Italian's death resulted from a similar commotion. Private detectives, escorting strikebreakers from the dye plant, commandeered a passing trolley car in order to get through an aggressive crowd of pickets. Strikers' passions broke into open hostilities. Empty beer bottles, grabbed from crates on the stoop of the saloon, were hurled at the blacklegs and their guards. Both the private detectives and, later, police investigators saw the attack as a premeditated design, "a concerted effort." Both pointed to the saloon and said, "There were two boys in there with two hats full of stones so that the men could use them; that is, they grasped the stones and slung them into the crowd, in addition to the bottles they were firing." The guards charged the pickets, firing wildly. In the melee, Valentino was mortally wounded.[22]

Disorders such as these bore the hallmarks of a pattern traditional to Paterson. They were rooted in the tightly knit community and work associations of the city's immigrant neighborhoods and, most important, reflected the autonomy of these groups. No Wobbly leaders were present at the killing of Valentino to direct picketing or to eschew violence, despite the notoriety of the area.

However, strike violence in 1913 also differed in important respects from the pattern of the late nineteenth century. Never before had relations between police and strikers been so poor. Nor had disorder ever been so fierce and prolonged. In 1913, the web of mutual interest and common assumptions previously shared by silk workers, police, and city authorities was in shreds. Its dissolution reflected a number of social and economic developments dating back a decade or more.

From the 1800s there was a rapid decline in the local economy. In that decade a significant number of Paterson silk manufacturers migrated to cheap labor "annexes" in Pennsylvania and the South. They protested against a hostile workforce and an uncooperative local government and were attracted by lower taxation, cheaper mill buildings, and lower wage levels in the "annex" areas. But most important, they moved to be "free of this everlasting labor question which in Paterson dominates the situation . . . the evident purpose being to diversify it so that labor troubles in one place will not control the whole industry."[23] William Strange again voiced the feelings of his fellow Paterson manufacturers:

Time and time again have the operatives of our mills, satisfied with their urges and treatment, been intimidated and compelled to abandon their employment by unchecked mob violence [which] could have been prevented had the proper authorities taken the necessary precaution [in the] incipient stages of the trouble.[24]

This exodus signaled the eclipse of Paterson as the center of United States silk manufacturing. By the opening decade of the twentieth century, local manufacturers were facing intense competition from the countryside. Paterson mills were surpassed in numbers employed, output, and value of product by their combined Pennsylvania competitors.[25] A city with a diversified economy might have weathered this loss of capital. In an industrial city dominated by a single industry, it was disastrous. Paterson businessmen and city officials were frightened by the economic stagnation. In 1913 their anxieties played a significant part in shaping opposition to the I.W.W. and the strikers. The "harm that was being done to the good name of the city" was frightening new investors away. Local boosters were appalled that business concerns "gave up the idea of coming here because they were really scared off the industrial unrest." There were those who were not directly affected by the loss, but

who were interested to maintain the good name and character of the city without having a disturbance and having the militia coming here and all that sort of thing which would only add to the notoriety which we had in the past.[26]

Paterson's notoriety as a center of unrest was bound up with another major factor in the strike of 1913: ethnic prejudice. From the mid-1890s, immigration to the city was principally Italian. As a workforce, Italian textile hands were not remarkably different from their British or French predecessors. Many had worked in the mills and weaving sheds of Italy's Alpine provinces. Like Macclesfield workers before them, most had left an industry technologically backward in comparison to that of Paterson. Biella, the wool manufacturing center of Piedmont, and the Como region, heart of Lombardy's silk industry, the principal sources of emigration to Paterson during the 1890s, were still undergoing the basic transformation from handicraft production to a mechanized factory system.[27] In the wool industry, modern forms of production were only slowly adopted. As late as 1900, one-half of the looms and one-third of the spindles in the industry were still hand-operated.[28] Silk weaving, too, was a predominantly handicraft industry, performed on handlooms in the household or small weaving sheds. The industry was part of a rural economy. The essentially pre-industrial work at the loom was frequently interrupted by the demands of the harvest or landowner. In 1890, handlooms still outnumbered the mechanical variety by four to one in the Italian silk industry.[29] Only in the throwing branch of the industry were factories common. But even here mills were usually located in rural regions, drawing upon a pool of child and female peasant labor.[30]

Organization among these workers reflected their backward and partially modernized industry. Unions, outlawed before unification, were unusual. Workers were more likely inclined to act through mutual aid societies, organized on a local basis.[31] Where organizations were established, they were often led by Bakuninist anarchists and based on specific local issues. They were also typically short-lived.[32] Violent outbursts rather than disciplined trade unionism characterized collective action in the region. An observer noted:

It is necessary to remember that in those pre-socialist times the working class was a crowd, not an army. Enlightened, orderly, bureaucratic strikes were impossible. The workers could only fight by means of demonstrations, shouting, cheering and cat-calling, intimidation and violence. Luddism and sabotage, even though not elevated into doctrines, had nevertheless to form part of the methods of struggle.[33]

Immigrants to Paterson from such a culture were not likely to submit to the new work discipline required of them in the city's mills. Their wayward-ness compelled a continuation of the harsh factory rules long familiar in the city. Tensions directly related to this same problem fueled the passions of both workers and mill owners in 1913.[34] Moreover, once out on strike, Paterson's Italians resorted to methods typical of a "crowd."

Nativist opposition to Italians was in part conditioned by the lack of organization amongst the new arrivals. Italians flooded Paterson mills in the opening decade of the twentieth century until, by 1913, they formed the largest ethnic group in the local silk industry. They displaced silk workers from the older immigrant communities and at a time when the "annex" movement was already costing jobs. Italians were seen as dragging down wage levels, resented by old-stock immigrants. English-speaking workers formed their own exclusive craft unions, anxious to keep at arm's length "immigrants coming into the trade who did not thoroughly understand the workings of our organization or had not become Americanized, and the foreigners hiring these foreigners at all kinds of wages."[35] Anti-Italian feeling was not confined to workingmen, however. A series of events at the turn of the century confirmed and perhaps extended it throughout the local community.

In July 1900, a Paterson Italian assassinated King Humbert in Italy. The assassin, Gaetano Bresci, was a member of a sizable contingent of Italian anarchists who had fled to Paterson following political persecution in their native land in the 1890s.[36] Although most worked in Paterson mills, these radicals were a secretive group, engrossed in the affairs of their homeland. Their journal, *La Questione Sociale*, showed little interest in American affairs and until 1900 was scarcely noticed in Paterson. The killing of Humbert quickly drew attention to the group, sparking off a "Red scare" in the city. New York newspapermen flocked to "Red City," picturing Paterson as a haven for foreign radicals in which law and order were main-tained only at the mercy of secret "subversive societies." City administrators and police shuddered at the reputation their city was gaining. They resolved to drive out this "murderous and bloody" collection of "stiletto carriers and blood loving swarthy devils."[37]

With the assassination of President McKinley in the summer of 1901, the situation worsened.[38] Finally, in 1902, Italian dye workers rioted during a general walkout, ransacking mill property and exchanging gunfire with city police officers. Paterson's mayor appealed to the governor for state militia, condemning the local police chief as ineffective. Strike leaders were jailed or forced to flee as the mayor pledged to destroy the "anarchist element," a mission he "would accomplish [even] if every Italian in the town had to be driven out."[39]

A new police chief, John Bimson, led the campaign that culminated in 1908 with the suppression of the Italian anarchist journal published in the city. "The fair name of the city" had been brought into question by the publication, Paterson's mayor explained in justifying his action, a matter that had "been the cause of great financial loss to this City and deep mortification to its citizens."[40]

This synthesis of nativist and antiradical sentiment was combined with long-term fears for the economic future of the city. It reached its peak in 1913. Police Chief Bimson's aim was to "nip the strike in the bud." His prompt suppression of strike meetings and bans on I.W.W. speech making were tailored to this end. But more important, in 1913, the press, Bimson's superiors in the government, and the local and county courts lined up behind him. A local editor explained the thinking prevalent amongst city officials:

New York with its big army of policemen can safely permit agitators to influence the passions of a few of its workers. Nothing serious can happen. A big strike in New York is merely an incident. A big strike in Paterson means business paralysis and a state of uneasiness for every resident in this community. New York can let professional labor agitators rant and roar because it does not affect public safety. A similar policy in Paterson would mean a constant menace to life and property.[41]

Thus, private detectives, brought into the city by mill owners, were "clothed with the authority of police." Two federal investigators noted, "The police authority of the State was, in effect, turned over to the mill owners."[42]

This campaign cannot be explained simply in terms of the I.W.W.'s lurid national image. Indeed, Wobbly personages were relatively unmolested while police and the local judiciary made the ethnic partiality of their actions obvious in a number of instances. Immigrant strikers complained that local judges were "kind of antagonistic" and "too severe" toward them. County Sheriff Amos Radcliffe agreed, explaining that immigrants were "a lower order of animals, unfit for free speech."[43]

Paterson police officers appeared to support the judiciary's stance. Missing was the traditional leniency toward mill hands, and in its place "animosity against the foreign nationality of the people." In an exchange before the federal Industrial Relations Commission in 1914, Adolph Lessig, a local strike organizer, pinpointed the change in relations between police and workingmen. He was asked, "Did you feel that the police conducted themselves as you would do as a policeman, or not?"

> *Lessig:*   Well, I thought I could have winked the other eye on many occasions. Many of them were silk workers themselves a few years ago.
>
> *Q.*   What do you mean by 'winked the other eye'?
>
> *Lessig*:   Looked the other way.
>
> *Q.*   Why?
>
> *Lessig*:   Give the other fellow a chance.
>
> *Q.*   What to do?
>
> *Lessig*:   Well, walk up and down. He was really doing nothing. They were simply too strict. No doubt about that.[44]

Lessig, a longtime resident of Paterson, judged police actions by reference to past disputes. Striker Ed Zuersher described the typical confrontation on the picket line:

They [the police] generally came with a drawn club, and sometimes with curses on their lips, especially if there were a foreign element on the picket line, and told them to get out of there, and called them Wops and Jews and such names as that, which incensed the workers a great deal.[45]

Recent immigrants predominated among arrested strikers. Of more than 1,100 arrested persons who can be characterized reliably, almost 50 percent were Italians. Jews (the city's other major group of newcomers) constituted another 25 percent. The vast majority were arrested in factory gate confrontations or for assaults on strikebreakers. To a remarkable extent their victims were from older immigrant groups and usually scabbing on the strike.[46] Manufacturers claimed that their English-speaking workers were "afraid of being called scabs," but fear of physical, not rhetorical, violence was the most effective deterrent against blacklegs. Reluctant strikers found their houses bombed or they were assaulted and intimidated from working. An Irish mill worker noted: "There was a lot that went on that did not appear of the disorder; threats and intimidation, and all that, that was done very quietly. At the same time it was very effective."[47]

The ethnic character of the strike was further illustrated by the nature of community support. As in the late nineteenth century, shopkeepers and saloon owners were the readiest source of assistance. Among those arrested in 1913 were barbers, bakers, shopkeepers, cafe owners, and even a "well-known contractor." A restaurant was provided as a relief center for strikers' families along with two horse-drawn wagons to distribute provisions. But in each case assistance came from within the immigrant community and was usually identifiably Italian. The main financial burden of the strike fell upon the Sons of Italy, a fraternal lodge including merchants as well as workers. Italians provided bail for the arrested Wobblies, Tresca, and Haywood, and an Italian lawyer was entrusted with their defense.[48]

The "Progressive" reform of Paterson's city government six years prior to the strike helps to explain why Italian workingmen, unlike their immigrant predecessors, could not count on the traditional friendship of the city. The city charter of 1908 removed municipal officers from popular accountability. Only the mayor was elected and he did not sit on the appointed commissions that supervised, among other things, the police department.[49]

The silk manufacturers had long pressed for commission government in Paterson and were a chief beneficiary of the charter. In 1913, the four-member police commission included a silk manufacturer, the superintendent of a machine shop supplying silk manufacturers, and a grocer with interests in silk manufacture. Their presence seems to bear out the observation of a recent historian that commission rule was "a plan to make government more businesslike and to attract business to government." It is inviting to see in the city commission evidence of the emergent "corporate state."[50]

In Paterson the case is ambiguous. The immediate effect of commission rule may have made government more businesslike, but it certainly did not disarm critics of industrial capitalism, promote class harmony, or regularize industrial relations. Two important aspects of commission rule are easily overlooked if we succumb too readily to the model of "corporate" rule. First, aside from local businessmen, the chief beneficiaries of municipal reform were old-stock immigrants. Many had strong links with the traditional political machine and quickly adapted to the new form of city government. "New" immigrants were notable in their exclusion from municipal posts under the new regime. Too recent in arrival to have been incorporated in the old electoral machine, they were now excluded from the new commissions and official influence. Second, the "gospel of efficiency," when translated into the programs of municipal officers, did not always reflect businessmen's interests nor the "corporate" concern to legitimize business rule and defuse class conflict. Both aspects had important bearings on developments in 1913.[51]

From the perspective of Paterson's Italians, the most important impact of "progressive" reform was its effect on the policing of the city. Not only was the police force now accountable to a nonelective board of commissioners, within the department a range of new appointments and responsibilities was instituted. The new board of police commissioners immediately increased the strength of the force by almost 50 percent. A mounted division was added to police patrols and a squad of detectives recruited that included the ominously titled "Italian Department." A general shakeup throughout the force was uncompromisingly announced by Chief Bimson, who declared his intention to root out "shirkers" and patrolmen who were "not on the level." The "efficiency of the department" became the keystone of police reform yet clearly denoted aims different from those of corporate manipulators. More "vigilant" patrolling of Italian neighborhoods, bound to provoke trouble, was prescribed. A new telephone system was to link patrolmen on the beat with force headquarters, and a precinct station was established in the heavily Italian Riverside section of the city. In addition, Bimson went to some lengths to recruit two Italians to the force in order that a more effective policing of the immigrant communities could be achieved. It was surely no coincidence that the suppression of the city's Italians' anarchist group followed shortly after these reforms, in 1908.[52]

When the strike erupted in February 1913, Bimson was well prepared to quell the disturbances. He ordered his whole force to headquarters. Cots were installed and a barbershop inprovised. The entire city fire department was sworn in as "special deputies." All policemen were assigned extra duties and expected to be available at a moment's notice.[53] Bimson was determined to suppress strike disorders and, freed from the shackles of a restraining mayor and an indignant middle class, he was plainly able to do so.

The new city administration, coupled with Bimson's internal reforms, marks another break with past handling of strike disorders in Paterson. Federal investigators noted of 1913:

The Board of Fire and Police Commissioners . . . were in sympathy with the mill owners. One member of the board was a silk manufacturer. As the board controlled the actions of the police and the Recorder, the instruments created for the administration of justice and the safeguarding of the rights of individuals became tools of oppression in the control of the few operators as against the 25,000 silk workers on strike.[54]

Bimson, in reflecting on the strike, was mindful of the assistance of his superiors on the board, for it was "through their arrangement with the sheriff" of Passaic County that he was empowered to recruit "special policemen" and "auxiliary deputy sheriffs" to assist his overburdened men. Many of these "specials" were mill owners' private detectives, as many as sixty "clothed with the authority of the police" and "employed not strictly as an adjunct to the state authority, but as a private army of the mill owners."[55]

Liaison between mill owners and city officials was often unofficial, the result of personal influence and favor. Adolph Lessig complained, "The day I got six months I saw a manufacturer walking out of the recorder's room.'' An automobile, owned by the national Silk Dyeing Company, was at the disposal of Bimson's officers. Individual silk manufacturers were sworn in as special deputies, while others directed the arrests of pickets.[56]

Bimson's restructuring of the police force paralleled the new influence of the city commission in removing the department from popular influence. Bimson's modernization of the police force emphasized the removal of officers from the popular pressures long evident in the city. The number of detectives—men not readily identifiable as policemen—was substantially increased. The numbers of motorized and horse-mounted officers likewise grew. Increasingly Paterson's police were concentrated upon specialized assignments, such as those in the "Traffic Squad" of the Italian Department. It was officers from this department who were frequently to infiltrate strike meetings in 1913, just as it was Bimson's mounted squad—dubbed "Cossacks" by strikers—that dispersed picket lines. Equipped with an efficient telephone system linking all units of his force, Bimson was able to locate trouble spots and to direct men to scenes of disorder.[57] Perhaps most important was the availability of police automobiles previously unknown during strikes in the city. In the past, escorting arrested strikers to headquarters was a hazardous mission. Culprits were frequently freed by jeering crowds. Moreover, if an officer was alone, it was easier to ignore minor infractions, particularly if friends were in the crowd. Patrol wagons put an end to such situations. Bimson's deputy, Captain McBride, emphasized the point when he wrote:

I would say that the facilities that we had with automobiles was *[sic]* more helpful to us. Had it not been for them we could never have gotten along. We could never have made the time. Between the telephone and the automobiles and the willingness of the men to work, is what made the thing successful.[58]

For the first time in the history of the city, the automobile made possible a policy of mass arrests.

McBride strenuously denied the accusation that ethnic prejudices influenced the police. The shared class origins of strikers and patrolmen, he argued, transcended ethnic barriers. Many patrolmen had relatives who worked in the mills, he said, and "all sympathize with the laboring men and women in getting better conditions."[59] This was, on the face of it, quite true. Almost half the men on the force in 1913 seemed to have had a relative working in silk or to be sharing lodging with a mill worker, and few did not live near mill workers. However, these were overwhelmingly English-speaking silk workers in the parts of the city where most of the strike breakers lived. The policemen themselves were old-stock Americans or "old immigrants"—Irish, British, or German, with the Irish clearly predominating. There were only two Italians on the force and no Jews. It was also a very young force, apparently almost a reflection of Bimson's conscious attempt to have a professional corps, free of community pressures. Bimson's recruits were not only ethnically hostile to the strikers, they were personally inexperienced in the city's traditions of industrial conflict.[60]

It is well known that, as in Lawrence, the I.W.W. did not "call" the Paterson strike of 1913. There was not even an I.W.W. branch in the city, although Daniel DeLeon's "Detroit I.W.W." was represented by a small local. A close examination of the incident, from a local perspective, indicates that this observation be carried a bit deeper. That is, the Paterson strike was never an I.W.W. strike at all, except inasmuch as the Wobblies claimed it to be so and were, in the national press and public eye, credited with it.

Of course, the issues were local. In addition, the patterns of worker action were deeply rooted in local tradition and resisted the efforts of the I.W.W. leadership to channel them according to approved Wobbly policy. The 1913 strike was "different." But the difference was not so much a result of the Wobbly celebrities (who failed miserably, after all, in their major publicity gimmick, the disastrous "Paterson Pageant"), but because of profound changes in Paterson itself over the preceding two decades: the partial emigration of the industry, the changed ethnic composition of the workforce, and the reform of local government, particularly the police department.

NOTES

1. W. C. Wyckoff, *American Silk Manufacture* (New York, 1887); N. Garber, "The Silk Industry of Paterson, New Jersey" (Ph.D. diss., Rutgers University, 1968).

2.   *Paterson's Population, 1850-1900*

Year	No. of Inhabitants	Rate of Expansion
1850	11,344	—
1860	19,586	42%
1870	33,570	71%
1880	51,031	52%
1890	78,347	53%
1900	105,171	34%

SOURCE: U.S. Bureau of Census, *Tenth Census of U.S., 1880* (Washington, 1884) 18, p. 721, *Eleventh Census of U.S., 1890* (Washington, 1895) 15, p. 240, *Twelfth Census of U.S., 1900* (Washington, 1901) 1, pp. 436, 628-29.

Paterson Silk Industry, 1860-1900 (Including Dyeing)

Year	No. of Establishments	No. Employed
1860	9	716
1870	27	2,551
1880	92	10,448
1890	112	12,862
1900	166	18,650

SOURCE: U.S. Bureau of Census, *Ninth Census of U.S., 1870* (Washington, 1872) 3, p. 624, *Tenth Census of U.S., 1880*, 2, pp. 430-31, *Eleventh Census of U.S., 1890*, 12, pp. 422-23, 426-29, *Twelfth Census of U.S., 1900*, 9, pp. 206-8.

3. *New York Herald*, March 8, 1880.

4. L. Brockett, *The Silk Industry in America* (New York, 1876), p. 178.

5. T. Greenwood, *A Tour of the United States: Out and Home in Six Weeks* (London, 1883), p. 139.

6. J. D. Osborne, "Industrialization and the Politics of Disorder: Paterson Silkworkers, 1880-1913" (Ph.D. diss., Warwick University, 1979), pp. 1-18.

7. *The Labor Standard*, July 3, 1880.

8. *Macclesfield Courier and Herald*, February 17, 1883.

9. Osborne, "Industrialization and the Politics of Disorder," pp. 19-75.

10. H. Gutman, "Class, Status and Community Power in Nineteenth-Century American Industrial Cities—Paterson, New Jersey," in F. C. Jaher, ed., *The Age of Industrialism: Essays in Social Structure and Cultural Values* (New York, 1968), pp. 263-87.

11. See S. P. Hays's important article, "The Changing Political Structure of the City in Industrial America," *Journal of Urban History* 1 (November 1974), 6-38, for some suggestive comments on urban politics in late-nineteenth-century America.

12. For numerous instances of like behavior, see Osborne, pp. 101-36. "Serenading" consisted of "blasts on tin horns, jeers and catcalls." It would often degenerate into wholesale physical attack. See New Jersey, Bureau of Statistics of Labor and Industries, *Twenty-Fourth Annual Report, 1901* (Trenton, 1902), pp. 437-38.

13. *The Labor Standard*, August 4, 1878.

14. *Paterson Daily Press*, March 14, 1894.

15. Hays, "The Changing Political Structure," p. 14.

16. *American Silk Journal*, June 1902.

17. For leading accounts of the dispute, see M. Dubofsky, *We Shall Be All: A History of the I.W.W.* (Chicago, 1969), pp. 269-90; P. Renshaw, *The Wobblies: The Story of Syndicalism in the United States* (New York, 1967), pp. 112-18; P. S. Foner, *The History of the Labor Movement in the United States: 4, The Industrial Workers of the World* (New York, 1965), pp. 360-72; J. R. Conlin, *Bread and Roses Too: Studies of the Wobblies* (Westport, 1969), pp. 88, 90, 128-31; J. Kornbluh, ed., *Rebel Voices: An I.W.W. Anthology* (Ann Arbor, 1964), pp. 197-226; G. Adams, Jr., *Age of Industrial Violence, 1910-1915: The Activities and Findings of the United States Commission on Industrial Relations* (New York, 1966), pp. 75-100.

18. E. G. Flynn, "The Truth About the Paterson Strike," in J. L. Kornbluh, ed., *Rebel Voices* (Ann Arbor, 1964), p. 216.

19. Osborne, "Industrialization and the Politics of Disorder," pp. 277-336. Unfortunately, all leading historians of the strike have ignored the local Paterson press in documenting the dispute. This has surely led to the woeful ignoring of violence perpetrated by silk workers. Surprisingly, the source forming the basis of most accounts of the strike, *Reports of the United States Commission on Industrial Relations*, also contains abundant evidence of the same.

20. Flynn, "The Truth," p. 218.

21. U.S. Congress, *Senate Commission on Industrial Relations: Final Reports and Testimony*, 61st Cong., 2d sess., 1915-1916, 3, pp. 2459, 2463, 2593. (Hereafter, *C.I.R.* 3.)

22. *C.I.R.* 3, pp. 2525, 2548, 2562, 2567, 2568.

23. U.S. Industrial Commission, *Reports on the Relations and Conditions of Capital and Labor, 1900*, 14, p. 680.

24. *Textile America*, October 23, 1897 (brackets are mine).

25. For the "annex" exodus and its effects on the Paterson silk industry, see Osborne, "Industrialization and the Politics of Disorder," pp. 137-72.

26. City Officers, Paterson, New Jersey, *Annual Report of the City Officers, 1912-1913* (Paterson, 1913), p. xxxv; *C.I.R.* 3, pp. 2553, 2580, 2581, 2584.

27. U.S. Congress, Senate, *Reports of the Immigration Commission*, 61st Cong., 2d sess., 1909-1910, vol. 11, pp. 18-19; C. C. Altarelli, "History and Present Condition of the Italian Colony of Paterson, N.J." (M.A. thesis, Columbia University, 1911), pp. 2-3; *La Questione Sociale* (Paterson), November 15, 1896, May 15, 1897.

28. S. B. Clough, *The Economic History of Modern Italy* (New York, 1964), pp. 15, 20-21, 62-64.

29. L. Cafanga, "Italy," in C. N. Cippolla, ed., *The Fontana Economic History of Europe: The Emergence of Industrial Societies* (London, 1973), p. 306; M. Neufeld, *Italy: School for Awakening Countries: The Italian Labor Movement in Its Political, Social and Economic Setting From 1800-1960* (Ithaca, 1961), pp. 141-42.

30. N. Hall Ets, *Rosa: The Life of an Italian Emigrant* (Minnesota, 1970) is a striking account of the Italian silk industry at the end of the nineteenth century.

31. Clough, *Economic History*, pp. 151-56; H. L. Gualtieri, *The Labor Movement in Italy* (New York, 1946), pp. 7-14; R. Hotstetter, *The Italian Socialist Movement: 1, Origins, 1860-1882* (Princeton, 1958); N. Pernicone, "The Italian Labor Movement," in E. R. Tannenbaum and E. P. Noether, eds., *Modern Italy: A Topical History Since 1861* (New York, 1974), pp. 197-227.

32. D. Horowits, *The Italian Labor Movement* (Harvard, 1963), pp. 38-41; Neufeld, *Italy*, p. 189.

33. "Rinaldo Rigola e il Movimento Opercio nel Biellese" (Bari, 1930), p. 19, quoted in E. Hobsbaum, *Labouring Men: Studies in the History of Labour* (London, 1964), p. 10.

34. J. Weed and L. Carey, "I Make Cheap Silk," *Masses*, November 1913; *C.I.R.* 3, pp. 2586-87, 2579, 2595, 2505-6; E. Koettsen, "Making Silk," *International Socialist Review*, March 1914, 551-55; E. G. Flynn, "Contract Labor in Paterson Silk Mills," in *Pageant of the Paterson Strike: Official Program* (New York, 1913),

pp. 29-31; *New York Times*, April 4, 1913. All provide striking evidence not only of the drudgery of life in Paterson mills but of the persistence of problems peculiarly associated with newcomers to industrial and factory toil. They could almost have been describing the conditions confronting immigrant hands forty years earlier.

35. *C.I.R.* 3, pp. 2612-14.

36. J. V. Ferraris, "L'Assassinio Di Umberto I E Gli Anarchici Di Paterson," *Rassagna Storica Del Risorgimento*, 50, March 1968; S. Merlino, *La Difoss Di Gattano Bresci* (Paterson, 1917); A. Cipriani, *Bresci e Savoia* (Paterson, n.d.).

37. *Paterson Daily Guardian*, July 19, 20, 24, 1900; *Paterson Daily Press*,, July 19, 20, 1900; *Newark Evening News*, July 19, 30, 1900; *New York Times*, August 3, 4, 1900; *Paterson Evening News*, July 31, 1900.

38. S. Fine, "Anarchism and the Assassination of McKinley," *American Historical Review*, 60, July 1955, pp. 777-99; N. Preston, Jr., *Aliens and Dissenters: Federal Suppression of Radicals, 1903-1933* (Harvard, 1963), pp. 30-34; *Outlook*, 68, August 10, 1901.

39. *American Silk Journal*, May and June 1902; *Freiheit*, June 14, 28, July 5, 1902; *Outlook*, 71, June 28, 1902; *New York Times*, June 19, 20, 23, 25, 27, 1902; A. N. Nishart, *The Case of William McQueen: Reasons Why He Should Be Liberated* (Trenton, 1905), pp. 3-14.

40. *Paterson Evening News*, November 14, 15, 1906; *Annual Report of the City Officers*, 1907-1908, pp. 41-44; L. Caminita, *Free Country* (Paterson, n.d.), pp. 21-29; *Paterson Daily Guardian*, February 28, 1912. The suppression of the journal was probably connected with the surveillance of anarchist groups carried out by the Immigration Bureau, the Secret Service, and local police forces in 1908. See Preston, *Aliens and Dissenters*, p. 33.

41. *Paterson Guardian*, February 27, 1913.

42. P. F. Gill and R. S. Brennan, *Report on the Inferior Courts and Police of Paterson, N.J.*; "Unpublished Reports of the Commission on Industrial Relations, 1912-1915; Records of the Department of Labor, R.G. 174, National Archives, Washington, p. 7.

43. *C.I.R.* 3, p. 2422; D. S. McCorkle to President Wilson, June 9, 1913; Department of Labor Files, R.G. 280, National Archives, Washington.

44. *C.I.R.* 3, p. 2463.

45. *C.I.R.* 3, pp. 2569, 2594.

46. N. Licht, "Young Immigrant Workers in Revolt—the Paterson Silk Strike of 1913" (Ph.D. diss., Princeton University, 1973). Licht's figures and information were taken from official arrest statistics of the Paterson police department, which were unavailable to the author. The author kindly acknowledges Licht's generosity in making the information available.

47. *C.I.R.* 3, p. 9420.

48. C. Mason, "Industrial War in Paterson," *Outlook*, June 7, 1913, p. 287; *Paterson Guardian*, March 6, 11, 13, 20, April 30, May 19, 21, 23, 24, July 9, 18, 1913; *C.I.R.* 3, pp. 2529-30.

49. For the campaign and effects of commission rule in Paterson, see Osborne, "Industrialization and the Politics of Disorder," pp. 233-76.

50. J. Weinstein, *The Corporate Ideal in the Liberal State, 1900-1918* (Boston, 1918), p. 97.

51. For examples of the bargaining groups and the manner in which bargains were struck for appointments to the commissions in 1908, see Osborne, "Industrialization and the Politics of Disorder," pp. 266-76.

52. *Annual Report of the City Officers, Paterson, N.J., 1907-1908*, pp. 24, 253-55; *Paterson Evening News*, April 10, 12, 15, 20, 25, 29, May 4, 9, 14, 22, 27, 29, 1907; *Paterson Guardian*, January 13, February 1 and 2, 1912; C. Vreeland, *Who's Who in Passaic County* (Paterson, 1917), p. 13.

53. *Paterson Guardian*, March 3 and 25, 1913.

54. Gill and Brennan, *Report on the Inferior Courts*, Records of Department of Labor, pp. 1-7, 20.

55. *Annual Report of the City Officers, Paterson, N.J., 1912-1913*, p. 296; Gill and Brennan, "Report on the Inferior Courts," p. 7.

56. *C.I.R.* 3, pp. 2463, 2524, 2592.

57. *C.I.R.* 3, p. 2498; *Paterson Guardian*, February 25, May 9, 1913.

58. *C.I.R.* 3, p. 2564.

59. *C.I.R.* 3, p. 2563.

60. The youth of the postreform recruits is, of course, relative to the then-existing members of the department. Their average age at time of recruitment (1907-1910) would have been about thirty years. By contemporary standards this may seem "mature" for new officers. At the turn of the century, their age was probably not regarded as unusual. A job on the force was a "desirable" and much sought after position. (See Osborne, "Industrialization and the Politics of Disorder," pp. 272-73.) Presumably a prospective policeman had to wait several years before selection was considered. However, if we accept thirty as a relatively advanced age, a number of intriguing questions are suggested. Among them: Was a policeman's lot such that mature men were better equipped to patrol city streets? Did the selection process merely reflect the age profile of Paterson's established ethnic groups? Most intriguing, and unfathomable: Was it the case that selection reflected reward, from the political machine or the civically influential, for past favors, a factor which surely would have excluded younger candidates?

PITTSBURGH, THE I.W.W., AND THE STOGIE WORKERS

PATRICK LYNCH

During the summer of 1909 a significant strike began in McKees Rocks, near Pittsburgh, Pennsylvania. The workers of the Pressed Steel Car Company demanded higher wages, the posting of wage rates, the end of a wage-pool system, and the creation of an acceptable grievance procedure. The company responded by ending credit at company stores, evicting strikers from company housing, using strikebreakers, deploying the state police, wooing AFL leaders, and attempting to divide the workers between native born and immigrant, skilled and unskilled.

Originally led by conservative, native American craft unionists, the immigrants rebelled and organized their own "secret committee," which effectively ran the strike despite the sixteen different nationalities involved. Seeking additional experienced leadership, the foreign strikers requested I.W.W. assistance. William Trautmann arrived quickly, then Joseph Ettor. During the long strike, violent confrontations occurred between the immigrant workers and state troopers. One worker was widely quoted as saying that one state policeman would die for every striker killed. Four strikers and three state troopers died after one clash and the violence declined sharply. Misled by management's vaguely worded promises, the strikers returned to work only to find conditions basically unchanged. Although their strike eventually failed, its drama kindled intellectual and worker interest throughout the country.

Some historians have described the McKees Rocks strike as the incident that inspired the revival of the I.W.W. in the East. Yet little attention has been paid to subsequent developments in the Pittsburgh area. This chapter briefly describes I.W.W. activities in the area from 1909 through 1913. It concentrates on the stogie workers' strike of 1913, an unorthodox I.W.W. strike that had the most enduring effects of any local I.W.W. actions.

Because of the I.W.W.'s newly gained reputation for militancy after

1909, workers across the country demanded organizers and formed locals. This was particularly true in Pennsylvania. By April 1910, Pennsylvania led all states with seventeen locals. (The State of Washington was second with fourteen.) Fifteen Pennsylvania chapters had been formed since the I.W.W.'s convention in 1908. The Pittsburgh area served as the location for no fewer than twelve of these and included in its membership meat packers, coal miners, car builders, and workers in steel, pipe, and tin mills.[1]

Western Pennsylvanian Wobblies demonstrated their enthusiasm on October 10, 1909, when twenty delegates from several locals met in McKees Rocks to organize the Pittsburgh-New Castle District Industrial Council, later shortened to the Pittsburgh Industrial Council. Delegates represented car builders, steel and tin plate workers, miners, railroad workers, and streetcar employees. William Trautmann, a founder of the national I.W.W. and still an important figure in it, opened the convention with a gavel from the fourth national convention. The delegates voted to establish an I.W.W. paper in New Castle to serve as a propaganda and educational organ for the region. Thus was formed *Solidarity*, one of the two journalistic buttresses of the union. Ben Williams, one of the I.W.W.'s leading theoreticians, soon became its editor. The delegates also agreed to expand their organizational work and to hold a district convention every three months.[2]

At the second district convention on January 9, 1910, the delegates selected Joe Ettor and Joe Schmidt for the posts of district organizer and assistant organizer. (The two men also worked together later in the anthracite region of Pennsylvania.) New district council members were elected and per capita taxes were assessed for organization work.[3] Local members obviously were determined to have a viable I.W.W. organization in the area. However, despite a few successes, the Wobblies were unable to create long-lasting locals in the vicinity.

In what was termed a free speech fight, most of the staff of *Solidarity* was imprisoned in New Castle under a legal technicality in 1910. Although other staff members continued the paper, the arrests weakened organization work in the New Castle area. Eventually Williams moved the paper to Cleveland.[4] About the same time, several thousand workers struck the Pressed Steel Company's plant at Schoenville,[5] and Ettor and Schmidt aggravated UMW officials by speaking to miners in Westmoreland County.[6] A meat packers' union was formed in November and a massive I.W.W. rally of 20,000 held in Pittsburgh in September. But by the second half of 1910, the Wobblies seemed to be fading away because of the declining economy.[7]

As poor economic conditions continued into 1911, the I.W.W. press continued to record few activities. The great success of the Lawrence strike, however, brought a revival. Wobblies cooperated with Socialists in rallies throughout the area for the Lawrence strikers and defendants in 1912. Bill Haywood addressed a giant gathering of 15,000 at Kennywood Park.[8]

Successful organizing and strikes took place among tobacco workers, department-store workers, tailors, furriers, and meat packers.[9] In August, Trautmann called on iron, steel, and coal workers for a general strike demanding an eight-hour day and higher wages. Several moderately successful small strikes occurred. The year ended with organized steel workers' committees and an appeal for a steel drive in 1913.[10]

Aside from the stogie workers' successful strike, 1913 was disappointing. *Solidarity* made a special appeal in March for steel workers to organize, but few did. Wobblies failed in strikes at McKeesport's Fort Pitt Steel Foundry and the Oliver Plant in Pittsburgh.[11] By the September 1913 national convention of the I.W.W., fellow Wobbly John Rhine of Local No. 215 of Pittsburgh said that, with the exception of the stogie workers, "the whole district looked like a cemetery with not a sexton to bury the dead."[12] The question arises as to why the I.W.W.'s longest-lasting success occurred in the stogie industry. The answers lie within the steel industry and the national and local I.W.W. organizations as well as with the stogie industry and its workers.

From an estimated 4,000 to 6,000 members in 1909, the McKees Rocks local had declined to only twenty members when it unsuccessfully attempted to reorganize in 1912.[13] By using a well-documented system of spies, thugs, and dismissals, the steel trust eleminated union activists.[14] George Speed, the Wobblies' national general organizer in 1913, accurately described the Pittsburgh steel situation in his report to the 1913 convention: "Thousands of slaves are guarded and watched over as a cat watches over a mouse. With its perfected spy system and thug police, it makes it well nigh impossible to get even a nucleus let alone a perfect organization."[15] Since steel dominated the region's economy, it was extremely difficult to organize any of the other basic industries in Pittsburgh, Without steel, any I.W.W. gains would be limited at best.

The local I.W.W. suffered from the same problems as did the national: an unfavorable economic cycle, lack of finances, and an insufficient number of experienced organizers. The fact that the Pittsburgh Industrial Council lasted from 1909 to 1914, probably the longest life span for an I.W.W. industrial council during this period, was due to the tenacity of the local membership. William Trautmann had served as the principal leader into 1913. By then local Wobblies had begun to criticize him as an ineffective organizer, a poor strike leader, and an immoderate drinker. National organizer Speed stated that Trautmann's industrial council records were in questionable array and pressured Trautmann into resigning.[16] He did so in April and joined the Detroit I.W.W. Demoralization was immediate. John Rhine, a Pittsburgh delegate, used Trautmann's alleged sins to urge decentralization during the 1913 national convention. National officials replied that Trautmann's transgressions were the fault of the district council that had employed him and not the responsibility of the national organization.[17]

The I.W.W. never reestablished itself in basic industry in Pittsburgh but, oddly, scored remarkable successes among stogie workers. Elizabeth Butler's fine chapter on the subject in her *Women and the Trades* volumes of the old *Pittsburgh Survey* series provides much detailed information on the structure of the stogie industry.[18]

The stogie provided the workingman with a cheap and enjoyable smoke. It began as "a long, loosely rolled cigar, made only of crumbled filler leaf and smooth, fine wrapper." Eliminating the binder leaf of a cigar lowered both the labor and material costs and allowed the best stogie to be sold at one-third to one-half the selling price of the cheapest cigar. The industry began in Wheeling, West Virginia, and soon spread to Pittsburgh.[19] The two remained the chief centers of the stogie trade into the 1920s, Wheeling for hand-made stogies and Pittsburgh for those made with a mold.[20]

During 1907 and 1908, a total of 3,527 workers (2,611 women and 916 men) labored in Pittsburgh's 32 factories and 203 sweatshops. The sweatshop doubled as a dwelling and a shop, whereas the factory's sole purpose was manufacture. Plants were found in the Hill District, the North Side, the South Side, and the central business section. Nine of the factories and 124 sweatshops were located in the Hill District and employed 1,046 men and women.[21]

Stogie manufacture involved several distinct processes: drying, stripping, bunching, rolling, and pushing. Women displaced men when the industry was mechanized. In a typical factory, leaves were naturally "air dried," slowly mellowing from a month to a year for the best quality handmade stogie. The cheaper molding process saved time and space by heating the tobacco to a high temperature in a closed and very dusty room. The resulting brittle tobacco could be shaped on a machine. Experienced men controlled drying processes.[22]

Women usually performed the next step, the stripping of the tobacco stem from the leaf. In dimly lit rooms, they wet the wrapper leaves, placed them individually over low, rounded stands, and carefully cut the stems from the leaves. The women weighed the leaves and tied them into one-pound packets.[23]

The handmade-stogie workers, usually Jewish men, were the aristocrats of the stogie labor force. They combined the processes of the bunchers and rollers of the molding system. The experienced handmade-stogie worker carefully cut the leaf, chose the correct amount of long filler, rolled, molded, and loosely curled the head. Each man had served an apprenticeship of about a year.[24]

Women dominated the positions for both the rolling and bunching of the molded stogie. After the buncher used her machine to change a handful of scrap filler and a piece of binder leaf into a bunch, she inserted the bunch into a "cigar-shaped transverse groove, six to eight inches long, cut in a wooden board."[25] After filling all of the grooves, she placed a matrix board on top of the first board and inserted both into a press until the molds were firm. Using a machine, the roller placed the wrapper leaf on a metal stand and followed the outlined pattern to cut the leaf held in place by suction. She then rolled the leaf around the bunch and placed it in a box. The more skillful roller did not use the machine, but carefully cut the wrapper leaf, fit it around the bunch, and finished it with curl or paste head.[26]

The packer quickly divided the stogies into groups of light, medium, and dark shades. After squeezing them under a press, she placed them into round tins or square boxes, and nailed the boxes shut. A bander reopened some of the boxes, individually banded the stogies, and reboxed them.[27]

The Hill District, the focus of the stogie industry, was located on a hilly area next to the central business section. It began as an Irish neighborhood and soon became the residence of many professionals and members of "society." During the period from 1870 to 1880, many Jewish refugees from Russia began to settle in the area.[28] Pittsburgh had a Jewish population of 15,000 in 1905 and 60,000 in 1919, with most centered in the Hill District.[29] The immigrants organized schools, synagogues, settlement houses, Zionist and Socialist groups, and branches of the Workmen's Circle. Small family businesses were central to the district's economy. "Kosher markets and dry goods stores spilled their contents over the stalls of the shops onto the streets." Peddlers filled the streets. Pittsburgh's *Gazette-Times* described one section of the Hill in 1905 as a "ghetto . . . the same as the East Side of New York City transplanted."[30]

The arrival of the East European Jews provided cheap labor and greatly stimulated the stogie industry. Friends and relatives found work in the trade for the newly arrived and unemployed. The stogie trade offered the promise of advancement. After a few years of experience, a hard-working immigrant could open his own shop.[31] Also, since most of the owners were Orthodox Jews, the workers could observe the Sabbath and Jewish holidays.[32] Besides, as one worker said, "What could one do in Pittsburgh?" Some believed that the management of the steel companies, mines, and other large Pittsburgh industries considered the East European Jews to be radicals and refused to hire them.[33] Therefore, people considered the stogie industry to be the Jewish trade of Pittsburgh, and "almost every Jewish family in Pittsburgh had someone in the stogie industry."[34] The Jews dominated the stogie workforce on the Hill, and the stogie industry ranked fifth among Pittsburgh's industries in the number of employees.[35]

Conditions were poor in the industry. Nervous tension pervaded the factories as workers strove to meet high speed requirements. Rollers were torn between the need for speed and the requirement for accuracy according to sliding scales. Some factory owners increased the tension by paying premium wages to the top two girls in each department, giving regular wages to those close to the best production, and docking the slower workers for their scrap. Other classifications of workers were paid by the pound without dockage or by the day. When women and men performed the same tasks, they received the same pay rates. Hill factory owners generally paid lower wages than employers of stogie workers in other parts of the city.[36]

In 1907, strippers averaged $.60 to $.80 a day, and under $5.00 per week. A machine buncher could make $1.40 per day. A top male hand buncher would reach perhaps $2.00 daily, and an average woman worker made $1.00 to $1.20 per day. Experienced rollers averaged $1.00 to $1.30 per day. Packers usually made $3.00 to $10.00 weekly. Handmade-stogie workers could earn $2.00 a day. The inability to maintain the rapid pace, the varying qualities of tobacco, and its irregular supply restricted and lowered the workers' pay.[37]

With the major exception of the handmade-stogie workers, the sweatshops generally paid lower wages than the factories. Wages were based on piecework, and workers performed at a more leisurely pace than in the factory. Although the sweatshop workers kept their own hours, they often worked overtime, which the factory workers rarely did.[38] Generally, the sweatshop's labor force consisted of the owner, his family, and possibly several outsiders. The owner usually did not consider his family's labor as part of the production cost in determining the price of his stogies.[39]

Working conditions were also extremely poor in the stogie industry. One factory, for example, had cracked walls, an unreliable fire escape, no dressing rooms—girls had to change in front of males—and toilet facilities were shared by both sexes with little privacy.[40] "In general, the workplaces on the Hill are characterized by a lack of cleanliness, by overcrowding . . . by an absence of ventilation and of sanitary accommodations."[41]

Dust from the drying tobacco permeated the air and the workers' lungs and frequently caused respiratory illnesses such as turberculosis.[42] "I sat opposite a pale, thin Yeshiva Bocher, who gradually coughed out his lungs into the tobacco dust. One day he didn't show up for work. We heard that he had died of consumption."[43] Testimony given at the Pennsylvania Industrial Board hearings on June 5, 1914, stated that cigar makers (including stogie makers) statistically suffered a very high rate of deaths from tuberculosis. A committee investigated and recommended clearner floors, more air space, and better sanitation.[44]

Elizabeth Butler also cited the effects of nervous exhaustion on young girls, stemming from the rapid pace of work and the demanding sliding scales of wages. Girls usually did not last more than six years in the industry. Many left to marry and raise families. For some, however, their weakened bodies led to underdeveloped children and poor households.[45]

Another issue was the use of child labor in the industry. In a 1908 article, Scott Nearing told of a four-year-old boy stripping tobacco in a sweatshop.[46] Although state laws forbade any minor under fifteen from working in the industry during school hours, Butler estimated that ninety to a hundred children from the ages of five to twelve stripped tobacco in sweatshops. Twice as many stripped tobacco after school.[47]

Several unions had attempted to organize the stogie workers. The Knights of Labor had concentrated on the handmade-stogie workers and only had support among the Germans on the South Side. The National Stogie Makers excluded women from its membership and had little local support. The Cigar Makers International Union (AFL) ignored the stogie workers until 1907 and then still preferred the highly skilled handmade-stogie workers. A local union, the Tobacco Workers' Protective Association, failed twice in 1899 and 1908 to be a viable organization. Members of the local Socialist party, perhaps fearing the I.W.W.'s Socialist Labor party elements, had opposed the I.W.W. and prevented it from organizing the stogie workers in 1906. The unions' lack of success was generally blamed on the "clannishness" and suspicious nature of the immigrants.[48]

The I.W.W., however, succeeded in organizing the Hill workers in 1912. In early spring, Fred Merrick and Jacob Margolis, two prominent direct-action Socialists, approached the stogie workers on the basis of organizing under the I.W.W. Less than two weeks before this proposal, the local AFL headquarters had refused to organize the stogie workers. Many of the stogie workers were "yellow Socialists" and opposed the I.W.W.'s ideology, especially sabotage. However, they agreed to affiliate with the Wobblies so that they could be unionized. On April 14, 1912, over 200 Hill workers signed I.W.W. membership applications, paid their dues, and formed the I.W.W. Tobacco Workers Local No. 101. Many regarded themselves as members of the I.W.W. Tobacco Workers Local No. 101, but not as members of the national organization.[49] This important mental reservation probably accounted for several of the policies subsequently adopted by the stogie workers.

In July, August, and September of 1912, Wobblies struck Hill shops for higher pay and better sanitary and safety conditions. The strikers generally won a cent increase per hundred stogies for bunching and the return of $.25 per week for spreading filler. Several factory owners promised to employ only I.W.W. members. In some plants a worker could not be discharged until a committee of workers had investigated the circumstances and had judged him as being inefficient.[50] Samuel Rabinowitz represented Local No. 101 at the 1912 national convention of the I.W.W. with three votes.[51] The stogie makers' union had made steady progress and earned prestige in 1912.

Because of their previous success, Hill workers pushed for higher wages in July 1913. Choosing the Industrial Cigar Company as a test case because of its large size and high status in the industry, a committee of fifty workers demanded $3.00 per thousand stogies for the molded-stogie rollers instead of the customary $2.25. After the owner's refusal to meet this term, the fifty workers struck. The Bosses' Association, an organization of the Hill District stogie factory owners secretly formed in 1912, attempted to smash the union by immediately declaring on July 3 "a lockout against all shops that are organized under the banner of the I.W.W." Since July and August represented the slowest months of the tobacco industry, the bosses expected minimal business losses while they starved the workers into submission.[52] The stogie workers' union found itself trying to organize support for all of its 1,200 members instead of the intended fifty workers.[53]

The local union, the Tobacco Workers Local No. 101, proved to be remarkably successful in defeating its opposition during the eighteen-week strike/lockout, which ended between October 18 and October 25.[54] The strikers themselves formulated and executed the strike strategy, although Matilda Rabinowitz, a national organizer for the I.W.W., and the Pittsburgh Industrial Council also helped. Rabinowitz spoke at several meetings and also wrote articles to radical papers. The Pittsburgh Industrial Council helped mostly by raising money. Bill Haywood also spoke to the strikers when he passed through town.[55]

The workers selected a strike committee of twenty-five members to organize and publicize the strike. Women were considered equals in the union, but few served as strike leaders. Men bunchers and rollers, such as Joe Mazer, Saul Rabinowitz, Max Swartz, and Harry Slawkin, dominated the strike committee. The committee met every day to plan its strategy. Large general meetings were conducted two or three times a week to maintain morale and to notify the membership of future plans or of any progress within the struggle. Open air meetings during good weather and dance benefits helped to build worker solidarity and mass support. Weekly parades on Saturdays from the Hill District to downtown also attracted much attention. One parade had over 2,000 participants.[56]

Attempts to have the newspapers publicize their strike had mixed results. Harry Slawkin recounts the following: "I went to the *Pittsburgh Dispatch* on Fifth Avenue and asked for publicity for our strike but the editor refused. He said we were a bunch of radicals." None of the capitalist Pittsburgh papers would mention the strike.[57] The workers instead made frequent use of the local direct-action Socialist paper *Justice* and such national I.W.W. papers as the *Industrial Worker* and *Solidarity* to publicize their strike.

Although the strike was called primarily for economic reasons, the tobacco workers used other issues to advance their cause. The I.W.W. firmly opposed child labor in both factories and sweatshops.[58] Workers especially criticized Goldsmit (the leader of the Bosses' Association) for using child laborers who were forbidden to talk while working under deplorable conditions. Strikers urged other workers to boycott Goldsmit's brand, "Dry Slitz," and the Russell cigar stores, which he partially owned. One article warned that "you smoke the blood of children if you smoke 'Dry Slitz.' ''[59] By the strike's end, the strikers claimed that the boycott had seriously affected both the "Dry Slitz" stogies and the Russell stores.[60]

Poor and unhealthy working conditions were also stressed. Matilda Rabinowitz wrote of how wet tobacco leaves continually dripped on the workers' heads and that their feet were always damp. Healthy-looking girls were unusual. Girls appeared mostly as "anemic looking, with sunken cheeks and flat chests. . . ." Rabinowitz warned that "cheap smokes are made by cheapening and shortening the workers' lives."[61]

Seven to ten workers reportedly contracted tuberculosis within one year at a Goldsmit factory. At one meeting the strikers resolved that "we would rather starve than go back in Goldsmit's Dry Slitz consumptive breeding hall and those like it." A float in a Labor Day parade displayed child labor and a worker dying from consumption.[62]

Although the workers had emphasized the evils of child labor and consumptive breeding conditions, they had little hope of major reforms in these areas. As Harry Slawkin remarked, "The father was a buncher, the mother was a roller, the kids and the grandparents were strippers and packers, and all combined they could sometimes not make a living." Due to economic necessity, the parents needed the children to work even after the proposed raises were won. But the issue was good for propaganda, illustrating the fact that the industry's low wages forced the entire family to work.[63] Although the strikers had also used the consumption issue primarily for propaganda purposes, they hoped to improve sanitary conditions and ventilation after the strike ended.

Because the strike lasted for eighteeen weeks, it was necessary to raise money to prevent the workers from being starved into submission as the owners had anticipated. Every Saturday a small band led a parade of strikers from the Hill District into downtown. The spectators tossed money in a sheet carried by four girls. Each week's contributions usually totaled over eighty dollars. The Workmen's Council also solicited funds. The Pittsburgh Industrial Council contributed a list of addresses to write to for donations. A week after the strike began, the I.W.W. Chicago headquarters circulated an appeal for financial support for the stogie workers. The I.W.W. cigar makers' local of Tampa, Florida, sent $118, and donations came from all parts of the country. Saul Rabinowitz appealed at the national convention for financial assistance, but the convention only promised to have six speakers conduct a mass rally and turn the proceeds over to the strikers. The strikers also formed the local Relief Conference for the Striking Tobacco Workers, on which labor unions and radical groups were represented.[64]

Some strikers went to work in Wheeling during the strike; others found temporary jobs in Pittsburgh. As small shops settled on the strikers' terms, the strike committee allowed workers to return to their jobs, but every worker had to contribute 10 percent of his wages to the strike fund.[65] This tactic of piecemeal settlements allowed men to work and decreased the number of dependents on the strike fund. All of these methods permitted the stogie workers to continue their strike.

The Bosses' Association had hoped to starve the workers out. As the strike continued, several owners resorted to having their stogies made in other towns, but the strikers gleefully claimed that the working class found these scab smokes to be poor smokes.[66] Pittsburgh Wobblies visited the Webster Stogie Company, a Pittsburgh satellite stogie factory in nearby Jeannette, and convinced the workers to join the strike. Goldsmit closed his Hill District plant and moved his operation to the North Side.[67] Smaller operators, unable to move and impressed by the working-class solidarity, began to meet I.W.W. demands. As Slawkin relates, the sweatshop owners usually did not present a problem to the strikers. A strike committee of several men would visit the owner and he would nervously agree to the terms.[68] Finally, in late October, the Bosses' Association, with the major exception of Goldsmit, agreed to the strikers' requests.

The bosses consented to the full recognition of the Tobacco Workers Industrial Local No. 101 and its shop delegates, the recognition of its grievance committees, no discrimination in rehiring, a fifty-four-hour week, better sanitary conditions, weekly pay, and no signed contract. New pay scales were established as follows: on 2-for-5¢ stogies, bunchers received 13¢ and rollers 17¢ per 100; on 3-for-5¢ stogies above six inches long, bunchers received 11¢ and rollers 11¢; on 3-for-5¢ cigars below six inches, bunchers got 10.5¢ and rollers 13.5¢; on scrap stogies, bunchers received 9.5¢ and rollers 13.5¢; on 5-for-10¢ stogies, bunchers made 13¢ and rollers 16¢; on special stogies, an increase of .5¢ per 100 was obtained, strippers of wrappers received 5.5¢ per pound on good tobacco and special rates on poor tobacco, strippers on binders received 3¢ per pound for heavy, and 4¢ per pound for light; fillers received 2¢ per pound for opening leaves, and 3¢ per pound for slinging leaves.[69] Altogether, the strikers had averaged about a $1.50 weekly raise.[70] The workers ratified the agreement and the strike was over.

The workers' conduct of the strike raises several questions. Fred Merrick severely criticized the stogie workers during the strike for their policy of piecemeal settlements. He declared that they had not learned anything from Paterson.[71] For I.W.W. unions to settle with individual owners was perhaps unusual but it was beneficial in this case. It strengthened the relief fund both by lessening the total number of people dependent upon it and by having the now-employed workers contribute 10 percent of their wages to the fund. Furthermore, the acceptance of the I.W.W.'s terms by many small proprietors added pressure on the larger owners to settle. Thus, the piecemeal settlements contributed to the strikers' victory.

A second issue is that the workers did not concern themselves with eliminating piecework pay. Their apparent conservative attitude was that since most of the work was piecework, each worker could pace himself at his own speed and determine his own earnings within the wage structure. The union, however, was there to protect the workers from the owners' changing the rates and causing a speed-up to earn the same wages.[72]

A third question asks why the I.W.W. was limited in its appeal to the Hill District, which had a minority of the stogie workers. The Hill's heavier concentration of both the industry and the politically more radical Jewish workers, as well as the lower pay scale, dictated that unionization efforts begin there. George Weinstein, a former Socialist party organizer in Pittsburgh, believes that many of Pittsburgh's Jewish immigrants had participated in Socialist activities in their native lands of Germany, Poland, and Russia. Their religion stressed social and economic cooperation with social obligations to the poor. This led to the strong Jewish support of and contributions to labor movements. Furthermore, the highly literate Jewish population read both Jewish and Socialist papers, which intensified their class consciousness.[73] Irving Howe, in discussing the East European Jewish immigrants in New York City, stresses that the idea of collective advancement and the intense search for knowledge advanced socialism. What the workers "learned from the Yiddish lectures, classes, rallies, and newspapers was incomplete, hazy, sometimes half-baked; but whatever remained was earned and felt."[74]

Perhaps many of the Socialist stogie workers did not agree with all of the I.W.W.'s ideology, but belonging to the I.W.W. with its emphasis on solidarity appeared to be the best way to advance their economic conditions in Pittsburgh. Slawkin estimates that 90 percent of the strikers in 1913 were Jewish, with sprinklings of other nationalities and blacks.[75] Matilda Rabinowitz wrote that "side by side, Jews and Negroes were fighting a common enemy, unmindful of racial and religious differences, and looking only to the betterment of their economic conditions."[76]

The Socialist party also helped the strikers. The Third Ward Socialist party, located in the Hill District, was largely Jewish and was considered the hotbed of Pittsburgh Socialists.[77] It raised $10,000 for the strikers, but the inner squabblings of the Pittsburgh Socialists complicated the strike. Two factions bitterly criticized one another: the direct actionists led by Merrick, editor of *Justice*, and the political Socialists commanded by W. J. Van Essen. Bitter enemies, each man was intolerant of the other's position. The conservative branch expelled over 400 members, including Merrick and Margolis, in 1913 over the question of sabotage and other issues. Both

factions had representation on the Relief Conference for the Striking
Tobacco Workers and criticized the other's proposals. Merrick untiredly
used *Justice* as a forum for the stogie worker strikers and his own ideology.[78]

The fact that so many Hill residents had relatives, neighbors, and friends
among the stogie workers ensured the community's support for the strikers.
During conflicts between Jewish workers and Jewish employers, a sense of
community and moral obligations usually prevented open class warfare and
helped to settle differences peacefully.[79] Leaders of the Irene Kaufmann
Settlement House and the business sector decided that the the strike had
seriously affected the community and its business life. Therefore, they
asked the strikers and the owners to select representatives and begin negotiations. This involvement directly led to the settlement of the strike.[80]

The other stogie-making sections of Pittsburgh were more economically
diversified, and the stogie factories employed workers of various nationalities including Italians, Slavs, and Germans.[81] These workers, as a result,
lacked the intense neighborhood economic, social, and political support
that the Hill District stogie workers enjoyed. Furthermore, when the I.W.W.
stogie workers had a successful Labor Day parade, the North Side factory
owners raised wages two cents per hundred stogies as an attempt to prevent
the I.W.W. from organizing in the North Side.[82]

Perhaps the location of much of the stogie industry in the Hill District
provided another advantage. Its distance from the steel industry and other
key industries lessened the strike's probability as a threat to the city's
major industries. The police department readily granted the necessary
permits for Saturday parades. Despite the I.W.W.'s reputation for violence,
little disturbance took place. An effort to organize the McKees Rocks
stogie factories had entirely different results. The police immediately
stopped the organizers and warned them to leave town, which they did.[83]

After the successful strike, the union maintained the terms of the settlement. Shop delegates made certain that the owners followed the agreement
and that workers belonged to the union. The shop delegate notified the
grievance committee of any problems during the weekly meeting of the
committee. Three to five men visited the shop to investigate complaints
about wages, safety, sanitation, and firings. The grievance committee had
to give its consent before an owner could fire a worker, and occasionally
it supported the boss. To ensure the continuation of good men serving on
the committee, the union paid the grievance committee members for any
work time they missed while performing union duties.[84]

The contract was maintained in some factories into World War I.[85]
Some owners sought to decrease their labor costs by increased mechanization. Others left the Hill and relocated their factories among a more docile
labor force. The increased competition from cigars and cigarettes also
lessened the number of available jobs in the Hill District and, consequently,

weakened the workers' position. The I.W.W. local disappeared by the end of the war, and the industry itself had largely left Pittsburgh by the early 1930s.[86]

The stogie workers' strike of 1913 was unusual. The workers gained community support, won the strike, and established the union shop and worker control of shop conditions. They also settled the strike without a signed contract and were able to enforce the provisions of the settlement for a reasonable time period. Although the I.W.W. had organized the workers, it was the support by the Jewish community in the Hill District that gave the stogie workers' local its strength.

NOTES

1. *Industrial Worker*, April 7, 30, 1910.

2. *Industrial Worker*, October 20, 27, 1909.

3. *Industrial Worker*, January 29, 1910. For Ettor's and Schmidt's roles in anthracite, see Patrick M. Lynch, "Pennsylvania Anthracite: A Forgotten I.W.W. Venture, 1906-1916" (M.A. thesis, Bloomsburg State College, Bloomsburg, Penn., 1974).

4. An interesting insight is provided in Ben H. Williams's "American Labor in the Jungle: The Saga of One Big Union" (paper, Wayne State University Labor Archives). Also see *Industrial Worker*, April 2, May 7, and November 2, 1910.

5. *Industrial Worker*, April 23, 1910, and the *Pittsburgh Post*, April 19 through April 26, 1910.

6. *Industrial Worker*, October 1, 15, 1910; *Solidarity*, August 27, 1910.

7. *Industrial Worker*, November 17, 1910, and *Solidarity*, September 10, 1910.

8. H. A. Goff, for example, both a Wobbly and a Socialist party member, was arrested in a Socialist party free speech fight in Homewood. See *Industrial Worker*, August 22, 1912; *Pittsburgh Post*, August 4, 11, 1912; Jacob Margolis, "The Streets of Pittsburgh," *International Socialist Review* 13 (October 1912), 313-20; *Solidarity*, October 1912. For the Lawrence rallies, see *Solidarity*, March 9, 23, July 13, August 3, 31, October 5, 1912.

9. *Industrial Worker*, May 1, August 15, October 3, November 14, 31, December 5, 1912.

10. *Solidarity*, June 22, August 10, October 12, 19, December 21, 1912; *Industrial Worker*, November 31, December 5, 1912; *Pittsburgh Post*, June 19, 1912; "Strikes in the Steel District," *Survey* 18 (August 3, 1912), 595-96.

11. *Solidarity*, February 1, 15, March 15, July 19, 26, August 16, 1913; *Industrial Worker*, February 20, April 3, 17, 1913; Celia Lepschultz, "Pittsburgh Traitors," *International Socialist Review* 13 (May 1913), 821.

12. I.W.W., *Eighth Annual Convention of the Industrial Workers of the World, 1913*, I.W.W. Collection, Box 2, Folder 1, Wayne State University Labor Archives, p. 48.

13. *Industrial Worker*, September 16, 23, 1909; Louis Duchez, "Victory at McKees Rocks," *International Socialist Review* (October 1909), 290; *Industrial Worker*, September 12, 1912.

14. Katherine Stone, "The Origins of Job Structures in the Steel Industry," *Radical America* 7 (November-December 1973), 19-61.

15. I.W.W., *Eighth Annual Convention*, p. 28.

16. Ibid., pp. 27-28, 48; *Solidarity*, May 10, 1913; Melvyn Dubofsky, *We Shall Be All* (New York: Quadrangle/The New York Times Book Co., 1969), p. 108.

17. I.W.W., *Eighth Annual Convention*, pp. 17-19, 48-57, 71, 115.

18. Elizabeth Butler, *Women and the Trades, Pittsburgh, 1907-1908*, ed. Paul Underwood Kellogg, *The Pittsburgh Survey* (New York: Charities Publication Committee, 1914), pp. 75-97.

19. Ibid., p. 75.

20. Eva Smill, "The Stogy Industry on the Hill in Pittsburgh, Pa." (M.A. thesis, Carnegie Institute, Pittsburgh, June 1920), p. 21.

21. Butler, *Women and the Trades*, pp. 76, 80, 385, 386.

22. Ibid., pp. 76-77.

23. Ibid., p. 77.

24. Ibid., p. 78.

25. Ibid.

26. Ibid., pp. 78-79.

27. Ibid., p. 79.

28. Alexander Z. Pittler, "The Hill District of Pittsburgh—A Study in Succession" (M.A. thesis, University of Pittsburgh, 1930), pp. 20-28.

29. Ailon Shiloh et al., *By Myself I'm a Book: An Oral History of the Immigrant Jewish Experience in Pittsburgh* (Waltham, Massachusetts: American Jewish Historical Society, 1972), p. 156.

30. Pittler, "The Hill District," pp. 29-32; Kurt Pine, "The Jews in the Hill District of Pittsburgh, 1910-1940" (M.A. thesis, University of Pittsburgh, 1943), pp. 12, 52-57.

31. Ida C. Selavan, "Jewish Wage Earners in Pittsburgh, 1890-1930," *American Jewish Historical Quarterly* 65 (March 1976), 274; Butler, pp. 81-82.

32. Shiloh, *By Myself I'm a Book*, p. 57.

33. Ibid., interview with Harry M. Slawkin, a former stogie maker, July 9, 1976.

34. Shiloh, *By Myself I'm a Book*, p. 56.

35. Butler, *Women and the Trades*, p. 80; Selavan, "Jewish Wage Earners," p. 274.

36. Butler, *Women and the Trades*, pp. 79-80, 84-86, 90-92.

37. Ibid., pp. 88-90.

38. Ibid., pp. 87, 90.

39. Smill, "The Stogy Industry," pp. 6-7, 10.

40. *Solidarity*, September 13, 1913.

41. Butler, *Women and the Trades*, p. 82.

42. Ibid., p. 95.

43. Shiloh, *By Myself I'm a Book*, p. 58.

44. "Minutes of Meeting of Industrial Board, June 5, 1914" and "A Preliminary Report of the Inspection of Tobacco Factories," *Monthly Bulletin of the Pennsylvania Department of Labor and Industry* 1 (August 1914), 29-37.

45. Butler, *Women and the Trades*, pp. 95-96.

46. Scott Nearing, "On the Trail of the Pittsburgh Stogies," *Independent* 65 (July 1908), 22-24.

47. Butler, *Women and the Trades*, p. 94.

48. Ibid., pp. 93-94; Smill, "The Stogy Industry," pp. 22-24.

49. *Industrial Worker*, May 1, 1912; Slawkin interviews, July 9, 1976.

50. *Industrial Worker*, May 1, August 1, August 15, 1912; *Solidarity*, August 10, September 7, 1912; Smill, "The Stogy Industry," p. 25.

51. I.W.W., *Seventh Annual Convention, Industrial Workers of the World, 1912* (microfilm copy, I.W.W. Collection, Wayne State University Labor Archives), pp. 1-2.

52. Slawkin interviews, July 9, 1976; *Solidarity*, July 19, September 13, 1913; *Justice*, October 11, 1913; Charles I. Cooper, "Stogy Makers and the I.W.W. in Pittsburgh," *Survey*, November 29, 1913, p. 214.

53. Cooper, "Stogy Makers," p. 214; Smill, "The Stogy Industry," pp. 25-26. Several sources such as Cooper list 2,000 to 2,500 stogie workers on strike. Slawkin disagrees. Soon after the strike began, he states, the workers on strike dropped below 1,000. Perhaps the I.W.W. inflated the strike statistics for effect; this would account for the discrepancy.

54. The exact date is not listed in the papers.

55. Slawkin interview, July 9, 1976; *Solidarity*, July 19, August 2, 1913.

56. Slawkin interviews, July 9, 28, 1976; Smill, "The Stogy Industry," p. 26; *Solidarity*, July 19, 1913; September 3, 1913; *Justice*, October 11, 1913.

57. Slawkin interview, July 9, 1976; Cooper, "Stogy Makers," p. 214; Selavan, "Jewish Wage Earners," p. 276.

58. Slawkin interview, July 9, 1976.

59. *Solidarity*, September 13, 1913; *Justice*, October 11, November 1, 1913.

60. *Solidarity*, September 27, 1913; *Justice*, October 25, 1913.

61. *Solidarity*, August 2, 1913.

62. *Solidarity*, September 13, 1913; Slawkin interview, July 9, 1976.

63. Slawkin interview, July 9, 1976; Selavan, "Jewish Wage Earners," p. 275.

64. Slawkin interviews, July 9, 28, 1976; *Solidarity*, October 4, 1913; *Justice*, October 11, 25, 1913; I.W.W., *Eighth Annual Convention*, pp. 16-17.

65. Slawkin interviews, July 9, 28, 1976.

66. *Solidarity*, September 27, 1913.

67. *Solidarity*, October 4, 1913; *Justice*, October 11, 1913.

68. Slawkin interview, July 9, 1976.

69. *Justice*, October 25, 1913.

70. Slawkin interview, July 9, 1976.

71. *Justice*, October 11, 1913.

72. Slawkin interview, July 28, 1913.

73. Interview with George Weinstein, August 2, 1976.

74. Irving Howe, *World of Our Fathers* (New York: Harcourt, Brace, Jovanovich, 1976), pp. 235, 238, 245, 246, 310, 311.

75. Slawkin interview, July 9, 1976.

76. *Solidarity*, August 2, 1913.

77. Weinstein interview, August 2, 1976.

78. Ibid.; Smill, "The Stogy Industry," p. 26; *Justice*, October 25, November 8, 1913.

79. Howe, pp. 302-4.

80. Slawkin interview, July 9, 1976.

81. Butler, *Women and the Trades*, pp. 83-84.

82. *Solidarity*, September 20, 1913.

83. Slawkin interview, July 9, 1976.

84. Ibid., July 28, 1976.

85. Ibid.

86. Ibid.; Smill, "The Stogy Industry," pp. 5, 9-12, 15-18, 25-30.

PART TWO

THE I.W.W. ON THE EXTRACTIVE FRINGE

RACE, CLASS, AND RADICALISM: THE WOBBLIES IN THE SOUTHERN LUMBER INDUSTRY, 1900-1916*

JAMES F. FICKLE

During the early twentieth century, the timber regions of the lower South erupted into conflict as blacks and whites united to challenge the institutions that kept them in common bondage. Centered in eastern Texas and western Louisiana, these struggles pitted the lumber workers against some of the most powerful forces in the region because of the premise that class interests transcend racial interests, and because of the affiliation of the workers with the "Wobblies."

The major conflict occurred during 1911 and 1912, and management was thoroughly triumphant. However, the experience was not soon forgotten by either workers or employers. The episode is an interesting southern chapter in the history of an organization whose activities in the industrial East and the West were much more highly publicized. Wobbly radicalism with a southern accent too often has been ignored or misinterpreted by students of the South and of American labor history generally. The details have been clouded by the perceptions, prejudices, and misconceptions of contemporary participants and observers as well as some later chroniclers.[1]

By the early twentieth century lumbering was the South's largest industry in terms of employees, geographical extent, and revenue. One of the industry's most important regions was the piney woods area of western Louisiana and eastern Texas, an area of magnificent stands of southern pine inhabited largely by an impoverished population of blacks and poor whites.

The people who labored in the lumber camps, woods, and mills eked out

*Portions of this chapter have been previously published in James E. Fickle, "The Louisiana-Texas Lumber War of 1911-1912," *Louisiana History*, 16, no. 1 (Winter 1975): 59-85. Reprinted by permission of *Louisiana History*.

a marginal existence in an industry noted for miserable working conditions even in an age of generally unenlightened labor policies. Wages were extremely low, ranging from $1.35 to $1.75 a day for a seventy-hour week, among many companies.[2] The company town with the attendant abuses of overcharges for rent and utilities was characteristic of the lumber regions. The company scrip-commissary system was commonly used, and excessive charges for inadequate medical services or insurance were frequent complaints. It should be noted, however, that despite the abuses, conditions in the company towns were often better than the alternatives available for the workers on the outside. Also, it is important to realize that in many cases the workers farmed and lived on their own land and labored in the woods and mills only part of the year. The perceptions, loyalties, and priorities of such workers and those of the people who worked only for the lumber companies obviously differed.

The labor force was racially mixed. Unlike some southern industries where factory labor was reserved largely for whites, in the lumber camps and mills blacks and whites labored side by side. This does not mean that they were treated equally. Blacks were generally relegated to the most menial jobs, and they were segregated in separate quarters in the company towns. They were often paid less than whites and their facilities were inferior. Despite the idealistic portrayals left by some contemporaries and later writers, it seems clear that while there were blacks and whites who realized that they faced common problems and sought to solve them by working together, there were many others before, during, and after the conflicts who were heavily influenced by racial animosity and distrust. There were whites and blacks who stuck by the companies and even acted as scabs during the strikes; there were blacks and whites who pulled together and supported the unions and the battles against management.

Lumber operators were plagued during this period by overproduction and great price fluctuations. While there were intermittent efforts to bring greater order to the industry, the common tendency was for the manufacturers to respond to an immediate short-run crisis by cutting back on hours of operation and employment. The burden of these "adjustments" fell on the workers in the mills and camps.

During the late nineteenth and early twentieth century, there were sporadic attempts to organize southern laborers into various unions, usually on a segregated basis. The Knights of Labor organized, occasionally on an integrated basis, and were involved in a number of strikes, including one in the Alabama lumber industry in 1890. In North Carolina the races were divided into separate assemblies. Efforts by the National Labor Union and other groups to organize blacks and whites in Texas during the late nineteenth century were generally unsuccessful and foundered at least in part because of racial prejudices.[3] Clearly there was a tradition of union activity in the South, including the occasional organization of workers across racial lines, but the record was one of virtually unmitigated failure.

The Knights made some efforts to organize Louisiana lumber workers without much success. However, a series of spontaneous strikes by local unions in 1902 did pressure the operators to move from a twelve- to an eleven-hour day.[4] These organizations soon disbanded, but union activity and strikes resurfaced again in 1906 and 1907 during a time of general depression in the lumber industry.

A typical manufacturer's response was reflected by a lumberman not directly located in the "infected" area: "We have let practically all our men go, and reduced salaries on those that will stay."[5] The employers' actions in dealing with the situation were predictable, but the workers unexpectedly responded by walking out en masse, with the trouble centered in eastern Texas and western Louisiana, especially around Lake Charles. The workers' action was largely spontaneous and no lasting labor organization resulted. A few AFL agents established craft unions in the area, but these soon died and the workers were eventually drawn back into the mills and camps with promises that their old wages and hours would be restored as soon as economic conditions warranted.[6]

The episode had important ramifications. While the workers were forced to return on the operators' terms, those around DeRidder, Louisiana, held out for several weeks after work resumed elsewhere. Later union activity in the piney woods stemmed at least in part from the animosity and strife generated in 1906 and 1907. When a lumber workers' union was finally organized, its greatest area of strength was in the DeRidder area.[7]

The labor disorders of 1906 and 1907 also spawned the manufacturers' organization, which vigorously fought unionization. Named the Southern Lumber Operators' Association, it was formed in September 1906 and dedicated to a single goal, "to resist *any* encroachment of organized labor." Within a few years it had grown to include eighty-seven companies with operations in Arkansas, Texas, Louisiana, Alabama, Oklahoma, Florida, and Mississippi. There was a Benefit Trust Fund for the relief of companies whose facilities were closed by labor difficulties, and members could be dismissed for only two reasons—nonpayment of assessment for the fund and failure to follow policies dictated by association directors.[8] From the start the organization attempted to associate the workers' cause with "foreign" and "radical" doctrines.[9]

In the immediate aftermath of the 1906 and 1907 outbreaks, despite the undercurrent of discontent, workers flocked back to the mills and camps of eastern Texas and Louisiana. The operators' association, complacent in victory, fell into somnolence. It was not until three years later that labor troubles erupted again.

The workers needed only a stimulus to bring them into revolt. They got two—another downturn in economic conditions that prompted shutdowns and wage reductions, and new leadership. The men who emerged to lead the embattled timber workers were Arthur L. Emerson and Jay Smith. Both were native southerners, although they were termed "outside agitators" by the operators. Emerson was a Tennessean who had drifted into the lumber industry working as a lumberjack, sawmill hand, and millwright in the South and on the Pacific Coast. During two trips to the western timber districts, he had seen "the discrepancy in wages between the Pacific Coast and the Gulf States" and "learned the need of organization."[10]

Emerson was a saint to the workers and Antichrist to the operators. He had been in trouble with the law frequently in the southern timber regions, according to Emerson because of a "relentless program of harassment designed to halt his organizing efforts . . . conceived by the lumbermen in collusion with local law enforcement officials."[11] Whatever the circumstances of his past difficulties with the law, there is no doubt that John Henry Kirby of Houston, a dominant figure among the operators, on one occasion prodded the authorities in a small eastern Texas town to reopen an old case against Emerson as a means of harassment.[12] Kirby described Emerson as a common criminal who had been fired by the Gulf Lumber Company at Fullerton, Louisiana, for "stealing blankets from the boarding house." According to Kirby, his nemesis was "a student of socialism and a man of more or less mental attainments and thoroughly unscrupulous."[13] He dismissed Smith as "a socialist and . . . by nature a criminal."[14]

Emerson's return to the South was inspired by his observations in other regions. He immediately began to scheme and work toward fomenting a great uprising of the southern timber workers, regardless of race, against the barons of the piney woods. He worked undercover at Fullerton among the laborers of the Gulf Lumber Company, testing and polling them about their willingness to support a union. Subsequently, in conjunction with Smith, Emerson formed his first local at Carson, in western Louisiana, on December 3, 1910. The movement spread and in June 1911, delegates from several fledgling locals assembled in Alexandria to unite in the Brotherhood of Timber Workers, which adopted a constitution and selected Emerson as its first president.[15]

The brotherhood's constitution stressed specific abuses. These included high rents for company-owned houses, long hours, high commissary prices, unfair insurance systems, hospital dues, and compulsory doctors' fees. The preamble was written in flowery, idealistic language, saying ". . . it is our aim to elevate those who labor—morally, socially, intellectually, and financially. . . ." The constitution referred to the rights of the employers, promising them "an absolutely square deal," and pledging that the workers were willing "to meet and counsel with those who employ us. . . ." The brotherhood, however, demanded "Recognition, Equal Rights, A Living Wage, A just consideration of abuses, [and] Exact and equal justice to those who work with their hands. . . ." The mill owners termed the union program "socialistic," "anarchistic," and "terroristic," and adamantly refused to yield a single point.[16]

While some of the workers involved in this early effort were sympathetic toward the Socialist party or the I.W.W., they do not seem to have been dominated or even primarily motivated by ideology. Whether for effect upon a particular audience or out of genuine conviction, Emerson preached a nonideological line. While he pushed the one-big-union concept, Emerson insisted, "I am not a Socialist, but I say I am a Union man." "If I were a Socialist," he continued, "that is my business." "I believe in union labor, I am going to talk for it. If that is socialism I am a socialist, if republican I am a republican, if democracy I am a democrat."[17]

If ideological considerations were not emphasized, racial realities could not be avoided. Over half the labor force of the southern lumber industry was black, concentrated in the lower occupational categories. In 1910 more than 7,200 of the nearly 8,000 blacks in the mills of Texas were common laborers. Obviously the Brotherhood of Timber Workers had to organize blacks if it was to succeed, but at the same time it had to avoid antagonizing white workers by violating the local segregation structure. Therefore, the union's constitution permitted black members, but provided for separate "colored lodges" that had to deposit all initiation fees and dues for safe-keeping with the nearest white local.[18] Union organizers and leaders addressing white audiences carefully noted that they were not promoting race-mixing or racial equality. As Emerson told an eastern Texas audience:

The negro is here and is here to stay and we can't get rid of him . . . you need not preach equality to me about the negro. Who put the negro in the saw mill. You are working side by side with the negro in the saw mill and you can't get around that. Let social affairs take care of themselves. Give the negro his lodge room but let him be under the management of the white man. We don't want social equality, let that take care of itself.[19]

The first year of brotherhood activity provoked an immediate response from the mill owners both through the SLOA and individually. Early in April 1911, the association prepared a yellow-dog contract to prevent unionization, and employing this tool the mill men began to require all employees to declare that they would not join the Brotherhood of Timber Workers. As a result, there were several strikes and a number of mills closed. In May, the operators began the "lumber war" by deciding that they would force the brotherhood to the wall by cutting operations to four days per week. The union, however, was not intimidated. The struggle began in earnest during June and July as the operators held secret sessions and planned strategy to combat the unexpected resistance.[20]

Some 150 lumbermen from Texas, Louisiana, and Arkansas attended a secret meeting of the SLOA in New Orleans on July 19 that was dominated by John Henry Kirby. The association ordered eleven mills around De-Ridder to close immediately, in effect locking out some 3,000 employees. The association was further empowered to shut down any of some 300 mills in the three states represented at the meeting if conditions warranted. During the next seven months, union men were excluded from all mills within the SLOA's jurisdiction.[21] The association issued a press release stating that "the lumber manufacturers are all determined that this apparently anarchistic organization [BTW] must not get any further both for the good of the lumber industry and for the good of the mill employees themselves."[22]

However, there was division within the operators' camp. C. B. Sweet of the Long-Bell Company said that his mills would not close down because he felt the company's men were loyal. While he would defend the "mutual interests of the fraternity," Sweet said the company would resign from the association rather than follow an unwise order.[23] Sweet's attitude encouraged others to resist, and Charles S. Keith of the Central Coal & Coke Comapny of Kansas City recommended that the order be rescinded. Kirby, however, stood his ground, and a conference in Sweet's Kansas City offices on July 27 resulted in an agreement that members would determine the union status of their employees, and "infected" mills would then be closed down beginning on August 7. It was agreed that employees would be forced to sign yellow-dog contracts or be dismissed.[24]

Still the operators were unable to present a completely solid front. On August 7, the very day that the new lockout was to begin, one of the "infected" mills, the American Lumber Company at Merryville in western Louisiana, reopened under a contract with the BTW. The agreement was reached with Sam Park, a part owner, over the objections of his partner. Feeling that Park "had betrayed us," said Kirby, "we forced him out and closed the door in his face."[25] However, defections were rare. On August 8, Kirby reported to C. B. Sweet that "aside from the action of Mr. Park, I have not heard of a disposition any where to refuse cooperation with us except from the Sabine Tram Company and Lutcher & Moore."[26]

The union's relatively strong showing during the summer of 1911 brought Sweet and Long-Bell into line. After learning that a majority of his company's men had refused to sign nonunion pledges, the Long-Bell leader came into the fight, dismissing union members and pressuring the local newspaper in DeRidder to alter its former prounion stance.[27] Kirby also picked up support from the president of the Atchison, Topeka, and Santa

Fe Railway System, which had close financial ties with his own empire and great interest in the affected area. The railroad leader said the union should be discouraged "in the interest of good citizenship." Although a shutdown of the mills "would be a serious matter to this company in loss of earnings," declared the president, the Santa Fe would cooperate, and "as to the particular relations of your company to ours—my voice would be in favor of granting all possible and reasonable assistance to you in the struggle. . . ."[28]

The union threat also prompted a reorganization of the operators' association and a refinement and systematization of its techniques. The headquarters were moved from New Orleans to Alexandria, which was more centrally located, and the part-time director, Oliver O. Bright, was replaced by M. L. Alexander, who served as the full-time executive secretary. By September work was under way to establish "a clearing house for saw mill labor." The president of the association requested members to submit full reports on their labor to the Alexandria office, which soon had a complete file on approximately 25,000 workers.[29] Individual owners also began to employ Burns and Pinkerton detectives, who submitted reports to the association's membership. The association itself began to augment its investigative forces. Detectives found it easy to infiltrate the brotherhood and some even succeeded in rising to high office. By late September, Alexander had a complete listing of the union's membership and the financial situation of each member.[30]

The operators' association was particularly concerned about the union's special appeal to blacks, "claiming that it is the only order ever organized in the South that looks especially after the Negroes and their families and gives them equality with the white wage earners on an industrial basis. This creates a complicated condition and one that is hard to combat. . . ."[31] Kirby corresponded with a black school principal in eastern Texas who promised that

. . . you may rest quite sure that they will not organize the Col'd people at this place while I am here. . . . I Mr. Kirby know their [*sic*] object in wanting the Nigro [*sic*]. They have an axe to grind & want him to turn the stone.[32]

Kirby responded that

the promoters of that Brotherhood have no concern about our colored citizenship except insofar as they can use the negroes for their personal advantage. . . . what Mr. Emerson and his cohorts seek to do is to get the negroes into this Brotherhood so that they can have their money in establishing the organization and that if they succeed in establishing the organization and getting control of the mills they intend to drive every colored man off the job and supply his place with some inferior white fellow. They would first tie the hands of the negroes by getting them into the so-called Union and get a part of their earnings for the support of the Union and as soon as the Union officers were in charge of the plants they would drive the negroes away and import rough necks and red bones from Louisiana and Arkansas to take their places. . . .[33]

On August 1, Kirby addressed a crowd estimated at 4,000 people at DeRidder. The day had a festive atmosphere. Kirby declared that there would be a holiday from toil and chartered special trains to bring workers from his Texas mills to the Louisiana town. Barbecued meat was served, and at the climactic moment the "Prince of the Pines" addressed the crowd from the guarded upper gallery of the local hotel. No known appeal to patriotism, Anglophobia, southernism, localism, God, or home escaped his attention.[34] The lumberman emphasized the interest and friendship between himself and his employees: ". . . the relation of employer and employee does not exist . . . except on payday; at all other times we are pals." However, their "pal" had a stern warning—if they joined the union, the mills would close down and they would be out of a job.[35] At the conclusion of Kirby's speech, A. L. Emerson climbed onto a wagon and challenged the lumberman to a debate. Kirby haughtily refused and ordered the local brass band to drown out Emerson's attempt to speak. The union leader then retreated to the local ball park with a large crowd following and listening unmolested. Kirby ordered the excursion trains to leave immediately with or without their passengers after Emerson announced his plans to speak. The day was somewhat of a success for the union since many workers joined the brotherhood after hearing Emerson.[36]

Kirby was enraged by Emerson's appearance at the rally, which he labeled "an impertinence," and he declared that he would have refused to speak if he had known he would be followed by "that wolf."[37] Nevertheless, the lumber baron also considered the day a success, although he believed that "since my DeRidder speech Emerson and his followers have determined upon a vicious attack at my plants and seem to be concentrating their efforts in that direction."[38] Kirby had in fact become recognized as the leader of the operators' association.

By the latter part of 1911, the operators' campaign was exacting a frightening toll on the brotherhood both financially and in membership. In October, the lumbermen again met secretly in New Orleans and discussed reopening the mills. The operators seemed to believe that the workers had been sufficiently disciplined and were under control. A number of plants were reopened with slight concessions in the form of somewhat higher wages and a ten-hour day, but the lockout at many mills continued until February 1912. There was absolutely no disposition to grant union recognition. Kirby reported that the fight was proceeding successfully and that "the mills seemed to be in better shape as far as their labor was concerned."[39]

Leaders of the brotherhood began to consider outside support and in September sent three delegates to the I.W.W. convention in Chicago. In order to keep their members' heads above water, they advised them to go underground—destroy their membership cards, sign the pledges or yellow-dog contracts, return to their jobs, but above all else pay their dues. Emerson and Jay Smith traveled to Chicago to confer with representatives of the Wobblies.[40]

Rumors and accurate reports from its operatives concerning the proposed affiliation of the brotherhood with the I.W.W. reached the operators early in 1912, and minor union organization successes in western Louisiana alarmed some of the lumbermen. However, Alexander argued that reports of union success were exaggerated. The rumor of I.W.W. entry into the piney woods provided the operators with powerful propaganda ammunition, for the Wobblies were regarded by middle-class Americans as radical and disreputable. Furthermore, the operators were in a stronger economic position. The lumber market began to improve toward the end of 1911, and the great stockpiles of lumber that had made shutdowns so attractive no longer existed. Securing nonunion labor was not a problem because of the large number of impoverished black agricultural workers in the South. For the first time the brotherhood was faced with a new menace—scab labor used on a large scale.[41]

Kirby sounded the theme of the new year's attacks when he said that Emerson's followers were made up of

farmers, and merchants and small men in trade who naturally sympathize with the laboring masses. . . . loafers and agitators and men who were not willing to work for a living. In some instances sound-headed and industrious day laborers about the mills were deceived into joining his organization but, as a rule, it was made up of the elements I have above stated and of negroes, dagoes, and other foreigners who are made socialists at heart through the oppressive institutions of the countries from which they came.[42]

Kirby was partially right. The entire countryside in the Louisiana-Texas piney woods seemed to be aflame in 1912, a year of violent conflict in which entire communities rose up to register their protest against the economic and political "establishment" in the dusty streets and at the polls. Covington Hall, a New Orleans Socialist and radical writer, joined the fray early in the year, and during his first interview with Emerson and Smith in April, he told them, ". . . this isn't a labor union you all have on your hands—it is an insurrection of all the people of Louisiana and East Texas under the Lumber Trust."[43]

Despite the desperate condition of the workers, they were buoyed by the hope of additional support and leadership from the I.W.W. In a euphoric mood, they met in convention in Alexandria in May to shore up their defenses and formulate structure and strategy. The meeting lasted for three days, and the delegates were addressed by both Covington Hall and Big Bill Haywood. One of the operators' spies said that Haywood delivered a "great speech" that was "strictly 'pizen,' and calculated to do a great deal of damage." Hall was described as being "as dangerous as a rattle snake. . . ."[44] The delegates voted overwhelmingly to affiliate with the Wobblies, and in an atmosphere replete with color, tension, and espionage, they planned to send new agitators into the timber belt to organize.[45] Interesting sidelights of the meeting were the successful efforts of Haywood and Hall to integrate the sessions, and the first of many reports that plans were afoot to assassinate the erstwhile lumberworkers' "pal," John Henry Kirby.[46]

The days after affiliation with the Wobblies were filled with feverish activity by both sides, which steadily built up until it erupted into violence. Signs that a major clash was in the offing were much in evidence. Rumors continued that Kirby would be the target of an assassin. On May 17, one lumberman reported that "the impression grows on me stronger from week to week that plans are being laid to assassinate Mr. Kirby."[47] Citizens' law and order leagues were organized throughout the "infected" area to guard against the "dangerous" ideas that might be spread through the efforts of the Wobblies or their "Socialist" sympathizers, and prounion speakers often found community meeting places unavailable for their use. If they persisted, local law enforcement agencies and citizens' committees did their best to dissuade the "agitators." Outright violence was not unknown. George Creel, editor of the *Rip Saw* and later the author of an exposé on Texas lumber company towns, was run out of Oakdale, Louisiana, on July 6, without making his scheduled speech, by a nearly successful assassination attempt.[48]

The day after the Creel episode brought the greatest physical clash of the entire "lumber war." The setting, in the small mill town of Graybow, Louisiana, south of DeRidder and toward the Texas line in the "infected" area, was not imposing. Graybow was the site of the Galloway Lumber Company's operations, and as early as May the town had become an armed camp with the BTW demanding union recognition. The owner had informed them "that he come [sic] there in a box car, a tramp and would leave the same way before he would be made to do anything."[49] Management's sentiments were echoed by a company guard who expressed his desire to "kill a union son-of-a-bitch."[50] The passions of both company officials and guards were further aroused and courage was buttressed on the fateful day of July 7 by generous portions of alcohol served from the company commissary.[51]

On the seventh, Emerson met with a group of men, women, and children in DeRidder and then led a group of some 200 to Carson where he spoke briefly. On the return to DeRidder he decided to go through Graybow and hold a meeting outside the gates of the Galloway Lumber Company on a public highway. As Emerson spoke, a gun battle erupted between the company owner and some of his men stationed in the mill office and a few of the union men. By the time the conflict subsided some ten minutes later, there were three union men dead with another mortally wounded and an additional forty injured. Each side blamed the beginning of the conflict on the other. M. L. Alexander of the operators' association charged that "the hostilities were brought on by the Union forces who were distinctly the aggressors."[52]

The authorities arrested union members who had been present at Graybow, as well as six company men. On July 23, a grand jury in Lake Charles indicted sixty-five unionists, while exonerating the company men. The presiding judge postponed their trial from August to October 1, and during the pretrial period the operators' association labored assiduously to find evidence and witnesses that would convict the defendants, employing some 100 Burns detectives in the process. Despite all of this, however, in early November nine union leaders charged with murder were acquitted, and the charges against the others were dropped. The outcome was a tremendous moral victory for the workers, but in the long run the lengthy legal battle contributed to the union's demise as a viable force.[53]

The financial burden was heavy as fifty-eight union men had spent the long pretrial period in the Calcasieu Parish jail, which union writers termed the "black hold of Lake Charles" because of its crowded and filthy conditions. The union had to care for their families, and its energies and attention were distracted from other needs.[54]

However, at the same time the anger and frustration engendered by the incarceration and trial brought a solidarity to the ranks of labor that Covington Hall said he had never seen "before or since."[55] Various organizations, including the I.W.W., AFL, railway brotherhoods, and Farmers' Union, lined up solidly behind the prisoners, with only the Socialist party notably failing to come to their support. Eugene V. Debs, traveling to New Orleans, did not even get off his train as it passed through Lake Charles, nor did he endorse the lumberjacks' stand. However, the feuding "Red" and "Yellow" factions in the Crescent City put aside their differences and held a mass meeting in Lafayette Square to demonstrate support. There were similar demonstrations in the piney woods parishes, including a mass meeting in Leesville.

In the western and upland parishes of Louisiana, the radicals made a vigorous effort to organize blacks and whites into a strong and cohesive movement.[56] They had some success. One black farmer pledged that "so long as I have a pound of meat, or a peck of corn, no man, white or colored, who goes out in this strike will starve, nor will his children."[57] Workers at

Bon Ami, previously frightened by company intimidation, threatened a general walkout unless Emerson was released.[58] They stated that if Emerson and his companions were convicted, they were "marching on Lake Charles and burning sawmills and lumberpiles as we come; and what's more, God Almighty will see more sawmill managers, gunmen-deputy sheriffs and Burns detectives hanging to trees in Western Louisiana and Eastern Texas than he ever saw in one place in all his life."[59]

By this time the union was promoting a more enlightened and forceful position with regard to the relationship between blacks and whites. "As far as the 'Negro question' goes," they argued, "it means simply this: Either the whites organize with the Negroes, or the bosses will organize the Negroes against the whites, in which last case it is hardly up to the white to dam the 'niggers.' Southern workers ought to realize that while there are two colors among the workers in the South there is actually one class."

"It is the object of this organization," they concluded, "To teach that the only hope of the workers is through industrial organization, that while the colors in question are two, the class is only one; that the first thing for a real workingman to do is to learn by a little study that he belongs to the working class, line up with the Brotherhood of Timber Workers or the Industrial Workers of the World, and make a start for industrial freedom."[60]

On the company side critical descriptions of conditions in the Lake Charles jail published in establishment newspapers in Houston and New Orleans created divisions. Captain J. B. White, one of the industry's most respected leaders, abhorred the negative publicity and determined that if there were some abusive practices it would be cheaper to eliminate them than to continue an expensive conflict. He noted that his companies alone were pouring thousands of dollars into the operators' association. Although there were some who shared White's view, they were not successful in persuading those who were directing the industry.[61] The lumbermen were determined to undertake a final drive to totally eliminate piney woods unionism.

The campaign revolved around the American Lumber Company of Merryville, Louisiana. Realizing that the union was under a tremendous financial burden because of the Lake Charles trial, the operators hoped to deliver the death blow by provoking a strike, which the union could ill afford. American Lumber Company management therefore dismissed and blacklisted all union men involved in the Graybow affair, and on November 11, 1912, after the company refused to alter its policies, the men walked out, officially beginning the only strike ever actually called by the BTW.[62]

The company erected a tall fence around the mill and company houses and began to recruit scab labor, especially blacks from Texas and Louisiana. According to labor sources, union appeals to the would-be scabs persuaded many to refuse to work for the company. They also claimed that the unity of black and white workers was so strong that it was cited by I.W.W. organizers as an object lesson for the entire working class. Nonetheless, by early January 1913, the company was back in full operation with nonunion labor.[63] The more ruthless operators wanted to close the plant permanently, giving the citizens of Merryville an "object lesson which they would not soon forget."[64]

As the strike continued, management resorted to strong-arm tactics, aided by a company-encouraged "Good Citizens' League." This culminated on February 16 when a mob led by league leaders and company gunmen went on a rampage, attacking and raiding union facilities and running most union people out of town during the next three days. This was the final blow to the union. Although the strike did not officially end until June 14, little happened in Merryville after the riot.[65] It was a crushing blow, for, as Covington Hall reported, ". . . as the Merryville Union had been, toward the last, the treasury of the Southern District, the loss of the strike left us practically bankrupt."[66] The defeat at Merryville was followed by other reverses at Fay, Elizabeth, Winnfield, Pollock, and Randolph.

Emerson was in bad health, due to his long stay in the Lake Charles jail, and in May 1913 he resigned as the leader of the union, which was now officially the National Industrial Union of Forest and Lumber Workers. He promised to return as a speaker and agitator if needed, but when he did come back on a speaking trip in the autumn of 1913, he was severely beaten in Singer, Louisiana, and fled the piney woods, never to return.[67]

Emerson was succeeded by Jay Smith, who led the union in one last brief skirmish against the "Sweet Home Front" mill of the Iron Mountain Lumber Company at Pollock, Grant Parish, Louisiana. Despite the efforts of union leaders and George Creel of the *Rip Saw*, who gained employment as a company bookkeeper and channeled information to the strikers, the effort gained no support. Workers in the surrounding camps and mills watched the struggle, saying that "if the Sweet Home men win, we'll strike too."[68] The strike was lost, and the workers' despair now seemed complete. Covington Hall reported that "the Sweet Home crew stood alone to the last," and the secretary of the once-powerful DeRidder local said that "it seems like the working class have gone to sleep. . . . The mill companies have taken all away from the workers that the union won for them. . . . the men who stay in the offices know how to keep the working classes scared half to death."[69]

Thus, by the spring of 1914 the Brotherhood of Timber Workers was virtually destroyed, and by early 1916 even the most dedicated unionists had to admit their organizations were dead.[70] Although the operators had overwhelmingly triumphed, the union had at least raised the issue of racial equality and cooperation in the interest of working-class solidarity. If its leaders were not always consistent in their advocacy and promotion of biracial cooperation, they had nonetheless left a legacy of practical black-white labor organization that was probably unmatched in any other southern industry.

NOTES

1. The best published accounts of early clashes in the southern lumber industry are in Charlotte Todes, *Labor and Lumber* (New York, 1931), a Marxist treatment; Vernon H. Jensen, *Lumber and Labor* (New York and Toronto, 1945); Melvyn Dubofsky, *We Shall Be All: A History of the Industrial Workers of the World* (Chicago, 1969); George T. Morgan, Jr., "No Compromise—No Recognition; John Henry Kirby, "The Southern Lumber Operators' Association, and Unionism In The Piney Woods, 1906-1916," *Labor History*, 10, no. 2 (Spring, 1969); F. Ray Marshall, *Labor in the South* (Cambridge, Mass., 1967); Merl E. Reed, "Lumberjacks And Longshoremen: The I.W.W. In Louisiana," *Labor History*, 13 (Winter 1972), 41-59; and Philip S. Foner, "The I.W.W. And The Black Worker," *The Journal of Negro History*, 55, no. 1 (January 1970), 45-64. Also see Merl E. Reed, "The I.W.W. And Individual Freedom in Western Louisiana, 1913," *Louisiana History*, 10, no. 1 (Winter 1969), 61-69.

2. Ruth Alice Allen, *East Texas Lumber Workers, An Economic and Social Picture, 1870-1950* (Austin, Texas, 1961), pp. 71-77.

3. For additional details concerning these early efforts, see H. M. Douty, "Early Labor Organization In North Carolina, 1880-1900," *The South Atlantic Quarterly*, 34, no. 3 (July 1935), 260-68; Frederic Meyers, "The Knights Of Labor In The South," *The Southern Economic Journal*, 6, no. 4 (April 1940), 479-87; James V. Reese, "The Early History of Labor Organizations in Texas, 1838-1876," *Southwestern Historical Quarterly*, 72, no. 1 (July 1968), 1-20.

4. Reed, "Lumberjacks And Longshoremen," 43.

5. Harold Lafayette Grant, Jr., "The Southern Paper Company, 1911-1928" (M.A. thesis, University of Mississippi, 1958), p. 4.

6. Covington Hall, "Labor Struggles in the Deep South," manuscript, Special Collections Division, Howard Tilton Memorial Library, Tulane University of Louisiana, New Orleans, Louisiana, pp. 129-30; H. Grady McWhiney, "The Socialist Vote In Louisiana, 1912: An Historical Interpretation Of Radical Sources" (M.A. thesis, Louisiana State University, 1951), p. 40; Todes, *Labor and Lumber*, p. 171.

7. Charles R. McCord, "A Brief History Of The Brotherhood of Timberworkers" (M.A. thesis, University of Texas, 1959), p. 16.

8. The material on the origins and early period of the operator's association is taken from scattered materials in the Kurth Papers, Box 102 (Forest History Collections, Stephen F. Austin State University Library, Nacogdoches, Texas), and from a paper by Professor George T. Morgan, Jr., of the University of Houston, entitled "No Compromise—No Recognition, John Henry Kirby, the Southern Lumber Operators' Association, and Unionism in the Piney Woods, 1906-1916," which was presented at the spring 1967 meeting of the Southwestern Social Science Association. Hereinafter cited as Morgan paper. A shorter version of the paper

appeared under the same title in *Labor History*, 10, no. 2 (Spring 1969), 193-204. Hereinafter cited as Morgan article. Several authors cite the formation of the operators' association in 1907, but materials in the Kurth Papers show conclusively that it was organized in 1906.

9. Allen, *East Texas Lumber Workers*, pp. 180-82; John M. Collier, *The First Fifty Years of the Southern Pine Association, 1915-1965* (New Orleans, 1965), pp. 129-33; Morgan article, pp. 196-97.

10. William D. Haywood, "Timber Workers and Timber Wolves," *International Socialist Review*, 15 (August 1912), 107. Hereinafter cited as *ISR*. Smith had worked as a sawyer in Texas, Louisiana, Arkansas, and on the Pacific Coast. J. H. Kirby to Edward P. Ripley, August 8, 1911, John Henry Kirby Papers, Box 221 (University of Houston Library, Houston, Texas). Hereinafter cited as Kirby Papers.

11. Morgan paper, p. 7.

12. C. H. Cain to John Kirby, August 17, 1911, Kirby Papers, Box 221; A. L. Reaves to Kirby, August 27, 1911, ibid.

13. Kirby to *American Lumberman*, August 8, 1911, ibid.

14. Kirby to Edward P. Ripley, August 8, 1911, ibid.

15. McCord, "History Of The Brotherhood Of Timberworkers," 17-18; Morgan paper, p. 8.

16. Morgan article, p. 195.

17. Transcript of speech by A. L. Emerson, January 16, 1912, in Kirbyville, Texas, pp. 20-21, Kirby Papers, Box 323. Hereinafter cited as Emerson speech.

18. Allen, *East Texas Lumber Workers*, pp. 54, 58; McCord, "History Of The Brotherhood Of Timberworkers," 19-20.

19. Emerson speech, pp. 16-17.

20. Jensen, *Lumber and Labor*, pp. 87-88; McWhiney, "Socialist Vote In Louisiana," 42-43.

21. McCord, "History Of The Brotherhood Of Timberworkers," 32-33; Morgan paper, p. 5. According to Jensen the operators in Mississippi refused to close their mills because "they were having to trouble and saw no reason why they should take such drastic action." Jensen, *Lumber and Labor*, pp. 87-88.

22. McCord, "History Of The Brotherhood Of Timberworkers," 33.

23. Morgan article, p. 197.

24. Ibid., pp. 197-98.

25. Ibid., p. 199.

26. John Henry Kirby to C. B. Sweet, August 8, 1911, Kirby Papers, Box 211. Even in the case of both of these companies there was great opposition to unions, and their refusal to join the operators did not in any way indicate a receptiveness to organized labor in their plants.

27. Morgan article, p. 199.

28. E. T. Ripley to John Henry Kirby, August 10, 1911, Kirby Papers, Box 221.

29. S. J. Carpenter to John Henry Kirby, September 5, 1911, Kirby Papers, Box 221; Morgan article, p. 200. Box 222 of the Kirby Papers contains a blacklist of the workers of the American Lumber Company at Merryville, Louisiana, breaking them down individually by name, race, and capacity employed, and containing descriptive remarks such as "union," "nonunion," "presumably union," "union—no good," etc.

30. Morgan article, p. 200.

31. M. L. Alexander to All Members, December 30, 1911, Kirby Papers, Box 221.

32. A. J. Criner to John Henry Kirby, August 10, 1911, ibid.

33. Kirby to Criner, August 11, 1911, ibid. On August 12, Criner replied that "my people all understand that you are their personal friend and they dont *[sic]* hesitate to say so. I dont *[sic]* believe that one of the number could be persuaded to sign any kind of paper for fear it was something against your interest at this place." Criner to Kirby, August 12, 1911, ibid.

34. Morgan paper, p. 198.

35. Ibid., pp. 198-99.

36. Ibid., pp. 7-8; Hall, "Labor Struggles in the Deep South," 132-33.

37. Morgan paper, p. 16.

38. John Henry Kirby to C. B. Sweet, August 8, 1911, Kirby Papers, Box 221.

39. Jensen, *Lumber and Labor*, pp. 88-89; McCord, "History Of The Brotherhood Of Timberworkers," 49; McWhiney, "Socialist Vote in Louisiana," 48.

40. M. L. Alexander to All Members, December 30, 1911, Kirby Papers, Box 221; Alexander to M. L. Fleishel, September 20, 1911, ibid.; McWhiney, "Socialist Vote in Louisiana," 45.

41. McCord, "History Of The Brotherhood Of Timberworkers," 54.

42. John Henry Kirby to R. L. Weathersby, January 13, 1912, Kirby Papers, Box 221.

43. Hall, "Labor Struggles in the Deep South," 125. Covington Hall was born in Mississippi, the son of a Presbyterian minister and a wealthy Southern belle. His childhood was spent in Terrebenne Parish, Louisiana, and he served for a time as adjunct general (national secretary) of the United Sons of Confederate Veterans. Beginning as a follower of William Jennings Bryan, Hall for more than fifty years was active as a writer, speaker, and publicity agent in farmer-labor struggles. Hall, "Labor Struggles in the Deep South," 137-38; Joyce L. Kornbluh, ed., *Rebel Voices: An I.W.W. Anthology* (Ann Arbor: The University of Michigan Press, 1964), pp. 259-60.

44. E. E. Sapp to C. P. Myer, May 10, 1912, Kirby Papers, Box 221.

45. M. L. Alexander to All Members, May 1, 1912, Kurth Papers, Box 265; Hall, "Labor Struggles in the Deep South," 140; Jensen, *Lumber and Labor*, p. 89; McWhiney, "Socialist Vote in Louisiana," 50-51; Morgan paper, p. 10.

46. Both Hall and Haywood were eager to claim credit for integrating the sessions. For differing accounts of how this was achieved see Haywood, *Bill Haywood's Book: The Autobiography of William D. Haywood* (New York: International Publishers, 1929), pp. 241-42; Hall, "Labor Struggles in the Deep South," 136-38; and McWhiney, "Socialist Vote in Louisiana," 51-52. An employers' operative who attended the sessions reported that "Mr. Kirby came in for a great deal of abuse, and it is my opinion that they will assassinate him in case the proper opportunity should present itself, and about the same thing will apply to R. A. Long of Kansas City." E. E. Sapp to C. P. Myer, May 10, 1912, Kirby Papers, Box 221.

47. J. A. Herndon to C. P. Myer, May 17, 1912, Kirby Papers. A letter addressed to Kirby from a close associate repeated the story that Haywood had called for the assassinations of Kirby and Long, and advised the lumberman that it would be wise to put his commissaries, hospital service, etc., on a basis that would at least look like they were designed for the welfare of the workers. The writer ominously warned Kirby not

to "ever go off on another special train to make any public speeches about this labor situation under any other conditions. . . . But at all events, don't you misjudge the present situation as involving your personal safety. I have been talking, or rather listening, to some of your close friends who all the time have their ears to the ground about this labor situation, and I am uneasy for you." W. W. Willson to Kirby, June 11, 1912, ibid.

48. Morgan article, pp. 201-2.

49. J. A. Herndon to C. P. Myer, May 17, 1912, Kirby Papers, Box 221.

50. McCord, "History Of The Brotherhood Of Timberworkers," 85-86.

51. *Times-Democrat* (New Orleans), October 20, 1912.

52. M. L. Alexander to C. D. Johnson, July 8, 1912, Kirby Papers, Box 221. For a union account, see Hall, "Labor Struggles in the Deep South," 152-53.

53. Reed, "Lumberjacks and Longshoremen," 50-51.

54. Covington Hall, "I Am Here For Labor," *International Socialist Review*, 13 (September 1912), 225; McWhiney, "Socialist Vote In Louisiana," 72.

55. Hall, "Labor Struggles in the Deep South," 158.

56. Ibid.; McWhiney, "Socialist Vote In Louisiana," 74-75.

57. Hall, "Labor Struggles in the Deep South," 149.

58. Grady McWhiney, "Louisiana Socialists in the Early Twentieth Century: A Study in Rustic Radicalism," *Journal of Southern History*, 20 (August 1954), 331. Hereinafter cited as *JSH*.

59. Hall, "Labor Struggles in the Deep South," 173.

60. *Voice of the People*, December 25, 1913.

61. J. B. White to Leonard Bronson, August 9, 1912; J. A. Freeman to Bronson, August 14, 1912; and C. D. Johnson to Bronson, August 31, 1912. All in Kirby Papers, Box 221.

62. Morgan article, pp. 203-4.

63. Reed, "Lumberjacks and Longshoremen," 51; Foner, "The IWW And The Black Worker," 55-56; Morgan article, pp. 203-4.

64. Telegram, E. P. Ripley to J. W. Terry, November 13, 1912, Kirby Papers, Box 221.

65. Reed, "Lumberjacks and Longshoremen," 51-53; Foner, "The IWW And The Black Worker," 56-57.

66. Hall, "Labor Struggles in the Deep South," 186.

67. Ibid., pp. 208-10; McCord, "History Of The Brotherhood Of Timberworkers," 100-101; Morgan article, p. 204. According to Hall, Emerson's injuries were so severe that he never fully recovered and remained an invalid. McCord says that the last word from Emerson was that he was in Lebanon, Tennessee.

68. Hall, "Labor Struggles in the Deep South," 191, 193-94.

69. Ibid., 192; McCord, "History Of The Brotherhood Of Timberworkers," 105.

70. McCord, "History Of The Brotherhood Of Timberworkers," 106; Morgan article, p. 204.

"RAUSCH MIT":*
THE I.W.W. IN NEBRASKA
DURING WORLD WAR I

DAVID G. WAGAMAN

A number of histories have chronicled the major events of the I.W.W.'s "first seventy years," including Wobbly activities in the grain belt and the suppression of the national union. The purpose of this chapter is to reconstruct in greater detail the I.W.W.'s organizational campaigns in Nebraska during the war years and to examine the justice department's raids in September and November of 1917 on the important Omaha headquarters of the union.[1]

The Wobblies attempted to organize grain belt workers soon after the Lawrence strike of 1912. But the soapbox method of the free speech fight era did not produce a lasting organization. In the spring of 1914, on-the-job organizing also failed because of competition among different I.W.W. locals and the lack of standard initiation fees and dues. In the fall and winter of that year, Wobbly leaders moved to develop a method that would succeed in reaching the agricultural workers.[2]

On April 15, 1915, an I.W.W. conference of representatives of local agricultural workers' unions in Kansas City created the Agricultural Workers Organization (AWO Local No. 400), "a recruiting or industrial union." The organizers were expected "to organize at the point of production" and "soapboxing" was banned. The following demands were formulated: a minimum wage of three dollars a day; fifty cents overtime for every hour worked above ten in one day; adequate room and board; and no discrimination against members of the I.W.W.[3]

By the end of 1915, the AWO claimed between 2,280 and 3,000 members, had over $14,000 in its treasury, and had opened offices in a number of mid-

*"Out with Them"

western cities, including Omaha. The AWO held its first annual conference in Kansas City on May 23, 1916, and immediately raised the stakes to four dollars for a ten-hour day and hiring of harvest hands through I.W.W. halls or delegates, as well as the overtime and room and board provisions from the previous year. The conference sent 300 delegates into the field to begin what Philip Foner calls "one of the most marvellous union organization jobs ever performed in the history of the world."[4]

After some successes in Kansas, an advance guard of approximately 155 Wobblies arrived in Hastings, Nebraska, on July 10 and 11, 1916. Organizers Ben Klein and J. A. Sullivan promised that an army of workers would enter the state within two weeks. On July 12, the *Hastings Daily Tribune* declared: "The Industrial Workers of the World have invaded the Nebraska harvest fields for the first time in the history of the state."[5]

Immediately there was trouble when John Madden was arrested for disturbing the peace after an altercation with one of the curb employment agents (whom the Wobblies called "job sharks") from whom Madden refused to buy a job. Klein and Sullivan acted as attorneys for Madden and won a suspended sentence from Judge Karl Beghtol. "Most people misunderstand us," declared Klein. "They say we don't wish to work. That isn't true. Every member must be a producer. The migratory class is a necessity, just as the steadier working classes are. We're producers even though we are migratory." Klein indicated that the AWO's principal fight was against employment agents: "I don't believe in any man paying for the privilege of working."[6]

For a while thereafter, Wobbly relations with the City of Hastings seem to have been almost cordial. Klein sent sixteen I.W.W. members to the chamber of commerce for farm employment and placed sixty-five others through his own efforts on July 11 alone. The *Tribune* commented that although the Wobblies wanted $4.00 a day, they settled for $3.25 and 3.50. At a convention in Hastings on July 14, the Wobblies resolved they would resist attempts to jail their members but the gesture was hardly necessary. Of an estimated 200 Wobblies per day who passed through the city during the week of July 10, seven had enough faith in Police Chief Carter to use his office as a "safety deposit box" leaving money and valuables in his care while they worked in the fields.[7]

In Lincoln, it was another scene altogether. On July 13, Sheriff Augustine Hyers mounted a campaign against harvest workers who had invaded the town. When Sheriff Hyers attempted to force thirty-five workers out of the city, five of them turned on the sheriff and struck his father with a frying pan. Deputy Sheriffs Claude Hensel and Bert Anderson quelled the uprising and jailed eight men: Phillip Strawbu, Ralph Bigelow, William Burns, Jeff Fogelson, Leo Landers, Harry Clifford, James King, and James Riley. The men attempted to send two telegrams—one to Kansas City asking for 500 men to come and help them, the other to Omaha requesting financial assistance. Sheriff Gus Hyers refused to send either telegram.[8]

On July 17, E. R. McNally, AWO counsel and organizer from Omaha, arrived in Lincoln to confer with Labor Commissioner Frank Coffey and Governor John Morehead, who were urging Sheriff Hyers to release the men. He refused to do so unless the governor put his request in the form of an order. The governor refused to interfere when Commissioner Coffey requested that he pardon the I.W.W. members. The governor said he would not pardon them unless Sheriff Hyers joined in the request.[9]

McNally stated that the I.W.W. had an interest only in the release of James Riley and James King, held on charges of illegally riding a freight, and none in the release of the men charged with assault and battery. McNally also was quoted as stating, "The authorities will release these men or you won't know the town in a short time." On the same day an estimated eighty I.W.W. members arrived in Lincoln as a protest against the jailing of their members. Some had stopped west of the city in the Lakeview area early in the afternoon. The men had committed no offenses and threatened no one. However, Lakeview residents were frightened by the presence of so many strangers, and they appealed to Lincoln Police Chief H. H. Antles for protection. It was reported that "men calling the police station, when asked what the workers had done, simply answered that 'the women are afraid of them.'" Other I.W.W. members arrived on a freight train from the West at around six o'clock that evening.[10]

Chief Antles did not interfere with the movements of the I.W.W. The same day, the estimated two to three hundred I.W.W. members in Lincoln held an "indignation meeting" at Thirteenth and K streets, marched to the statehouse grounds, and, failing to gain the release of the prisoners, voted to stay until the men were freed. Reportedly, one worker said menacingly, "Blood will flow," and another, "What do we care for lives?" The men then proceeded to the Rock Island yards where they stayed the night in cars and on the ground.[11]

When a group of Wobblies congregated outside the county jail, Sheriff Hyers told them that Theodore Carr of Rokeby wanted four workmen and would furnish transportation to and from Lincoln. No Wobbly accepted the invitation. Then the group attempted to "invade" the county jail, and Sheriff Hyers "beat them back with his gun butt." Approximately seventy-three Wobblies lined up before the county attorney's office and asked to be jailed on the same charge as Riley and King—stealing rides on freight trains. Their request was denied. The men then began to beg in the streets, but the onlooking law officers refused to arrest them on vagrancy charges.[12]

Having met defeat in his attempts to have Riley and King released, McNally threatened to telegraph Omaha and Kansas City requesting that Wobblies descend on Lincoln in support of their jailed comrades. "We will

have these men out of jail,'' said McNally, ''or the people of Lincoln will
suffer the consequences.'' When asked if he feared another attack on the
county jails, Sheriff Hyers responded, ''They ought to see the stock of
firearms we have first.''[13]

On July 19, the *Omaha Evening Bee* headlined: ''I.W.W. Signs Peace
Pact at Lincoln.'' According to Sheriff Hyers, hundreds of citizens called
to assure him of their help if I.W.W. members attempted to charge the
county jail. However, the occasion to defend the jail never arose. McNally
and Hyers came to an understanding whereby King and Riley, after finishing
their assigned task of cleaning the courthouse, were released. McNally
again stated that he and the I.W.W. members had no interest in the remaining prisoners. He assured the police that no more violence would occur
and agreed to station an I.W.W. organizer at the jail to ensure that end.

According to the newspapers, most local labor union members had little
sympathy for the Wobblies passing through Lincoln.[14] Other hostility took
the form of support for the ''Utah Plan,'' which reputedly included arresting I.W.W. members, forcing them to work on county roads for a dollar
and a half a day, and boarding them at the county jail for fifty cents a day.[15]

Other locals, however, such as F. F. Johnson, were able to see the ''hobo
question'' with a remarkable clarity. In a letter to one of Lincoln's leading
newspapers, he wrote:

I notice the annual ''gab fest'' about hoboes, labor and harvest fields is in full swing
again. As usual only some of the most glaring inconsistencies are mentioned and
most of the primary facts are left out.

First, these harvest field jobs are of short and uncertain duration. The cost of
transportation to and from these ''summer outing jobs'' (as some think), if paid
would use up a good share of the wage harvest. Another nice attraction is you only
work about twelve to fourteen hours of the day at it.

Second the idea advanced by I. W. Jacoby of providing county work for all
itinerants wouldn't do. The same opportunity would have to be extended to all who
are out of employment. This would do away with the surplus supply of labor and
give every family a chance to have a respectable living. This would upset our whole
economic system and put the ''kibosh'' on speculative business. A great many
aristocratic loafers might have to go to work and ''hired girls'' would be scarce.

Third, as a writer in The Journal, July 22 says, ''transportation has a great deal to
do with the 'wander about' habit.'' This writer uses the term ''hobo'' for all tramps.
I think there is more back of all this. Human beings do not generally like disagree-
able and unhealthful surroundings, nor arduous work under a tyrannical boss and
where there are little comforts in connection with the work. Little wonder they drift
to life of freedom, relief from car, pure air to breathe and occasionall free water to
fish and take a swim in—(I didn't say bathe.)

Fourth, again is the question of employment. A large per cent of the jobs in the
industries only last for the season or a greater or less part of the year. A larger per
cent of laborers work by profession or trade and dislike to tinker with strange work.

When the question of steady employment has been solved it will go a long way toward solving the hobo and kindred problems.[16]

Meanwhile, Omaha police had taken action. On July 15, they arrested more than 150 "vagrant" Wobblies who "contented themselves by spending the night singing songs and parodies of their organization."[17]

On July 16, according to the *Bee*, Omaha "doomed . . . two hundred vagrants, Industrial Workers of the World, and other unwanted flotsam to exile" by loading them into two North Western freight cars and shipping them to South Dakota. The decision to rid Omaha of "undesirables" via banishment to the harvest fields was made by Commissioner Albert Kugel, Commissioner Walter Jardine, and Acting Police Magistrate Charles H. Kubat. North Western Railroad Police Chief W. T Dineen arranged for the railroad cars that carried the men from town. The local secretary of the I.W.W. agreed that "a little work would not harm the members much," and he sanctioned the trip.

Even the little town of Holdrege did not escape the invasion of the Wobblies. On July 14, harvest workers there demanded $5.00 per twelve-hour day and a ten-minute recess each hour for "a smoke." Going wages in the area were reported at $3.50 per day. On July 15, approximately eighty-five Wobblies were in control of a Burlington freight as it passed through Alma heading west. On July 16, about 150 Wobblies riding another train decorated the Alma depot with their emblems.[18]

By July 17, 1917, the Wobblies seemed to be all over southwest Nebraska. In Wilsonville, a score of them allegedly stole three crates of cantaloupes from the railroad platform "in broad daylight." They again descended on Holdrege and in groups of "two or four" asked housewives for handouts. At Minden, they refused to work for farmers at $4.00 a day. In Axtell, in numbers exceeding the local male population over fifteen years of age, they refused to work but insisted on being fed. At McCook, a couple of young men from Pittsburgh were allegedly robbed by I.W.W. members who had refused to work. In Kearney about eight Wobblies camped on the lawn of the Union Pacific Hotel prior to returning to Lincoln. During a previous incident, Chief of Police Pickerell had escorted Wobblies from Kearney and pointed them in the general direction of Grand Island. In Fremont, sixty-three Wobblies were rounded up and jailed when they refused harvest work at $3.00 to $3.50 per day. After a night in jail they were started westward along the railroad tracks.[19] Across the Missouri River from Omaha, Council Bluffs, Iowa, was invaded by "200 hoboes, most I.W.W.'s" who congregated around the North Western Railroad yards near Big Lake on July 18. A score of Negroes were in the group.

All this I.W.W. activity prompted Victor Rosewater, editor of the *Bee*, to comment:

Nebraska is just now having its first real experience with the I.W.W., the outcome of which is to be determined. Other western states have been visited and more or less disturbed by this band of migratory irresponsibles, whose inverted system of social economy makes tham a problem as well as a nuisance. Ordinary treatment, such as confinement or repression, has little effect upon them other than to invite further visitations. Because of this, the remedy for them is not easy, but our peace officers may be depended upon to see that order is maintained and the law supported. Men with a constitutional grudge against all society, although not easily dealt with, must not be permitted to overturn all that man has accomplished. Nothing really serious has developed in connection with the I.W.W. in Nebraska, but the presence of these men itself is a menace, and authorities must be vigilant.[20]

Still, it continued. On July 20, approximately fifty Wobblies invaded Oxford. The editor of the *Oxford Standard* noted that although they called themselves harvest hands, ". . . they are always looking for work when there is nothing to do, and when opportunities are plentiful they put the price so high they can't work."[21] Ostensibly, the Wobblies held down a shady section of the street curbing during the afternoon, repaired to a pile of tires in the early evening, and headed east on an evening freight train.

On the same day, Wobblies allegedly attacked three Omaha men who had Carson and Norman Pearl of Cadiz, Kentucky, serving as lookouts for sixty-five men riding Rock Island freight no. 94 from Colby, Kansas, to Omaha, were attacked by four armed bandits near Fairbury. On July 21, the *Bee* observed that in Omaha "about a half dozen men" were beaten up by their own members, seemingly without provocation, though it seemed to have been an I.W.W. method of forcing doctrine on individuals. On the same day, John Carlson, a member from St. Paul, Minnesota, was charged with assault and battery by Herbert Berg of Council Bluffs.[22]

Wobblies riding Burlington trains were passing through Seward "by the dozens" by July 22—as many as eighty-five on one train, with "only one robbery" being reported. Violence flared at Beaver City when two men claiming to be I.W.W. members killed a fellow harvest hand who refused to join the organization. On July 25, Omaha policemen Sergeant Carl Madsen, Detective John Holden, and Officer Coleman Fimple arrested A. S. Bartlett, G. P. Ranson, and S. O. Hall, who were carrying I.W.W. cards as well as revolvers and blackjacks. On the same day, 150 men were arrested in various railroad yards in the city on charges of trespassing and interfering with workmen. Wobbly officers said only fifteen of those arrested were "their" men; the others were "plain bums." One of those arrested was J. J. Rogers, secretary of the local Omaha I.W.W. He was sentenced to fifteen days in the workhouse. On July 26, Rogers and one other I.W.W. member were pardoned on the recommendation of Commissioner Jardine. The other men arrested on July 25 were arraigned before Judge Kubat and given the choice of serving five days in jail or leaving town; most left town. On the same day, six masked men, suspected Wobblies, boarded North Western train no. 290 near Craig and robbed the crew.[23] At the same time, "Red" Moyer, freight conductor for the Rock Island Railroad, had a run-in with alleged Wobblies in the Lincoln yards. Moyer learned that the leader of a group of approximately twelve Wobblies had announced his intent to ride the caboose of the outgoing freight regardless of state, city, or railroad policy. According to the *Fairbury Journal*:

Mr. Moyer informed the leader that they could ride in the caboose if they had either money or tickets . . . otherwise, he opined that riding there might be uncomfortable.

The leader of the small army didn't quite get the drift of Mr. Moyer's argument, or if he heard correctly he didn't understand what follows argument when Moyer talks. He motioned his men to board the caboose and himself started to get on. At about the same time he collided with a club in the conductor's hand, and instantly the club swung again for anyone who desired to follow the leader. The leader was down, out, and followerless. The engineer answered the highball sign and the train moved out of the station with no I.W.W. passengers in the caboose.[24]

Victor Rosewater pointed out that not every "suspect I.W.W." was a member of the organization, that "in most cases I.W.W. is merely a convenient cover for the ordinary genus tramp who wants to make a living off the community without giving any return in work."[25] Victor Rosewater's valid observation was generally ignored.

On July 29, the *Bee* said that the Wobblies were "shaking the dust of Omaha from their feet." It also sarcastically observed: "Plenty of pure drinking water and a loaf of the staff of life is the diet upon which the I.W.W. guests at the city jail were being fed." "Heavy food is very detrimental during heated periods," intoned Ben Keegan, supervising architect of the city workhouse in an article on how to keep healthy in the summer.[26]

While the Wobblies were, indeed, shaking Omaha's dust from their feet, they were doing so while heading across the river toward Council Bluffs. On July 27, they began filtering into the hobo camp in the Big Lake vicinity of Council Bluffs, and soon there were approximately 500 "harvest hands" encamped there. According to police who visited the camp, the crowd was orderly until noon. Only a few signs, some reading "four dollars a day or nothing," were seen around the camp that bordered on the North Western Railroad yards. After noon, however, Park Policeman John Gibler sent in a riot call. A battle had begun between Wobblies and "bodies of independents" when Wobblies began using "terrorist methods" to force others to join their ranks. Some twenty-five to thirty Wobblies took possession of a North Western freight and refused to permit nonunion members to ride, including Herbert Crawford and Ford Wilson, both of Shenandoah, Iowa. They were told to leave the yards if they did not join.[27]

Crawford replied that he did not have the initiation fee. "When he made this clear to the men who were pressing him he got a crack in the jaw and was told to beat it. The instant the blow was struck, Wilson pulled a revolver and began shooting wildly. The shots were returned and he fell with a nasty wound in the chin."[28] Wilson then reloaded the revolver and "standing over his prostrate friend held the angry crowd of I.W.W.'s at bay until reinforcements of independents came to his aid." The shooting then became widespread, with Wobblies lying on top of freight cars returning the fire of the independents. Railroad men on the scene "dodged behind anything that afforded protection from the flying bullets, and all escaped injury." By the time police officers led by Detectives Frank Lee and Elmer Lane arrived, the Wobblies had disappeared, and only trainmen Crawford and Wilson and a crowd of "ten or fifteen badly frightened independents" were left in the yards.[29]

The Wobblies disappeared from the headlines of the Omaha area papers on August 12, 1916, on the following sour note: A "postal card addressed to 'the chief of police' and signed 'I.W.W.' was delivered to Omaha's Acting Chief M. F. Dempsey via 'the crack beneath the door' route." The letter contained "threats of due calamity to the city and its officials." The writer called the chief and his minions everything except "scolars *[sic]*, gentlemen and diamonds in the rough." The I.W.W. left the pages of the *Hastings Daily Tribune* on a somewhat different note. On August 7 the paper carried the following story:

The last issue of the *Industrial Worker*, the official organ of the I.W.W. organization, contains a letter in its columns from one of the members complimenting Chief of Police Bob Carter of Hastings. The member's name is F. A. Neary from Giltner. He refers to the chief as the only decent cop I every seen or heard of. Not only did Chief of Police Carter win the confidence and cooperation of the leaders of the I.W.W. organization in the task of handling an unprecedented number of harvest hands but those who have watched the situation closely during the movement of the workers through the city have expressed themselves as being pleased from the public safety standpoint. With a daily average of upwards of 200 harvest hands passing through the city, there was comparatively little street disorder and no robberies which might be attributed to the strangers. Mr. Carter is one of the few police officers in Nebraska or Kansas who handled the movement of harvest hands with no trouble and still maintained law and order. The Hastings Chief is to be congratulated.[30]

The events of the latter part of July 1916 seem to have somewhat tempered the editorial position of Victor Rosewater's *Bee*. In his July 31 editorial, "Problem of the Migratory Worker," he displayed remarkable insight into the problems of the migratory laborer and the appearance of the I.W.W. in the harvest fields. In part, he stated:

As was noted in *The Bee*, by no means all the migratory workers are members of the I.W.W., nor are all the offenses against law and order reported committed by these men. One of the most marked of phenomena attending social growth within the last decade has been the development of a class of migratory workers, properly so designated because of the habit of life forced on them by circumstances.

These men come from the unskilled and untrained, and are held in their social disadvantage by the fact that opportunity to rise rarely comes to a man whose only possession is ability to perform the rougher and distasteful kinds of work. And as this work is seasonable in its nature, with no possibility of permanency of employment, these workers become wanderers. They do not belong to the "hobo" class although many end in that classification. Ambition has little place among them, and often a rooted resentment against what they deem the injustice of their situation possesses them.

What to do, *not with, but for them* is one of the biggest questions to be faced. Industrial readjustment is inevitable but it can not be made satisfactorily workable, until the growing army of migratory workers is given its proper place in relation to the whole. "Unemployment" and "vagrancy" are involved in this, and will be settled when the better balance is applied to our working methods. Then the I.W.W. will vanish, or at least retreat to the condition of mere annoyance.[31]

In October 1916, the AWO reported 18,000 members had been initiated since April 1915. By November 1916, the AWO was receiving dues from 20,000 members, a third of the I.W.W.'s enrollment. For fiscal 1916, the I.W.W. had an income of $49,114.84 compared with $8,934.47 for fiscal 1915. During 1916, the I.W.W. issued 116 charters, the most ever issued in a comparable period. The tenth convention of the I.W.W. was held in Chicago from November 10 through December 1, 1916. A revised constitution was adopted under which the I.W.W. was structured into industrial departments, industrial unions and their branches, and recruiting unions, the latter "to be composed of wage workers in whose respective industries no industrial union existed."[32]

The convention also established Big Bill Haywood in firm control of the union. Walter Nef, "the creator and guiding genius of the AWO," had already resigned as secretary-treasurer to move to Philadelphia to establish an I.W.W. local there. Vincent St. John, Joseph Ettor, and Ben H. Williams faded into the background. Elizabeth Gurley Flynn and Carlo Tresca were headed for a split with Haywood. No one was left to challenge Big Bill, who, along with convention delegates, began to soft-pedal soapboxing and free speech fights, while emphasizing the "virtues of employment, of improving conditions on the job, and of organizing new members." The I.W.W. was beginning to function as a labor organization for the first time since Lawrence. In March 1917, AWO Local No. 400, stripped of its nonagricultural members, was rechartered as Agricultural Workers' Industrial Union No. 110. It was restricted to organizing only agricultural workers, and its members became known as the "one-ten cats."[33]

Despite the chartering of No. 110, I.W.W. activity lagged in Nebraska during 1917 while it increased elsewhere among miners, lumbermen, oil field workers, and maritime workers. However, its presence was still felt in the state. On June 25, 1917, the Nebraska State Council of Defense received a request from Robert Graham and Ira E. Tash of Alliance to organize a volunteer guard. The letter stated in part:

The need is imperative. This being a railroad center, with large round house, stock yards and machine shops, to say nothing of the three large warehouses, filled with binding twine, and harvesting machinery it is a temptation to the I.W.W.'s and pro-Germans. We have two of them in jail now. A dozen I.W.W's could take the city and cause havoc, with our inadequate police protection.[34]

On July 3, 1917, the *Omaha Evening Bee* ominously reported that I.W.W. strike leaders at its Bisbee, Arizona, headquarters "claimed to have received telegrams . . . from the agricultural division of the Industrial Workers of the World offering support to the strike and stating that 'workers in the field are going to use Industrial Workers of the World tactics.' "[35]

Fremont had an experience with the I.W.W. on July 11. William Russell, who carried credentials as a job delegate, and Albert E. Anderson, a companion, were arrested for vagrancy in the railroad yards. Russell was sentenced to twenty days in the county jail by Police Judge Mahlin, while Anderson drew five days in the city jail. Russell threatened the judge that Fremont would "hear from the I.W.W.'s." The judge replied that the town was ready to receive them.[36]

On the evening of July 14, some forty Wobblies passed through Lincoln without incident. They claimed to be on their way to Omaha and, eventually, the harvest fields of South Dakota. Lincoln Police Chief John Dee and a squad of officers made sure that they did not get off the train.[37]

But the incident, coincident with the Bisbee and Jerome, Arizona, deportations of July 10 through 12, were enough to arouse newspapers and law officials in the state to new activity and well-laid plans to meet the invasion.[38]

The Bisbee affair apparently did send many Wobblies to Nebraska. The justice department assured the state that it was prepared to assist state authorities in meeting the augmented menace.[39] In fact, however, the I.W.W. created no chaos during the harvest of 1917. Indeed, an incident in Lincoln in August proved to be a sign of a change of fortune for the union. About August 10, Curt G. Wilckens, a German-born I.W.W. member who came to the United States in 1906, was arrested by watchmen for the

Burlington. Wilckens was accused of making treasonable remarks, declaring that he would not fight for the United States. When jailed, Wilckens denied having said anything against Uncle Sam; however, he stated that he did not want to fight for any country. However, a letter written by Wilckens to a New Mexico friend fell into the hands of authorities in Omaha; it contained statements considered disloyal and on August 24, Federal District Attorney T. S. Allen ordered Wilckens interned at Fort Douglas, Utah.[40]

At about the same time, the Nebraska State Council of Defense stepped up its interest in the I.W.W. At the council's tenth session on September 18, the governor's secretary said that "special agents" were watching the organization.[41] The Wobblies were decentralizing, the council was told, in an effort to elude the council's efforts.[42]

July and August of 1917 saw federal troops of vigilantes raid I.W.W. offices throughout the country. However, it was not until September that the justice department moved openly against the I.W.W. While the I.W.W. had not advocated "draft-dodging," it had, through its general antiwar and anticapitalist stance, alienated public opinion, and only a minority of the population objected to the government violation of Wobblies' First Amendment rights, which began in earnest at this time. On September 5, 1917, Federal Bureau of Investigation agents raided simultaneously I.W.W. headquarters, locals, and residences of members throughout the nation. Sixty-four I.W.W. headquarters yielded tons of membership lists, pamphlets, books, and letters.[43]

On September 5, 1917, federal authorities raided the I.W.W. headquarters at 1301 Douglas Street in Omaha. No arrests were made in connection with the raid but several large barrels of I.W.W. literature were confiscated as officers searched for seditious material. Also raided on the same day was the home of Michael Barry (603 South Thirtieth Street), business agent of the Common Laborer's Union of the AFL. Barry protested that he was in fact an active enemy of the I.W.W., but to no avail.[44]

The Agricultural Workers' Industrial Union called a special convention for Omaha on November 12, 1917. Ostensibly, the convention was called as a response to the treatment of workers who were tarred and feathered by Tulsa, Oklahoma, citizens on November 8, 1917. However, according to a reporter ". . . delegates who arrived early for the convention stood around in a room at I.W.W. headquarters smoking corncob pipes and discussing the high cost of eating and traveling." Tom A. Jenkins, local I.W.W. secretary, stated that only a business meeting and smoker was to be held. He denied reports of a huge influx of members and predicted nearer 400 than the 4,000 that had been speculated, although twenty branches or industrial unions of the I.W.W would be represented.[45]

Richard Metcalfe, Governor Neville's secretary, and Omaha Mayor James Dahlman held a conference on November 11 at the Fontenelle Hotel, after which Dahlman said he would allow no demonstrations. Marshal Eberstein, chief of the Federal Bureau of Investigation, cautioned: "They have a perfect right to hold a meeting if they desire. . . . We have no authority to molest them unless a law has been violated or there are reasonable indications of such a fact." Mayor Dahlman went on: "One thing certain . . . Omaha is not going to be made a dumping ground for the I.W.W's from other cities of this country."[46]

On November 12, the bulletin board at the I.W.W. headquarters at Thirteenth and Douglas streets announced a business meeting and smoker for that evening. Admission was fifty cents, and a ticket entitled the holder to I.W.W. membership. Chief of Police Henry Dunn sent two policemen disguised as members into the headquarters. They reported everything calm and only about seventy-five "strangers" in attendance. A number of women in the Hanscom Park area telephoned the *Bee* to report Wobblies begging, and one asked, "Couldn't we people of Omaha follow the fine example of the Oklahoma vigilantes who tarred and feathered them?"[47]

Despite an orderly convention with no seditious remarks, the justice department raided the headquarters on November 13 and confiscated materials found. The raid, "authorized in Washington," was led by U.S. Marshal Thomas J. Flynn under the direction of Chief Marshal Eberstein. Police Captain Henry Heitfeld led the "morals" squad that assisted Flynn. Among the sixty-four alleged Wobblies arrested were T. A. Jenkins, local secretary who arrived after the raid was in progress; Mrs. Elmer Buse of St. Louis, the only woman arrested; E. F. Dix, chairman; Albert Watkins, of Sidney, Australia; Dan Thompson, "a well-known Omaha character"; Joseph Ratti, a painter from Omaha; Jack St. Clair, a British subject; and William Smith, Otto Olsen, E. Wydell, D. O. Anderson, John Stine, and William Eike.[48] Those arrested were from Missouri, Indiana, Nebraska, North Dakota, South Dakota, Minnesota, Oregon, Texas, California, Colorado, Illinois, Australia, and Great Britain. Upon arrest, the Wobblies were searched and about $250 was taken from them. No weapons were found, but one bottle of carbolic acid was confiscated. Twenty-five of the prisoners were taken to the city jail where "in the best of spirits" they broke out "in chorus several times." Thirty-nine prisoners were taken to the county jail because of the overcrowding in the city jail.[49]

Approximately two tons of literature were confiscated in the raid. A "great variety" of pamphlets were found, including one on the "gentle art of sabotage," as well as I.W.W. songbooks, dues stamps, money orders, account books, several typewriters, a phonograph with many records, and membership lists. The *Bee* commented that "machinery for bringing in cash from members is shown to be especially complete," and "in some cases it cost a man as much as $9 to become a member." It added sarcastically, "The 'capitalist' class couldn't improve on that . . . the receipts . . . appear to have been sufficient to satisfy any capitalist."[50]

Also confiscated were pictures, "chiefly caricatures showing the down-trodden workingman and the diamond-studded capitalist." One drawing was entitled "The Blanket Stiff"; behind the framed picture of Joe Hill, legendary I.W.W. martyr, was an envelope containing grains of his body's ashes. At the time of the raid, I.W.W. leaders refused to open the head-quarters' safe, then relented. Its contents included a vast number of blank I.W.W. membership cards, $78,000 in cash, and a letter from a prisoner in a Minneapolis jail requesting a copy of a pamphlet entitled "Speeches from the Dock."[51]

From the vast number of filled-out and empty membership cards, U.S. Attorney T. S. Allen theorized that Omaha was to be the next national headquarters of the I.W.W. Previous raids in Kansas City, St. Louis, St. Paul, and Chicago pointed to Omaha as a likely candidate. The vast number of filled-out indexed membership cards, several gunnysacks of red cards, and other material too great for local use pointed to this possibly.[52]

The events surrounding the activities of the I.W.W. throughout the nation in 1917, and the entrance of the United states into World War I, brought about a minor reversal in the editorial position of Rosewater's *Bee*. On November 15, he stated:

The prompt action of the federal authorities in arresting the I.W.W. gang assembled in Omaha will have the approval of right minded folks. These brazen advocates of disorder openly advertised their gatherings here, announcing plans for their meetings and promising a demonstration that happily has been checked. What the outcome might have been can only be conjectured, but experience of other communities is warrant for believing that Omaha has been spared a serious infliction by the act of the United States Marshal in getting the "delegates" behind bars. A visitation of these malcontents and apostles of disloyalty is unwelcome at any time and particularly now is their presence for any purpose undesirable. Sympathy for men in their industrial position must not blind any to the danger that follows allowing them freedom of action. Our government is alive to a full sense of the menace from this source and we trust the move made here will aid in some way the efforts being made to render the I.W.W. harmless. America suffers enough from Bolshevikism in time of peace and the doctrine and its advocates are alike intolerable in time of war.[53]

Chicago attorney Samuel Block, on order of Acting Secretary E. F. Doree of Chicago, was sent to Omaha to defend the imprisoned Wobblies. On November 16, without having communication with the prisoners, Block stated that none of the imprisoned men were disloyal; none had made seditious remarks; all were "fundamentally opposed to imperialism and autocracy in any form"; and none were in sympathy with the German cause, as implied by the government. The Wobblies attempted to convert other prisoners to the I.W.W. cause in their initial week of imprisonment. On November 27, the justice department began the slow process of releasing the Wobblies. Mrs. Elmer Buse, when questioned by Assistant District

Attorney Howard Saxton and Chief Marshal Eberstein, said she had only affiliated with the I.W.W. a few days before the convention for the purpose of serving refreshments and should be released. The justice department also released Albert Watkins, who claimed he had "been induced" to join and attend the convention.[54]

Thanksgiving dinner proved a "memorable event" for the jailed Wobblies. The *Bee* observed: "Previous Thanksgiving day feeds of the fraternity of conscientious objectors to honest labor have consisted of beans à la tomato can, cooked jungle style near convenient tracks." The sheriff, Michael Clark, however, regaled the prisoners with turkey and cranberry sauce on the fifth floor of the courthouse. "Fainting Bertha," one of the "social leaders" present at the meal, was observed by Sheriff Clark to be one of the most fluent conversationalists he had ever entertained in "his marble halls." After dinner the Wobblies were returned to their cells where they "held song service until the fire hose was unlimbered. Not wishing to bathe immediately after dinner the meeting was adjourned."[55]

George F. Vanderveer, the Seattle attorney who was defending Wobblies indicted in Chicago, visited Omaha on November 30 to confer with Chief Eberstein and Assistant District Attorney Saxton, and to visit the prisoners. Afterward Vanderveer outlined what was to be the Wobblies' defense in all its wartime trials: the I.W.W. was not violent if, for no other reason, than "the minute they start violence the troops are called out, and they fail to gain their ends." When Vanderveer was confronted with confiscated I.W.W. pamphlets advocating sabotage, he declared the I.W.W. publication house merely printed and sold them but didn't "put any official endorsement on them." Before he left Omaha, Vanderveer attempted to obtain records seized in the raid; however, U. S. Commissioner Robert D. Neely refused to grant him an order.[56]

On December 1, twenty imprisoned Wobblies were held over to a federal grand jury after a hearing before Commissioner Neely. They were charged with conspiracy to violate the Selective Draft Law, the Espionage Act, and the President's Proclamation. Bond was set at $5,000 each. None of those initially bound over gave Omaha addresses. On December 11, thirty-one more were held over for the grand jury. Among those prisoners released on this date was Dan Thompson, who sent messages to authorities stating he cared nothing for the I.W.W. and wanted to "leave them and go to work in the smelter." E. J. Burkhart, who was jailed when the raid occurred, was also released. William Smith, E. Wydell, D. O. Anderson, John Stine, and William Eike were given the opportunity to enlist in the army—at their own request. After they passed examinations, complaints against them were dropped. Otto Olsen, when released on January 9, 1918, stated that the first thing he was going to do was "get a square meal." On the same day, Jack St. Clair renounced all I.W.W. sentiments and was escorted to the local British recruiting mission by Sergeant Joiner to enlist in the British army. The fifty-one Wobblies held over were not brought to trial in 1918 because the justice department knew it had a weak case and did not want to jeopardize its case in Chicago with a dismissal, acquittal, or reversal in Omaha.[57]

The I.W.W.'s activities as a labor organization in 1917 did not go unnoticed by the state government in Nebraska. The *Fifteenth Biennial Report of the Bureau of Labor and Industrial Statistics of the State of Nebraska* included a section on the I.W.W. in its year-end report published in 1918. It concluded:

But of the I.W.W. this fact is patent: The organization is growing each year in numbers, and each year is the cause of more strife and hindrance in the amicable solution of labor problems. When resisted the organization becomes more bold and defiant. How to deal with them, how to meet their demands, just and unjust, presents a problem which calls for deliberate thought and cool and impassionate action.[58]

The Nebraska State Council of Defense also was concerned with the I.W.W. and its sympathizers. As early as July 1917, the council had directed the attention of the Board of Regents of the University of Nebraska, Lincoln, to "several professors who had persistently given encouragement, publicly and privately, to those who are out of harmony with the American cause." The council's activities, which were spearheaded by Richard Lee Metcalf, chairman of the council, led to a bitter feud in which charges, countercharges, and innuendos were made. Initially, accusations of unpatriotic attitudes were directed at five university professors who publicly defended themselves with the support of the board of regents.[59]

Metcalfe and a joint conference of the state and county defense councils called for the resignation of Regents P. L. Hall and Frank L. Haller, chairman of the board. Haller responded by calling for Metcalfe's resignation. Metcalfe and others accused Haller of writing unpatriotic letters signed under the pseudonym of "Patricia Newcomb."[60] Most Omaha and Lincoln newspaper editors tended to support the regents and university professors. But the entire matter simmered over the winter and in the spring, on April 19, 1918, the state council of defense "advised action" on the part of the regents, who arranged a public hearing.[61]

At the hearing, a "Committee on the University Matter" agreed to confront the regents with statements made by citizens concerning the conduct of certain professors. The committee, headed by Richard Lee Metcalf, made complaints against twelve instructors:

This evidence discloses partiality on the part of more than one instructor for the another, assumed an attitude calculated to encourage among those who come under their influence, within and without the University, a spirit of inactivity, indifference, and opposition towards this war and an undesirable view with respect to the several fundamental questions inseparable from the war.

This evidence discloses partiality on the part of more than one instructor for the I.W.W., an organization that is practically at war with America. You will find where one instructor spoke "very feelingly" in regard to the treatment of the I.W.W. referring to "tyranny" in this country and the alleged misuse of the common people and presenting excuses for the behavior of the organization against which our government is now proceeding. Another instructor declined to subscribe for Liberty Bonds, explaining his unwillingness on the ground that he was opposed to all war and for that reason could not support the government. On one occasion when an instructor (hereinafter referred to) announced that he intended to write a paper in defense of the I.W.W., this instructor urged him to prepare the paper and expressed entire sympathy with his views. Another instructor made many apologies and excuses for the attitude and behavior of the I.W.W. . . . This . . . instructor announced that he intended to prepare a paper in defense of the I.W.W., asserting that they were misrepresented and mistreated, and that there was a concerted effort to discredit them. He insisted that the I.W.W. were misjudged and maligned. The general attitude of this instructor has been distinctly out of sympathy with the war and with questions relating to it.[62]

On May 28, 1918, the council of defense released the names of ten faculty members against whom charges were brought. Of the original ten charged, three were eventually directed to resign for being "negative, halting or hesitating in support of the government." They were Dr. G. W. A. Luckey, professor of education; C. E. Persinger, professor of American history; and Erwin P. Hopt, professor of agriculture. In addition, two instructors, F. M. Fling and Mrs. Minnie Throop England, were asked to resign for being conservative "agitators" in the university faculty and for "casting suspicion" on their fellows. They, however, remained on the faculty.[63]

Between June 6 and June 27 of 1918, Albert Hansen, new I.W.W. secretary in Omaha, was arrested three times, the final occasion on vagrancy charges along with Charles Casey, A. L. Super, Fred Peterson, and Steve Zinger. Provost Marshal Crowder gave them a "work or fight" ultimatum. By July 8, these five Wobblies and one nameless one decided that Crowder's order was no joke and agreed to work if sedition and vagrancy charges were dropped.[64]

During the remainder of the summer, fall, and winter of 1918, I.W.W. activities in the Midwest declined. Not wanting to prejudice the case of their leaders standing trial in Chicago, the Wobblies refrained from attention-getting activity despite the fact that I.W.W. membership was estimated at between 100,000 and 250,000.[65]

In early February 1919, the *Bee* reported strikes in Butte, Montana, and Seattle, Washington, involving the I.W.W. At the same time, on February

6, 1919, a bill directly aimed at I.W.W. activities was introduced by the Senate Judiciary Committee in Nebraska. The bill was identical to a syndicalism bill passed into law in Colorado with, however, amendments that broadened the law to make not only criminal syndicalist acts aimed at producing industrial or political *revolution* illegal and subject to imprisonment for one to ten years and/or a fine of $1,000, but also syndicalist acts aimed at attaining industrial or political *ends*. The bill was passed into law by the Nebraska House on March 29, 1919, with only one dissenting vote.[66] The syndicalism law stayed on the books in Nebraska until 1977, when the entire criminal code was rewritten. Since 1919, no case had ever been successfully prosecuted under it.[67]

Shortly after the passage of the syndicalism law, between April 10 and 30, the Wobblies imprisoned in Omaha for a year and a half were released. Of all the Wobblies arrested in November 1917, this was the only group not prosecuted. As to why the Omaha group was not prosecuted, Melvyn Dubofsky speculates, "Perhaps some of them [Justice Department officials] had pangs of conscience about the propriety of sentencing another large group of probably innocent men to prison." William Preston comments:

After holding the trial in abeyance, the Omaha Office eventually cancelled the prosecution, probably believing that public opinion had by then been satiated. Allen himself felt self-rightously content. Dismissal of the proceedings, he reported, would prove to the radicals that when the government did have a weak case, "it was ready to recognize that fact."[68]

On May 1, 1919, the Socialist party and the I.W.W. scheduled a joint meeting at the Swedish auditorium in Omaha. Circulars announcing the meeting were signed "First of May Committee, Socialist Party of America, Twenty-fourth and Cuming; Industrial Workers of the World, 104 North Thirteenth street." One side of the circular read: "International Labor Day, first of May. May Day—the day of labor's international and never before a May day so thrillingly significant."

Edmund R. Brumbaugh of the local Socialist committee stated the program would include "written addresses" by Eugene V. Debs, Kate Richards O'Hare, William D. Haywood, Rose Pastor Stokes, Victor Berger, and four other men sentenced for violation of the Espionage Act. Mayor Edward P. Smith declared he would not allow the meeting to take place. He had previously attempted to distinguish the Socialist party from the I.W.W., he said. However, since they presumably were now working for a common cause and adopting common policies, he stated he would treat them alike:

I want the I.W.W. to understand . . . that there is no place for them in Omaha. I was disgusted at the action of the mayor of Sioux City when he gave an address of welcome last week to these people. We don't propose to have these fellows sow seeds of discord in Omaha. There never was a time in the history of Omaha when relations between employers and employees were better. . . . Any meeting that seeks to glorify Debs, O'Hare, Haywood, and Mooney must not be held in the City of Omaha.[69]

The mayor wrote Police Commissioner John Dean Ringer requesting him to instruct Chief of Police Eberstein that the Swedish auditorium was not available for the proposed meeting, nor was he to permit the I.W.W. to meet elsewhere in Omaha. The mayor also wrote Victor Danielson, manager of the auditorium, requesting him to cooperate in the ban and Danielson complied. Nevertheless, the arrangements committee pushed on, and, on the evening of May 1, more than five hundred men and women met at Tel Jed Sokol Hall, at Thirteenth and Dorcas streets, to hear Anton Novotny, head of the Bohemian Socialists in America. On the instructions of Kate Richards O'Hare, red carnations were worn, and many persons signed a petition protesting the imprisonment of Eugene V. Debs.[70]

Although Mayor Smith had warned against the use of any language but English, Novotny spoke in "Bohemian." Three policemen attending the meeting arrested no one for violation of the mayor's instructions, as Novotny used mildly inflammatory rhetoric:

"I am a bolshevist" he shouted in a voice pitched high with excitement. Every eye in the house was riveted on the speaker. "I am a socialist," he continued with all the emphasis of his nature, and a deafening roar of applause bespoke the unanimous approval of the audience. He continued: "I protest the imprisonment of Eugene V. Debs, Kate Richards O'Hare, and all others who expressed their sincere and candid opinion about the war. The war is supposed to be over. The most autocratic European nations have released their political prisoners. Only here in the United States does a 'democratic' administration still throw men and women into prison for having spoken their honest convictions. I demand freedom for all political and industrial prisoners. I demand this freedom without delay."[71]

The anarchist bombings, many attributed to the I.W.W., that swept across the United States in May 1919 did not go unnoticed in Omaha. Postmaster Charles E. Fanning stated: "We are watching Chief of Police Eberstein's mail very closely . . . as the chief, before leaving the department of justice, arrested 40 I.W.W.'s who were recently released." Acting Mayor George Dayton of Lincoln announced on May 5 that no Wobbly would be permitted in the city after an advance man a few days previously had posted notices of a forthcoming meeting in Lincoln. Police notified the advance man that "the roads out of Lincoln were in condition and that he better make use of them as quickly as possible and he accepted the invitation." Dayton added that returning World War I soldiers would be called on to drive Wobblies out of town if necessary.[72]

On July 24, 1919, the Omaha area had one of its last encounters with the Wobblies. Eugene Maddox, a Negro harvest worker, was jailed in Council Bluffs for possession of a concealed revolver. He claimed he bought it for protection after being robbed of fifty-six dollars by Wobblies and charged that only belligerent Wobblies could ride the freights in safety. The same day, George H. Salow, a harvest itinerant and discharged veteran from Montgomery, Alabama, was arrested in Council Bluffs by North Western Railroad detectives. He said he was awakened from a nap in a freight car near Valley, Nebraska, by Wobblies who stole his money and attempted to brand him with their insignia. He escaped but received cuts, bruises, and a closed eye when thrown from the train. The *Bee* commented that incidents of Wobblies branding harvest hands on the chest or arm had been reported elsewhere.[73]

While the I.W.W. seems never to have had the spectacular impact in Nebraska that it had in other states, its presence was still felt in 1919. In a speech entitled "Some of the Activities of the State During 1919," Governor S. R. McKelvie included this reference to the I.W.W.:

Though Nebraska is an interior State, and its industrial activities are fairly limited, it became none the less apparent that the radical elements, particularly the I.W.W., were gaining a foothold here. Therefore instructions were sent out to county attorneys to enlist the services of local police officers in apprehending these radicals and taking them into custody. The last legislature passed quite a comprehensive act, bearing upon this subject, and it is our purpose to see that it is enforced to the letter. If relief cannot be obtained through this channel, then these radicals will be turned over to the Federal Government. Nothing is being left undone to prevent their operating in this state.[74]

The effect of May Day 1919 also carried over in 1920. Governor McKelvie proclaimed May 1, 1920, Americanization Day in response to "the recurrence of May 1 demonstrations by radicals who are opposed to organized government and the enforcement of law."[75] By the fall of 1920, the I.W.W. had entered a downward spiral—"almost half a century of declining virility and approaching senility." The I.W.W. was never again a vital presence on the American radical scene, nor was its presence as a labor organization felt appreciably again in the Midwest. In the words of Taft and Perlman, "The marvel is not that the I.W.W. declined but that for seven terrible years it was able to survive without crumbling into dust."[76]

Other authors have analyzed Wobbly activities throughout the United States. Activity in Nebraska was strongly dominated by agriculture and the railroad network. Nebraska's agriculture-dominated economy made permanent, long-term organization difficult for the I.W.W. Little industry existed outside of Lincoln and Omaha; and in Omaha and Lincoln, meat packing tended to dominate. Lumber and mining were of little significance in Nebraska's economy, and Lincoln and Omaha were the major urban centers.[77]

Therefore, most I.W.W. organizing activities or work stoppages occurred in the harvest fields or involved incidents in railroad yards during the harvest season. Wobbly activities tended to be of relatively short duration, sporadic in nature, and followed grain harvesting activities or railroad freight traffic. Apparently the only semblance of a long-term organizational base in Nebraska was established in Omaha, the largest urban center.

The identification of the I.W.W. as a pro-German, antiwar organization engaged in sabotage swayed public opinion against it in Nebraska, although the union's interest in organizing agricultural workers and the annual intimidating presence of even unorganized hoboes were quite enough to aggravate Nebraskan sensibilities. However, it was surely the war issue that accounts for the persecution of pro-I.W.W. university professors.

Compared to newspaper treatment of the I.W.W. elsewhere, Nebraska newspapers and editors (particularly Victor Rosewater) seemed to present somewhat evenhanded coverage of I.W.W. activities. Somewhat surprisingly, the *causes* of I.W.W. activities, as well as legal remedies, were emphasized in the press.[78]

The importance of the strong individual as well as philosophical and personality differences and the effect on I.W.W. activities is clear in the events in Nebraska. Examples are the actions of Police Chief Robert Carter of Hastings as opposed to those of Sheriff Gus Hyers of Lincoln and Acting Chief M. F. Dempsey of Omaha. When confronted with somewhat similar situations, Hyers and Dempsey heightened the tension between local residents and the Wobblies, whereas Carter, who maintained relative calm, was even respected by the Wobblies. Another example is the exchange between Regent Haller and Richard Lee Metcalfe, which certainly did not help the position of university professors.

The existence of the I.W.W in Nebraska seemed to act as a spur to AFL organizational drives in Omaha in 1917. Only one reference labeling the AFL "the lesser of the two evils" is cited in this paper, yet newspaper accounts of militant I.W.W. activities and conservative AFL craft-union activities in Nebraska give the impression that the AFL gained a better image in Nebraska because of its relative conservatism. The Lincoln press seems to have reported approvingly of the local AFL craft unions' non-support of I.W.W. activities.

While the I.W.W. was not strong numerically, its presence was felt, as the incidents, editorials, speeches, proclamations, and activities of the Nebraska State Council of Defense abundantly attest. Yet, prosecution of the I.W.W. leaders, its identification as "anti-American," the breakdown of the organization in the 1920s, the introduction of improved farm machinery—replacing much of the migratory labor—and the introduction of the automobile tended to dissipate any long-term impact in the Midwest.[79]

The ability of the federal government, along with the oil, mining, and lumber interests, to brand the I.W.W. as a threat to the war effort—advocating draft-dodging, pacifism, and sympathy for Germany—was the major element turning public opinion against the I.W.W. in 1917. This shift in public opinion permitted the justice department and local vigilantes to violate the I.W.W.'s First Amendment rights without causing a public outcry. This carried over into the Omaha case, where Wobblies were arrested and jailed for one and a half years with little cause.

By the end of 1920, the stigma left on the I.W.W. by the prosecution of its members and leaders was so heavy that the remnants of the organization were never again able to mount an effective organizational campaign in Nebraska. Indeed, the predominant theme of the period in Nebraska—"Rausch Mit"—became the I.W.W.'s reality.

NOTES

1. The phrase is taken from the book by Fred Thompson and Patrick Murfin, *The I.W.W.: Its First Seventy Years, 1905-1975* (Chicago: Industrial Workers of the World, 1976). The earliest historical works are by members of the I.W.W.: Vincent St. John, *The I.W.W.: Its History Structure* (Chicago, I.W.W. Publishing Bureau, revised, 1919); *The I.W.W. in Theory and Practice* (Chicago, I.W.W. Publishing Bureau, 1921). Early works on the I.W.W. are: Paul F. Brissenden, "The I.W.W.: A Study of American Syndicalism," *Studies in History, Economics and Public Law*, 88 (New York, 1919); John S. Gambs, *The Decline of the I.W.W.* (New York, 1932); more recent works on the I.W.W. are: Philip S. Foner, *History of the Labor Movement in the United States, The Industrial Workers of the World, 1905-1917* (New York, 1965); Patrick Renshaw, *The Wobblies: The Story of Syndicalism in the United States* (New York, 1968); Melvyn Dubofsky, *We Shall Be All* (Chicago, 1969); Len DeCaux, *The Living Spirit of the Wobblies* (New York, 1978). See also: Philip Taft, "The Federal Trails of the I.W.W.," *Labor History*, 3 (Winter 1962), 57-91; Philip Taft, "The Bisbee Deportation," *Labor History* (Winter 1972), 3-40; William Preston, Jr., *Aliens and Dissenters: Federal Suppression of Radicals, 1903-1933* (Cambridge, 1963); Philip Taft, "The I.W.W. in the Grain Belt," *Labor History* (Winter 1960), 53-67; Philip Taft and Selig Perlman, *History of Labor in the United States, 1896-1932*, 4 (1935), pp. 386-432. George Griesel compiled one of the earliest general analyses of the personnel of the I.W.W. in the Midwest; George Henry August Griesel, "Study of the Personnel of the I.W.W. Movement" (M.A. thesis, University of Nebraska, 1920).

2. Foner, *I.W.W.*, pp. 462, 474-75.

3. Dubofsky, *We Shall Be All*, p. 315; Stuart Jamieson, *Labor Unionism in American Agriculture*, Bureau of Labor Statistics, Bulletin No. 836 (Washington, 1945), pp. 399, 400. AWO No. 400 was a "sardonic I.W.W. comment" on Mrs. Astor's ballroom and New York City society's famous "400." Haywood considered

that "the new union was being formed by the elite of the working class," the migratory harvest worker who was going to carry out the more difficult tasks of organization and regeneration of the labor movement. Joyce L. Kornbluh, *Rebel Voices: An I.W.W. Anthology* (Ann Arbor, 1964), p. 230; Taft, "The I.W.W. in the Grain Belt," 59; Renshaw, *Wobblies*, p. 135.

4. Foner, *I.W.W.*, pp. 477, 478, 484; Dubofsky, *We Shall Be All*, pp. 315, 316; Taft, "The I.W.W. in the Grain Belt," 60.

5. *Hastings Daily Tribune*, July 12, 1916, p. 8. According to the *Tribune*: "The demand upon Kansas farmers which finally brought the $3.50 wage last year include a minimum wage of $4.00/day of not more than 10 hours; double time for each hour overtime worked above the ten hours constituting a day; good clean board; good clean places to sleep in, with plenty of clean bedding; no discrimination against union men [I.W.W.]."

6. The information on the Hastings incident is largely based on a summary of a *Tribune* story entitled, "The Wobblies: A Labor Story," *Historical News*, Adams County Historical Society, 5 (October 1972), 1, 5.

7. This underscores the predominance of bandits, tinhorns, and gamblers hiding in the I.W.W. and "harvesting the harvesters"; Taft, "The I.W.W. in the Grain Belt," 62; Foner, *I.W.W.*, pp. 477-478; *Lincoln Daily Star*, July 14, 1916, p. 11.

8. *Lincoln Daily star*, July 13, 1916, p. 1; July 19, 1916, p. 1; *Omaha World-Herald*, July 14, 1916, p. 1; *Omaha Evening Bee*, July 14, 1916, p. 10. While the various newspapers claim seven men were arrested, eight names appear. The *Bee* refers to Philip Strawbu as Philip Strauer.

9. *Nebraska State Journal*, July 19, 1916.

10. *Omaha Evening Bee*, July 18, 1916, p. 1; *Nebraska State Journal*, July 18, 1916, p. 6.

11. *Lincoln Daily Star*, July 18, 1916, p. 1; *Omaha World-Herald*, July 19, 1916, p. 1.

12. *Nebraska State Journal*, July 21, 1916, p. 6; *Lincoln Daily Star*, July 18, 1916, p. 1.

13. *Lincoln Daily Star*, July 18, 1916, p. 1; *Omaha Evening Bee*, July 18, 1916, p. 1. It had been reported by the *Omaha Evening Bee* that Lincoln Chief of Police H. H. Antles had received a letter from Kansas City stating I.W.W. official T. J. Thorne would invade Lincoln with 500 Wobblies. However, the *Lincoln Daily Star* reported that E. R. McNally stated there was no official of the I.W.W. by the name Thorne in Kansas City and that he, McNally, was the spokesman for the I.W.W. in Lincoln at this time. The *Journal* carried a slightly different account of the relationship between Counsel McNally and Sheriff Hyers: "This afternoon, after a conference between E. R. McNally, counsel of the industrial workers of the world, and Sheriff Hyers, the situation in regard to the I.W.W. was practically settled. Mr. McNally in coming to the city was very peaceable in his movements, lawful, and used good diplomacy. There was no time that he and the sheriff were at swords' points, nor were there words used that would throw any insinuation for or against the Community or the men." *Nebraska State Journal*, July 19, 1916, p. 7.

14. *Nebraska State Journal*, July 19, 1916, p. 7.

15. *Nebraska State Journal*, July 18, 1916, p. 4; July 21, 1916, p. 6; July 22, 1916, p. 6; July 23, 1916, p. 9; July 31, 1916, p. 4. The editor of the *Nebraska State Journal* offered the following description of the average Wobbly and his activities:

"The I.W.W. immigrants who have just passed through Lincoln are a mixture of western miners and tramps. There are very few genuine harvest hands among them. Practically all are between twenty and forty-five years of age. They are roughly dressed and have radical ideas about labor and property. Now and then a man of brains or talking ability is found who delights to burn up 'capital" with fiery invective. It is not slandering the present bunch to say that none of them have been known to accept bona fide offers of employment. They get money for food and tobacco largely by collecting from the real harvesters who want to travel on the freight trains. The I.W.W. crowd will throw these boys off unless they pay $2.50 or so for admission to the ranks. Once admitted, the boys are forbidden to work for less than $3.50 a day. Not wishing to be beaten up the real harvesters become tramps also until they are able to get away from under the I.W.W. It is feared that a good many of them become infected with the idea that they can scare society into supporting them and lose their taste for honest labor. The average traveller of the I.W.W. class wears coarse, servicable clothing, with the khaki color prominent. He has in his pocket a piece of soap, a razor, a spoon, a handerchief, a time table of the road he is following, an identification note book, an I.W.W. card and an I.W.W. song book. They all pretend to be workers on the way to the wheat fields of the north and east."

16. *Nebraska State Journal*, July 25, 1916, p. 4.

17. *Lincoln Daily Star*, July 19, 1916, p. 4; *Omaha Evening Bee*, July 16, 1916, p. 1; July 19, 1916, p. 14.

18. *Omaha Evening Bee*, July 16, 1916, p. 3; July 17, 1916, p. 3; *Lincoln Daily Star*, July 14, 1916, p. 11.

19. *Omaha World-Herald*, July 18, 1916, p. 4; July 19, 1916, p. 3; *Kearney Morning Times*, July 19, 1916, p. 1.

20. *Omaha Evening Bee*, July 19, 1916, p. 8.

21. Editor of the *Oxford Standard*, as quoted in the *Beaver City Times-Tribune*, July 27, 1916, p. 1.

22. *Omaha Evening Bee*, July 20, 1916, p. 7. On the same day an intriguing "infiltration" of the I.W.W.'s ranks occurred. After witnessing a brawl in Hastings, a Lincoln police officer "donned a black shirt and some overalls" and pretended to I.W.W. members involved in the fracas that he wanted to join the organization. No delegate being in Hastings to enlist him, he rode eastward toward Omaha with about forty Wobblies, where he could pay a $2.50 entrance fee—and 10 cents per month dues. Soon after leaving the station, a committee appointed to bar non-union members from the train forced about twenty men to leave. The officer learned from the train crew that the railroad never attempted to collect fares from the Wobblies or throw them off the train because of the "power of their I.W.W. numbers." While on the train, the officer was forced by Wobblies to agree not to work for less than $4.00 per day in Nebraska. The officer also observed other traits of his fellow Wobblies: Their average age was twenty-five; some were educated, some illiterate; all were followers of the Socialist party. Their conduct was good, and they claimed respect for law; they even abstained from alcoholic beverages. The officer, abandoning his "plan" to join the I.W.W., left the train when it stopped in Lincoln. *Lincoln Daily Star*, July 21, 1916, p. 1.

23. *Omaha Evening Bee*, July 21, 22, 25, 26, 27, 1916; the *Kearney Daily Hub*, July 22, 1916, p. 1.

24. *Fairbury Journal*, July 27, 1916, p. 6.

25. *Omaha Evening Bee*, July 22, 1916, p. 4.

26. *Omaha Evening Bee*, July 29, 1916, p. 1. The Missouri Pacific Railroad offered its own solution to the "wobbly problem." Its construction department "had $5,000 left over from its July budget because laborers were hard to hire." The line would have liked "to impress 2 to 3 hundred I.W.W.'s to work on the roadbed between Omaha and Kansas City." *Omaha Evening Bee*, July 27, 1916, p. 1.

27. *Omaha Evening Bee*, July 29, 1916, pp. 1, 5; July 30, 1916, p. 1.

28. *Omaha Evening Bee*, July 30, 1916, p. 2.

29. *Omaha Evening Bee*, July 30, 1916, p. 2. The *Bee* noted that the police found a bottle of whiskey in Wilson's pocket, and Crawford admitted both had been drinking. Other witnesses also stated that Wilson had been "flourishing" his revolver before he was cracked in the chin. The *Bee* also noted (July 29, 1916, p. 5) that, up to this time, the Council Bluffs police had "found very few weapons among the thousands of men who passed through the city."

30. *Omaha Evening Bee*, August 12, 1916, p. 1; *Historical News*, Adams County (October 1972), 5; *Hastings Daily Tribune*, August 7, 1916, p. 5.

31. *Omaha Evening Bee*, July 31, p. 4. Emphasis supplied. The editor of the *Kearney Daily Hub* agreed that the I.W.W would and should vanish. He speculated that they would disappear much as pests in vegetable gardens often do—when a parasite destroys them. *Kearney Daily Hub*, August 15, 1916, p. 2.

32. Taft, "The I.W.W. in the Grain Belt," 62-63; Foner, *I.W.W.*, pp. 479, 484; for a chart of the revised structural organization of the I.W.W. see Brissenden, "The I.W.W.: A Study of American Syndicalism," appendix 3, p. 351. This chart can be compared with the chart of the I.W.W.'s structure in 1912, found in Vincent St. John, *The I.W.W.: Its History, Structure and Methods* (Chicago, 1912), p. 2.

33. Dubofsky, *We Shall Be All*, pp. 317, 334, 345; Foner, *I.W.W.*, pp. 550-51; Kornbluh, *Rebel Voices*, p. 232; Jamieson, *Labor Unionism*, p. 339; Taft, "The I.W.W. in the Grain Belt," 63, 64; Haywood exercised his power to increase the centralization of the organization. Foner also notes that many of the able organizers, therefore, were not available for the 1917 campaign.

34. *Nebraska: State Council of Defense*, Series 3, Box 15, folder 28, "Correspondence: Home Guard, 1917," Nebraska State Historical Society, Manuscript Collection.

35. *Omaha Evening Bee*, July 3, 1917, "Special Sports" edition, p. 1. The *Nebraska State Journal* also reported these incidents: July 8, 1917, p. 2; July 8, 1917, p. 3A; July 9, 1917, p. 1.

36. *Fremont Tri-Weekly Tribune*, July 14, 1917, p. 1; *Lincoln Daily Star*, July 12, 1917, p. 9. The *Fremont Tri-Weekly Tribune* provided a lengthy description of Russell and Anderson: "Russell, who is about 30 years of age, and Anderson, a seaman with papers showing that he has served on a British merchant ship, were picked up in the railroad yards yesterday by members of the police force. Russell had a letter from another organizer telling of conditions in North Dakota in which laborers were referred to as 'La-Bores,' and especial attention called to the spelling and the pronunciation. He had several receipts from the headquarters office at Kansas City for money he had collected for memberships and sent in. Pictures, membership cards, and other literature depicting the 'hardships' to which the members are subjected were found in the papers taken from the pockets of Russell

and Anderson. A poem denouncing Sheriff McCrae of Everett, Washington, and informing him that he had been 'marked' by the Wobblies was found in Russell's pockets. Just before sentence had been pronounced Russell, in answer to a question regarding the poem, stated that Sheriff McCrae is 'the lowest cur on earth.' Sheriff McCrae led a company of officers and citizens of Everett when a gang of Wobblies were run out of that town with fire hose.''

37. *Nebraska State Journal*, July 15, 1917, p. 11A. While the train was stopped in Lincoln, three new men tried to join the Wobblies. "Search them for guns and their I.W.W. cards," commanded the delegate or leader. When the cards were displayed and no guns were found, the three men were allowed to board the freight.

38. *Omaha Evening Bee*, July 14, 16, 1917.

39. *Omaha World-Herald*, July 19, 1917, p. 1.

40. *Omaha World-Herald*, July 19, 1917, p. 1; *Lincoln Daily News*, August 24, 1917, p. 1; *Lincoln Star*, August 12, 1917, p. 2.

41. The state councils of defense were similar in nature to the Council of National Defense. They were created in the spring of 1917 and became operational on May 3, 1917. Their purpose was to coordinate the war activities of each particular state. "Report on the Organization and Activities of State Councils of Defense, June 18, 1917," 1, *Nebraska: State Council of Defense*, Series 1, Box 1, folder 1, Nebraska State Historical Society, Manuscript Collection. Also "Report on Settlement of Packinghouse Workers," *Nebraska: State Council of Defense*, Series 1, Box 1, folder 3, Nebraska State Historical Society, Manuscript Collection. For further information on the strikes by the AFL unions in Omaha in the summer and fall of 1917 see: "Partial Report, Board of Mediation and Investigation of the Labor Troubles in Omaha: June 18 to August 1, 1917," Department of Labor, State of Nebraska, August 1, 1917; Russell Lowell Beebe, "History of Labor Organization and Legislation in Nebraska to 1918" (M.A. thesis, University of Nebraska, 1938).

42. "Minutes of the Tenth Meeting of the Nebraska State Council of Defense," September 18, 1917, p. 3, *Nebraska: State Council of Defense*, Series 1, Box 1, folder 3, Nebraska State Historical Society, Manuscript Collection.

43. The *Nebraska State Journal* listed examples of cases prosecuted under the Espionage and Selective Service acts: "The alien enemies who offend are interned. They are locked up and kept behind detention bars without any hearing. Several cases will illustrate the operation of this law. John Gerbert, an I.W.W. agitator, was arrested on the charge of urging farm hands to strike unless they were given $5 a day. Gerbert was formerly a member of the Prussian army, belonging to the One Hundred and Seventy-first regiment of the Fifteenth corps. He is now in the federal detention camp at Fort Douglas, Utah, and will be kept there until after the war is over. Then he will be deported. John Fentrohs "turpentined" a man named Walker in Blaine county because he hung out an American flag and talked for America. He was at one time an officer in the German navy, and told the federal authorities that the turpentine treatment was given men in the German navy who did not obey regulations. He is also at Fort Douglas, and after the war is over will be escorted out of the country. L. W. D. Schald, an I.W.W. and a German citizen, is also at Fort Douglas, He was making speeches against the war and advising young men not to enlist. He also made disloyal statements. Rev. William George Krauleidis, the River-dale Lutheran Minister, will either be interned or paroled. The latter course will

probably be taken. His presiding elder and friends have rallied to his defense and have asked permission to file a number of affidavits to show that his conduct had not been disloyal. The gun found in his house was not loaded and he had no cartridges. It is admitted that he prayed for the kaiser, but that he was included in a petition along with other rulers. Anyway, it is urged there is Biblical authority, St. Paul, for praying for your enemies." *Nebraska State Journal*, August 10, 1917, p. 1.

44. *Lincoln Daily Star*, September 7, 1917, p. 8.

45. For more information on this incident, see Kornbluh, *Rebel Voices*, pp. 332-34; *Omaha Evening Bee*, November 10, 1917, p. 2; *Omaha Evening Bee*, November 12, 1917, p. 9; *Nebraska State Journal*, November 12, 1917, p. 1; Dubofsky, *We Shall Be All*, p. 442; Taft and Perlman, *History of Labor*, p. 418; *Nebraska State Journal*, November 12, 1917, p. 1.

46. *Omaha Evening Bee*, November 12, 1917, p. 1; November 13, 1917, p. 4; *Nebraska State Journal*, November 13, 1917, p. 1; Governor Neville also empowered Mayor Dahlman to call in the troops from Fort Crook if the situation warranted. *Omaha World-Herald*, November 13, 1917, p. 4.

47. *Omaha Evening Bee*, November 13, 1917, p. 1. Federal authorities admitted it was orderly. Preston, *Aliens and Dissenters*, p. 137.

48. The actual count of Wobblies taken varies: the *Bee* originally sets it at 69 or 65, the *Omaha World-Herald* and the *Chicago Tribune* at 63, the *New York Times* at "about fifty." However, Preston gives it as 137, Dubofsky, 442, and later *Bee* editions say 64. *Omaha Evening Bee*, November 14, 1917, p. 1; November 27, 1917, p. 1; December 12, 1917, p. 4; *Omaha World-Herald*, November 14, 1917, p. 1; December 15, 1917, p. 9; *New York Times*, November 14, 1917, p. 4; *Chicago Tribune*, November 14, 1917, p. 3.

49. *Omaha Evening Bee*, November 14, 1917, p. 1; *Omaha World-Herald*, November 14, 1917, p. 1.

50. *Omaha Evening Bee*, November 14, 1917, p. 1; *Omaha World-Herald*, November 16, 1917, p. 5.

51. *Omaha Evening Bee*, November 14, 15, 1917.

52. In addition to the raids on I.W.W. headquarters throughout the nation, Wobblies were rounded up "on the job" in many areas, especially in Kansas oil fields. Approximately fifty were rounded up in Butler County, Kansas, between November 19 through 21. For details on this incident, see Taft, "The Federal Trials," 79; "Amnesty for Political Prisoners," testimony of Caroline A. Lowe, *House Judiciary Committee on House Resolution 60*, 67th Cong., 2d sess., pp. 31-37; *Omaha World-Herald*, November 21, 1917, p. 2; *Chicago Tribune*, November 21, 1917, p. 3; Winthrop P. Lane, "Uncle Sam: Jailer," *Survey*, September 6, 1919, 812, 834; *Omaha Evening Bee*, November 15, 1917, p. 1.

53. *Omaha Evening Bee*, November 15, 1917, p. 8. Rosewater's statement concerning the I.W.W. promise of a "demonstration" seems unfounded. Tom Jenkins, local secretary, stated, "I can tell you one thing, though—all this stuff about this being a big general convention is all rot! There's just a few delegates here to talk over a little business. The chairman will be elected from the floor. The meeting may last a day or a week or a year—I dunno!" *Omaha World-Herald*, November 13, 1917, p. 4.

54. *Omaha World-Herald*, November 16, 1917, p. 5; November 17, 1917, p. 7; November 28, 1917, p. 5; *Omaha Evening Bee*, November 22, 1917, p. 1.

55. *Omaha Evening Bee*, November 29, 1917, p. 9.

56. *Omaha Evening Bee*, November 30, 1917, p. 4; December 1, 1917, p. 1; *Omaha World-Herald*, December 2, 1917, p. 5.

57. *Omaha Evening Bee*, December 12, 1917, p. 4; January 9, 1918, p. 1; *Omaha World-Herald*, January 10, 1918, p. 1; Preston, *Aliens and Dissenters*, p. 137.

58. *Fifteenth and Sixteenth Biennial Report of the Bureau of Labor and Industrial Statistics, State of Nebraska, 1917-1918*, pp. 15, 16 (Lincoln), 39, 40.

59. *Nebraska State Journal*, July 13, 1917, p. 9.

60. *Lincoln Daily Star*, July 18, 21, 1917, pp. 1, 4; September 5, 1917, p. 10; *Nebraska State Journal*, July 20, 1917, p. 6; September 5, 1917, p. 4.

61. *Nebraska State Journal*, July 14, 18, 19, 20, 1917; *Lincoln Daily Star*, July 18, 19, 1917.

62. *Nebraska: State Council of Defense*, Series 1, Box 1, folder 3, "Minutes of the Twenty-fifth Meeting," May 17, 1918, pp. 1-2, Nebraska State Historical Society, Manuscript Collection. It should by no means be assumed that the twelve instructors were "complained against" only because of their views on the I.W.W. and the nature of war in general. A number were vocally defensive of the German position.

63. "Minutes of the Twenty-fifth Meeting," p. 2.

64. *Omaha Evening Bee* (final evening edition), June 28, 1918, p. 1; July 8, 1918, p. 1.

65. Dubofsky, *We Shall Be All*, pp. 445, 450.

66. *Omaha Evening Bee*, February 6, 1919, p. 1; February 7, 1919, p. 1; February 9, 1919, p. 1; February 10, 1919, p. 1; *Omaha World-Herald*, February 6, 1919, p. 4; Nebraska *Senate Rolls* 1919, amendments to Senate File No. 200; *Lincoln Daily Star*, March 29, 1919, p. 1; Nebraska *House Journal*, Sixtieth Day, March 29, 1919; *Reissue Revised Statutes of Nebraska*, 1975, 28 §815-28 §817.

67. This is according to Lieutenant Governor Roland Leudtke, a prime sponsor of LB38. For more information on criminal syndicalism laws passed during this period, see Eldridge Foster Dowell, *A History of Criminal Syndicalism Legislation in the United States* (Baltimore, 1939).

68. The exact date is not known. It has been narrowed to this three-week period from the data in Preston, *Aliens and Dissenters*, pp. 136, 138, and the *Omaha Evening Bee*, May 1, 1919, p. 1; Dubofsky, *We Shall Be All*, pp. 442, 443; Taft, "The Federal Trials," 76.

69. *Omaha Evening Bee*, April 30, 1979, p. 1.

70. Eberstein left the justice department to become chief of police in Omaha sometime between January 1918 and April 1919. *Omaha Evening Bee*, April 30, 1919, p. 1; May 1, 1919, p. 1; May 2, 1919, p. 1.

71. *Omaha Evening Bee*, May 2, 1919, p. 1.

72. The *Omaha World-Herald* stated that no I.W.W. or Socialist meetings were held; while more than 1,000 people clustered around the Swedish auditorium, no meetings or any violence occurred on May 1; the meeting Novotny addressed was not held by the Socialists or the I.W.W. However, the *Herald* offers no alternative to the *Bee*'s translation of Novotny's speech, which seems to indicate a pro-Socialist

position. *Omaha World-Herald*, May 1, 1919, p. 3; May 3, 1919, p. 12; *Omaha Evening Bee*, May 1, 1919, p. 1; May 5, 1919, p. 4.

73. *Omaha Evening Bee*, July 25, 1919, p. 4.

74. *Governor Samuel R. McKelvie: Speeches and Proclamations*, 1919-1922, Series 2, Box 5, folder 2, "Some of the Activities of the State During 1919," pp. 13, 14, Nebraska State Historical Society, Manuscript Collection. The act passed can be found in *Nebraska Session Laws*, 36th (extraordinary) sess., 1918, House Roll No. 5.

75. *Governor Samuel R. McKelvie*, 1919-1922, Series 2, Box 2, folder 2.

76. Dubofsky, *We Shall Be All*, p. 473; Taft and Perlman, *History of Labor*, p. 432.

77. James C. Olson, *History of Nebraska* (Lincoln, 1966), p. 271. Generally, see also Richard Edward Olson, "Some Economic Aspects of Agricultural Development in Nebraska, 1854-1920" (Ph.D. diss. University of Nebraska, 1965).

78. Gambs, *Decline of the I.W.W.*, pp. 47, 49, 52; Dowell, *History of Criminal Syndicalism*, p. 37-44; Joseph R. Conlin, *Bread and Roses Too: Studies of the Wobblies* (Westport, 1969), p. 66. Carlton H. Parker observed that few analysts looked beyond legal remedies for the causes of I.W.W. activities. Carlton Parker, *The Casual Laborer and Other Essays* (New York, 1920), pp. 94, 95. One of the first analysts of I.W.W. activity, George Griesel, also mirrored the Parker position; he stated: "What is the I.W.W.? It is simply one expression of the social and economic conditions of the times. It is the radical or 'left wing' manifestation in America of the unrest that has been developing for a number of years among portions of our laboring class. It is that portion of the laboring class who are proclaiming the overthrow and destruction of the present order of society with the hope that some organization of society better for their class will develop. It is therefore not the sign or manifestation of this unrest which we should attack but it is rather the cause of these conditions which should be removed." Griesel went on to list solutions to the problems causing unrest: (1) educate and americanize foreigners, (2) bridge over seasonal demand for labor, (3) improve work and home environments of labor, (4) instead of employees giving as little labor as possible, they should give as much as possible within their ability, (5) employers should pay as much as their ability will allow, not as little as possible. Griesel, pp. 110, 111.

In addition to the articles already recounted, the *Lincoln Daily Star* ran an article by J. D. Crown recounting an interview with William D. Haywood on August 26, 1917. On July 25, 1920, The *Sunday State Journal* ran an article by William Oeschger entitled: "In the Home of the I.W.W.—A Study of I.W.W.-ism." Both articles were relatively evenhanded in their presentation of I.W.W. ideas, activities, and tactics.

79. Gambs, *Decline of the I.W.W.*, p. 1; DeCaux, *The Living Spirit*, pp. 5, 6; Thompson and Murfin, *The I.W.W.*, p. 95.

THE UNITED STATES v. C. W. ANDERSON et al.: THE WICHITA CASE, 1917-1919

EARL BRUCE WHITE

When the United States entered World War I in April 1917, the I.W.W. had already embarked on a new strategy. Big Bill Haywood was reorganizing the union into industrial organizations he could control efficiently from Chicago headquarters. The industrial unions would abandon free speech fights and "brass band" tactics in favor of organizing on the job. The important thing to Haywood was getting the I.W.W. to the point of production. The unions were making some progress in the northern timber regions and the western copper mines and with maritime workers, construction labor, and oil workers in the Mid-Continent Oil Field of Kansas and Oklahoma when wartime legislation, patriotism, and hysteria were turned against them.

Timber workers were harassed; miners were deported from the Bisbee, Arizona, copper mines; Frank Little was lynched in Butte; and the federal government turned its forces against the I.W.W. Federal raids on I.W.W. locals during September 1917 resulted in four indictments at Chicago, Sacramento, Omaha, and Wichita. During 1917 and 1918, the defendants were charged with conspiracy to impede the war effort. The counts were similar, if not identical; much of the evidence was repetitious; and select groups of government prosecutors were put in charge of the cases. The Wichita trial, however, was unique among the I.W.W. prosecutions of this period.

Historians have emphasized the unsanitary and inhumane jails in which the defendants were incarcerated for over two years while awaiting trial. The men were forced to abide those conditions because the government's first two indictments were faulty, and a third set of charges was necessary before the case could go to trial. Although these circumstances were seemingly peculiar to Wichita, jail conditions were a source of I.W.W. complaints in the other federal cases, and multiple indictments also occurred in the Sacramento case. The Wichita prosecution is different from other I.W.W. cases because it was the only successful federal prosecution specifically directed against the I.W.W.'s concept of industrial unionism. The defendants were in the midst of an organizing campaign in the Mid-Continent Oil Field when they were arrested. The Chicago defendants represented the I.W.W. leadership and were convicted as the principal force behind the union; Sacramento represented a venting of prewar grievances against Wobbly agricultural workers, but the Agricultural Workers Industrial Union No. 400 (AWIU) was not on trial. Members of the Construction Workers Industrial Union No. 573 (CWIU) were indicted at Omaha, but the charges were eventually dismissed. Only in Kansas would industrial unions be tried and convicted as such. The Oil Workers Industrial Union No. 450 (OWIU) was a fledgling organization controlled by the AWIU, and the two organizations were so intertwined that both were prosecuted in Kansas. After the conviction of the Wichita defendants, the state obtained a permanent injunction enjoining the AWIU and OWIU from operating in the state. The I.W.W was convinced, however, that the case was an attempt by Standard Oil to end its efforts in the Mid-Continent Oil Field.[1]

The Mid-Continent Oil Field consisted of a series of pools located in two states. The Kansas wells were centered in the Butler County towns of Augusta and El Dorado east of Wichita. The Glenn and Cushing pools were west of Tulsa, Oklahoma. Geographically, the field approximated an ellipse, although there were a few pools outside of this main field. The field became a major oil-producing area in 1912 when the Cushing Pool began pumping 1,500 barrels per day. The city of Cushing boasted forty-six new oil wells by November 1912, and the nearby town of Drumright was equally active.[2] Most of the field was developed initially by either Standard Oil or its subsidiary companies. Standard's Prairie Oil and Gas had been operating in Kansas since at least 1910.[3] Carter Oil was acquired by Standard in 1908, and it entered Oklahoma in 1913 and Kansas in 1915.[4] The Kansas portion of the field began with a high production well in Augusta in December 1915, which was soon followed by the neighboring community of El Dorado. As new wells were drilled, the Wichita-based Empire Gas and Oil Company moved into the area. Soon its wells alone were producing 20,000 barrels a day in the Augusta-El Dorado area.[5] This new source of employment was not lost on the I.W.W., and many timber workers from the unsuccessful Texas-Louisiana Timber War of 1912-1913 went to the Oklahoma oil fields.[6]

From 1914 through 1917, there were three distinct phases of I.W.W. activity in the Mid-Continent Oil Field. The initial attempt to organize workers began in 1914 and 1915, shortly after the field began producing large quantitites of oil, but was very limited in scope or objectives. The second phase started in January 1917, when the AWIU chartered a new branch union, the Oil Workers Industrial Union No. 450 (OWIU), at Tulsa. Shortly after the formation of the OWIU, William D. Haywood assumed his greater control over the industrial unions. As part of his increased power and responsibility, he appointed Phineas M. Eastman to head the AWIU-OWIU local at Augusta, Kansas. In making the appointment, Haywood recognized Eastman's past loyalty to the I.W.W. as an agitator and saboteur in the Louisiana timber regions. Eastman held the post until September 1917, or just prior to the federal raids that led to the Chicago indictment and the arrest of Haywood. The final period began in October 1917, when C. W. Anderson became secretary-treasurer of the AWIU. He launched an organizing campaign in the Mid-Continent Oil Field by directing a newly elected AWIU committee until they and other members of the AWIU-OWIU were arrested in Kansas and Oklahoma during November 1917.

During the first phase, over 300 members were claimed by the financial secretary at the I.W.W. local in Tulsa in 1914. The union's complaints were typical of most labor organizations which objected to poor housing, food, and the twelve-hour day, but the I.W.W. knew it faced difficulties in organizing the oil workers to change conditions. "The skilled workers . . . are the most conservative and enslaved of the lot, owing to their fancied superiority over the common laborer," the financial secretary wrote. However, in those prewar days, the union's goal was simply to organize to the point where it could demand an eight-hour day.[7] It should be noted that this limited objective preceded the formation of the Agricultural Workers Organization No. 400 (AWO).

As the AWO became a stable industrial union in 1915 and 1916, it expanded I.W.W. goals. The Minneapolis, Minnesota, headquarters of the AWO housed the offices and controlled the activities of struggling industrial unions in mining, construction, and timber. A red AWO membership card allowed members to freely transfer between any of the other industrial unions.[8] The advantages of this transfer system apparently appealed to some migrant laborers in the Mid-Continent Oil Field. In either December 1916 or January 1917, some I.W.W. oil workers in the Tulsa area requested a charter from AWO headquarters. Apparently few in numbers, this group was the first to call itself the Oil Workers Industrial Union No. 450 (OWIU). Under the direct control and tutelage of the AWO because the new industrial union lacked sufficient members and funds to be an independent organization, the AWO intended to conduct OWIU business only until such time as it was large enough to become a separate industrial union.[9] However, a series of circumstances, both internal and external, interfered with this process. Bill Haywood would reorganize the I.W.W. and the federal government destroy the OWIU with the Wichita case.

Bill Haywood was considering reorganizing the I.W.W. at about the same time the OWIU was added to the growing ranks of the AWO. He planned to centralize control of the industrial unions from his Chicago headquarters rather than allow Minneapolis to dominate the scene.[10] One contemporary stated that Haywood moved in this direction because he believed he was losing control of the I.W.W. to the AWO.[11] When the AWO met for its semiannual convention in June 1917, it was renamed the Agricultural Workers Industrial Union No. 400 (AWIU) and stripped of all the other industrial unions except the OWIU.[12] However, leaving the OWIU with the AWIU may have been meaningless since Haywood had already assumed some control over the oil workers' union.

In February or March of 1917, after personal correspondence between the two men, Haywood appointed Phineas Madison Eastman secretary-treasurer of the Augusta, Kansas, AWO-OWIU local. At best a pitiful example of an I.W.W hall, the headquarters consisted of a large tent (although three members owned a small home were personal property and union literature were sometimes stored).[13] Yet the unimpressive local was to be the focal point for organizing the Mid-Continent Oil Field for the I.W.W because Eastman brought a militancy to Augusta that would set the tone for its entire existence. He established and enforced some questionable policies in dealing with organizing the oil fields that lasted until his resignation in September 1917.

Phineas Eastman was a mature man of forty-six with approximately a decade's experience as an I.W.W. organizer when, apparently, he solicited the Augusta post from Haywood. Slight of build and short of stature, Eastman was a relatively handsome man with slightly graying, dark hair and sideburns. Whatever physical attractiveness he possessed, however, was offset by the southerner's cold, gray-blue eyes.[14] He was born on December 25, 1871, in Clinton, Mississippi, and both of his parents were dead by 1881. He was adopted by a schoolteacher aunt, Kate Eastman, and his aunt and uncle, Judge and Mrs. H. B. Kelly of New Orleans. After finishing public school in 1890, he began an odyssey that took him wandering from job to job only ending in 1937 with his death.[15]

Eastman worked at various positions for short periods of time during the 1890s. In Birmingham, Alabama, he was an office employee in a hardware store, a shipping clerk, and a judge's clerk. In 1893, he worked in an Arkansas plantation store but returned to New Orleans in 1894 and briefly served as clerk and messenger for his uncle, Judge Kelly. In 1895, he left for the timber regions of western Louisiana, where he was shocked and disgusted by the brutality employers showed their laborers. He quit his job because he could not tolerate the conditions under which timber workers labored and went to Memphis, Tennessee, as a salesman. He returned to Arkansas in 1896 to manage another plantation store and claimed he would have remained there if the Spanish-American War had not occurred.[16]

During his stay in Birmingham, Eastman had joined the Alabama militia. In a feeling of patriotic fervor he left Arkansas in 1898 to rejoin his militia company, the "Jefferson Volunteers." As a private in Company G, First Regiment of the Alabama Infantry, he served at both Mobile, Alabama, and Miami, Florida, from June 11 to October 25, 1898, when his company was mustered out of service.[17] In 1902, after working at various jobs in several states, he returned to the Louisiana timber regions. He described his own career as "jumping from milltown to milltown," from 1902 until 1915, although he did marry schoolteacher Mary Hoskins in December 1907.[18] Not finding inner peace, however, Eastman turned to the solace of alcohol and radicalism.

In 1917, Eastman described how he drifted into the labor movement. He wrote Haywood that he had been outlawed from "so-called genteel jobs and have been for some time (12 years) a real working stiff. I can thank whisky primarily for this, which I do fervently." Continuing his story, he related how his drinking had estranged him from his "aristocratic people and bourgeois association," and allowed him to become a Wobbly, "whiskey having been accredited (innocently it's true!) with guiding my footsteps into the paths of Industrial Unionism and the only life."[19]

Eastman had come to the I.W.W. via the Brotherhood of Timber Workers (BTW). Organized by A. L. Emerson in southwestern Louisiana in about 1907, the BTW affiliated with the I.W.W. in 1911. Haywood went to Louisiana in 1911 to solidify the amalgamation during a particularly bitter I.W.W. strike, and Eastman probably came to his attention at that time because of his militancy during the walkout.[20] There is no question that Eastman was considered one of the leading agitators in a later I.W.W. timber workers' strike.

A series of walkouts known as the Texas-Louisiana Lumber War of 1912-1913 provided Eastman with the opportunity to show his worth to the I.W.W.[21] Involved in the Lake Charles and Merryville strikes in southwestern Louisiana, Eastman's activities came to the attention of the timber companies. On February 13, 1913, a group of strikebreakers and company gunmen subjected him and three colleagues to a beating with clubs and gun butts, forcing them to take the next train out of town.[22] Undoubtedly this physical abuse resulted when the timber producers learned or suspected that Eastman was a saboteur, because he later bragged to Haywood that he and two friends had sabotaged railroad cars in Merryville.[23] Although his importance to the total BTW-I.W.W. movement in Louisiana has been underrated with organizers A. L. Emerson and Covington Hall receiving most of the notoriety, Eastman's union activities impressed the Wobblies.

In 1913, he became a member of the I.W.W.'s ruling circle, the General Executive Board. Eastman later claimed that he had remained in that position for a very short period of time.[24] He did stay, however, in Louisiana and in his own words, "After the organization went to pieces, I stayed on and with the help of my wife, tried in every way to fan the dying embers into something like a blaze." He related how he worked and lived "on the ragged edge down there for two years [1913-1915] and finally to keep from starving or getting murdered, sold out what we owned for enough to get to Cushing."[25] In 1917, he once again attracted Haywood's attention.

Eastman was ready for another I.W.W. assignment. Although the available correspondence is incomplete, it appears that Haywood wanted him to return to the South as an organizer. It is not clear whether Eastman had written Haywood for a job or Haywood had sought him out for a position. In any case, Eastman made it very clear that he did not want a post in the South.[26] He made a counteroffer asking Haywood for the post of secretary-treasurer for the AWO-OWIU local in Augusta. Eastman tried to convince Haywood of his loyalty to the I.W.W. and his own personal worth to the order. In one letter he bragged of the sabotage he had committed at Merryville in 1913 when others had been afraid to do anything and ended the missive, "Without bragging want to say that I am not afraid of anything or any person in the world." A few days later he wrote Haywood, "I am not contented unless I am raising hell with the boss, and will do anything, go anywhere where I can serve the organization." To bolster these sentiments, he told Haywood, "It surely makes me feel good to hear and see so much Hell being raised by workers everywhere."[27] Haywood, obviously convinced of Eastman's loyalty, organizational abilities, and previous activity as a saboteur, sent him to the Augusta local in February or March of 1917.[28]

At the time Eastman assumed the Augusta post, the chain of command within the I.W.W. was also in the process of redefinition because of Haywood's centralization program. Although there is no question that Eastman was Haywood's personal choice for the Kansas job, it is not known whether Eastman was directly responsible to Haywood and followed his orders for organizing the Mid-Continent Oil Field. However, if Eastman was taking his instructions from Haywood, then there is evidence that the I.W.W. pursued a policy that was in fact detrimental to the war effort, as the government later claimed.

In May 1917, Eastman sent two letters that became the basis for the Wichita case. The first communication was an antidraft resolution allegedly adopted by the Augusta membership.

Resolved, That all members of the I.W.W. resist conscription by refusing to join any band of potential murderers, or by any other effective method deemed advisable. Copies of the motion to be sent to W. D. Haywood, secretary and treasurer, and Forrest Edwards, secretary and treasurer of the AWO.[29]

Haywood marked his copy "File" and did not reply, but Edwards informed Eastman that the action was satisfactory to the AWO and that headquarters would try to implement the resolution.[30] The resolution was later used as evidence of overt acts in all of the federal cases against the I.W.W. At the Chicago trial, a witness named Clark testified that he was a member of the Augusta local when the resolution was allegedly passed and denied any knowledge of it. He maintained that "Phineas Eastman, then the secretary there, had been taken to task and relieved from duty as [an] official by the membership because of strong anti-war talk."[31] Eastman believed that "the I.W.W. put [a] witness on stand at Chicago Trial in 1918, thru *[sic]* whose perjured testimony I was portrayed as the one solely responsible for that resolution, passed by members at Augusta, Kas. against the draft act; [the] fact was just the oposite."[32] Later Eastman wrote, "This resolution was afterwards saddled upon petitioner to screen men whose former records dare not be placed before a jury."[33] The resolution undoubtedly aided in the conviction of I.W.W. members at Chicago, Sacramento, and Wichita. Unfortunately, the available evidence does not indicate whether Eastman was used as a scapegoat to protect others, possibly Haywood who requested such a resolution, or he merely forwarded the resolution to headquarters as ordered. If the resolution's purpose, however, was to prompt the I.W.W.'s general executive board into taking a stand on the draft question, then it failed because there was never any official I.W.W. statement on the draft.[34] Eastman's second letter, however, cannot be interpreted as a prompting but rather as a vicious threat.

During the latter half of May, Augusta's chamber of commerce received an unsigned threat:

Sir: Your damned speaker from Missouri in a speech to you and your members advised you to take steps to unlawfully suppress the W.C.U. [Working Class Union] and all organized workers, who are against your blood sucking, cowardly conscription. We warn you that the first dirty move that you make against the workers, whether they be organized or unorganized, we will reply with a handful of matches and numerous sticks of dynamite and nitro.

At your first move up go your homes and pipelines and tanks. One box of matches can whip the whole country.

Take notice and do not start anything with the worker. Just leave us alone and everything will be fine and dandy.[35]

Although written in a disguised hand, a government handwriting expert at the Wichita trial later identified the letter as Eastman's penmanship.[36] Undoubtedly it was this kind of radicalism that may have prompted Haywood to appoint Eastman to head the struggling Augusta local, the gateway to the

Mid-Continent Oil Field. However, even if Eastman can be viewed as Haywood's representative, he was assisted by AWO-sponsored organizers.

The key to building the successful AWO and its successor AWIU had been organizing on the job and not "brass band" tactics, as threats like Eastman's were called by the I.W.W. At least as early as April 1917, Frank J. Gallagher was sent to the Mid-Continent Oil Field as a traveling delegate or organizer for the AWO-OWIU. Apparently during the transition period when Haywood was consolidating his power over the industrial unions, the AWO still controlled the organizers in the field. The brawny thirty-six-year-old Gallagher, also known as John Shannon and John King, was reportedly one of the first I.W.W organizers in the Mid-Continent Oil Field.[37] He had worked in the Oklahoma oil fields for a number of years and may have believed that he understood the labor situation there better than the southerner Eastman. Whether there was an actual conflict over policy or merely friendly opposition between the two men is not known.[38] However, Eastman retained his post nearly as long as Haywood was in power.

Eastman resigned September 1, 1917, and left Augusta on the eleventh or twelfth. Haywood might have warned him of the impending federal raids of I.W.W. locals that did occur on September 5, or his wife's health may have necessitated a change of climate as he later claimed.[39] Regardless of the truth of the matter, shortly after his departure Eastman was indicted in Chicago but remained a fugitive until 1919 while Haywood and his companions awaited trial.[40] With Haywood and the heads of the various industrial unions in jail in Chicago, a new secretary-treasurer was elected to head the AWIU-OWIU and oil operations in the Mid-Continent Oil Field.

Charles W. Anderson, better known as C. W. Anderson, was elevated from shipping clerk to secretary-treasurer of the AWIU-OWIU, replacing the indicted Forrest Edwards. The thirty-one-year-old Anderson had been with the I.W.W since 1913. Of average height but stockily built, he had flattened facial features, but his piercing blue eyes and dark hair took attention away from that fact. A lifetime resident of Minneapolis, Anderson was not familiar with the petroleum industry.[41] As the sole head of operations in the Mid-Continent Oil Field, he turned away from Eastman's "brass band" tactics to the on-the-job organizing with which he was familiar. As part of this new strategy, a new AWIU-OWIU organizing committee was elected in October and sent to Augusta to bolster Frank Gallagher's efforts in the Mid-Continent Oil Field. The experienced agitators and organizers from previous AWO-AWIU union drives in the grain belt were Oscar E. Gordon, Wencil Francik, and Michael Sapper.[42]

At age thirty-one the short, stocky Gordon was a leader of men. He had served two tours of duty in the Philippine Islands as an army sergeant prior to joining the I.W.W. in 1915. His facial features were those of the classic stereotype of a boxer, and his extensive tattoos added to the image of a tough individual. An excellent soapbox orator, Gordon had organized for the AWO in the Dakotas, Nebraska, and Kansas.[43] Wencil Francik was a large, raw-boned man who stood over six feet tall and weighed over 200 pounds. His relatives were Iowa farmers, but he had left them in 1909 to join the I.W.W. At age thirty-five, Francik was a fierce looking and sounding man with a rumbling, gravelly voice. A prominent nose and hooded eyes added to the frightening effect. His work was typically migratory and took him all over the West. He had last been in the copper mines at Bisbee, Arizona, when he arrived in Augusta.[44] Thirty-two-year-old Sapper was a Russian immigrant with a mixed work record. Of medium height and weight, he had the bored look of a man beyond caring for anybody or anything.[45] Gallagher, however, was not satisfied with the men or the situation in the Mid-Continent Oil Field.

In late October 1917, Gallagher explained his position to C. W. Anderson:

. . . Now, I hope you will not misunderstand me and think I have cold feet. That is not a complaint I was ever troubled with, but this is the way I feel about the oil fields. As you know, I have spent lots of time trying to organize the oil workers and this has turned out to be a personal matter with me. In fact, my greatest ambition is to see the oil fields line up solid with the I.W.W. and would like to be in at the finish, that is active until the last man is lined up. I know I am flirting with my liberty, and I am willing to take a chance, but I want to know I have accomplished something; otherwise it would be foolish to take a chance on a long jolt without the satisfaction of knowing it was worthwhile. I am willing to do anything at any time for the organization, and do not understand the position taken by the three committeemen [Gordon, Francik, and Sapper]. Gordon also informs me that some of the committeemen are oil workers. I don't know anything about Sapper, but I do know that Francik and Gordon are not, and I have my doubts Sapper being an oil worker. I know every one of the oil slaves, but never knew of Sapper working in the oil fields. He may have worked in the oil fields one winter, but that does not say he understands the industry. Well, to sum up, if they will meet me, I will be foolish and go down there and will work for a master.[46]

It is obvious from this letter that Gallagher was concerned about the inexperienced AWIU organizers conducting an oil field organizing campaign. He also feared personal retaliation because of harassment shown Wobblies earlier in the year. Government agents estimated that there were approximately 2,000 Wobblies in Kansas and Oklahoma during the summer and fall of 1917. In Butler County, Kansas, alone, between 300 and 400 had been arrested on vagrancy charges.[47] In Oklahoma the pressures were of a different nature.

On October 29, the Tulsa home of J. Edgar Pew was dynamited. Because Pew was manager of Carter Oil, it was assumed by some of the local authorities and oil companies that the act was one of Wobbly revenge for the recent arrest of members of the Working Class Union, an allegedly I.W.W.-affiliated organization.[48] On November 5, city police broke into the OWIU hall without a search warrant and arrested eleven men on vagrancy charges. The accused requested a trial, which was conducted during the night of November 8. The defendants produced six witnesses but were found guilty and each assessed a $100 fine. When they would not pay, they were remanded to the county jail along with their witnesses! The seventeen men were loaded into touring cars, which were soon halted by a robed and hooded group calling themselves the "Knights of Liberty." Those vigilantes escorted the prisoners to the outskirts of the city, where they were stripped to the waist, whipped with a rope, and tarred and feathered. The victims were sent on their way with a volley of rifle shots and the message, "Don't let the sun shine on you in Tulsa."[49] However, no one was arrested for the brutality and Tulsa newspapers openly condoned the violence.[50] Members of the OWIU no longer felt safe in Oklahoma and fled, either for their safety or as a base for retaliation against the oil producers, to Augusta. Shortly before this incident, known as the "Tulsa Outrage," Anderson had made the decision to launch a major organizing campaign in the Mid-Continent Oil Field.

In October, Anderson called Gallagher back to Minneapolis headquarters for orders and instructions. Evidence indicates that he was to meet with committeemen Gordon, Francik, and Sapper in Kansas City but became ill. Then, on November 2, Anderson ordered Gallagher to meet with the trio in Augusta to outline plans for organizing the oil workers. Either Gallagher ignored or misread his instructions, because he went to Ardmore, Oklahoma, instead of Augusta. He requested that the committee meet him at Arkansas City, Kansas, nearly on the Oklahoma border, on November 8.[51] Although the government would interpret this meeting as evidence of a conspiracy to control oil production in the Mid-Continent Oil Field, Gordon's account of the session did not give that impression. He wired Anderson a report of the meeting, "Sapper left Ark City 5:25 P.M. for Drumright, and Francik for Tulsa . . . Shannon [Gallagher] went to Healton *[sic]* fields. In our meeting we decided to give lots of publicity to papers, get out some new leaflets one after the other and try and have # job Del on every job," he closed.[52] Entering Oklahoma at the very same time as the "Tulsa Outrage" meant the possibility of personal danger because of the increased hostility toward the I.W.W. after the incident.

Francik and Sapper quickly reported their progress to Anderson. Writing on the tenth, Sapper stated that the I.W.W. hall in Drumright had been raided by the police, windows and furniture smashed, literature seized, and some members arrested on vagrancy charges. "I had to leave Drumright on threats of death if I didn't leave before sundown. Cushing is just as bad . . . they are very hostile through here," he wrote. He continued, describing how the police went to boardinghouses and searched itinerants for I.W.W. cards, adding that the newspapers were "full of threats and advocating violence and the master tools are sure practicing it. Nearly every job is some gunmen *[sic]*." He concluded on a very negative note, "So you see it is impossible to do any active work for a traveling delegate. The country through here is flooded with work, and the only way to get back at the barbarians is on the job."[53] Francik's letter of the twelfth commented on the dismal situation in Tulsa. He was concerned that the I.W.W. hall could not remain open because of local hostility and thought that an experienced organizer should replace him, "Some member like Gordon should have charge of this place." He was so discouraged that he wanted to leave Tulsa but was told to stay.[54]

Anderson had either inadvertently selected the worst time to organize the Mid-Continent Oil Field because of increased hostility toward the I.W.W., or he was acting out of desperation to continue union activities with the main I.W.W. leadership incarcerated in Chicago. Anderson believed that he had no choice but to keep the I.W.W. active after the Chicago indictment or the union would perish.[55] Although his conclusion is understandable, federal authorities soon instigated action against the OWIU anyway.

Both federal and local authorities coordinated a raid on the Augusta and El Dorado locals on the nights of November 20 and 21, 1917. Local police arrested between 250 and 350 area Wobblies but quickly released most of them. Butler County District Attorney Robert McCluggage held forty-two of the men on "John Doe" warrants charging them with vagrancy. Federal officers were armed with a search warrant for the purpose of collecting evidence implicating Eastman in the Chicago case.[56] Over three mailbags of union correspondence, newspapers, and literature were seized in the raid. The Wichita case came into being with these searches and arrests. The basic question, however, asks why the raid and arrest took place when and where it did.

The prevalent historical interpretation of the Wichita case is that local oil companies insisted on the arrests, and an overzealous U. S. District Attorney initiated the prosecution.[57] Historians also have criticized prosecutor Fred Robertson for assuming a broad interpretation of wartime legislation that justified his prosecuting the I.W.W. in the northern section of the Mid-Continent Oil Field while his counterpart in the southern section at Tulsa, W. P. McGinnis, refused to act against the Wobblies without conclusive evidence.[58] The lack of prosecutions in Oklahoma seems to support this interpretation, and two seemingly irrefutable documents are frequently cited as supporting the other half of the theory. In 1922, Miss Caroline A. Lowe testified before a U. S. Senate Hearing Committee on the I.W.W. cases. As cocounsel for the Wichita I.W.W., Lowe related her belief that agents of the Carter, Theda, Sinclair, and other oil companies operating in

Butler County, Kansas, suggested to County District Attorney Robert McCluggage that he arrest I.W.W. oil workers to protect their properties from destruction.[59] While it is true that her partner, Fred H. Moore, attempted to solicit from McCluggage at the Wichita trial the answer that the oil companies suggested the arrest, he carefully avoided giving Moore that answer.[60] There is no question, however, that Fred Robertson wired the U.S. attorney general requesting that an agent be sent to the oil producing region near Augusta:

County attorney at Eldorado, Kansas [McCluggage], makes alarming claim that over three thousand industrial workers of world are assembled in oil field threatening riots and pillage as soon as soldiers stationed there leave for training at Fort Sill I suggest special agent be ordered there immediately.[61]

However, other considerations and explanations may detract from the culpability of Robertson and McCluggage in the initiation of the Wichita case.

It is unfair to criticize Robertson's I.W.W. prosecution by comparing his with the actions of W. P. McGinnis in Oklahoma. Vigilante pressure and mob violence against the I.W.W. in Oklahoma have been largely ignored by historians writing about the Wichita case. One writer briefly describes other incidents such as the Bisbee deportations and the lynching of Frank Little but ignores the Tulsa Outrage. This incident signaled open violence against the I.W.W. and OWIU in Oklahoma.[62] McGinnis did not have to respond to alleged pressure by oil companies to prosecute the I.W.W.; as at least one contemporary newspaper noted, extralegal violence had already driven the active OWIU organizers and members into Kansas.[63] However, when given a similar set of circumstances in Oklahoma, evidence indicates that McGinnis would have acted with more zeal than did Robertson in Kansas. During July and August of 1917, there were a series of arrests in Oklahoma of allegedly I.W.W.-affiliated groups for conspiring to violate the draft. When McGinnis prosecuted one of these groups, the Working Class Union, in August, one of his first comments to the press was that "where evidence was sufficient, he would ask for the death penalty."[64] Although Robertson would make some strongly patriotic statements to the press, he never approached this rhetoric.

Another interpretation is that the Wichita case was the natural result of a second wave of federal raids on I.W.W. locals. Evidence seized in the September raids and forwarded to Chicago may have been interpreted by the federal government as revealing plans by some industrial unions to violate wartime legislation. This would explain arrests in November at Omaha that temporarily halted the activities of the Construction Workers Industrial Union No. 573, and the raids in the Wichita and Tulsa vicinities crippled the OWIU's plan to organize the Mid-Continent Oil Field. A better explanation, however, involves Eastman.

The search warrant for the federal raid at Augusta was clearly captioned *U.S. versus Phineas Eastman*. There is a distinct probability that the Wichita case would never have been initiated by the federal government if Eastman had not sent the antidraft resolution to both Minneapolis and Chicago headquarters. Because of this action, Eastman was indicted in Chicago, and a search for evidence in that case led to the Augusta raid. With new evidence obtained in the raid, the decision was made in Washington to initiate a new I.W.W. prosecution, and Robertson merely became the instrument of prosecution.[65] Eastman became the focal point of the government's new case, and its representatives were nearly obsessed with him.

Fred Robertson and Special Agent Thomas J. Howe considered Eastman the controlling I.W.W. force in the Mid-Continent Oil Field. Howe told the press that Eastman "was regarded by the government as the guiding hand of the organization in the Midcontinent oil fields and the Western agricultural regions." Robertson described him as "the most dangerous of those on trial," adding that "Eastman is the nerve center of that ganglion of twisted intellects."[66] Although these comments were made to the press at the time of the Wichita defendant's trial, both men expressed even stronger sentiments at a much later date in official correspondence not intended for the public. Nearly two years after the trial, Robertson recounted Eastman's activities for his successor.

. . . He [Eastman] is a vicious character. . . . Our proof in the case showed this man to be a confirmed opponent of law and order, thoroughly dissatisfied with our government and its institutions, and imbued with the ideas that a government of anarchy offered the only opportunity for a laboring man to get justice. There are in the District Attorney's office many exhibits which were actually introduced in evidence upon the trial showing that long before the war this man, with others, was engaged in Mississippi and elsewhere in acts of outlawry. . . . Eastman told Haywood of his ability to "raise hell with the boss" and further advised Haywood of some of the crimes he had committed for that purpose in the southern part of the United States. *In those letters he outlined to Haywood how he could cripple the government by an organization of harvest hands and of oil workers, and assured Haywood that all he wanted was a chance. This sort of correspondence resulted in his selection as Manager of the local branch of I.W.W. at Augusta, Kansas* [emphasis added]. . . .

I cannot take further time or space in discussing this man. Hours could be devoted to a disclosure of his many vicious characteristics. *Suffice it to say that every fact and circumstance which cropped out through out long investigation of this situation which grew up in Kansas and Oklahoma in 1917, tends on all occasions, stamps Phineas Eastman as an active, vicious leader of the anarchistic elements which undertook to capture the Midcontinent oil field for the purpose of depriving the government of the petroleum and petroleum products then being produced in that field* [emphasis added].[67]

Howe was even stronger in his condemnations in 1923. In writing a series of reports to U. S. Pardon Attorney James Finch, Howe initially outlined his relationship to the I.W.W. prosecutions and continued with an unsolicited comment about Eastman.

> . . . I prepared all the evidence in the Chicago and Kansas cases and assisted somewhat in the Sacramento, California case, in all there being some two hundred defendants. . . .
>
> On my arrival in Kansas [1923] I found that the defendant Phineas Eastman was pardoned [he was paroled]. *In my opinion he was the most vitriolic and vicious of all the defendants in the three cases* [Chicago, Sacramento, and Wichita]. . . . He was the leader of the Kansas group. [Emphasis added][68]

Thomas J. Howe's opinions were particularly important because he was responsible for indexing the evidence and preparing the final indictments in the Chicago, Omaha, and Wichita cases. He also sent evidence to Sacramento, where fellow officer George Murdock wrote the final Sacramento indictment. Both men had worked together in Chicago, and Murdock's responsibility was California and Howe's the Midwest.[69] It is not surprising, therefore, that all of the final indictments were nearly alike in all the I.W.W. cases, much of the evidence identical, and some of the same prosecution witnesses appeared in the trials. The government carefully coordinated its efforts with a few key personnel.[70] The I.W.W. also worked with a basic defense team.

Fred H. Moore had been general counsel for the I.W.W. since 1909, when he first defended Wobblies in the Spokane free speech fight of that year. In 1916, he was called to Everett, Washington, to defend members accused of murder in the so-called "Everett Massacre." He employed a local attorney, George F. Vanderveer, to assist him there and soon was joined by a neophyte lawyer and former Socialist lecturer, Caroline A. Lowe.[71] The trio won the Everett case and later formed a legal team that was to defend against federal charges in all the I.W.W. cases. Moore, however, suffered a nervous breakdown in August 1917 and mysteriously disappeared for over a year.[72] In his absence, Vanderveer became chief counsel at the Chicago trial, assisted by Lowe and Otto Christensen, among others. While they were engaged with the Chicago defense, an elderly Oklahoma attorney, R. H. Towne, defended both the Omaha and Wichita defendants.[73] After the Chicago case, Moore reappeared and was assigned to Kansas and Oklahoma. At various times he was assisted by Vanderveer, Towne, and Christensen, but he and Caroline Lowe basically defended the Wichita I.W.W. Towne, however, handled the first indictment.

On March 14, 1918, the Wichita defendants were indicted for the first time. Charged with conspiracy to violate various wartime measures including the Selective Service, Espionage, and Lever acts, the men were held on high bail.[74] Towne filed a motion to quash the indictment, which was exactly what the government wanted because Robertson had been ordered not to commence his case until the Chicago trial was completed.[75] Judge John C. Pollock ordered a continuance of the case until September, giving both adversaries time to answer and file new motions.[76] When September arrived a new indictment was filed.

On September 24, 1918, the second indictment was delivered. The charges were expanded, but basically the case against the defendants remained unchanged.[77] Towne, Moore, and Lowe filed objections, but the case was set for trial in March 1919. Vanderveer came to Wichita to defend the the men in March, filed more objections, and arguments were to be heard by June 1919.[78] In June, the third indictment was delivered.

Judge Pollock quashed the second indictment early in June, and Robertson quickly assembled a new grand jury. On June 7, the new indictment was drawn listing four counts of conspiracy and modeled very closely after the Chicago indictment.[79] Trial was set for September 1919. Moore hired a prominent Kansas City attorney, John Atwood, to assist him. Considered strictly a political move, Atwood was hired because he was a prominent Democratic politician, and Moore hoped that he could persuade Washington to drop the case.[80] Newly appointed U. S. Attorney General A. M. Palmer appointed a special U.S. district attorney to assist Robertson.

In August 1919, Colonel Sam B. Amidon of Wichita joined the prosecution. Amidon was also a prominent Democratic politician and personal friend of Palmer, President Wilson, and Wilson's son-in-law, McAdoo.[81] Amidon and Atwood faced each other at the September term of court, filing motion and countermotion. On the defense's request, the trial was postponed until December 1, 1919, and moved to Kansas City, Kansas.[82] However, by this time most of the defendants had been incarcerated for nearly two years awaiting trial and began to take advantage of the situation.

When the second indictment was delivered in September 1918, defendant Stephen Shurin cut his throat from ear to ear in a fit of depression over continued incarceration in the Sedgwick County Jail in Wichita.[83] Although he survived, I.W.W. complaints concerning jail conditions began to build after the attempted suicide. Defendant E. M. (Ed) Boyd complained to the National Civil Liberties Bureau (NCLB) not only about the Sedgwick County Jail, but its seemingly unique rotary unit.[84]

A section of the jail contained a rotary jail unit. The cells were constructed out of heavy sheet metal and formed a cylinder that was placed inside of another cylinder of latticework iron and steel bars. Of two-tier construction, each level contained ten wedge-shaped cells approximately two feet six inches wide at the rear, seven feet six inches at the front, and eight feet high and deep.[85] Only one combination exit-entrance was provided in the latticework, making it necessary to rotate the entire unit either to place a prisoner into it or release him. The NCLB immediately complained to the justice department about the jail conditions in Kansas generally and the rotary jail in particular. After a great deal of correspondence and denials of poor jail conditions, the justice department admitted that the Sedgwick County Jail was not fit for prisoners.[86] The NCLB, however, did not wait for the government to act and in the fall of 1918 hired Winthrop D. Lane of *Survey* to investigate Kansas's jails.[87] Lane's most startling article appeared in the fall of 1919 at about the same time the defendants were to go on trial in Wichita.[88] Because of the adverse publicity, Judge Pollock ordered an investigation of the Sedgwick County Jail and found it unfit for prisoners.[89] Undoubtedly this finding was one of the key factors in changing venue for the trial to Kansas City. Also, Lane's article was the only piece of major publicity on a national scale that the Wichita case received. However, if the article did help the defendants, other developments did not.

The employment of John Atwood by the defense failed to get the dismissal Moore had hoped for. Still believing Atwood would receive more sympathy in Kansas City than he would, Moore apparently left the preparation for trial to Atwood and left Wichita with Caroline Lowe. They went to Tulsa in October 1919 to defend Wobbly Charles Krieger against charges of the Pew dynamiting in October 1917. They were partially successful; on November 11, 1919, a Tulsa jury could not reach a verdict and was dismissed. At the same time, John Atwood resigned from the Wichita case.[90] Available evidence does not indicate why he resigned, but his decision left Moore and Lowe little time to prepare for trial on December 1, 1919.

Moore attempted to delay the trial with various motions but was overruled. He played for time by intensely examining and dismissing prospective jurors until Judge Pollock insisted that a jury be selected at the end of the fifth day of the trial.[91] The case went as expected, with the prosecution introducing evidence from the Chicago trial and many of the same witnesses who had been used there. Moore attempted to shake their testimony but for the most part failed. His greatest shortcoming, however, was with former Chicago star witness Frank G. Wermke. Wermke was a former Wobbly who testified to personal knowledge of I.W.W. violence and destruction.[92] On cross-examination, Moore damaged his case when Wermke testified to specific acts of I.W.W. sabotage in Kansas and Oklahoma. Although there is a tendency to blame Moore for bringing out this damaging testimony, George F. Vanderveer had not done any better in his cross-examination of Wermke in Chicago.[93] After nearly two weeks of prosecution testimony, the government rested its case. Moore surprised the packed courtroom by declining to offer a defense. He told reporters that his clients had voted to rely on his summation to the jury as their hope for acquittal. The case went to the jury December 18, 1919, and a verdict was reached the next day. All of the defendants were found guilty on all counts. Sentencing was on the nineteenth as follows:

C. W. Anderson, 9 years
Albert Barr, five years
A. M. Blumberg, 4 years
E. M. Boyd, 5 years
Harry Drew, four years
Phineas Eastman, 7½ years
Samuel Forbes, 5 years
Wencil Francik, 7½ years
Frank Gallagher, 8 years
O. E. Gordon, 7½ years
Fred Grau, 3 years
Morris Hecht, 5 years
Michael Sapper, 7½ years
Ernest Henning, 3 years
S. B. Hicok, 4½ years
Peter Higgins, 3½ years
E. J. Huber, 3½ years
Paul Maihak, 3 years
Harry McCarl, 3½ years
Frank Patton, 3½ years
Robert Poe, 3½ years
Carl Schnell, 3 years
Leo Stark, 4½ years
John Wallberg, 3½ years
George Wenger, 3 years
J. Gresbach, 3½ years[94]

All the men were sent to Leavenworth Federal Penitentiary immediately. However, some of them had escaped punishment. Stephen Shurin and John Caffrey were adjudicated insane and sent to the Kansas State Mental Hospital where they were soon released.[95] V. W. Lyons pleaded guilty at the end of the evidence and was sentenced to an additional day in county jail.[96] James Gossard died of influenza in October 1918.[97] The Wichita I.W.W. case was finished, or so it seemed.

Fred Moore requested ninety days to file a Bill of Exceptions for an appeal to a higher court and Judge Pollock granted his request.[98] However, Moore failed to file the motion. His major blunder did not allow the Wichita defendants to have their trial reviewed. When Haywood learned of Moore's failure to file the motion, he immediately investigated the situation. Moore was called to Chicago in April 1920 and resigned as an I.W.W. attorney.[99] Caroline Lowe maintained that Moore was not negligent but suffered from aphasia and was not responsible for his action.[100] The I.W.W.

quickly assigned Otto Christensen to the appellate work in all I.W.W. cases. Christensen argued the Wichita case before the Eighth Circuit Court of Appeals in 1921 and won a partial victory. The court overturned the first count of the indictment and thus freed twenty-one of the defendants. Judge Pollock had placed the longest sentence on the first count for these men; therefore, they were automatically released.[101] Other Wichita prisoners were released by commutation and parole in 1922 and 1923. The Christmas Amnesty of December 1923 released Wencil Francik and Frank Gallagher, the last of the Wichita prisoners.[102] Francik had refused conditional commutation of his sentence earlier in the year, and Gallagher had not been offered his freedom.[103]

The Wichita case, however, had other ramifications. In 1920, Butler County's district attorney obtained a permanent injunction against the AWIU-OWIU operating in Kansas. Eventually the I.W.W. was able to get the injunction removed through a series of related cases brought before the Kansas Supreme Court.[104] Fred Moore went on to create international publicity and notoriety for the Sacco-Vanzetti case. His personal humiliation for failing to file the Bill of Exceptions and then being dismissed by the I.W.W. after more than a decade's service must have left him in a desperate professional predicament. When approached by Elizabeth Gurley Flynn to defend Sacco and Vanzetti in 1920, he undoubtedly welcomed the case as his last hope of regaining his reputation.[105]

NOTES

1. *Defense News Bulletin* (I.W.W.), January 12, 1918. Hereafter cited as DNB.

2. Carl Coke Rister, *OIL! Titan of the Southwest* (Norman: University of Oklahoma Press, 1949), pp. 120-22, 137.

3. Ibid., p. 137.

4. Ibid.

5. H. Craig Miner, *The Fire In The Rock: A History of the Oil and Gas Industry in Kansas, 1855-1976* (North Newton, Kansas: Mennonite Press, 1976), pp. 54-67, *passim*.

6. Joyce L. Kornbluh, ed., *Rebel Voices: An I.W.W. Anthology* (Ann Arbor: University of Michigan Press, 1964), p. 252.

7. "In the Oil Fields," *International Socialist Review* (May 1914), pp. 664-67.

8. C. W. Anderson, DNB, June 1, 1918.

9. Ibid.

10. Joseph R. Conlin, *Big Bill Haywood and the Radical Union Movement* (Syracuse: Syracuse University Press, 1969), p. 172.

11. E. W. Latchem to Professor Donald J. McClurg, University of Colorado, May 1, 1963. Mr. Latchem was one of the founders of the AWO and wrote, "Earlier

Chaplin [member of the I.W.W. general executive board] had mentioned that Haywood felt that he was losing control after the upsurge of the I.W.W. as a result of the formation of the AWO No. 400." Carbon copy in the possession of Fred Thompson, Chicago, Illinois.

12. DNB, June 1, 1918.

13. Transcript, *U.S.* v. *C. W. Anderson et al.*, Pardon Attorney File No. 39-242, Records of the Pardon Attorney, Record Group 204, National Archives Washington, D.C., pp. 151, 158, and 159. This document is the only known trial transcript of the Wichita I.W.W. case but does not contain the exhibits.

14. "Prison File and Photograph of Phineas M. Eastman," Federal Penitentiary, Leavenworth, Kansas.

15. *St. Tammany Farmer* (Covington, Louisiana), December 24, 1937. Eastman obituary.

16. "Phineas Eastman File," Records of the Pardon Attorney, Record Group 204, National Archives, Washington, D.C. This file contains over 150 pages of letters, petitions, and various documents, many of which are in Eastman's own handwriting. Hereafter cited as Eastman Pardon File.

17. Ibid.

18. Ibid.

19. *Kansas City Times*, December 13, 1919. This was an exhibit or evidence used in the Wichita trial and reported by the press. The Kansas City newspapers are the only known source of most of the exhibits that do not appear in the trial transcript.

20. *Kansas City Star*, December 12, 1919.

21. Phineas Eastman, "The Southern Negro and One Big Union," *International Socialist Review* (June 1913) pp. 890, 891.

22. Merl E. Reed, "The I.W.W. And Individual Freedom in Western Louisiana, 1913," *Louisiana History* 10 (Winter 1967), 64.

23. "Parole Report," U. S. District Attorney Fred Robertson to Parole Board President Dickerson, February 9, 1920, Official Letters Sent by U. S. Attorneys, Record Group 118, Federal Records Center, Kansas City, Missouri. These reports were actually written by Chicago Department of Justice Agent Thomas J. Howe. Hereafter cited as Parole Report.

24. Eastman Pardon File.

25. *U.S.* v. *C. W. Anderson et al.*

26. Ibid.

27. *Kansas City Star*, December 13, 1919.

28. Fred Robertson to A. F. Williams, December 1, 1921, Eastman Pardon File.

29. *Kansas City Star*, December 12, 1919.

30. Thomas J. Howe to Claude R. Porter, November 4, 1918, Case File Number 189152, General Records of the Department of Justice, Record Group 60, National Archives, Washington, D.C. Hereafter all documents in this group will be cited as DJ 189152.

31. Harrison George, *The I. W. W. Trial: Story of the Greatest Trial in Labor's History by one of the Defendants* (Chicago: I.W.W. Publishing Bureau, n.d.; reprint ed., New York: Arno Press, 1969), p. 97.

32. Phineas Eastman to Ned Rightor, April 3, 1921, Eastman Pardon File.

33. "Application For Executive Clemency," October 10, 1921, Eastman Pardon File.

34. Kornbluh, *Rebel Voices*, pp. 317, 318.

35. *Kansas City Times*, December 13, 1919.

36. *U.S.* v. *C. W. Anderson et al.*, pp. 677-87, *passim*.

37. Parole Report, 9 February 1920.

38. *U.S.* v. *C. W. Anderson et al.*, p. 922.

39. Eastman Pardon File.

40. George, *The I.W.W. Trial*, p. 11.

41. "Prison File and Photograph of C. W. Anderson" and Parole Report.

42. Parole Report.

43. Ibid. and "Prison File and Photograph of Oscar E. Gordon."

44. "Prison File and Photograph of Wencil Francik," and personal letter from Catherine Francik Leehman, March 31, 1977. Mrs. Leehman is Francik's niece and remembered his frightening appearance and voice when he visited her parents' home in the 1920s.

45. "Prison File and Photograph of Michael Sapper."

46. Frank Gallagher to C. W. Anderson, October 31, 1917, PA 39-242.

47. *U.S.* v. *C. W. Anderson et al.*, pp. 193, 194, 402.

48. Ibid., pp. 920, 921, and "Information," *State of Oklahoma* v. *Charles Krieger*, Criminal Case No. 1576, County District Court, Tulsa, Oklahoma, Tulsa County Court House, Tulsa, Oklahoma.

49. Tulsa victim E. M. Boyd to the National Civil Liberties Bureau, undated, American Civil Liberties Union Papers, Princeton University Library, New Jersey, volume 35. Hereafter cited as ACLU.

50. Numerous letters, reports, and personal accounts of the "Tulsa Outrage," ACLU vols. 28, 35.

51. "Indictment," *U. S.* v. *C. W. Anderson et al.*, June 7, 1919, U. S. District Court, Wichita, Kansas, Federal Records Center, Kansas City, Missouri, pp. 24, 25.

52. Ibid., p. 26.

53. Ibid., p. 27.

54. Ibid., pp. 29, 30.

55. C. W. Anderson to Arthur Boose, October 28, 1917, Parole Report.

56. "Search Warrant," *U. S.* v. *Phineas Eastman*, November 19, 1917, DJ 189152.

57. Clayton R. Koppes, "The Kansas Trial Of The I.W.W., 1917-1919," *Labor History* 16 (Summer 1975), 339 and 340, and William Preston, Jr., *Aliens and Dissenters: Federal Suppression of Radicals, 1903-1933* (Cambridge: Harvard University Press, 1963; Harper Torchbooks, 1966), pp. 130, 131.

58. Preston, *Aliens and Dissenters*, pp. 130, 131.

59. "Amnesty for Political Prisoners," *Testimony of Caroline A. Lowe before House Judiciary Committee on H. Res. 60*, 67th Cong., 2d sess., p. 32.

60. *U.S.* v. *C. W. Anderson et al.*, pp. 390-414.

61. Robertson to attorney general, August 17, 1917, DJ 189152.

62. Preston, *Aliens and Dissenters*, pp. 93, 110.

63. *Denver Post*, November 21, 1917.

64. Charles Bush, "The Green Corn Rebellion" (M.A. thesis, University of Oklahoma, 1932), p. 53.

65. William C. Fitts to Fred Robertson, November 23, 1917, DJ 189152. This was the first time the Wichita case was given a department of justice case file number. Previously correspondence was filed under the Chicago case file number 186701 and at a later date was renumbered as 189152. This is a clear indication that with this letter Washington decided to initiated a separate I.W.W. prosecution in Wichita.

66. *Kansas City Star*, December 13, 1919.

67. Robertson to Williams, December 1, 1921, Eastman Pardon File.

68. Howe to U.S. Pardon Attorney James Finch, April 2, 16, 1923, Pardon Attorney File No. 39-242.

69. Howe to Porter, September 25, 1918, DJ 189152.

70. William C. Fitts, Claude R. Porter, Robert P. Stewart, George Murdock, and Thomas J. Howe were directly responsible for all the federal prosecutions of the I.W.W.

71. Lowell S. Hawley and Ralph Bushnell Potts, *Counsel For The Damned: A Biography of George Francis Vanderveer* (Philadelphia: J. B. Lippincott Co., 1953), pp. 182-89.

72. Fred H. Moore's widow, Lola D. Moore, to Eugene Lyons, February 4, 1937. Original in the possession of Mr. Lyons, New York, New York.

73. Howe to Porter, November 4, 1918, DJ 189152.

74. "Indictment," *U.S.* v. *C. W. Anderson et al.*, March 14, 1918, U.S. District Court, Wichita, Kansas, Federal Records Center, Kansas City, Missouri.

75. Fitts to Robertson, January 21, 1918, DJ 189152.

76. "Order," *U.S.* v. *C. W. Anderson et al.*, March 16, 1918.

77. "Indictment," *U.S.* v. *C. W. Anderson et al.*, September 24, 1918, U.S. District Court, Wichita, Kansas, Federal Records Center, Kansas City, Missouri.

78. *Wichita Eagle*, March 15, 1919.

79. "Indictment," *U.S.* v. *C. W. Anderson et al.*, June 7, 1919, U.S. District Court, Wichita, Kansas, Federal Records Center, Kansas City, Missouri.

80. Fred H. Moore to Roger Baldwin, July 24, 1919, ACLU vol. 86.

81. *Wichita Eagle*, May 9, 1925. Amidon obituary.

82. Ibid., September 26, 1919.

83. *New Solidarity* (I.W.W.), November 16, 1918.

84. Boyd to Baldwin, October 1918, ACLU vol. 89.

85. "Architectural Plans Sedgwick County Jail," Pauly Jail Co. Archives, St. Louis, Missouri.

86. Numerous letters between National Civil Liberties Bureau and Department of Justice officials, ACLU vol. 89.

87. Albert DeSilver to Fred Moore, November 20, 1918, ACLU vol. 89.

88. Winthrop D. Lane, "What's the Matter with Kansas? Its Jails! Uncle Sam: Jailer," *Survey* (September 6, 1919), 806-12, 834.

89. *Wichita Eagle*, September 24, 1919.

90. Atwood may have been pressured by the government to quit because Amidon complained to Attorney General Palmer that Atwood was also a Special U.S. District Attorney in another case and did not think it proper to have the I.W.W. defended by a U.S. Attorney. Amidon to attorney general, September 5, 1919, DJ 189152.

91. *Kansas City Star*, December 4, 1919.

92. Transcript, p. 745 and following pages.

93. The Chicago defendants were still found guilty despite Vanderveer's efforts to shake Wermke's testimony.

94. *Kansas City Times*, December 19, 1919.

95. Personal letter from Osawatomie State Hospital, January 5, 1976. Caffrey was discharged February 27, 1920, and Shurin June 18, 1920.

96. *Kansas City Star*, December 19, 1919.

97. *New Solidarity* (I.W.W.), November 16, 1918.

98. *Kansas City Times*, December 19, 1919.

99. William D. Haywood to Roger Baldwin, May 5, 1920, ACLU vol. 136.

100. Caroline Lowe to Albert DeSilver, May 11, 1920, ACLU vol. 136.

101. *Anderson et al.* v. *United States*, 273 F. 20 (Eighth Circuit Court, 1921).

102. "Announcement," December 15, 1923, U.S. President, *Calvin Coolidge Papers,* Library of Congress, Washington, D.C., Case File 111.

103. "Report," attorney general to President Harding, June 19, 1923, PA 39-242.

104. See annotations in *Kansas Statutes Annotated*, sec. 21-301.

105. Elizabeth Gurley Flynn, *The Rebel Girl: An Autobiography—My First Life (1906-1926)*, rev. ed. Edited by James S. Allen. (New York: International Publishers, 1973), pp. 302-3, 311.

PART THREE

THE I.W.W.
AFTER THE FALL

YAKIMA AND THE WOBBLIES, 1910-1936

JAMES G. NEWBILL

> They had made piles all along the edge of the field . . . and soon the air was
> full of flying rocks, up to fistsize. . . . You took that old sledgehammer and
> you let somebody have it, just putting it as hard as you could go. They were
> just layin' all over. . . . You had to step over 'em to get through anywhere.
> . . . They were that thick on the pavement . . . both sides.[1]

These observations were made by two of the participants in the "Congdon
orchards battle" of August 24, 1933, the most dramatic confrontation
between strikers and farmers in the history of the Yakima Valley. The
defeated I.W.W.-led strikers were marched five miles to town by their
farmer escort and placed in a hastily built stockade. The prisoners were held
there until mid-December, when their lawyer negotiated their release.
Attendant on the Congdon situation were the mobilization of the national
guard, the full participation of the state patrol, surveillance of the railroad
and highways, and the organizing of farmer groups from one end of the
valley to the other.

In many ways this climactic event represented the immediate frustrations
and hopes of depression-burdened farmers, of underpaid fruit workers, and
of a very small but still militant union, the Industrial Workers of the World.
But the battle also has a larger significance. Therefore, Part I of this chapter
will briefly describe a number of confrontations with the I.W.W. in Yakima
prior to 1933. Part II sketches several labor problems in early 1933. Part
III is a description of fruit rancher-laborer difficulties in July and August
1933, immediately before the Congdon incident, and Part IV deals with the
actual battle and its aftermath. A final section consists of conclusions.[2]

I

The 1933 Congdon battle was not an isolated incident in Yakima Valley history. It was the successor to a series of earlier disputes between local residents and the itinerant workers who were often led by the I.W.W. These disputes began before World War I.

The rapid increase of I.W.W. activity and notoriety from its 1905 beginnings is well known, as is the fact that Washington state was the scene of significant Wobbly action. In 1909, there was a strike of farm laborers in Waterville and the famous Wobbly free speech fight in Spokane. In 1910, "small 'fights' were conducted in the spring and summer in Wenatchee and Walla Walla, . . ."[3] Yakima had its contact with the I.W.W. in 1910; local reactions were reflected in the newspaper headline: "Industrial Workers Not Wanted."[4] It seems that two Wobblies, Joseph Gordon and John W. Foss, had attempted to speak on Front Street[5] but were arrested and fined for vagrancy. Their pleas that they were exercising their constitutional rights of free speech fell on deaf ears, but it seems that their statement that they had a permit from the mayor did not. Police Chief William Kelly replied, "You didn't have any permit from me." When Foss tried to explain the situation, Judge Bounds interrupted, "That is the trouble with you fellows; you explain too much." They were to work off their fines while in jail, but the two Wobblies and five other prisoners refused. Chief Kelly immediately separated Foss and Gordon from the other five and the two were given bread and water. Kelly then carried out Judge Bounds's instructions to shackle them with ball and chain so that they would, as the local paper put it, "experience as many as possible of the sensations of working."[6]

According to Brissenden, 1912 was the "high tide of I.W.W. activity" but the wave only hit Yakima in 1916. The Wobblies had established temporary headquarters on Front Street in September and had evidently begun organization activities when eleven were arrested by the police. Ranchers had complained about the I.W.W. hindering their hiring activities on Front Street. The local hatred for the union is revealed by the *Yakima Morning Herald*'s alarmist headline, "Anarchistic Body Is Nipped in Bud," and by Judge R. B. Milroy's admonition to the eleven men, "There is no room in North Yakima [then the name of the city] for an I.W.W. camp."[7] The men were finally released, the judge warning them to work while they were in town. Less than a week later, Police Chief McCurdy secured a letter written by an I.W.W. leader in Spokane, a letter that grandiosely threatened Yakima with "twenty thousand members of the Industrial Workers of the World . . . if activity of the organization are [sic] interfered with." The police chief said no "agitation" would be allowed and that 100 businessmen and other citizens had volunteered to assist the police. Mayor

Barton declared that, if necessary, invaders would be deported forcefully.[8]

A major confrontation occurred at 7:30 P.M. on September 24. The Wobblies were having a street gathering at Second Street and Yakima Avenue. The police tried to stop the singing and speeches, finally arresting several participants. However, the police were confronted with a standard Wobbly free speech tactic of immediately replacing each arrested speaker with another, who usually got no further than "Brothers, . . ." when he would be arrested—to be replaced by yet another volunteer. This went on until forty-six were arrested, placed in commandeered autos, and carted off to jail. The fervor of the Wobblies did not subside in jail; they made so much noise that the guards had to remove the other prisoners who were "liberally decorated with I.W.W. stickers." The Wobblies also threatened that Yakima soon would be hit with a "flying Squadron" of them. The next morning the prisoners broke out of their cells, and fire hoses were called into play. Two hundred local citizens gathered, armed with pick and axe handles, and then marched to the jail. They took the prisoners to the nearby railroad yards and loaded them into two refrigerator cars, but the railroad would not move the cars. Thwarted, the vigilantes took the prisoners back to jail and the city authorities.[9]

They were brought before Judge Milroy and given jail sentences of fifteen to thirty days and "were made to understand that the real charge against them was they were members of the I.W.W." The judge said, "We are running things here. We don't want you to butt in and tell us what to do. The people here don't want your organization. You can't organize here." When some of the men contended that their constitutional rights were being abridged, the judge responded that "the majority rules. That's one of the fundamental things in the constitution. The majority of the people here don't want your organization and you can't organize here." Several days later a committee of local citizens, including a minister and two labor officials, met with the mayor and emphasized that the prisoners were being deprived of their rights. They pointed out that the Salvation Army was not disturbed in its street meetings. After several days of such negotiations with the committee and with the prisoners, it was agreed that the prisoners were to work or leave town and that the I.W.W would not hold street meetings. The men were then released singly from the jail.[10]

"It is accurate to say that it was World War I that did in the I.W.W.," writes Joseph Conlin. War hysteria found the I.W.W. a favorite target. Some critics called them "Imperial Wilhelm's Warriors."[11] The famous I.W.W. conspiracy trial occurred in 1918 in Chicago and resulted in long prison terms for the national leaders of the union. Any organizational or strike efforts by the I.W.W. during this period were greeted with suspicion or, most generally, open hostility. This was certainly true in 1917 in the Pacific Northwest and specifically in Yakima. Throughout July and August, the Yakima papers carried front-page stories, often highlighted with two-column headlines, of I.W.W. activities throughout the nation. Whether it was a strike in the mines of Pennsylvania or in the lumber mills of Washington, the tone was obviously critical and strongly suggested that there was some involvement with the German war effort.

This fear of internal subversion during the war led to the sending of federal troops to Yakima. During the morning of July 9, 1917, they raided the local I.W.W. hall on Front Street, arrested forty-four Wobblies, and confiscated the literature found in the hall. According to the local paper, the prisoners were to be charged by federal authorities with "interfering with the production and harvesting of crops." The editor supported the arrests, explaining that free speech "does not mean that any radical may promote anarchy and lawlessness. There is such a thing as abuse of free speech. . . . The present war crisis has brought the danger and this danger must be suppressed." The next day's headlines referred to "I.W.W. Agitators . . ." and a "Reign of Terror in Idaho." There were also articles describing vigilante actions. All of the valley's railroads and major highways were being patrolled, with transients being questioned. The Yakima Valley Producers' Protective Association had organized in every community in Kittitas, Benton, and Yakima counties with its members prepared to resist the I.W.W. "threat" by physical means if necessary. A page-one article in the *Herald* editorially commented that "Yakima, according to all reports, has set the pace for the nation in the handling of the I.W.W. situation."[12]

The Yakima raid was coordinated with similar efforts throughout the state. Simultaneous raids were made in Ellensburg and Cle Elum. All railroad passes and tunnels were patrolled by troops who were to arrest anyone stealing rides on trains. A state council of defense was organized with chairmen appointed in each county. The governors of the states of Washington, Oregon, Idaho, Montana, Utah, and Wyoming conferred and discussed special sessions of their state legislatures "to empower the authorities to proceed vigorously in controlling any I.W.W. disturbance."[13]

The Wobblies imprisoned in Yakima hardly were passive spectators at these events. They sang their songs, tried to pass messages about I.W.W. reinforcements, and on July 29, almost three weeks after being arrested without charge, they demonstrated in jail. Some damage was caused before order was restored by several soldiers with drawn pistols and bayonets. Seattle attorney George F. Vandeveer was retained by the Seattle and Spokane I.W.W. locals to defend the Yakima Wobblies. He concentrated his efforts on the fact that no formal charge had been brought against the prisoners, and he claimed there was no federal law under which they could be charged. The army slowly released the prisoners after each signed a "statement to the effect that he will remain at useful employment and avoid agitation among workers." A few days after the release of the prisoners, a threatened I.W.W. strike was greeted by equally ominous "summary action" by local county officials and ranchers. The strike did not materialize.[14]

The last overt I.W.W. incidents in Yakima before 1933 occurred in 1919 and 1920. Seven men were arrested in November and December of 1919 for "criminal syndicalism." Five were brought to trial and found guilty in June 1920. They were sentenced to two to ten years at the Walla Walla Federal Penitentiary.[15] However, the convicted men's lawyers, one of whom was George Vandeveer, appealed the case to the state supreme court, and the decision was reversed on the grounds that "hearsay evidence" was used. This was April 1921, and the Yakima County prosecutor subsequently had the case dismissed since the prisoners had been in jail for almost the duration of their minimum sentence.[16]

The preceding incidents indicate quite clearly that Yakima, like many parts of the country, had a strong anti-I.W.W. tradition long before 1933. This tradition was reinforced by local elected and police officials who were willing to use their positions against the Wobblies and by local private citizens who, on at least two occasions—in 1916 and 1917—formed vigilante groups or "protective associations" to prevent Wobbly organizational and strike activities.

II

A combination of depression economics and racism led to mass meetings and eventual violence in the spring of 1933. These events, which occurred in the Lower Yakima Valley, are mentioned because they point out that the dire farm problems of 1933 did produce almost spontaneous mass meetings and then violence almost six months before the Congdon orchards battle. The one main difference between the two situations was the "opponent" the farmers faced. In Wapato, it was the contracted Filipino workers and, to a lesser extent, the local Japanese; in August it would be the I.W.W.[17]

The first overt act in the Wapato area occurred the evening of March 1, when 250 farmers met in order to discuss action agaiont Filipino workers and the Japanese who often employed them. Walter Brandt, who was elected secretary of the group, said, "We want no trouble if it can be avoided, but we are determined that the Filipino must go. . . . They are taking jobs that belong to white men, contributing nothing to the support of the community and are an undesirable element." He added, "Our activities right now are devoted only to getting rid of the Filipinos. However, if we are successful with this we will probably turn our attention to the Japanese problem." It was also reported that the Filipinos were not only unfair competition with white labor, but were "mingling" with white women. Nine three-man committees of farmers were formed to "call on" local farmers to "demand" that they refuse to hire Filipinos.[18]

A week later another meeting of 200 Wapato area farmers met to hear the reports of their nine committees. Cooperation was general, it was reported; however, "strong-arm methods would be resorted to in the event [further] negotiations failed. Loud cheers greeted a proposal that all produce harvested by Filipinos be dumped and destroyed." A petition to various state and federal officials condemned the presence of Filipinos and Japanese as "creating an ever increasing problem for the white farmers and laborers." The petition also pointed out that the living standards of these minority groups "are such that the white men are unable to compete with them either in farming or labor." The reference to the Japanese led one farmer to blurt out, "The Japanese situation is just as bad as the Filipino's [sic]. They don't pay any taxes and they live cheaper than we do." Third and fourth meetings were held in the next few weeks. It was reported that the speeches were fiery, threats were made, and "mob action was narrowly averted."[19]

In late March and early April, the "direct action" included the burning of six tons of hay and the bombing of property (a truck, house, shed, and fence) owned by Japanese who employed Filipinos. In less than a week the county sheriffs had arrested seven Wapato men, two of them elected officials of the earlier farmers' meetings. Several of them eventually pleaded guilty to charges of "unlawful use of explosives" and second-degree arson.[20] That ended the mass meetings in Wapato and the violent destruction of Filipino and Japanese property. There would continue to be opposition to these people, but it did not produce such violence.

The Wapato situation had barely subsided when trouble broke out in the hop fields, trouble that would set the stage for the confrontations in the fruit ranches. The center of the hop industry then and now was Moxee, a small community about five miles east of Yakima. There was also considerable acreage in hops in the Ahtanum Valley and around Selah, but the Moxee and Terrace Heights farmers were the principal targets of the I.W.W.-led strikers.

On May 16, one hundred pickets appeared at the B. D. McKelheer hop yard. Smaller numbers picketed other yards, including some in Selah. It seems that most of the pickets were local people, but it is clear that the strike was organized and led by the I.W.W. An article in the *Industrial Worker* described the low pay in several of Yakima's industries, including hops, and concluded, "This is a good place for a few IU No. 110 [Agricultural Workers' 'Industrial Union'] to get busy and start a little action. In the next issue, another article concluded, "But, look out hop growers, the I.W.W. will organize your slaves. . . . So come on, fellow workers. Help organize the hop workers and give us a hand in this battle for the cause. Get in the box car and via for Yakima Valley."[21] A report by Joe Clohessy, an organizing official of IU No. 110 and one of those arrested later at the Congdon orchards battle, was filed at the June 1 Annual Spring Conference of the union. Clohessy wrote, "Already a campaign of organizational work is taking place in the Yakima hop fields where a strike has taken place among the hop pickers. This is an I.W.W. strike with I.W.W. tactics being used that promises to being good results in the near future. A call went out from those members holding the firing line in Yakima for men and money. The #110 members in Omaha [at the annual conference] not having money, did the next best thing—twenty-five members are rushing to Yakima to re-enforce *[sic]* those already on the firing line." The IU No. 110 conference also passed motions transferring their drive to the state of Washington and told Clohessy to notify Frank Grad, also to be arrested at the Congdon fight, that "#110 is coming and to hold the fort in the meantime."[22] Further and more important evidence of the Wobbly role was the fact that a number of the pickets who were eventually arrested were card-carrying members of the I.W.W.

The strikers, through their signs and handbills, demanded an eight-hour day, an end to child labor in the yards, and a minimum wage of thirty-five cents an hour for both men and women. It was, of course, this last demand that really rankled the growers as the current wage for common labor was ten to twelve cents an hour. Although the hop growers did raise wages to twelve and one-half cents, they were adamant in their assertion that they could afford no more. The Wobblies contended that the growers were reaping big profits as a result of the end of Prohibition and that they could easily afford to pay much more. This controversy must be examined in some detail.

A congressional act legalized 3.2 percent beer and wine on April 7, 1933. By June 22, fourteen states had repealed the Eighteenth Amendment, and the electorate in nineteen more were scheduled to vote by November 7. Washington State's decision was set for August 29. The effect on hop prices was dramatic. They sold for eleven to fourteen cents a pound in 1932. In April and May of 1933, valley papers reported sales of the remaining uncommitted 1932 crops at forty to fifty cents, and the *Yakima Morning Herald*, in its "Local Markets" column, showed prices going to seventy-five cents for about a month. Twenty to thirty cents was being paid for the forthcoming 1933 crop. Three- and four-year contracts were being signed for eighteen to twenty-five cents. These prices help to explain this somewhat jealous comment by the editor of the *Zillah Mirror* (Zillah was and is a fruit-growing area twenty miles from Yakima): "The paper says that farmers over in Moxee have paid off the delinquent drainage bonds since the advent of 3.2% beer. Just wait until the new hop yards come into bearing and those guys will pay off the entire national debt, besides paying last year's taxes."[23]

The hop farmers argued that few of them were profiting from the high prices on the remaining 1932 crop, that they had lost money for several years, and that "The hop game is an up and down gamble." They were certainly correct in describing earlier low prices and in predicting fluctuations in the price—in 1934 the price slipped to about twenty-five cents, still a profitable figure, and in 1935 to eight cents with earlier contracts being canceled for a fraction of their original value. But their optimism was still strong enough in the spring and summer of 1933 to spend $80,000 on nineteen new kilns. At any rate, for reasons imagined or real, the hop growers refused to pay more than twelve and one-half cents an hour, and they combined their strength with those of the authorities to make the picketing largely ineffective.[24]

On May 17, the second day of the strike, Sheriff Lew Evans and Prosecuting Attorney Olaf Sandvig contacted Washington State Patrol Chief William Cole, asking for immediate aid. Twenty-two officers were on hand the next morning. They and county sheriffs moved in on the pickets who "molested" workers trying to enter the hop yards. The local paper reported, "Some of the pickets would jump upon running boards of a car, grab the wheel of the machine and turn off the switch." Eight pickets were arrested and charged with either trespassing or unlawful assembly. The sheriff's office indicated that picketing would be allowed as long as there was no "abusing persons, calling profane names or threatening or interfering with persons going about their work." Picketing continued without interruption until May 31, when three carloads of sheriffs' deputies, aided by a special deputy hired by the hop growers, arrested eighteen pickets at the Andrew Slavin ranch in Moxee. "Shouts of 'You're nothing but dirty scabs,' 'You're taking the food away from our women and children by working for such wages,' and profane and obscene remarks addressed to persons working along the edges of the hopfields preceded the arrest."[25]

The I.W.W. had retained attorney Mark M. Litchman, an experienced defender of labor groups, including the Wobblies. He and Claude Erwin, an I.W.W. official, immediately contacted the prosecutor, and a compromise was arranged whereby all pickets were to be released on their own recognizance with future picketing to be by pairs separated from others by at least twenty-five feet. Also, "officers of the law . . . [must] confer with the strikers when the farmers phone in their complaints, instead of coming out to arrest the strikers on such information." Litchman suggested to the prosecuting attorney and the sheriff that he would like to talk to the hop growers to see if he could bring about "a peaceful settlement of the strike." He got no response from the growers. The strike had run its course with little success against the organized efforts of growers, sheriffs, state patrol, and the sympathy of Yakima's chamber of commerce. The effect of the strike efforts—and of the burning of several hop kilns, presumably by arsonists—put all farmers on their guard against more strike activity.[26]

Before moving away from the hop ranches, it is necessary to emphasize the very active role taken by the law enforcement officers, a role repeated in August during the picketing of fruit ranches. First, the Yakima sheriffs were very sympathetic to the hop growers' position. Lew Evans was sheriff and H. T. "Army" Armstrong the chief criminal deputy. Both of them were in telephone and written contact with State Patrol Chief William Cole. It was Armstrong who contacted the local growers to send letters to Governor Clarence Martin, thanking him for the help of the state patrol, and it was Armstrong who reported attending a meeting of Moxee growers to encourage them to finance a night hop patrol. He commented in a letter to Cole, "Many of the growers request that a force of at least six men be here during the harvest as some eight thousand savages, head hunters, niggers, and whites will be in the valley."[27]

William Cole was appointed patrol chief by newly elected Governor Clarence Martin. The patrol had just recently been given powers to make arrests for crimes other than traffic violations. The new chief used this new power very widely in 1933 and 1934, particularly against any "agitators." In a typical "memo" from Cole to Governor Martin, the patrol chief states,

The committee sent to Port Angeles from the strike headquarters was taken care of and I don't believe there will be a strike called at that point. The strike delegation sent to Yakima and Wenatchee have been taken care of and I feel those two places will be quiet until the hop picking in Yakima. I am keeping in touch with all strike delegations being sent to other counties and see they are received in the proper manner before they have time to incite a strike.[28]

The Clarence Martin papers and the state patrol's "General Correspondence of 1931-1934" contain numerous "memos" and letters from Cole indicating that he was closely following the meetings and the movements of any group of "agitators," be they Socialists, Communists, or Wobblies. During the years 1933 and 1934, in addition to the places mentioned in the previous quotation, Cole also reported either watching or impeding the activities of various groups in Grays Harbor, Aberdeen, Astoria, Bellingham, Cle Elum, Everett, Spokane, Seattle, Tacoma, Olympia, Whatcom County, and Skagit County.

III

Although the June 3 hop strike had been called off, the I.W.W. was anything but discouraged. A. J. Farley,[29] the I.W.W's "stationary delegate" in Yakima, in a June 16 letter to the Chicago headquarters wrote,

Send me ten blank job credentials as we need them badly here. Everything looks rosey here for a good organizational drive. All the old members are certainly surprised with all the sentiment for the I.W.W. Very large attentive street meetings and getting line-ups at every one of them. We are lining up meetings in every town around here. The slaves are waking up here. They want to do something.

And at least eleven public meetings were held in late June, July, and August in Naches, Toppenish, Wapato, Buena, Selah, and Yakima.[30]

The *Industrial Worker*'s editorial staff, headed by Ralph Chaplin, obviously did all they could to focus attention on Yakima and encourage I.W.W. efforts there. Between May 2, 1933, and January 23, 1934, the weekly newspaper contained hard-hitting and often front-page articles in every issue but two. The "articles" were usually editorials and revealed the determination to win in the Yakima Valley. This concluding paragraph of a three-column front-page article entitled, "Yakima Valley Agricultural Slaves Looking to AWIU 110 For Pro-Worker Organization," is typical of their enthusiasm: "This summer promises to be a great season for Yakima. With the four thousand slaves in the valley confused with the I.W.W. on one side, and the reactionary farmer and the local benighted petty bourgoisie on the other. It will be great fun."[31] It turned out to be anything but fun for the Wobblies.

On August 14, several dozen men (estimates vary from a few dozen to 100) parked their cars at the Sunnyside Canal bridge on Lombard Loop. The spot is two miles north of Sawyer or about fifteen miles down the valley from Yakima. Some of these men drove onto the neighboring Anna Mitchell place where the peach harvest was in progress and, after asking for the foreman, went into the orchard where they talked to the pickers about wages. One of the men blew several blasts on a whistle and they left the orchard, returning the short distance to the canal bridge. Mrs. Mitchell's pickers left their work, too, most of them stopping at her packing shed where they indicated that they would return to work when the visitors were gone. Mrs. Mitchell's foreman, her nephew Edgar, drove past the bridge on his way to Sawyer and remembers the men as not being residents of the area. One of the ranchers described them as "total strangers" and as "a rough looking bunch of middle aged, older men."[32] The men at the bridge tried to discourage other workers from crossing the bridge, and a speech was given from a truck.

Using the party-line telephone system, word was quickly spread among the neighboring farmers who gathered on both sides of the strikers, soon outnumbering them. Both sides were armed with various homemade clubs or tree limbs. Cecil Clark, one of the farmer leaders, said:

We told them to move on. "We don't have to. There is no law to compel it," they replied. "Oh, yes there is," I answered. "We just passed it" and proceeded to force them to move out, which they reluctantly did. . . . One big burley customer said, "No S. O. B. is going to make me go." So, brother Ted [another farmer] and I took him on. "Throw him in the canal. That will cool him off," I told the boys. He was a hard man for even the three of us to handle. Some not too hard wollops *[sic]* on the shins with a pick handle helped to subdue him. In the hassel *[sic]* his pants were mostly torn off and without underwear he was not exactly presentable. "I'll go," he said and we let him loose to head down through Cronkhite's orchard.[33]

Cecil's younger brother, Ted, seemed to be sympathetic to Mrs. Mitchell. "If they want to pick on men—fine," he said, "but if they wandered down there and pick on a widow woman, we'd help her. We did." He described his role in the fracas by saying, "This guy didn't move out and he got it right across the seat of his pants [with a mop stick]. He moved out! We were young and tough . . . 23 years old and I was a pretty tough farm boy."[34]

The only thing the strike effort accomplished was to complete the organization of valley farmers, a process that had begun months before "when signs of labor trouble first appeared." Farmers from Grandview (fifty miles down the valley) to Lower Naches (ten miles above Yakima) were meeting, dividing the valley into districts, appointing leaders, and securing weapons. One hundred and fifty growers around Sawyer gathered right after the Mitchell ranch fight and issued a formal statement stating, in part,

Certain individuals have seen fit to invade our premises and to threaten and intimidate workers in an effort to prevent harvesting our crops. Regardless of any grievances that these individuals may have against society, we assert that the responsibility for their misfortune does not belong to us because we have paid labor its fair share of what our crops have sold for, and we still are. In view of the belligerency manifested by malcontents in threatening our lives and property, we have no recourse but to defend out belongings to our utmost ability and resources.

The same message, though stated more bluntly, was given by another rancher: "We do not intend to let a bunch of hoodlums run our business and we are not going to tolerate interferences with the labor we hire. We are paying as high wages as we can possibly pay in view of economic conditions."[35] On August 15 and 16, the I.W.W. made attempts to mobilize strikes in the Lower Valley, but they were completely unsuccessful. The well-organized farmers, now aided by the county sheriffs and the state patrol, were just too strong.

Were the ranchers' pleas valid? Could they have easily raised wages from ten or twenty cents an hour to the thirty-five or fifty cents demanded by the I.W.W.? The answer would be emphatically no according to several farmers who looked back the thirty-five to forty years to the Great Depression. Cecil Clark, whose ranch was north of Sawyer, said that tempers were high in the valley because the farmers' livelihood was being threatened. He wrote, "Those were tough times. . . . Ranchers were struggling as hard for survival as were the workers." Carroll Hull still has the fruit ranch he owned when he helped escort the defeated Wobblies to town after the Congdon fight. Hull, discussing the economics of the time, said that money was so scarce that he finally got to the point of giving "time slips" to his employees which they would exchange for food at the nearby Ahtanum store. Chad Karr's father, Arthur, was one of the leaders of the Congdon farmers. Chad writes, "About twenty years ago I saw his financial statement for 1934 which showed a net worth of minus $8,000. Some of the orchard property was in my mother's name; otherwise, the family would probably would have been forced into bankruptcy." Arthur Karr's daughter, Mrs. Jane Van Eaton, said that her father's place was mortgaged to the limit and that he finally had to go to the Home Owners Loan Corporation for money. Charles Morrison and his sons still have fruit orchards in the Buena area where, in 1933, he and his employees were prepared to physically confront the Wobblies who picketed a nearby ranch. Discussing finances, Morrison said,

We had heard about the I.W.W.'s who were dissatisfied, and as I look back on it now you couldn't blame them for being dissatisfied with wages . . . because the farmers at that time were absolutely broke. We couldn't pay our taxes. . . . It got to the point where I told those I was buying from, "if you want to take the land, why go ahead and take it. I can't do anything about it. . . . But if you want me to take care of it until we see what is going to happen, why I'll do my best. When I get something, I'll share it with you." So, all the fellows I was buying from—six or seven real estate contracts at that time—[said] "keep it." So, we were strung tight-as-a-wire, of course, And it didn't get any better until 1940.[36]

These plaints appear to have been justified. The Yakima Valley fruit rancher had been in dire economic straits for several years before the summer of 1933. Although the prices of some fruit crops were higher in 1933 than in 1932, conditions were still bad and would remain so for several more years. One observer, W. D. Lane, in a reply to an inquiry from the American Civil Liberties Union for whom he had worked at one time, indicated that he was now working for a Washington state agency, but could give the ACLU some information about the labor and economic problems in Yakima. In part, he wrote,

I may say that our department which is really a public service commission this spring held several hearings in Eastern Washington on rates for electric power for irrigation pumping. We found conditions such that we issued an emergency order prohibiting the companies from cutting off power for non-payment of bills for this last year or two. The plight of the orchardist was nothing short of pitiful. Last year they did not get enough for their apples to pay [the] cost of picking, packing and marketing. They had run behind from hundreds to thousands of dollars last year. To have had their power cut off meant nothing short of ruin. Asked about what wages they were paying they confessed with shame that it was 15 or 20¢ an hour.

In a second letter to the ACLU, Lane wrote that the orchardists "have been going behind for two years, and soft fruit's a poor crop this year. Apples will be a good crop, but do not come in until later, and not a good prospect for a good price."[37]

What is the statistical evidence on fruit prices? The weighted United States price per bushel of apples was as follows: 1929, $1.39; 1930, $1.02; 1931, $.65; 1932, $.62; and 1933, $.72. The weighted price of Washington state apples averaged $.53 per bushel in 1932 (compared to 1926-1930) and $.68 in 1933. Examining specific varieties, all showed a drastic drop between 1929 and 1933. Two popular varieties in the Yakima areas were Winesaps and Jonathans. The 1929-1930 price of Winesaps on the New York market was $2.67 and in 1932-1933 it was $1.50. Jonathans sold for $2.64 in 1929-1930 and fell to $1.44 in 1932-1933. The Selah newspaper reported Jonathans (fancy and better) sold for $1.50 a box in late August, for $.90 in September, $.50 in October, and $1.00 in December. These are undoubtedly prices to the grower rather than New York market prices. On a more optimistic note, the *Yakima Morning Herald* reported on December 31 that Yakima Valley apple growers got "twenty-five to 50 cents a box more" than in 1932.[38]

A similar price pattern held true for pears. The average price per bushel in Washington state in 1932 was $.30 and in 1933 $.40, or $20.00 a ton. This corresponds to the reports in several valley newspapers. In addition, only $1.00 a ton was being paid for culls, some of which, according to complaining farmers, were being used by canners as "No. 1" fruit. The December 31 issue of the *Herald* reported an average price for canning pears of about $17.50 a ton, which was an increase over the disastrous 1932 receipts. The pattern for peach prices is similar.[39]

Other economic factors also must be considered. Federal loans from several agencies played a very important role in keeping many Yakima farmers from bankruptcy. It was reported that ". . . the government will be the only source of finance for the farmers and fruit growers" and that "the Yakima Valley has accounted for more than one eighth of the farm loans applied for in Washington, Idaho, Oregon, and Montana under the emergency farm mortgage act." In addition, the value of farm real estate decreased more in Yakima County between the years 1930 and 1935 than in any other county in the state except neighboring Benton County. Farm real estate taxes for the state increased slightly during the 1920s, then increased rather sharply in 1931 and 1932. There is no breakdown of these taxes by county, but newspaper references to delinquent taxes would suggest that Yakima County was a part of this general real estate structure. While national statistics indicate that wage rates for hired farm labor had fallen dramatically during the early years of the depression, it is also clear that the agricultural wages paid in the Yakima Valley in 1933 were as high or higher than the national average. The statistics seem to support the conclusions of the fruit farmers.[40]

IV

As has been indicated, the confrontations in the Lower Valley in mid-August were followed by increased activity by both farmers and workers. Farmers throughout the valley formed committees, chose leaders, determined strategy, and collected weapons. The I.W.W. increased its meetings in and around Yakima. On a Wednesday evening, August 23, several hundred workers gathered in Selah, elected a strike committee of seven, and demanded an eight-hour day and fifty cents an hour. They also voted to strike at eleven o'clock the next day.[41]

In the early morning hours of the twenty-fourth, about twenty pickets gathered at one Selah ranch and sixty at another, but local farmers and sheriffs quickly patrolled the area, keeping the pear harvest in operation. At about eleven in the morning, a group of sixty to one hundred pickets gathered at the large Congdon orchards ranch, three miles west of Yakima, where pears were being picked. They carried signs calling for a strike and for other workers not to "scab." Two sheriff's deputies were called, and they found the pickets on the Yakima Valley Transportation track right-of-way, which runs through the Congdon orchards. The pickets were told to get off the tracks as it was private property. The pickets moved off to the edge of the nearby highway or into the orchards where some attempt was made to get the pickers to quit. Having no success there, the picketing continued with some strikers gathering at the grassy and tree-shaded "triangle" of land in the middle of the intersection of what is today Nob Hill and Sixty-fourth avenues. In the meantime, using a prearranged telephone system, farmers within a ten-mile radius were contacted to come. As one man described it, ". . . when the call came we picked up our 'weapons,' a couple of seasoned apple-wood limbs, and joined a neighbor who had volunteered his car, as he was not physically able to engage in 'combat.' When we arrived . . . there were a few farmers assembling, and the pickets were patrolling the outskirts of the orchard, and watching the growth of our group somewhat apprehensively." Several people—either witnesses, participants, or those who later talked to participants—believe that sheriff's officers were near the scene. One participant said he stood "right behind Bannister [one of the farmer leaders] and . . . [Deputy Sheriff] 'Army' Armstrong told Bannister, 'If you drive these people out of here, drive them clear out of the county and I'll come along and pick up the injured.' . . . Bannister said, 'Let's go!' " This was at approximately 12:30 P.M.[42]

The farmers began to move toward the pickets at the triangle. Witnesses are not clear as to exactly how the fight began. It seems that several of the leaders of the ranchers, including Edward Bannister, Arthur Karr, and Ellis Bounds, stepped forward and told the pickets to move out of the area. Blows were struck and men went down. Who struck the first blow will undoubtedly remain in dispute, but there is no question that a full-scale, bloody melee erupted immediately, involving at least two hundred men. The farmers were armed with tree limbs, baseball bats, pickax handles (many of which had been secured earlier from the Yakima Hardware Company), ax handles, and one farmer had a homemade weapon, the "business end" being an eighteen-inch chain within a rubber hose. The pickets had limbs, galvanized pipe, and all the rocks they could gather. Several of the farmers said that the rocks came like "hail" or that it was like a "snowstorm." "They just didn't seem to run out of rocks." During the battle, the farmers were reinforced by those coming from greater distances.[43]

After about fifteen minutes of fighting, the pickets who had not escaped through the orchards were herded together. By this time the farmers easily outnumbered the remaining sixty to seventy pickets whom they surrounded. One farmer said,

> . . . there was a lot of argument of what to do with them. . . . I tell ya they were hot and they were mad. . . . They were just about ready for anything. One talk was to lock them in boxcars . . . and order the railroad not to let them out 'til they got I don't know where. . . . They even talked about taking them to the river. There was just all kinds of talk going on. But, finally, they got 'em started for town and the farmers completely surrounding them with these axe-handles all poised and ready to clobber somebody.[44]

The farmers on foot were aided by several on horseback (from the Congdon cattle ranch), a number in cars that followed the caravan, and by two state patrolmen who led the procession. At least two escape attempts were made during the five-mile walk, one being thwarted at Nob Hill and Sixteenth avenues by the horsemen who recaptured the man.

During the march down Nob Hill Avenue, a number of Moxee and Terrace Heights farmers reinforced the escorts and evidently added some heated threats to the situation. The caravan, however, continued following a path to Third Avenue, to Yakima Avenue, and then east to Front Street where several scuffles occurred. An onlooker, who one witness said was picketing at Congdon's prior to the battle, yelled to the passing prisoners to "Lay down!" One of the Moxee farmers quickly turned toward him, swung a chain over his head and down on the man, yelling, "I'll teach you to lay down, you son of a bitch!" The man fell into the street. By the time the caravan had finished its route—north on Front Street and then east on B to the county jail—the number of prisoners had grown, as some of the curious and/or sympathetic spectators were added to the group. At the courthouse the farmers told the sheriffs, "Here they are. You take care of them." Because of the large number of prisoners and about a thousand spectators, it was quite a task even to book the prisoners and get them inside a wire fence before putting them in jail. One deputy remarked, "It was a mad house there . . . just like a bunch of milling cattle."[45]

The prisoners were behind the wire by three o'clock, and by four o'clock Deputy Sheriff Armstrong called out the national guard. Most of the seventy-four local guardsmen were assembled in only thirty minutes. "We're going to stop this agitation if we have to string a barbed wire fence all around the county," declared Armstrong. "There will be no more picketing in the county. We have the right to stop it because we know it will lead to disorder. If we can't do anything else, we can lodge a state vagrancy charge against everyone who attempts to picket the orchards."[46]

Armstrong's prediction was accurate. There was no more picketing in Yakima County. It is easy to see why. For a short time, guardsmen had a thirty-caliber machine gun mounted at the main intersection in Selah and two at Yakima Avenue and Front Street in Yakima. They used tear gas and displayed fixed bayonets in Yakima the evening of the twenty-fourth to clear out a large crowd in the Front Street area. They helped patrol the railroad yards and some of the hobo "jungles" along the river, bringing every suspicious transient to the sheriff's office for questioning. They were aided, of course, by the city police, the full contingent of sheriffs, and, on the twenty-fifth, by forty state patrolmen brought in personally by Chief William Cole. Every road into the valley was watched, with all cars stopped that carried men who might be potential trouble. All trains were searched for transients. There were usually many of these men, most of whom were encouraged to stay in the yards until their train resumed its journey and then to leave the valley. Local vigilantes, on two different occasions, grabbed several prisoners just as they were released, took them miles into the country, beat them, and, in one situation, applied tar and feathers to the victims' bodies and put linoleum cement in their shoes.[47]

Additional pressure was applied as County Charity Commissioner H. C. Davis cut off relief to any man refusing to work. Other strategy included having the county health department condemn the I.W.W. camp on the Yakima River, the sheriffs then sending the ten men and one woman out of the area and confiscating all the goods they could find (including some guns and ammunition). Also, the I.W.W. postal box was watched, and three Wobblies were arrested when they appeared at the post office to collect their mail.

Arrests continued when some Wobblies and a few local Communists persisted in their objection to the actions being taken locally.[48] In a few days, the number arrested for assault, vagrancy, or criminal syndicalism rose to 114, the most ever housed in the county jail for more than one day. The jail was jammed, so the county began the construction of a special stockade for the prisoners. Two county crews, in twelve-hour shifts, worked continually to put up an enclosure, built of fourteen-foot high three by twelves and topped by barbed wire and a catwalk for the guards. A bunkhouse was built within the walls. The construction work was accompanied by occasional jeers from the prisoners looking out of the jail windows. Over sixty of the prisoners would be put into the stockade, and thirty-two of these would stay there until their release on December 16.[49]

Mark M. Litchman, the Seattle attorney who had secured the release of the hop pickets in May, was again retained by the I.W.W. He arrived in Yakima the evening of August 29 and immediately went to work interviewing the prisoners. Robert Blankenbaker, who had gone out to the Congdon orchards "for lack of something better to do," had been arrested and jailed. His reactions to his first meeting with Litchman are as follows:

I'll never forget. He walked up—I don't believe he was over five feet one or two, a little bit of a short Jew—and he says, "Blankenbaker?" and I says, "Yeah." And he says, "My name is Mark Litchman and I'm a sheeny from Seattle and I'm a damned good one!" And I said, "Yeah?" And he said, "Well, now you don't belong to the I.W.W., but I been retained by the I.W.W. and anybody whose ever arrested in any activities on their behalf . . . they like to take care of it. And if you want, I'd like to represent ya." And I said, "Well, I guess that would be alright." He said, "I'll have you out of here in a couple of days."[50]

True to his word, Litchman got Blankenbaker released in about a week. Working very hard, Litchman also secured the release of several dozen others who obviously had no connection with the I.W.W. At the same time, he continued to interview prisoners, get depositions, and search for witnesses for the impending trial of the remaining Wobblies. He realized, however, that if the trial was ever held in Yakima, the defendants would "have the proverbial chance [of] . . . a 'snow-ball in hell.' " Therefore, he filed motions for a change of venue and for the case to be transferred to a federal court. These motions and others were denied. Litchman also secured from Prosecutor Sandvig the names of several influential valley farmers and invited them to a dinner meeting to see "if the matter can be settled."[51] He received no positive response to his invitations. But tempers had cooled. As the date for the December trial neared, Litchman got the support of several community leaders to end the affair short of what would be a prolonged and expensive trial.[52] On December 16, 1933, an agreement was reached with Sandvig for the immediate release of the remaining thirty-two Wobblies. The conditions were that most of the prisoners were to leave the county within ten days and not return before a year and that twelve of the men were to plead guilty of vagrancy, but were to be immediately released since they had been in custody for more than the ninety days usually given for vagrancy.[53] The twelve pleaded guilty and all were released. The concerted efforts of the I.W.W. in the Yakima Valley had ended.

V

The view I.W.W. organizers held of their own strength and chances of success was distorted by their earlier, distant national successes and by the romantic rhetoric of their movement. And, for some of the leaders, this distorted view was not even corrected after 1933 as they continued to see their role as being the saviors of the agricultural workers in the fight with "Farmer Jawn."

The view Yakima farmers held of the Wobblies was in many ways inaccurate. Fear was a real component in their reactions to the I.W.W., fear based on the commonly accepted view that the Wobblies were violent, wild-eyed radicals. This fear also was heightened by the sharply worded demands of the I.W.W. and by the pressing economic problems of the depression. This fear helped produce both the excessive, and sometimes illegal, reactions as well as the self-perception some farmers held that they were either re-playing some heroic role of frontier vigilantes fighting the invading outlaws, or the patriotic minuteman rising to defend home, traditions, and especially their property.

Considering the economics of the depression year of 1933, there seems no way to avoid the conclusion that the fruit ranchers of the Yakima Valley were in bad condition. They had made little, if any, money for several years, faced increased taxes, lower property values, and had little hope of immediate profits. Prices of some crops did rise during the end of the harvest season, but there seems no evidence that anyone was anticipating the increases in August. They did increase their wages somewhat, partially as a result of the I.W.W. strikes, but there is no justification in assuming that they could have increased them anywhere near the fifty cents an hour demanded. The conditions of the hop industry in 1933 are more complicated because 1) it was an industry with highly fluctuating prices, 2) the prices immediately before 1933 were low, and 3) the end of Prohibition in 1933 brought big profits for that year. Certainly the I.W.W. was justified in its belief that the hop growers could afford to pay more than the twelve and one-half cents an hour due to the profits that the end of Prohibition seemed to be bringing and the grower optimism that led to the their investing thousands of dollars in the contruction of new kilns.

The opponents of the Wobblies were many and were well organized. The farmers, sheriffs, national guard, state patrol, city police, Yakima chamber of commerce, and valley newspapers were united in their efforts to prevent any union activity. Their cooperation was increased by the fact that some men were members of two or more of these groups.

The Yakima Valley had an antiunion, and particularly an anti-I.W.W., tradition covering a quarter of a century. From 1910 to the late 1930s there were recurring, if not continuous, conflicts between union organizers and the valley's farmers and community leaders. Although it is beyond the scope of this chapter, it must be noted that the current antiunion bent of many Yakima Valley farmers, if less vocal and less fear filled than that of earlier decades, remains very real. The I.W.W. and the depression are gone, but certain traditions, undergirded by the economic peculiarities of agriculture, maintain this posture.

NOTES

1. G. R. LeVesconte, letter to the author, March 29, 1974; David Zier, interview with the author, July 31, 1973.

2. A few observations on the research: first, it would not have been possible without the aid and encouragement of many, including my colleague Bill Scofield, Mrs. Virginia Santini, director of the Yakima Valley College Library, Mrs. Ardelle Madden of the Yakima County Clerk's Office, Mr. William Lindberg of the Washington State Archives in Olympia, several people at Camp Murray and at the libraries of the University of Washington and Wayne State University, the National Endowment for the Humanities, whose grant supported the initial stages of the research, and, of course, the several dozen people who graciously answered my questions by interview and letter.

This cooperation produced a great deal of information, but some misinformation as well. Forty-year-old memories were sometimes dim; or they brought back details that were strikingly out of place with the general story and with the accounts of other eyewitnesses. Also, newspaper stories, particularly in-house organs such as those published by the I.W.W. and by state farm groups, had to be analyzed with some care to sift fact from propaganda. I have tried to include only that oral and printed information that could be confirmed from other sources or was completely consistent with other known evidence. Material that could not be confirmed and was obviously divergent from the general story was omitted. This is orthodox methodology, of course, but must be emphasized here because of the emotion that was, and still is, associated with the story. Few persons refused to grant interviews, but one of the reasons given by those who did was that the "truth" would not be told.

For example, one former Wobbly who now lives in the lower Yakima Valley phoned a local teachers' union to discuss the author's attitude toward labor. He must have assumed that my not being a member of that particular union precluded any chance of the "truth" being written, for he then withdrew his offer of an interview. The man's information would probably not have been critical to the completion of this research since he indicated that he had not participated in any of the confrontations, but his refusal to grant a formal interview indicates that the fears and emotions of 1933 are not dead.

3. Paul F. Brissenden, *The I.W.W.: A Study of American Syndicalism* (New York: Russell and Russell, 1919), pp. 261, 265.

4. *Yakima Daily Republic*, July 11, 1910, p. 1.

5. Front Street in the vicinity of the Yakima Avenue intersection was and still is a place to which transient workers come for "rest and recreation."

6. *Daily Republic*, July 11, 13, 14, 1910. The article of July 13 commented that "it became apparent that I.W.W. meant 'I Won't Work.' " This derogatory title was mentioned to the author by numerous persons he interviewed on the affair of 1933.

7. *Morning Herald*, September 16, 1916.

8. *Morning Herald*, September 23, 1916.

9. *Morning Herald*, September 25, 17, 1916.

10. *Morning Herald*, September 25, 28, 30; October 1, 4, 5, 6, 1916.

11. Joseph R. Conlin, *Bread and Roses Too: Studies of the Wobblies* (Westport: Greenwood Press, 1969), p. 140.

12. *Morning Herald*, July 10, 18, 1917; Carl F. Reuss, "The Farm Labor Problem in Washington, 1917-1918," *Pacific Northwest Quarterly* 34, 4 (October 1943), 344.

13. *Morning Herald*, July 11, 1933; Reuss, "Farm Labor Problem," 344, 345.

14. *Morning Herald*, August 15, 19, 1917. The I.W.W. had a widespread reputation for violence, but, it seems, this was based on their earlier open use of the term "sabotage" and on the use of agents provocateurs by their enemies, particularly in the lumber industry. While it cannot be said that Wobblies never employed violent methods, Joseph R. Conlin points out that "despite dozens of prosecutions and the investigatory powers of a dozen states, the Federal Bureau of Investigation, the Immigration Bureau, and the Justice Department, no Wobbly was ever proved to have committed an act of violence. . . . On balance, the I.W.W. must be characterized as a nonviolent union." Conlin, *Bread and Roses*, pp. 111-12; see also Eldridge Foster Dowell, *A History of Criminal Syndicalism Legislation in the United States* (Baltimore: Johns Hopkins University Press, 1939), pp. 29-36.

15. The Washington law passed in 1917 and revised in 1919 prohibited the advocating orally or in print of "crime, sedition, violence, intimidation or injury as a means . . . of affecting or resisting any industrial, economic, social or political change . . . ," the organizing, giving of aid to, being a member of "or voluntarily assemble with any group . . . formed to advocate . . ." the above, and it also prohibited "any owner, lessee, agent, occupant, or person in control of any property" from permitting the use of that property for acts illegal in the above section. Washington state's c. s. law was similar to those passed in twenty states and two territories. All were passed in the period of war hysteria, 1917-1920. These laws were not aimed only at the I.W.W. They were a product of a nationwide antiradical and antilabor drive that is sometimes generally termed "The Red Scare." The Washington law was repealed in 1937. See Dowell, *History of Criminal Syndicalism*, p. 152, for the complete text of the legislation.

16. Interestingly, the $450 bail bond was paid in U.S. liberty bonds by the I.W.W., some indication that the Wobblies were not so totally opposed to the war as they have often been pictured as being. *Yakima County Criminal Cases* Nos. 2039, 2052; *Morning Herald*, 1920 and 1921, *passim*.

17. For similar difficulties in 1928 in Toppenish and Cashmere, Washington, see Marion Hathway, *The Migratory Worker and Family Life: The Mode of Living and Public Provision for the Needs of the Family of the Migratory Worker in Selected*

Industries of the State of Washington (Chicago, University of Chicago Press, 1934), pp. 92-95.

18. *Daily Republic*, March 2, 1933.

19. *Daily Republic*, March 9, 16, 1933.

20. Yakima County Criminal Cases Nos. 4087, 4089, 4090, 4091, and 4092.

21. *Industrial Worker*, May 2, 16, 1933.

22. *Minutes of the Agricultural Workers Industrial Union No. 110*, Omaha, June 1, 1933, Box 44, folder 44-17, I.W.W. Collection, Labor History Archives, Detroit.

23. *Yakima Valley Optimist* (Selah), May 4, 1933; *Sunnyside Sun*, May 4, 1933; *Morning Herald*, April 30, 1933; *Zillah Mirror*, June 1, 1933.

24. *Morning Herald*, May 17, December 31, 1933; September 1, 1935. Leon La Framboise, who has been associated with the hop business for over forty years, indicated that the long-term contracts basically protect the dealer rather than the grower. If the market prices were low while the contracts were high, dealers became very particular about the quality of the hops delivered. "You're going to have quite a time delivering those hops." Interview with La Framboise, February 5, 1974. It should also be added that there were wild fluctuations in prices before 1933, too. The following December 1 prices illustrate this: 1916/17, 12¢; 1917/18, 33.3¢; 1918/ 19, 19.3¢; 1919/20, 77.4¢; 1922/23, 8.6¢; 1925/26, 21.8¢; 1929/30, 11.4¢; 1932/33, 17.5¢. *Yearbook of Agriculture, 1934*, U.S. Department of Agriculture, Milton S. Eisenhower, ed. (U. S. Government Printing Office: Washington, 1934), p. 570. It might also be noted that the cost per pound of raising hops in 1930 was approximately 15¢. Carl F. Reuss, Paul H. Landis, and Richard Wakefield, "Migratory Farm Labor and the Hop Industry on the Pacific Coast, with Special Applications to Problems of the Yakima Valley, Washington," *Rural Sociology Series in Farm Labor*, No. 3 (State College of Washington Agricultural Experiment Station: Pullman, Washington, August 1938), 15.

25. William Cole, memorandum to Governor Clarence D. Martin, May 19, 1933, Administrative Papers, State Governors, File 10, Washington State Archives, Olympia; *Yakima Daily Republic*, May 18, 31, 1933.

26. Claude Erwin, letter to Lucille B. Milner (secretary of the American Civil Liberties Union), June 19, 1933, and Mark M. Litchman, letter to Milner, July 3, 1933, in "Selected Papers on Washington State and Related Subjects" from the American Civil Liberties Union Archives in Princeton University Library, microfilm, University of Washington. The *Minutes of the Board of Directors of the Yakima Chamber of Commerce* for May 24, June 14, July 26, and August 30, 1933, clearly indicate an interest in vigilante organizations across the country, which were working in "cooperation between hops growers and business interests" and in using a 1932 plan for "identification cards" so that employers could hire only local workers.

27. H. T. Armstrong, letter to the Honorable William Cole, May 23, 26, 1933, in Washington State Patrol General Correspondence, 1931-1934, Washington State Archives, Olympia.

28. Cole, letter to Martin, July 31, 1933, Administration Papers.

29. Farley was arrested on August 27, 1933, charged with criminal syndicalism, and released on November 4, 1933. Yakima County Criminal Case No. 4139.

30. A. J. Farley in "Report of Marion Simovic," *G.E.B. Bulletin* No. 115, June

30, 1933. The *Industrial Worker*, June 27 and July 4, 1933, indicated that Farley and Guy B. Askew were often the leaders. Askew, nicknamed "Happy Jack," was an active I.W.W. organizer and was arrested during the Congdon battle on August 24.

31. *Industrial Worker*, July 11, 1933.

32. Edgar Mitchell, interview, August 13, 1973; Ted Clark, interview, August 17, 1973, and letter to the author, November 7, 1973.

33. Cecil C. Clark, letter to the author, February 12, 1973.

34. Ted Clark, interview, August 17, 1973.

35. *Morning Herald*, August 17, 1933; *Zillah Mirror*, August 15, 17, 1933; *Wapato Independent*, August 17, 1933.

36. Cecil Clark, interview, February 20, 1973, and letter to the author, February 7, 1974; Carroll Hull, interview, December 21, 1973; Chad Karr, letter to the author, December 3, 1973; Jane Van Eaton, interview, July 3, 1973; Charles Morrison, interview, August 17, 1973.

37. W. D. Lane, letter to ACLU, New York, September 8, 19, 1933, Selected Papers.

38. *Yearbook of Agriculture, 1934* (Department of Agriculture, 1934), pp. 498, 499, 503; *Yakima Valley Optimist*, August 17, September 14, October 5, December 7, 1933; *Morning Herald*, December 31, 1933.

39. *Yearbook of Agriculture*, pp. 527, 580; *Zillah Mirror*, August 3, 1933; see also Harold F. Hollands, "Washington Pears on the New York and Chicago Fruit Auctions," Bulletin No. 361 (State College of Washington Agricultural Experiment Station: Pullman, Washington, July 1938), 29-30.

40. *Yakima Valley Optimist*, March 23, July 6, 1933. For a detailed description of the various federal loans, see *Proceedings of the Twenty-ninth Annual Meeting of the Washington State Horticultural Association, Yakima*, pp. 10-13; Carl. P. Heisig, "A Graphic Presentation of Changes in the Agricultural Experiment Station: 1935" Bulletin No. 341 (State College of Washington Agricultural Experiment Station: Pullman, Washington, December 1936), 12; *Yearbook of Agriculture*, pp. 706, 709, 714-15; *Selah Valley Optimist*, March 9, 1933.

41. Mike Capelik in *G.E.B. Bulletin No. 117*, August 1933, 23.

42. Emory Hale, interview, July 26, 1973; Dward W. Melton, interview, July 26, 1973; Eugene Thomas, interview, July 19, 1973; G. R. LeVesconte, letter to the author, March 29, 1974; Chad Karr, letter, December 3, 1973; Bert Guns, letter, July 24, 1974; John R. Mosebar, interview, February 16, 1974; George Martin, interview, August 6, 1973; Cecil Brackett, interview, August 14, 1973.

43. Of the dozens of men who were bruised and cut, the most seriously injured were Wobbly Chester Zook, whose jaw was fractured, and two farmers, J. C. Young, whose skull was fractured, and Arthur Karr, who received a blow to his back, the probable cause of the paralyzing syringomyelia that eventually led to his death in 1946. Chad Karr, letter, December 3, 1973; David Zier, interview, July 31, 1973.

44. Caroll Hull, interview, December 21, 1973.

45. Eugene Thomas, interview, July 19, 1973; Emory Hale, interview, July 26, 1973.

46. According to the county prosecutor, the local sheriff had the authority to call out the guard in an emergency situation. With Lew Evans out of town, Chief Criminal Deputy Armstrong took action. *Seattle Post-Intelligencer*, August 25, 1933,

p. 1, and the *Spokesman-Review*, August 25, 1933, pp. 1-2. Although there is a brief indication in the August 25 issue (p. 5) of the *Morning Herald* that "Governor Martin issued an order yesterday granting sufficient funds to keep the guardsmen on the job until they are no longer needed," the national guard records at the Washington State Archives in Olympia and at Camp Murray in Tacoma contain no records that H Company (machine gun company) or the headquarters company of the 161st Infantry were officially called into duty. The "Morning Reports" show that H Company had four training periods in August, but not on the twenty-fourth, and there are no records of rosters, activities, payrolls, or requisitions for the emergency Yakima situation. *Seattle Post-Intelligencer*, August 26, 1933.

47. "Only one shot was fired by any guard during the campaign. That one left its mark in the armory ceiling and was due to over-zealousness in demonstrating." *Daily Republic*, August 28, 1933. However, the local editor did little to calm things when he wrote on August 25, "A number of agitators have been beaten up by the vigilance committees, and no one need be surprised if a few are strung up if they do not let up."

48. The three Communists arrested were local residents: Charles Goold, his son, Clifford, and his twenty-three-year-old daughter, Mary. All three had been outspoken supporters of the Soviet Union for several years, and Mary, an attractive young lady, received particular attention for her speeches and then her arrest. Other Communists tried, through front organizations like the Northwest Congress of Farmers and Workers, the United Farmers League, and the International Labor Defense, to affect the labor situation in August, but they had no success. Either their own weaknesses, the local organized opposition after August 24, or the opposition of the I.W.W. rendered them ineffective. The Wobbly opposition must be stressed. It was continual and aggressive as they had no love for those they called "comrats." See the *Morning Herald*, July 14, 1933, p. 16, for a description of a Yakima street fight between the Communists and the I.W.W. Also see Joyce Kornbluh, ed., *Rebel Voices: An IWW Anthology* (Ann Arbor: University of Michigan Press, 1964), p. 361, for an interesting anti-Communist cartoon. The following indicate similar strong sentiments: The *Industrial Worker*, July 4, September 5, October 3, 10, December 19, 1933.

49. Sheriff Lew Evans was still out of town when Armstrong ordered the construction of the stockade. The structure remained for over a decade. Some residents described it as a good warning for troublemakers; others called it an eyesore. According to Bert Gunns, the only other time it was used as a jail after December 1933 was to hold drunken Indians the next fall. Bert Gunns, letter, July 24, 1974.

50. Robert Blankenbaker, interview, August 8, 1973.

51. Litchman, letters to Olaf Sandvig, October 27, 1933, and George R. Dunn, October 11, 1933, in Mark M. Litchman papers, Manuscript Collection, University of Washington, Seattle.

52. On December 18, 1933, after the prisoners' release, Litchman wrote a letter to the owner/editor of the *Republic* and *Herald*, Colonel W. W. Robertson, thanking him for his recent support (which was certainly a contrast to his paper's summer-long criticisms of the "agitators") of the release. "For your civic mindedness, the people of Yakima County owe you a debt of gratitude. For myself I want

to publicly thank you for your encouragement of my early aim to amiably settle the I.W.W. case." Litchman letter to Robertson, December 18, 1933, in Mark M. Litchman papers. Yakima County Criminal Case No. 4135.

53. Yakima County Criminal Case No. 4135. The I.W.W. did hold some meetings in Yakima in 1934, but the Wobblies were few in number and seemed to spend about as much time on local internal bickering as on organizing. The March 1935 national annual convention of IU No. 110 was held in Spokane and its minutes reflect the general weakness of the union. Motions and speeches for more activity were made—some by men who had been in the Yakima stockade in 1933—but they were made to a total of twenty-one Wobblies. I.W.W. *Collection* at Wayne State University. And it might be appropriate to add here that during this same period—1935 to 1936—the farmers in Yakima had organized a "Citizens' Protective Association" that issued blue membership cards to each member (Bert Gunns letter of July 24, 1974) and a public proclamation that concluded, "What we have, we have worked for through long hours and by self-denial. We propose to keep it at any cost. These are fighting words and we know it. We purposely use them in preference to the weasel kind. Make no mistake about our meaning. All who aid and abet practices which threaten our well being, are included in our list of natural enemies." It was signed by W. B. Armstrong, secretary (and father of deputy sheriff H. T. Armstrong). *Morning Herald*, July 26, 1936, and July 24, 1974, letter from Bert Gunns, who worked in the CPA.

"RANG-U-TANG": THE I.W.W. AND THE 1927 COLORADO COAL STRIKE

RONALD L. McMAHAN

'Rang-u-tang,
'Rang-u-tang,
Siss boom ba,
Who in the hell,
Do you think we are?
Wobblies,
Wobblies,
Ha, ha, ha.

We're rough,
We're tough,
We never take a bluff.
Of free speech
We never get enough.

We're Wobblies,
Wobblies,
Wobblies.

1927 Colorado Strike Rallying Song

During the fall of 1927, 12,000 Colorado coal miners went out on strike. Early on the morning of Monday, November 21, 1927, the state militia opened fire on a group of nearly 500 unarmed picketers, killing six and wounding at least twenty more during a demonstration at one of the few mines that continued to operate during the strike. The incident, known as the Columbine Mine massacre, occurred in the small Rocky Mountain Fuel Company town of Serene, Colorado. On the surface, the 1927 Columbine massacre might appear to be just another incident in the Colorado coal miners' long and often frustrated struggle to gain better working conditions and the right to organize and join a labor union. Beginning with the strike of 1893-1894, through the strike of 1903-1904, and the 1913-1914 strike, which culminated in the Ludlow massacre, the coal miners had attempted time and again to challenge the absolute power of coal companies who refused to even negotiate with them.

However, despite its obvious similarities with prior strikes, the 1927 strike stands out as a unique, indeed critical, event in the social and economic history of the West. There are at least three features that distinguish this strike. First, the strike was not organized by the United Mine Workers of America (UMWA); rather, it was led by the revolutionary syndicalist union, the Industrial Workers of the World (I.W.W.). The UMWA, having lost the 1913-1914 coal strike, had suffered considerable financial loss in Colorado, and because of the executive board's decision to concentrate organizing efforts in the eastern coal fields, the UMWA was unresponsive to the needs of the Colorado miners.

Second, the miners of the state were not at the time of the strike without any means of redress. After the 1913-1914 strike, John D. Rockefeller, Jr., who controlled the Colorado Fuel and Iron Company—the leader of the coal industry in Colorado—had implemented a self-fashioned "company union" known as the Rockefeller Industrial Plan of Employee Representation. It was to a large degree the gross inadequacies and failures of the Rockefeller plan, not simply the cutthroat competitive conditions that typically surrounded laissez-faire capitalism, that set the stage for the 1927 strike.

Third, because of the I.W.W.'s success in organizing the strike and the threat of future radicalism in Colorado, one of the state's major coal operators felt it prudent to invite the more conservative UMWA to negotiate a labor contract, thus stifling the potential for future Socialist-led organizing activity in the western coal fields.

The very features that distinguish this strike accentuate some very important issues concerning the ways in which the social order in the West was shaped by the labor movement. Both John R. Commons and Selig Perlman, the principal exponents of the Wisconsin school of labor history, identified the frontier as one of the keys to American labor conservatism.[1] Perlman contends that although the violent industrial struggles in the mining regions of the West between 1890 and 1930 appear to show a picture of class warfare as conceived by Marx, these labor struggles proceeded from no theory of revolution, but from the general characteristics of the frontier. Westward expansion and land availability generated a sense of optimism and opportunity that militated against class consciousness and a genuine sense of labor radicalism. Yet, it must be noted that at the same time the American Federation of Labor was embarking on its course of "pure and simple" unionism, events in the West led to the formation of the powerful Socialist union, the Western Federation of Miners, and then to the syndicalist I.W.W. During the early part of the twentieth century, a large segment of the western working class did find radicalism relevant.

A detailed analysis of the 1927 Colorado coal strike, the last major strike organized by the I.W.W., raises some very specific questions concerning the forces that impelled the miners in a part of the American West to adopt socialism and syndicalism, and provides a concrete framework for the consideration of these questions:

1. What were the conditions that created the environment enabling the I.W.W. to organize a massive strike in Colorado?
2. What were the goals of the I.W.W., and how effectively did their tactics in Colorado serve as a means to these ends?
3. To what extent does the Colorado strike serve to shed light upon the more general questions concerning the decline and virtual disappearance of Socialist influence within the American labor movement?

To date, there have been few scholarly studies of the 1927 Colorado coal strike. Harry O. Lawson offers an analysis that concludes that the Colorado strikers' militancy was not grounded in what Marxists would view as the necessary reaction to the unchallenged power of the coal companies and the increasing immersion of the working class. Rather, he portrays the events as the product of a resurgent Jeffersonianism.[2] Daniel McClurg presents an historical description of the specific organizational tactics employed by the I.W.W. in Colorado.[3] Baynard contends that the 1927 strike is at best slightly distinguishable from earlier strikes in the state.[4] All of these works are based upon rigorous study of historical documents such as newspaper articles, company records, and reports issued by investigating committees.

The study upon which this chapter is based is grounded in a methodological approach quite different from that of Lawson, McClurg, and Baynard. Both the ethnographies and oral histories of persons who have lived and worked in the state's coal-mining regions and the analyses of scholars are blended together in order to create a more comprehensive picture of the past. By conducting hundreds of hours of tape-recorded interviews, it was possible not only to document coal miners' subjective recollections of the major historical events, but also to paint a picture of what day-to-day life was like. Interviews were conducted with an open-ended format, which allowed people to set their own direction and to talk about what they and their peers saw as important occurrences. These people were well aware of their own value perspectives and were eager to discuss both the internal and external conditions that shaped their lives.

It is important to understand a few things about coal miners, about the nature of the coal-mining community. Their communities are more than a cluster of buildings at the side of the road. They are historic entities. People in their communities talk to one another; they have their own sensibility. And while standards of sensibility change, people's lives remain relentlessly sensible. Within the community, history is constantly being spoken

and respoken in an endless process called "making sense" or "verstehen."
The researcher's job is to note the ways in which persons make sense of their
lives and share that sense with others. The researcher is not in the position
of providing a framework, structure, or standards of objective truth through
which others can come to an understanding, but rather to listen, to notice,
and to record those aspects held in common.

To seek enlightenment concerning the important issues of the 1927 strike
solely through the use of newspaper articles, company records, and other
such sources of "recorded history" is incomplete at best. The people who
made the history carry with them an understanding of their history. The
people who fought and lost strikes, who experienced the conditions in the
local camps, who dealt with the political questions of radical syndicalism,
socialism, and "pure and simple" unionism are able, indeed eager, to share
their understandings. This discussion employs all availabe sources of information—the historical record, ethnographic accounts, and scholarly
works—in an attempt to get at the heart of the issues raised by the 1927
Colorado coal strike.

The appearance of the United Mine Workers of America coincided with
the emergence of a national industrial economy using coal as its basic fuel.
There is a general consensus among labor historians concerning the development of relations between miners and management.[5] During the early years
of coal development, anarchistic competition characterized the industry.
The coal companies often resorted to wage cuts as a competitive weapon,
and miners were quick to realize that they were the victims of the fierce
competition that resulted from overproduction. Their response was typically to try to organize all of the mines in a given area and negotiate with the
operators in an attempt to stabilize the situation by setting a uniform wage
and reducing the effect of the downward wage-price spiral as a competitive
weapon. But this strategy remained ineffective as long as mines outside the
organized region continued to slash wages and prices. It became more and
more evident to the miners that they would have to organize an industry-
wide union with a single policy implemented by a central body with sufficient
power to put this policy into effect. John Mitchell, president of the union
from 1898 to 1908, was a strong leader, and although there had always been
a Socialist element in the UMWA, it was his commitment to the reform
strategy of "pure and simple" unionism that was to set the course the union
would follow in the future.[6]

Due to the inability of the fiercely competitive coal operators to stabilize
their industry, it fell upon the miners to take the initiative. This fact pro-
foundly affected the UMWA. While other unions in other industries were
afforded the luxury of engaging in active debate and experimentation
concerning the course unionism should take in relation to growing industrialization, and while the ideas of socialism and syndicalism were the subject
of much discussion, the course of the UMWA was in a sense determined by

the nature of their industry.[7] The men indulged periodically in arguments about the necessity of a radical course of action, but if they meant to remain a viable organization able to secure the most minimum safety standards and a living wage for their members, Mitchell felt that they had no choice but to assume a greater amount of the responsibility for making coal an industry that could function efficiently and return a profit on investment. While claiming that the trade union is "not irrevocably committed to the maintenance of the wage system, nor is it irrevocably committed to its abolition," Mitchell urged the workers to accept the interdependence of labor and capital and their permanent status as wage earners and to forget the class struggle.[8]

The I.W.W. would, of course, have none of this. They were committed to direct action as the means of both making the revolution and improving workers' daily lives. Once introduced to the coal fields of Colorado, such a policy was inevitably to have significant effects.

By 1900, the western coal and iron industry was centered in Colorado. The Colorado Fuel and Iron Company (CF & I), of which John D. Rockefeller, Jr., was the major stockholder, was one of the largest steel mills west of the Mississippi. This vertically integrated corporation controlled the bulk of the coal mines in Colorado, and although there existed two other large coal companies in the state, the Rocky Mountain Fuel Company and the Victor American Fuel Company, CF & I was clearly the industry leader.

At this time there were 34,000 coal miners in the state, and the numerous mining camps and company towns in the region were quite different from those in Appalachia. There existed a unique blend of the Old West and the emerging industrial society. During these early days of economic expansion, while the industrialists amassed private fortunes, the miners worked under hazardous conditions for substandard wages in a situation that might best be called industrial feudalism. The companies not only controlled the workplace, but they also owned the mine towns—the houses, stores, saloons, churches, medical facilities, and schools, The miners were powerless in the face of the companies' all-encompassing control.

There were strikes in Colorado—violent, bloody frontier strikes in 1883, 1893-1894, and 1903-1904. In 1903 the staunch antiunion sentiments of Rockefeller were exemplified when, through his personal directive, his representatives refused to even meet with the striking miners. The CF & I company's hired gunmen and the state militia joined forces to crush the statewide coal strike. In the process, the operators came near to crushing the UMWA in Colorado; thereafter, they preferred foreign-born labor. By importing immigrants from Italy, Greece, Yugoslavia, Mexico—from all over the world—the coal companies were able to eliminate their reliance upon the predominantly Welsh and English miners who had led so many strikes in the past. However, by 1910, even this new labor force began to resist the absolute power of "King Coal." The immigrants found themselves on the periphery of the American promise, and the UMWA once again found the Colorado coal fields to be fertile ground for renewed organizing activity. On the eve of the 1913 strike, the demands of the miners were no different from those that had led to earlier strikes—an eight-hour workday, increased wages, the right to be paid in currency instead of scrip, the right to trade where they wished, the right to be paid for "dead work," but, primarily, the right to organize and join a union.

Exactly as in the past, the companies refused even to negotiate with the miners, seeing this as an unacceptable concession and a forfeiture of their rights as owners. When the miners called a strike, the owners immediately evicted them from their company homes, and the miners prepared to face the Colorado winter in tent colonies. Baldwin Felts gunmen were hired by the companies to protect the nonunion miners who kept many of the larger mines operating. When it became clear that the strike would not be broken quickly, the companies convinced the governor to call out the state militia in order to carry out strikebreaking duties. Throughout the winter there occurred scattered incidents of violence in which miners, scabs, and militiamen were killed. Finally, in April of 1914, when tension had risen to a peak, the militia attacked a tent colony of unarmed miners and their families near the town of Ludlow. They set fire to the tents, totally destroying all of the miners' property and killing two women and eleven children who had taken refuge from the gunfire in a cellar dug beneath the floor of a tent. It was this "Ludlow massacre" that turned national attention to Colorado. Public sentiment was clearly on the side of the miners. The miners quickly armed themselves, and thus began an all-out war between the militia and the miners that lasted for ten days until federal troops were called in to stop the fighting.

When the smoke had cleared from Ludlow, the miners found themselves in a familiar position. Their strike was broken, their funds exhausted, and the United Mine Workers union forced to withdraw.

Perhaps the most important aspect of this strike was that John D. Rockefeller, Jr., began to reevaluate his attitudes toward labor. Against the grim background of the Ludlow massacre and the ten-day war—considered by some to be the prime example of outright class warfare in the United States[9]—the Rockefeller Industrial Plan of Employee Representation was born.

Wiley points out that by the First World War most of the operators in Appalachia, Pennsylvania, and the Midwest had signed with the UMWA, generally facilitating the rationalization of the coal industry.[10] But what he fails to discuss is the fact that the conditions in the West were considerably different. With respect to the union, the executive board of the UMWA was not only disinterested in pursuing further organizing activities in Colorado, but it went so far as to place District 15 under trusteeship, removing from office John R. Lawson and the other militant organizers of the Colorado strike. Coal miners had battled and lost to the Rockefeller interests on no fewer than four occasions over the last twenty years. Since there was little likelihood that shipments of coal from the isolated western fields could ever be competitive in the East, regardless of wage scales in Colorado, the UMWA leadership in Indianapolis reasoned that the union's energies and funds would be better spent in the East.

On the side of capital, Rockefeller remained stubbornly committed to his "great principle" of antiunionism. In fact, he stated that he would rather lose all the millions invested in the coal fields rather than recognize the union there.[11] The position of his CF & I company remained strong. Rockefeller was still the largest coal operator in the West, and the defeated miners, without any union support, again provided him a massive labor pool. The stabilizing role played by the UMWA in the East was irrelevant in the West. Rockefeller's mines were largely "captive" mines whose primary market was the CF & I steel works; the Victor American Fuel Company in the south and the Rocky Mountain Fuel Company in the north supplied the bulk of the state's growing industrial and domestic markets. Because of Colorado's geographic isolation, the mining industry in the West would operate under "classic" competitive conditions long after the eastern mining industry moved into its corporate phase.[12]

Yet, guided by his desire to improve the company's public image as well as his desire to avoid future disruptive labor disputes, Rockefeller made concessions—but on his own terms. He commissioned McKenzie King, Canada's minister of labor, to develop a plan for employee representation both in the coal mines and in the steel mills. The plan King designed was the first, and certainly the most famous, of American company union plans.[13] It called for miners' representatives to be elected annually from each of the company's mines in proportion to each mine's labor force under a formula of one representative per 150 employees.[14] These representatives were supposedly spokesmen for their constituency regarding working and living conditions, and they served on six-man committees involving 1) industrial cooperation and conciliation; 2) safety and accidents; 3) sanitation, health and housing; and 4) recreation and education. However, these committees had no power other than to bring up issues for discussion with the "proper officer of the company," meaning primarily the mine superintendent—the same de facto procedure the miners had always employed. The miners were theoretically allowed to appeal grievances through the bureaucratic hierarchy to the president of the company, but in an evaluation of the plan commissioned by the Russell Sage Foundation, Selekeman reported that this grievance procedure was totally ineffective.[15] In fact, the miners still—justifiably—feared reprisals if they actually tried to appeal beyond the pit boss or mine superintendant. Even though CF & I claimed that the company's policy would be to keep wages in line with those of UMWA mines, the miners themselves still held contempt for the plan.[16]

In short, the plan had done little more than change what had been frank autocracy into corporate paternalism. Selekeman concluded the plan was at best "an incomplete experiment and that the enforcement of the agreement between the company and the employees, may be said to be . . . almost exclusively a function of the managerial officials."[17] In the final analysis, the Rockefeller plan was nothing more than a weapon against the UMWA. Miners realized that only an independent union could meaningfully represent their interests, but they had been made totally powerless first by the defeat of the strike and then by the company union.

During World War I, the demand for coal and hence its price, rose quickly, and this stimulated a nationwide expansion of demand and a rapid expansion of output. By 1920 coal production hit an all-time high and both union, and nonunion miners enjoyed high wages. But the industry was greatly expanded, and a postwar recession pulled the bottom out from under the coal market at the end of that same year. The response of the coal operators in Colorado, as in the rest of the country, was to cut wages. Throughout 1924 and 1925, the three major coal companies in Colorado circulated petitions among their miners requesting that the State Industrial Commission grant the companies permission to cut wages. By presenting the commission with petitions signed by the employees, the companies could demonstrate that the wage cuts would not lead to labor disputes. Many miners were reluctant to give up the gains they had achieved, not through a strong collective bargaining posture, but rather through the war-generated economic boom. Sporadic wildcate strikes were called throughout the state, and many miners refused to sign the petition.[18] But, legally, Rockefeller's company union plan had vested in the owners the right to cut wages if economic conditions dictated, and as it became clear that the UMWA was neither willing nor able to launch an organizing effort in Colorado to protect wages, the miners were forced to sign the wage-cut petitions rather than sacrifice their jobs to men willing to work under a lower scale.

The miners who were working in the Colorado coal fields during this time agree that not until 1924-1925 did they truly begin to feel betrayed by the UMWA. It was at this time that employees began to perceive the inadequacies of the company union plan. Once again they were forced to accept the fact that it was the workers who were the first to feel the effects of economic slumps in a competitive capitalist economy.

The I.W.W. was quick to notice the reemerging consciousness among the Colorado miners, and Wobbly organizers began to come to the state with the intention of offering an alternative and providing leadership to the state's coal miners. In 1925, however, the Wobblies were themselves in a much weaker position than they had been prior to World War I and the subsequent "anti-Red" movement in the United States. The I.W.W. had expended nearly all of its funds for the defense of leaders who had been imprisoned as a result of the famous Palmer raids. Internal dissension in the Wobbly organization left little hope for the union's old goals of one big industrial union. Yet the organizers who came to Colorado remained committed to the same strategy and tactics which had been employed in earlier strikes from Lawrence to Paterson and in the lumbering country of the Northwest.

Among the first Wobbly organizers to come to Colorado in 1926 was A. S. Embree. Over the previous ten years, he had been in jails in Arizona and Montana. Embree's own words, written in prison, indicate the attitude of the Wobbly leaders on the eve of their organizing efforts in Colorado: "The end in view [the revolution] is well worth striving for, but in the struggle itself lies the happiness of the fighter."[19]

From the beginning, organizing efforts in Colorado bore this distinctive I.W.W. mark. During the late summer of 1927, after some preliminary organizing efforts in the smaller "fringe" mining camps, I.W.W. organizers called for a three-day work stoppage in conjunction with a nationwide protest against the conviction of Sacco and Vanzetti. To the surprise of everyone, including Embree, 1,132 of the 1,167 miners in the Walsenburg District stayed out of the pits,[20] making the Colorado demonstration the most successful in the nation. When the I.W.W. leaders learned that the Colorado attorney general's office planned to issue an injunction against the strikers during the second day of the protest, Embree urged the miners to vote to go back to work. He realized that the success of this demonstration stemmed neither from the miners' sympathy with Sacco and Vanzetti, nor from an informed understanding of the revolutionary principles of the I.W.W., but rather from deeply held and explosive grievances against the coal companies. The tactical decision of the Wobblies was to give ground on this occasion in order to intensify organizing efforts for a statewide strike.

Detailed preparations were made for a strike. In September, 187 delegates from forty-three mines in the state's southern fields met in order to draft a list of strike demands. The demands were no different from those of any other strike in the state: wage levels, working conditions, and the right to organize. From the outset, the democratic principles of the Wobbles were demonstrated by the fact that all committees were composed only of miners; all ethnic factions were represented; and the I.W.W. organizers served only as nonvoting members. The Wobblies were careful not to impose Socialist demands, such as the abolition of the wage system or the right of the workers to control the workplace, since this would certainly have turned the attention of the government, the companies, the Colorado Federation of Labor, and the media toward the radicalism of the I.W.W. rather than the real grievances of the miners. The Wobblies were content to leave the education of the workers to the "I.W.W. Preamble," which was printed on the inside cover of the membership card, mimeographed leaflets, and personal conversations with the rank-and-file organizers. The philosophy of the Wobblies had long been that the experience of organizing and of developing solidarity was the best radical education the miners could receive in preparation for the general strike.

A reading of the preamble underscores the reasons why the Colorado miners were—at least on the surface—sympathetic. The indictment of the capitalist class was pertinent in the eyes of the miners since their living and working conditions and their relative wage rates had remained virtually unchanged over the past twenty-five years. While the owners enjoyed the good things in life, the immigrants who had come to America in search of a dream went further into debt to the company stores each year, and their children were deprived of the upward mobility for which the parents had made so many sacrifices. In addition, the Wobblies' indictment of the trade unions fell upon receptive ears considering the fact that these miners had been abandoned by the UMWA, the very union for which they had fought on so many occasions.

On September 8, 1927, when the miners voted to call a strike for October 8, they informed the State Industrial Commission of their demands and intentions in compliance with the thirty-day notice provisions of the law. Again the tactics of the I.W.W. were to work within the law in order to deter accusations of anarchism that would displace the demands of the miners. However, the commission immediately declared the proposed strike illegal, claiming that the I.W.W. did not represent the miners. The arbitrariness of this decision served to anger even the established labor organizations, and spokesmen of the Colorado Federation of Labor interpreted it as an affront to all organized labor in the state.[21] Upon receipt of the commission's decision, the strike committee decided to go ahead with the strike, but, according to Lawson, they moved the date to October 18 in order to have more time for organizing the northern fields and increasing the strike's scope and effectiveness.[22] On the first day of the strike, 6,340 miners, or just about half of the state's 12,690 miners, walked out. By the time the strike reached its full momentum, approximately 12,000 miners were on strike, making it the most successful strike in Colorado's history.[23]

Even the coal companies' gesture of a nonnegotiated raise of sixty-eight cents per day did not deter the miners' commitment. Throughout the state, however, opposition to the I.W.W. was active and direct. Newspapers such as the *Rocky Mountain News, Denver Post, Trinidad Chronical-News, Walsenburg Independent*, and *Boulder Daily Camera* launched fervent attacks on the Wobblies, reigniting the postwar, anti-Red campaign. Six mayors in southern Colorado communities ordered the I.W.W. out of town, and on at least two occasions, in Walsenburg and Aguilar, citizens' committees marched on I.W.W. halls and wrecked them.[24]

On the surface, the UMWA, which had forbidden its members to join the I.W.W. at its 1918 convention, remained neutral. There was no way by which the union could condemn the strike without also condemning the demands for which the miners were striking. But agents of the UMWA carried out overt actions against the strikers. In their accounts, miners tell of how persons affiliated with the UMWA participated in vigilante raids on I.W.W. property and served as informants to the state police.[25] On at least three occasions, the UMWA's District 15 president denied accusations that his union was sabotaging the strike, but the recollections of participants contradict him.[26]

In the face of this opposition, the I.W.W. implored the strikers to act in a peaceable manner:

You are not to abuse anyone. You are not to strike anyone. Tell them they are hurting themselves as well as the rest of us. There will be no rough stuff on the job. The sheriff's orders to his men are that they must not shoot or abuse anyone. If anyone is to be killed, let it be one of our men first.[27]

The Wobblies would be "selectively law-abiding." As McClurg points out, "Laws were broken, but selectively and with care; the antipicketing law for instance was violated consciously and regularly. The I.W.W. contended that the statute was an unconstitutional infringement of personal liberty and vigorously sought to test it."[28] Thus, picketing was the major weapon used in the strike; daily, the miners got together in efforts to close down the few mines continuing to operate. In addition, the miners in the northern field devised the tactic of organizing car caravans to carry the message of the strike to the miners in Freemont County, where only a handful of the miners had orginally responded to the strike call. Not only did this tactic spread the strike, but it also actively involved the miners in strike activity, thus maintaining the morale of idle men. The success of this tactic in Freemont County led to its use in El Paso County. By mid-November, western slope miners had gone out in Gunnison and Routt counties, bringing the state's coal production to a virtual halt.

This was the situation on the eve of the Columbine massacre. The miners, committed to peaceful action, broke no laws other than the antipicketing laws. When outbreaks of violence erupted, the strikers were quick to retire, thus taking the force out of the companies' pleas for the governor to call out the National Guard. But at just the time when the companies were being forced into a position of having to recognize the I.W.W. as a legitimate representative of the miners and opening negotiations, the current abruptly changed.

It is ironic that the major scene of violence occurred at the Rocky Mountain Fuel Company's Columbine mine. That company, long the industry leader in the northern fields, had been feeling the effects of the prolonged recession in the coal industry. The death of the company's president, John J. Roche, in January 1927 had thrown the control of RMF into question. Roche's daughter, Josephine, had been educated in the East and had been openly sympathetic to the cause of unionism since the 1913-1914 strike. She was a personal friend of John R. Lawson, the leader of that strike. After her father's death, Josephine wished to take over the operation of the company. In her own words: "Realizing the needless waste of the bitter, long established, antiunion policy in the state . . . I was convinced that a sound union program must be worked out by the Rocky Mountain Fuel Company with resulting benefit to all concerned."[29] But the members of the board disagreed with her views, and before she had time to actually gain control of the company's stock, the 1927 strike policy had been set. It was necessary to continue to operate the Columbine mine through the strike in order to prevent the company from going into receivership. However, Josephine was emphatic in her orders to the superintendent of the mine that picketing *would* be allowed and that the state and county law enforcement officers were not to take action against strikers on her property. She stated that she intended to avoid any acts that might provoke violence.[30] But without her knowledge, the events at the Columbine were already out of control.

Captain Louis Scherf, an operative and cohort of the same Major Pat Hamrock who led National Guard Troop A in the Ludlow massacre, had been appointed commander of a small group of state "rangers," many of whom had also been present at Ludlow. In a memorandum Josephine Roche told of how other operators—primarily CF & I's Jesse Welborn—convinced the governor that the miners needed to be kept in their place and that history would chastise him for not at least dispatching the rangers to the troubled areas.[31] Consequently, without the knowledge of Roche, Captain Scherf and a detachment of twenty state police arrived at the Columbine on the evening of Sunday, November 20. An armed attack upon the Columbine picketers was planned by the rangers and the operators.[32] When word reached Roche that the police were at her mine, she contacted the governor, who assured her that he had not given Captain Scherf orders to leave the southern fields. In spite of repeated attempts, the governor was unable to reach Scherf that night to tell him to leave the Columbine.

"Recorded history" states only that the noise of a party was heard at the Columbine mine that night,[33] but men who were there tell of how the rangers were drinking heavily all through the night and talking of how they planned to deal with picketers in the morning.[34] On the morning of Monday, November 21, the Weld County sheriff, who knew of Scherf's plans, stood on the running board of his roadster outside the gates of the Columbine pleading with the 500 picketers to forgo their demonstration for just that day. He dug his hand into his pocket and threw a few dollars onto the ground telling the miners that that was all he had and to take it and go home. With little reason to heed his warnings, the unarmed picketers poured through the gate and charged into the point-blank range of the state police's machine guns. By the time the shooting ended, five were dead, one fatally wounded, and at least twenty other strikers lay on the ground along with spent cartridges and empty beer bottles.

The miners retreated, and the I.W.W. leaders issued orders for all strikers to stay home so as not to antagonize the authorities. The Wobblies were convinced that the state police's actions were meant to lure the strikers into retaliatory action that would justify more severe repressive measures. But the damage had been done. Within a few days the blame for the Columbine incident was officially placed upon the miners, the national guard was called in, and the "repressive" measures came in spite of the retreat.

The presence of the militia, coupled with the miners' reluctance to hold mass meetings and demonstrations, served effectively to curtail strike activity, and most mines in the north reopened. But the violence had not ended. Scherf and his men, vindicated of wrongdoing at the Columbine, were at the center of several disorders in the southern fields in the months that followed. Three more miners were killed and scores injured during demonstrations in Trinidad, Walsenburg, and Aguilar.

Although the strike was not officially called off by vote of the strikers until February 20, 1928, it was the turn of events at the Columbine and the use of martial law that turned the advantage to the antistrike forces. By the time the strike was terminated, both the coal companies had suffered considerable financial losses. Jesse Welborn, president of CF & I, estimated that labor and industry had lost almost ten million dollars as a result of the strike.[35]

The miners voted to go back to work for three reasons. First, Embree and the strike committee had set February as the target date for termination since the miners could still find some work before the summer shutdowns. Second, the Rocky Mountain Fuel Company had made gestures indicating they might be willing to consider unionization; the miners assumed that the other operators would follow suit. And third, the operators, via the industrial commission, had offered a dollar-a-day increase in wages. Technically, the I.W.W. had not won the strike—its list of demands was never even negotiated. But the miners came away with the most substantial gains they had ever received in Colorado as a result of strike activity. In fact, although their wage increase was awarded by the operators, on the companies' own terms, it was the only such increase reported between 1928 and 1930 in any American coal field.[36]

The 1927 Colorado coal strike is unique in the labor history of the state, and it provides essential clues concerning not only the ultimate fate of the I.W.W., but also some of the reasons for the decline in effectiveness of radical influence in the American labor movement.

The Wobblies entered the Colorado fields during a period of union inaction and employee discontent. At the national level, the I.W.W. leadership was split over what had grown into a bitter dispute over the union's future. On one hand, there was the faction that was becoming increasingly aligned with the Communist party and felt that the only hope for the union's future lay in affiliation with the Soviet-based Red International of Labor Unions (RILU). On the other hand, the Wobblies who remained committed to the old anarcho-syndicalist ideology were hostile to the RILU's directive of abandoning the strategy of dual unionism and dissolving the I.W.W. so as to "bore from within the AF of L."[37] But, in spite of this split, the Wobblies were able to conduct a massive strike in Colorado.

In Colorado, whatever differences existed among the I.W.W. leaders, the strike leadership responded effectively to the dictates of the specific situation. Even though Embree and the other strike leaders agitated and organized, it was the miners themselves who made decisions about objectives and tactics and who engaged in meeting with the industrial commission.

Anarcho-syndicalists in general and the Wobblies specifically have consistently been criticized for their "impossibilist" tactics. At the heart of their philosophy was the notion that workers had to be free at all times to strike, and, thus, by signing time contracts with their employers, the workers sacrificed their right to strike spontaneously. As Dubofsky points out, ". . . without the unreserved right to strike, the I.W.W. could not wage the class war, and without the ongoing class struggle, there could be no revolution and no cooperative commonwealth."[38] Along the same lines, the Wobblies spurned the idea of union recognition by the companies as a token of cooperation with the capitalists through which the workers would certainly be exploited. The issues of time contracts and union recognition proved to be the Wobblies' Achilles' heel every time they organized a successful strike. Once the strike had tactically been won and the operators ready to come to terms, the I.W.W. withdrew, leaving the employees to negotiate, thus sacrificing an ongoing organization recognized by the operators. In many instances, as was to be the case in Colorado, the workers felt abandoned by the very organization that had led them into battle. This often resulted in outright hostility toward the I.W.W., since they resented the departure of the organizers at the time when they were most needed.[39] Again Dubofsky states: "If the I.W.W. could offer its members nothing but perpetual industrial warfare, how could it maintain its membership, let alone increase its ranks? On the other hand, if the I.W.W. did sanction contracts, win recognition, and improve its members' lives, what would keep them from forsaking revolutionary goals and adhering to the well-established AF of L pattern?''[40]

There was one major incident during the Colorado strike that has been given only passing attention by historians, but serves to shed light on the evolving goals of the I.W.W. Midway through the strike, when A. S. Embree was jailed for inciting picketing, Tom Conners came to the state to replace him. Before long, friction developed between Conners and the supporters of Embree stemming from Conners's desire to learn from past defeats and reevaluate the union's "impossibilist" tactics. Conners recognized that the industrial commission was ready to recognize the I.W.W. as the legitimate representative of the strikers and would soon force the operators to begin negotiations. But the companies were aware of the I.W.W.'s prior no-contract principle and, hence, used it as a lever in their own favor. Conners believed that if the strikers could hold out until February, the financially troubled coal companies—especially Rocky Mountain and Victor American —would have no choice but to recognize the I.W.W., and the faltering union would gain new life through the membership of the state's 12,000 strikers. But it was more than simply the stubborn commitment to the I.W.W.'s dogma that led Embree's old guard to oppose—and finally overcome—Conners's revisionism. Embree was concerned with the welfare of the strikers; he argued that the strike should terminate in early 1928 before the seasonal decline in demand for coal was felt and while the strikers could still find jobs in the mines. He felt that there was no way the miners could survive the entire season without wages or a strike fund. As Conners, partially through his own initiative and partially with the support of one faction of miners, made overtures toward the industrial commission, Embree accused him of resorting to politics and used his influence with the General Strike Committee to put an end to Conners's efforts.

In a sense, it is unfortunate that not until the Colorado strike were the Wobblies' "impossibilist" tactics seriously challenged from within. For in a situation not clouded with the tangential question of the length of the strike, perhaps the no-contract principle might have been more seriously debated. Conners's challenge was not new. Early in the history of the I.W.W., there were those who conceded the possibility of signing contracts in an effort to establish an organization that could systematically engage in the education of the workers rather than leaving this process of education to chance after the I.W.W. had moved on. They argued that the workers need not feel committed to the contract since "the contract between an employer and a workman is no more binding than the title deed to a negro slave is just."[41]

However, it should be noted that Embree was not unwilling to employ new tactics in Colorado even though his stance on time contracts and union recognition followed old lines. Like Conners, he realized that there was little to be lost through experimenting with innovative actions in Colorado. One such tactic employed early in the strike was to send the idle miners to operate some abandoned mines in the Walsenburg District.[42] Through such action, the miners would not only gain finances to sustain the strike, but would also demonstrate their ability to engage in production independent of the capitalists. Even though the CF & I company had abandoned this property, their attorneys were able to launch legal maneuvers sufficient to frustrate this effort. Incensed at the I.W.W.'s action and claiming that it was simply a propaganda tactic, two independent operators issued a challenge. To prove the "false philosophy" of the I.W.W., they offered to turn over their mines to the Wobblies providing they could post the safety bond required by state regulations within twenty-four hours. However, the I.W.W.'s treasury, which was incapable of even providing relief to the strikers, lacked funds for financing such an experiment.

All of the I.W.W.'s tactics were designed to maintain the morale of the strikers by involving as many of the miners as possible in strike activity. The car caravans, picketing, and mass meetings (organized and conducted by the strikers themselves) illustrate the I.W.W.'s basic tenet of mass organization.

The I.W.W. leadership was extremely flexible in Colorado, and they realized where they had been vulnerable in the past. As expected, the anti-strike forces in Colorado—namely the companies, state government, media, and conservative labor unions—found it to their advantage to focus attention on the I.W.W.'s radical politics and to characterize the strike as an attack on the social fabric. The I.W.W. countered by emphasizing the traditional bargaining issues of the miners and condemning any acts of violence or sabotage on the part of the strikers. Embree and the other leaders knew that if the state police or the companies were able to draw the strikers into acts of violence, not only would the miners feel the greatest losses in terms of physical injuries, but their real grievances would become secondary issues.

In spite of the Wobblies' sensitivity to these issues, the old antiradical mood prevailed. The press, whose sentiments ran in favor of the conservative AFL unions, was quick to place the blame for the strike upon the failure of the Rockefeller plan. They used the Colorado strike as a means of demonstrating that the logical outgrowth of the "unenlightened capitalists'" stubborn resistance to labor unions naturally resulted in the workers resorting to more radical action that represented, in fact, a very real attack upon the social fabric and the American industrial system.[43] In effect, these "progressive" publishers condemned the western coal operators for resisting the current of change exemplified by their counterparts in the eastern fields.

By stubbornly clinging to what had come to be an outdated philosophy of classic competitive capitalism (as analyzed by Marx), the western operators created an environment that permitted successful Socialist organization of the workers. To wit, in an editorial, the *St. Louis Post Dispatch* claimed:

In the West, there exist bad conditions and a limited work force. Having no alternative, the miner opts for the I.W.W. which offers him a chance to use a method of industrial warfare which constructive unionism frowns upon. The miner, of course, is in error in allowing himself to be thus misled, and he will no doubt pay dearly for his mistake. The false philosophy and destructive tactics of the IWW have no place in our industrial order. But it is well to remember that if some of the mine owners had used wiser policy with regard to unionism, the western miner would never have erred.[44]

The common analysis of the press, the State Industrial Commission, and the Colorado Federation of Labor was that the miners were pawns who had been misled by the I.W.W. The Wobblies' success in Colorado was considered to have been a result of the failure of the company union plan and the operators' stubbornness—not the miners' radicalism.

Since the question of labor's radicalism and class consciousness has typically been the central issue in the analyses of labor historians, it becomes pertinent to focus upon the nature and sources of the Colorado miners' radicalism. Specifically, there exists a debate among scholars revolving around the question of whether western working-class militancy was grounded in class consciousness (in the Marxian sense), or whether it was simply the logical response of pioneer individualists to frontier conditions.

Lipset, in his analysis of the American labor movement, approaches the question of working-class consciousness by isolating two determining American values—equality and achievement. He suggests that the equalitarian-achievement orientation of American workers excluded a working-class ideology, emphasized immediate material goals, and, at times, even encouraged militant tactics.[45] In other words, he employs Merton's classic concept that the pressures generated by the interplay between America's basic values and the facts of social stratification result more in an emphasis upon approved *ends*—particularly pecuniary success—than with the use of approved *means*. Hence, American laborers have resorted to militant tactics solely as a means of attaining success and status, not because of a realization of any inherent shortcomings in the American system.

This view is supported by Lawson in his analysis of the 1927 Colorado coal strike. He concludes that this conflict was the result of a "violent expression of Jeffersonian populism," not a class-conscious labor force challenging the tenets of the social and economic system.[46]

Perlman and Taft fully describe the history of violent class warfare in the American West (including, of course, the Colorado Coal Wars).[47] They, and their disciples in the Wisconsin school of labor history, characterize these conflicts as arising from "the independent and lawless spirit of the frontier," the lack of respect for the social distinctions of a settled community, a disregard by labor for the "elementary amenities of civilized life," and the absence of farmers, a neutral middle class, and others who might keep matters within bounds. These scholars conclude that the bitter disputes arose from the "general characteristics of the frontier" and "quick on the trigger" employers and employees.[48]

In contrast to this point of view, Dubofsky points out that by 1893 the mining West had passed well beyond the frontier stage, and working-class radicalism was a predictable response to the general nature of early industrial capitalism.[49] By the end of the nineteenth century, the coal communities in Colorado and other western states were not wide-open, lawless frontier towns; they were established mining and industrial centers, tightly controlled by the companies. The "foot-loose" transient worker was the exception, not the rule. By and large, the immigrants who came to work in the coal camps brought with them their wives and children in order to start a new life in America. As mentioned earlier, the immigrant miners who came West held preconceptions of what life in the new country would be like—in short, the American dream. Lipset's notion of the equalitarian-achievement orientation is perhaps an accurate description of the preconceptions the immigrants held, but the reality of life in the company towns and coal camps soon forced the miners to reevaluate their situation.

The miners' own accounts of the early years of industrial struggles provide the most credible source of information concerning the nature of their radicalism and class consciousness. Among those miners who were active in organizing and strike activity, there is general agreement about, and a common understanding of, their shared situation.

The miners did, indeed, come to share a common awareness of their status as a class apart from capital. In the earliest years of organizing activity, the miners believed that if they were to go out on strike, the operators would realize the seriousness of their demands and at least engage in dialogue, if not actual negotiations concerning hazardous working conditions and lower-than-subsistence wage levels. How, they wondered, could they ever come to realize their aspirations if they were forced deeper into debt to the company each year? The companies responded to the miners' action by resorting to lockouts, evictions from company houses, and by importing new immigrants to act as strikebreakers. At first the strikers directed their hostility toward the scabs, with whom they often did not share a common language. But the strikers came to understand that the operators were using this tactic not only to keep the mines operating, but also to channel the strikers' hostility away from the company and toward the foreign strikebreakers. The result was that the miners became even more spiteful of the capitalists, and they responded by infiltrating the closed camps and converting the scabs to their cause rather than fighting them. Inevitably, the strikes turned into wars of attrition, destined to be lost by the strikers, who were financially unable to hold out for long.

Even after the strikes had ended, the miners tell of how the operators tried to exploit ethnic divisions in order to diffuse the unity of the miners. The foremen would assign men to work shifts by ethnic groups. They would then try to convince successive shifts that conditions were poor because the group that had worked before them had failed to do the dead work, left the working face in disorder, or left dangerous conditions for the relief crew. But the miners, who admit that they at first fell for this ploy, eventually came to realize that it was not their fellow workers who were the source of their misery. They identified the capitalists as their adversaries and overcame ethnic divisions. The miners did not simply form coalitions among ethnic groups; rather, they came to develop a class awareness that transcended all such barriers. They shared a common hostility toward the operators.

As the early years of the twentieth century passed by, the miners became increasingly disillusioned with the American promise. Those who rationalized their situations by hoping that their sacrifices would result in a better life for their children soon came to see their sons, educated in company schools, forced to follow them into the pits as soon as they were old enough to handle a pick and shovel. Every time the miners attempted to assert their claim to a more decent treatment and a better place in the American system, they found themselves up against not only the unyielding capitalists, but also the coercive agents of the government—e.g., state militia, local sheriffs, and federal troops—who consistently came to the aid of the operators.

The miners defined themselves as radicals. Although their sense of the term "radical" incorporated no sophisticated notion of Socialist ideology, they shared a working-class consciousness in the classic Marxian sense. The western coal fields represented a prime example of the type of capitalist exploitation of which Marx and Engels had spoken. The massive labor pool, i.e., reserve army of labor, kept wages at, or near, the subsistence level. Even during periods of economic boom in the coal industry, the relative life-style of the mine laborer remained virtually unchanged. The coal industry in Colorado was far behind other industries throughout the nation in moving from the competitive to the corporate stage. While the influence of the UMWA in the eastern fields functioned to stabilize the coal industry by placing a floor under wage levels, the wages in the West fell with the pressures of competition.

Throughout World War I, the boom in the coal industry created a period of relative stability for all coal miners, including those in Colorado. But the recession of the 1920s again led to pay cuts and less work for the Colorado miners. The Jacksonville pay scale, to which Colorado operators had voluntarily conformed during good times, was the first casualty of the recession. The series of pay cuts in the years preceding the I.W.W. strike served to reignite the consciousness and radicalism of the Colorado miners. Hence, it is not at all surprising that these men found the leadership of the I.W.W. particularly relevant within this specific historical, social, and economic context. The miners were not, as asserted by commentators of the time, simply "pawns" who had been "misled by the false philosophies of the I.W.W." Rather, the Colorado miners represented a segment of the working class with a long history of exploitation and frustrated struggle. They were disillusioned, desperate, disenfranchised men who willfully chose a radical course of action. The failure of the Wobblies to establish and maintain a viable organization in Colorado resulted from the anarcho-syndicalist ideology and strategy of the I.W.W, not from the absence of class consciousness and radicalism among the miners.

NOTES

1. John R. Commons, *History of Labor in the United States* (New York: Macmillan, 1918); Selig Perlman and Philip Taft, *History of Labor in the United States, 1896-1932* (New York: Macmillan, 1935).

2. Harry O. Lawson, "The Colorado Coal Strike of 1927-1928" (Master's thesis, (University of Colorado, 1950).

3. Daniel J. McClurg, "The Colorado Coal Strike of 1927—Tactical Leadership," *Labor History* (1966).

4. Charles J. Baynard, "The 1927-1928 Colorado Coal Strike," *Pacific Historical Review* (August 1963).

5. Sam H. Schurr, *Energy in the American Economy* (Baltimore: Johns Hopkins, 1960); Lloyd Ulman, *The Rise of the National Trade Union* (Cambridge: Harvard University Press, 1955); Peter Booth Wiley, "The United Mine Workers and the Rationalization of the Bituminous Coal Industry, 1945-1960" (Master's thesis, University of Wisconsin, 1960); Morton Baratz, *The Union and the Coal Industry* (New Haven, 1955).

6. William M. Dick, *Labor And Socialism in America* (New York: National University Publications, 1972), p. 68.

7. Dick, *Labor and Socialism*, p. 76.

8. John Mitchell, *Organized Labor: Its Problems, Purposes, and Ideals* (Philadelphia: American Book and Bible House, 1903), pp. 186-95.

9. Barron B. Beshoar, *Out of the Depths* (Denver: Denver Trades and Labor Assembly, 1942); Frank L. Palmer, "War in Colorado," *The Nation* (1928); Saul Alinsky, *John L. Lewis: An Unauthorized Biography* (New York: Putnam's, 1949).

10. Wiley, "The United Mine Workers."

11. "Bloody Colorado," *The Nation* (1927), 534.

12. Until the late 1920s, when the overall drop in demand for coal began to be felt in the West, the three major coal companies in Colorado were able to remain competitive with one another by absorbing or crushing smaller independent companies that encroached upon their market.

13. Ben M. Selekeman and Mary Van Kleeck, *Employees' Representation in the Coal Mines* (New York: Russell Sage Foundation, 1924), p. 27.

14. John D. Rockefeller, Jr., *The Colorado Industrial Plan* (n.p., 1916), pp. 63-95.

15. Selekeman, *Representation*, p. 149.

16. Several miners stated that the company's wage plan was arbitrary, that the employees could not participate in any way in determining wages, and that the miners had no means of enforcing the wage clause. They felt they were benefiting from UMWA activity without contributing to it. Interviews with Michael Freil, Walsenburg, 1975; Victor Bazanell, Ludlow, 1976; Mike Livoda, Denver, 1975.

17. Selekeman, *Representation*, p. 149.

18. The miners at first felt that if they all refused to sign the wage-cut petitions, the State Industrial Commission would force the companies to maintain the prevailing wage levels. But, in the absence of a union that could serve as a bargaining agent for the miners, combined with the threats of being fired if they did not sign, the solidarity of the miners quickly broke down. Interviews with Arlow Wilson and Louis Bougger, Louisville, 1975.

19. Quoted in Melvyn Dubofsky, *We Shall Be All* (Chicago: Quadrangle Books, 1969), p. 484.

20. *Walsenburg Independent*, August 9, 1927.

21. *Colorado Labor Advocate*, September 22, 1927.

22. Lawson, "Colorado Coal Strike," p. 66.

23. *Rocky Mountain News*, October 19, December 3, 1927.

24. McClurg, "Colorado Coal Strike," 76.

25. Interview with Walt Celensky, Boulder, 1976.

26. *Colorado Labor Advocate*, October 20, 27, 1927; *Walsenburg Independent*, October 18, 1927.

27. *Trinidad Chronical-News*, October 19, 1927.

28. McClurg, "Colorado Coal Strike," 91.

29. Josephine J. Roche, "Memorandum Describing Columbine Incident," Roche Collection, Denver Public Library.

30. Ibid.

31. Ibid.

32. Frank Thurman, interviewed in Boulder in 1976, had been operator of the Black Diamond mine near the Columbine and confirmed the fact that the operators had conspired over the weekend to attack the miners on Monday, November 21.

33. McClurg, "Colorado Coal Strike," 84; *Colorado Labor Advocate*, December 24, 1927.

34. On Sunday, November 20, 1927, Lawrence and Claude Amiceralla, striking miners, were summoned by their parents, who lived inside the camp at the Columbine. When they arrived, they were warned by soldiers who had been drinking heavily that if the strikers attempted to picket in the morning, they were in for a surprise. Interview, Lafayette, 1976.

35. *Rocky Mountain News*, February 15, 1928.

36. Dubofsky, *We Shall Be All*, p. 447.

37. Patrick Renshaw, *The Wobblies: The Story of Syndicalism in the United States* (New York: Doubleday, 1967), p. 252.

38. Dubofsky, *We Shall Be All*, p. 165.

39. Even workers who had been active in the I.W.W. felt that the Wobblies were running out on them when leadership was most needed. They went so far as to accuse I.W.W officials of leaving the state with strike funds. Interview, Brugger.

40. Dubofsky, *We Shall Be All*, p. 165.

41. *Solidarity*, June 4, 1919.

42. Baynard, "The 1927-1928 Colorado Coal Strike," 242.

43. *San Francisco Chronicle*, November 23, 1927; *Rocky Mountain News*, November 27, 1927; *Denver Post*, November 26, 1927; *New York Times*, November 23, 1927; *Colorado Labor Advocate*, November 23, 1927; *Denver Evening News*, November 23, 1927.

44. *St. Louis Post-Dispatch*, October 2, 1927.

45. Seymour Martin Lipset, *The First New Nation* (New York: Basic Books, 1963), pp. 170-99.

46. Lawson, "Colorado Coal Strike," 184.

47. Perlman and Taft, *History of Labor*, *passim*.

48. The Wisconsin school analysis is based upon idealism and accidentalism: it is not a theory of western working-class radicalism.

49. Melvyn Dubofsky, "Origins of Western Working-Class Radicalism, 1890-1905," *Labor History* (1966).

THE I.W.W. AND THE BOULDER CANYON PROJECT: THE DEATH THROES OF AMERICAN SYNDICALISM

GUY LOUIS ROCHA

Nevada witnessed the birth and death of the Industrial Workers of the World. After the I.W.W.'s founding in July 1905, the radical labor union had staged its first major organizational campaigns, in Tonopah and Goldfield, beginning in the latter part of that year and extending through early 1908. There, in south-central Nevada, the anarcho-syndicalist I.W.W. suffered its first substantial defeat at the hands of local businessmen and mine owners, state officials, and a contingent of federal troops.

Over two decades later, the final significant organizational activity of the I.W.W. in the state terminated on August 16, 1931, with an unsuccessful strike at the Boulder Canyon Project. This abortive action at the federal government's dam project in southern Nevada stands out as one of the last important I.W.W.-related activities in America. Syndicalism, as embodied in the I.W.W., was in its death throes.[1]

The union was true first to last to its commitment to the unskilled workers. At the I.W.W.'s founding convention in 1905, Big Bill Haywood had shouted, "We are going down into the gutter to get at the mass of workers and bring them up to a decent plane of living."[2] At the Boulder Canyon Project, the organizers were likewise devoted to protecting the unskilled workers from exploitative contractors and bettering their immediate conditions, and not particularly in promoting class warfare and revolution. For example, in reference to the numbers of injuries and deaths projected by the I.W.W. as a result of dam construction over a seven-year period, a Wobbly —after describing a recent premature dynamite explosion that critically injured two workers—graphically articulated the I.W.W.'s objectives at the dam site:

Our job is to organize, make it safe, make it fit to work on, and make it a source of decent living for ourselves. . . . When the Simplon Tunnel was finished in 1901 a statue was erected to the workers killed on the job. They may do it here. It is up to the workers to chose between a red union card and a statue.[3]

Little attention has been given to the labor problems, much less the role of the I.W.W., at the Boulder Canyon Project during the first spring and summer of construction. Conditions were extremely hazardous, the heat unbearable, and an open-shop policy was practiced by the six private firms contracted to build the gigantic concrete impediment to the Colorado River. At the same time, many of the dam workers found themselves without adequate housing because the project was begun six months earlier than originally planned. As the depression became more critical in the latter half of 1930, President Herbert Hoover, and Secretary of the Interior Ray Lyman Wilbur, determined it was necessary to employ some of the vast number of jobless workers in America as soon as possible. President Hoover then requested Elwood Mead, director of the Bureau of Reclamation, to proceed on the dam construction with the "utmost dispatch possible." Bureau of Reclamation engineers rushed the completion of project plans and specifications and bids were let in December. The price of such a measure was to begin building the dam before the construction of Boulder City, the proposed model government town some seven miles from the dam site.[4]

The original building contract, a project of over ten years of Colorado River control planning that included federal passage of the Boulder Canyon Project Act in December 1928, included only three stipulations in regard to labor. "Mongolians" could not be hired; preference was to be given veterans; and, what later proved to be one of the most important issues associated with labor-management relations on the project, 80 percent of the laborers hired by the contractors had to be housed in company buildings in Boulder City. Shortly after obtaining the construction contract with a bid of $48,890,995.50 on March 11, five million less than the nearest of two competitors, the Six Companies, Inc., of San Francisco ("Big Six") found that the latter stipulations had been temporarily suspended with the government's decision to begin dam operations before Boulder City was built.[5] Paul Kleinsorge, in his work *The Boulder Canyon Project*, wrote:

Construction was begun in the spring of 1931, and engineers and contractors alike rushed the start of the work, although the existing conditions were most unsatisfactory. Instead of adhering to the usual practice of having small crews prepare adequate facilities before the main body of men was put to work, hundreds of men were given jobs in 1931 even though Boulder City was a barren desert. The inevitable result was severe hardships for those employed, especially since the summer temperatures for 1931 were twelve degrees above normal.[6]

Another problem in addition to the lack of adequate housing resulted from the government contract. Dam construction was divided into two major phases. The first phase entailed the digging of four tunnels, each 4,000 feet long and 50 feet wide, with two on each side of the river to divert the water around the dam site after the cofferdams were built, thus drying the area for work. The contract specified that the tunneling had to be finished by October 1, 1933, or a $3,000 find would be imposed for every day over the deadline. The second phase included the actual building of the dam, and the deadline for completion in this case was June 15, 1936. Again the same penalty would be imposed for every day over the deadline. The entire project, including the power plant, was to be completed by May 1, 1938. The impending deadlines led the Big Six in the first years of construction to a job speed-up, where safety precautions, on many occasions, were neglected to save "all-important" time and money.[7]

In late March 1931, the Big Six initiated work on the dam section of the railroad linking Las Vegas to the project. The section connecting the Boulder City camp to the Union Pacific siding seven miles west of Las Vegas (Bracken) had been completed by another contractor. The Lewis Construction Company was presently building the short stretch between the Boulder City camp and the dam section of the railroad. Construction had already begun on the dam highway as well, which when finished would connect Las Vegas to Boulder City and the dam site. Both the railroad and the highway, like Boulder City, were to have been originally completed before the awarding of the Boulder Canyon Project contract.[8]

On April 9, while in Las Vegas to sign the Big Six building contract, Raymond F. Walter—chief engineer of the reclamation bureau's Denver office—expressed the government's priorities regarding the Boulder Canyon Project. Walter announced "that under the revised plan, everything is working out on schedule except the construction of Boulder City, which has been temporarily sidetracked to make way for the more necessary work." Paradoxically, Louis C. Cramton, appointed by Secretary of the Interior Wilbur to oversee the construction of Boulder City, recognized the value of adequate housing and living conditions for the dam workers, but not the immediacy. "Our plans for the city," Cramton proclaimed, "will be in the best interests of the workmen employed on the job, for satisfied workers means greatly increased efficiency, lack of labor difficulties, and saving of both time and money in construction of the dam project." Cramton's observations in early April later proved to be an unconscious prognostication of future labor strife due in large part to the delay of Boulder City's construction.[9]

With the signing of the building contract by Bureau of Reclamation Director Mead in Las Vegas on April 13, and by Secretary of the Interior Wilbur in Washington on April 20, actual dam operations began. During April, 800 workers were employed on or near the dam site, and the large, unorganized workforce attracted the I.W.W. Wobbly headquarters in

Chicago sent organizers representing Construction Workers Industrial Union No. 310 (IU No. 310) to establish a local in Las Vegas. With the small desert town of just over 5,000 residents as a base, the organizers were then to hire on with the Big Six and other contractors, solicit on the job, and agitate for better conditions.[10]

The I.W.W., no longer a powerful labor organization as a result of the devastating federal and state repression during and after World War I, as well as the internal dissension and schisms that plagued the union in 1919 and 1924, now planned in the depression year of 1931 to make a comeback as a viable union. In addition to the coal strike in Harlan County, Kentucky, the I.W.W. focused its resurgent organizational activity on the Boulder Canyon Project. Frank Desmond Anderson, recently elected a general organizer committee member for IU No. 310, was selected as head Wobbly organizer in the crusade to make the dam project and nearby Las Vegas an I.W.W. stronghold.[11]

Anderson arrived in Las Vegas sometime in early May and proceeded to the project, where he obtained a job at the river camp as a truck tender. Shortly thereafter, on May 16, construction began at the dam site when the first dynamite charges were exploded "at the portals of two adits driven into the abutments of the projected dam, one on each side, to intersect the diversion tunnels." The 400 men, including Anderson, employed at the Big Six river camp to work on the tunnels were housed in crude, wooden dormitories similar to army barracks. Perched precariously on the canyon wall at "Cape Horn," the river bend just above the dam site, the camp had little to offer in the way of common comforts. Showers were unavailable in the dormitories, forcing dam laborers to bathe in the river. Drinking water was drawn directly from the silt-laden Colorado River, stored in large tanks, and, with no water coolers, it was soon tepid or even hot. As temperatures increased, the water, with its high bacteria count, began making the workers sick.[12]

At the same time, there were no facilities for cooling the dormitories. Daytime temperatures were constantly on the rise, and by the end of July the average daily maximum temperature was 119.9 degrees. After an eight-hour shift dam workers were totally exhausted. They would return to the river camp only to swelter in the evening heat, which by the end of July averaged 95 degrees. With the hottest summer days and nights reaching 128 and 103 degrees respectively, and only warm or hot water to drink, it is a wonder that the river-camp laborers could sleep, much less work.[13]

Dr. Elwood Mead, paraphrasing a March 9, 1931, Department of the Interior press release in an address at the Massachusetts Institute of Technology, described the brutal summer heat:

This project, like Panama, has a climate. The summer wind which sweeps over the gorge from the desert feels like a blast from a furnace. At the rim of the gorge, where most of the work must be done, there is neither soil, grass nor trees. The sun beats down on a broken surface of lava rocks. At midday they cannot be touched with the naked hand. It is bad enough as a place for men to work. It is no place for a boarding house or a sleeping porch.[14]

Mead was aware of the inhospitable conditions associated with housing men in the canyon during the summer, yet did little to remedy the immediate situation. Apparently he assumed that the men could survive the first summer without great losses and occupy the Boulder City housing scheduled for completion in the fall. "Next year," declared Mead, "there will be an entirely different story."[15]

Meanwhile, Frank Anderson and other Wobblies employed at the dam project were outraged, not just over housing conditions, but more because of the growing number of injuries and deaths related to poor working conditions. Although some of the casualties appeared to be careless accidents on the part of the workers involved, the Wobblies quickly publicized the situation as "capitalist exploitation" and a job speed-up through their national weeklies, *Industrial Solidarity* (Chicago) and *Industrial Worker* (Seattle). IU No. 310 local headquarters in Las Vegas wired all dam information via Western Union to Chicago and Seattle. After the radical newspapers were received in Las Vegas, Wobblies would sell them on downtown street corners, in front of casinos, and smuggle them into the Boulder City and river camps on the federal reservation. The I.W.W. hoped that workers would join the union by dramatizing the working and housing conditions at the dam site, and advocating a six-hour day to reduce the work load and employ more men.[16]

Such was not the case. According to the *Las Vegas Evening Review Journal*, twenty-six persons died on the dam project between May 16 and August 4—approximately one person every three days—and a majority of them from heat prostration. Yet, for a dam worker to join a labor union, especially a union with the I.W.W.'s national image, on an open-shop job was not considered a wise decision in the midst of the nation's worst depression. Single men and married men with their families had traveled by the thousands to Las Vegas in hopes of finding a job on the dam project. The lawn in front of the downtown Union Pacific depot served as the home for many of the desperate job-seekers. The rest moved on to "Ragtown," located between the Boulder City camp and the dam site, where they lived in cars, trailers, tents, makeshift shelters, and out in the open, while the men "rustled" for jobs. With employment at a premium, few dam workers, despite the miserable working and housing conditions, desired to join the I.W.W. and jeopardize their livelihood.[17]

The Wobbly local had no problems attracting hostility and suppression in nearby Las Vegas, although IU No. 310's organizational campaign in the Clark County seat, and at the Boulder Canyon Project, had met with only limited success at best. At 9:00 P.M., on July 10, Deputy Sheriff Eddie Johnson, a part-time Boulder Club bouncer, arrested Frank Anderson in front of the casino. Anderson recently had been laid off from his job as truck tender at the project and was now working evenings in Las Vegas. Most of his free time was spent selling Wobbly newspapers both at the dam site and in town. Subsequent to Anderson's arrest, the July 11 headlines of the *Las Vegas Age* proclaimed, "I.W.W. Group at Dam Revealed." A quote attributed to Anderson read that he forecast Wobbly control of Boulder City, organized twenty-one members in one month, and boasted of 300 workers as I.W.W. members. Further, the article claimed that the labor union's objective at the dam project was to organize a large enough body of workers to call a general strike.[18]

Obviously sensationalist journalism was used to arouse public antagonism. The *Las Vegas Evening Review Journal* criticized the *Age* for its inflammatory story and claimed that there was no real Wobbly threat at the Boulder Canyon Project. Local IU No. 310 headquarters denied the statements credited to Anderson, as well as charges that they forced workers to join the I.W.W. organization. The construction workers' local argued that "its primary purpose is not to call a Boulder Dam strike but to organize for better pay, hours, and so on, and that if a strike is necessary the men will have the power of unity to fight it to successful issue."[19] The I.W.W. was conducting itself more like a "bread and butter" union than an anarcho-syndicalist organization, but that did little to change its subversive image in the minds of Las Vegas officials.

On Saturday morning, July 11, I.W.W. organizers Louis Gracey and C. E. Setzer were arrested as they left the Western Union telegraph office. Gracey and Setzer had just wired Herbert Mahler, I.W.W. general secretary-treasurer, in Chicago informing him of Anderson's arrest and requesting defense funds. A Western Union operator apparently tipped off the police, although the manager of the telegraph office denied the Wobblies' accusation. Las Vegas IU No. 310 then took steps to secure an attorney to fight the vagrancy charges lodged against the three organizers, while town officials planned an investigation of the radical union.[20]

Local officials approached Assistant U.S. Attorney George Montrose, in Las Vegas that Saturday on federal business, about the possibility of government prosecution in the Wobbly cases. Montrose's response was that the matter was "wholly and solely in the hands of county and city officials." No government action would be forthcoming unless overt acts were committed on the federal reservation, or construction of the dam delayed by disruptive union activities. With no cooperation from the U.S. Attorney's office, city officials decided to prosecute the three I.W.W. organizers on the vagrancy charges.[21]

Saturday night witnessed a wholesale roundup of Wobblies selling

Industrial Solidarity and *Industrial Worker* in front of the Boulder Club.
Evidently staging a protest against Anderson's, Gracey's, and Setzer's arrests,
W. F. Burroughs, R. A. McFarland, Bert King, K. Mather, and Barney
Savilonis were arrested by Eddie Johnson and incarcerated in the city jail.
IU No. 310 planned to continue selling newspapers, and as fast as Wobblies
were arrested, other union members would take their place. Using tactics
similar to the bygone free speech fights between 1909 and 1916, the I.W.W.
hoped to fill the city jail and inundate the court docket.[22]

Eight Wobblies found themselves spending Sunday and Monday in the
Las Vegas jail. Although the I.W.W. members probably capitalized on their
predicament and exaggerated conditions in the jail, it still appears that the
facility lacked a swamp cooler and adequate bedding in the crowded cell.
Daytime heat was stifling, and the floor proved to be a poor substitute for a
mattress. Besides these obvious discomforts, the Wobbly cell was the drunk
tank. Early Monday morning, two Wobblies were told they had to work
and carry boxes through the streets of Las Vegas. The men refused on the
grounds that they had not been tried and convicted of any crime. The eight
Wobblies' only meal that Monday was a couple of sandwiches given them
at 9:00 A.M. When Police Chief Clay Williams was interviewed by the
Evening Review Journal about the food problem, he replied that "he was
giving I.W.W. members no assurance as to how much they would be fed
when housed in the Las Vegas city jail."[23]

On the morning of July 13, the eight Wobblies were arraigned before
Municipal Judge W. G. Morse. They pleaded not guilty to the vagrancy
charges and declared that they were going "to stand upon their constitutional rights and demand jury trials." With the arresting officers absent,
Judge Morse rescheduled the hearing to 4:00 P.M., Wednesday, July 15.
Postponement was granted all defendants except Barney Savilonis. He was
fined ten dollars, which could be worked off on a five-day street job.
Refusing to pay the fine or work, Savilonis was returned to his cell and had
to endure a diet of bread and water. City Attorney Frank A. Stevens took
the matter of jury trial into consideration. Having no provision in the city
ordinances for a jury trial in municipal court, a favorable decision meant
that the case would go to a higher court.[24]

In the meantime, Wobblies continued to sell I.W.W. newspapers on the
streets of Las Vegas. On Monday evening, three more men were arrested on
vagrancy charges and jailed with their fellow workers. Later that night the
eleven Wobblies were separated from the other prisoners and given no food.
All efforts by union members to provide the incarcerated men with outside
food were prevented by the police. In addition to the problems with city
officials, the Western Union held up a telegram addressed to Secretary-
Treasurer Mahler for four days. The overt suppression of the Las Vegas
IU No. 310 organizers and members, and subsequently the denial of a jury

trial by the city attorney, appeared to set the stage for increased troubles associated with the July 15 hearing.[25]

Surprisingly, however, the case was decided in favor of the I.W.W. Frank Anderson, represented by T. Alonzo Wells—attorney for the Wobblies—was called before the court Wednesday afternoon. Eddie Johnson was sworn in as a witness. He testified that he was a Clark County deputy sheriff and was working at the Boulder Club as a bouncer at the time of Anderson's arrest. Johnson stated that he had seen the defendant three times between July 1 and July 10 and on one occasion overheard Anderson criticize labor conditions at the dam site. Anderson's entering the Boulder Club on two occasions, and his selling of I.W.W. newspapers at the time of his arrest, were introduced into evidence.[26]

Well's cross-examination of the witness destroyed the grounds for vagrancy. Although Anderson earned twenty-eight dollars a month as a member of the IU No. 310 General Organizer Committee, Johnson admitted he knew nothing about Anderson's means of support at the time of his arrest, had never read a Wobbly newspaper, and that he arrested the defendant because "Bud" Bodell, chief deputy sheriff and owner of the Boulder Club, told him to do so. Counsel for the defense made a motion for dismissal following Johnson's testimony which Judge Morse denied.[27]

Frank Anderson then took the stand. City Attorney Stevens attempted to discredit Anderson's testimony in the cross-examination, but to no avail. When Stevens redirected his questions and argument, and cited court precedents in similar Texas and Ontario, Canada cases, Wells protested on the grounds he came prepared to defend Anderson on a vagrancy charge and not as a Wobbly. Ironically, Anderson and the other defendants might have been prosecuted under the 1919 Criminal Syndicalism Law, which outlawed the distribution and sale of subversive literature among other proscribed activities. The Wobblies were fortunate for it seems the Las Vegas city attorney either neglected to research his case properly, or realized that no I.W.W. member had ever been convicted of violating Nevada's anti-syndicalism law. At 5:15 P.M., Judge Morse took the case under advisement until 9:00 A.M. of the following day.[28]

On the morning of July 16, Judge Morse ruled that the City of Las Vegas had failed to prove the charges against Frank Anderson and ordered that he be released. On motion of City Attorney F. A. Stevens, the remaining cases were dismissed. Barney Savilonis was released at the same time, even though his sentence was unfinished. The I.W.W. had won an important legal battle in the southern Nevada town. The newly freed Wobblies returned to selling their newspapers, organizing dam workers, and agitating on and off the job for better conditions. The Las Vegas Central Labor Council now recognized the I.W.W. construction workers' local and invited a delegate to address their next meeting on Tuesday evening, July 21. After his release, W. F. Burroughs wrote in *Industrial Solidarity* that "much fine sentiment among the local people had come to light as a result of the affair. Nevadans have not forgotten the workers' condition in the unparalleled Goldfield which was controlled by the I.W.W."[29]

The Wobblies' success in Las Vegas may have influenced the Big Six and the federal government to upgrade conditions on the dam project. By early August, cooling systems were being installed in the bunk and cook houses at the Boulder City camp, and at the river camp's cook house. The powder room at the dam site was moved to the Arizona side of the river from its previous location thirty feet from the blacksmith shop. Drinking water was transported from Las Vegas to the river camp, although the Wobblies claimed there was not enough. And a Frigidaire water cooler was placed in the river camp cook house. This improvement also had its limitation according to I.W.W reports. With only one electric coil, and the water cooler's constant use, little cold water was available.[30]

IU No. 310 was not satisfied with these small concessions. They demanded a six-hour day, or "eight hours from camp to camp," on the grounds that Boulder City camp workers spent eleven hours on the job, and river camp workers nine to ten, when travel was included to and from the actual work site. Other demands made were: "a cooling system in every bunk house; water flushed toilets; health inspected camps; food clean and wholesome; water clear and pure."[31]

Whether or not a food problem existed was a questionable issue. An *Industrial Solidarity* article reported that the Anderson Brothers Board and Supply Company, contracted by the federal government to feed project employees, did not provide enough food and that the food served was of poor quality. According to the Wobbly (card No. x81482) writing the exposé, on one occasion at the river camp there had been widespread ptomaine poisoning due to bad pork, and four or five men had died as a result. The Anderson brothers were also charged with not hiring enough kitchen help, and those hired were men just waiting for construction jobs. The irate Wobblies demanded three full-time dining room crews.[32]

Yet other reports conflicted with *Solidarity*'s account of the food problem on most counts. One itinerant worker who found a job as a waiter for the Anderson brothers at Lewis Construction Camp "B" reported in the *Nation* that he was definitely overworked, but "there can be no legitimate complaint about the food, either as to quantity or quality, and I would say that it was well chosen to suit climatic conditions." The consensus at the project was that the food was generally good.[33]

The *Las Vegas Age* did report one outbreak of ptomaine poisoning at the river camp which affected twenty-seven workers, but all rapidly recovered. The ptomaine poisoning that allegedly killed four or five workers may have been covered up, but it is much more likely that the Wobblies, in their zeal to organize dam workers and rectify real problems, sometimes exaggerated already bad conditions at the camps.[34]

The I.W.W. did not have to exaggerate the Big Six wage cut on August 7, 1931. As the swing shift on the dam project went to work that afternoon, they saw a notice stating that tunnel workers would receive a wage reduction. According to a Wobbly report, muckers, nippers, and cherry pickers were to have their daily pay reduced from $5.00 to $4.00, cabletenders from $5.60 to $4.00, and brakemen from $5.60 to $5.00. The Big Six, and later the federal government, argued that a new mucking machine rendered some unskilled tunnel labor less valuable and that the pay cut only affected about thirty men. The workers, on the other hand, immediately protested against the wage cut charging that the Big Six was trying to take advantage of the unlimited labor supply in Las Vegas and Williamsville (another name for "Ragtown"), and that 180 workers suffered from the wage reduction. They argued that the construction company would threaten to hire other laborers if the present men affected did not capitulate and accept the lower wage. Ironically, just three months earlier, the president of the Big Six proclaimed that the company "was anxious to cooperate with the government in its desire to maintain or raise the wage scale throut [sic] the nation."[35]

Aroused by the wage cut, the swing-shift workers met the day crew coming off work at the boat landing and discussed the situation. Two Wobblies addressed the gathering and exhorted the workers to hold a mass meeting to consider strike action. The day and swing crews agreed to meet at the river camp cook house at 5:00 P.M. The debate there was brief. The 400 workers in attendance voted unanimously to strike. A committee was elected to draw up strike demands and then travel to the Boulder City camp and solicit workers to join the walkout.[36]

The meeting at the Boulder City camp began at 7:00 P.M. Nearly 600 workers attended and after hearing about the wage reduction voted to go out on strike. After a second strike committee was organized, the river and Boulder City camp committees were to present the strike demands to Big Six Superintendent Frank T. Crowe the following day at 10:00 A.M. All work was brought to a standstill.[37]

The first and only major labor-management confrontation on the Boulder Canyon Project had begun. On Saturday, August 8, the two Las Vegas daily newspapers featured banner headlines announcing the strike. The labor unrest even made the front page of the *New York Times*. The *Las Vegas Age* had interviewed Frank Crowe by telephone the night of the strike. Crowe's opinion at that time was that the "protest" would have little effect on the project, "was largely the result of I.W.W. agitation . . . and that the company would be glad to get rid of such." The committee when interviewed stated that the walkout was a spontaneous action stemming from the wage cut, and did not result from I.W.W. action or any other labor organization. "We wish to make it plain," committee members emphasized, "that the strike has nothing to do with the I.W.W.s or the United Mine Workers—it is a matter distinctly among the workmen on this project. We're not Wobblies and don't want to be classed as such." Although Frank Anderson and other IU No. 310 organizers and members tried to promote the strike at the dam site and in I.W.W. newspapers, the overwhelming majority of unorganized workers reasoned that to openly associate themselves with the small contingent of Wobblies would undermine their cause by giving the strike action a radical image.[38]

L. L. "Red" Williams, head of the strike committee, verbally presented Superintendent Crowe the strike demands Saturday morning. The demands included:

1. A pay raise from $4.00 to $5.00 for surfacemen; $5.50 for tunnel workers; $6.00 for miners; and $6.00 for carpenters.
2. Improvements in the sanitary conditions of the river camp.
3. That all men be returned to their jobs without discrimination.
4. That workers be supplied with ice water until drinking fountains were installed.
5. That rates for board be set at $1.50 flat per day.
6. Strict adherence to Nevada and Arizona mining safety laws.
7. That dry rooms be installed at portals in tunnels.
8. An eight-hour day from camp to camp.
9. That a safety miner be placed in each heading.

Crowe told the strike committees he would take twenty-four hours to consider the demands and announced a general shutdown. With 1,400 men, including skilled laborers, out on strike by that time, Crowe's action meant little to the protesting workers.[39]

In an interview for the *Evening Review Journal*, Superintendent Crowe claimed that if the laborers had not gone out on strike they would have had electricity in the river camp dormitories that night for fans and lights, and that Frigidaire water coolers were already in operation there. He denied there were any delays in transporting workers to and from the construction camps. Crowe even stated that the company's July records showed no reported accidents. The death of seven Big Six employees—five from heat prostration, one drowning, and one from an appendicitis attack—must not have been considered accidents by Crowe.[40]

The Wobblies associated with the strike accused "Speed-Up" Crowe, as he was derogatorily called, of lying about conditions. According to a report in *Industrial Solidarity*, electricity could not have been provided that night because the walkout began at 4:00 P.M., and the electricians had already stopped work. The article also claimed that there were no fans or water coolers in the river camp and no preparations in the dormitories for water coolers. Travel to and from the Boulder City camp for dam workers was not just one hour as Crowe announced, but between three and four. Another accusation was directed toward Crowe's statement regarding the absence of accidents involving Big Six employees in July. "There are six men drawing compensation for July," the I.W.W. argued, "and if they aren't accident cases why are Nevada and Arizona paying compensation?" Whether or not Superintendent Crowe's or the Wobblies' stories reflected actual conditions at the dam project, the fact remained that the striking workers themselves believed immediate conditions had to be upgraded.[41]

At 10:00 A.M., August 9, Crowe responded to the strike demands by closing down the project indefinitely. He refused to make any concessions and told the committees that the striking workers must vacate the federal reservation. William Wattis, president of the Big Six, when asked in San Francisco about strike demands for an increase in pay, cold water, and a safety inspector at all tunnels, candidly replied, "We do not mean to be arbitrary, but we will not discuss the matter with them. They will have to work under our conditions or not at all."[42]

Many workers picked up their paychecks and left the area for Las Vegas after word spread that federal troops were in readiness and might be called by Walker R. Young, the government construction engineer in charge of the dam project. Superintendent Crowe announced that he would hire new crews as soon as all strikers had left the federal reservation. The strike committee countered Crowe's plans by keeping as many workers as possible on the project to continue the strike. Sympathetic Las Vegas merchants donated food and money to the remaining strikers, and the siege began with the protesting workers determined to obtain their demands.[43]

The Big Six was just as determined to clear the federal reservation of strikers. Shortly after Crowe's announcement in Boulder City of an indefinite shutdown, Big Six strikebreakers traveled to the river camp to deport any workers found there. The strikers at the dam site, including I.W.W organizer Fred Fuglevik, were rounded up at gunpoint and loaded into company trucks. Fortunately for the laborers, a U.S. deputy marshal arrived on the scene and ordered the vehicles unloaded. After arresting one strikebreaker for carrying a weapon, the deputy marshal told the strikers the Big Six had no authority to move them without a warrant. A successful strike seemed a distinct possibility as long as the federal government maintained a neutral stand.[44]

Yet subsequent events demonstrated that federal officials would abandon their neutral position to support the interests of the Big Six. At a 6:00 P.M. meeting held in the Boulder City government warehouse on August 11, Walker Young ordered the strikers to vacate the federal reservation at 8:00 A.M. the following day. After a discussion of conditions on the project, the recently amalgamated General Strike Committee, desiring no confrontation with government authorities, agreed to comply with the order if transportation was provided.[45]

Early Wednesday morning, Young, U.S. Marshal Jacob H. Fulmer, and Assistant U.S. Attorney George Montrose proceeded to the river camp where between 150 and 200 strikers, including the Wobbly contingent, were holding out. Congratulating the workers for the nonviolent manner in which they had conducted the strike, Young told the men that the reservation was to be cleared, and that government trucks would take them to Las Vegas if they so desired. The striking laborers assumed the federal authorities were acting as a neutral body and left the project peaceably. Yet they reminded government and Big Six officials that the strike was still on. The strikers established "Camp Stand" eight miles southeast of Las Vegas on the nearly completed Boulder City highway, where they planned to picket the reservation.[46]

The Las Vegas Central Labor Council openly supported the strikers. After an organizational meeting Tuesday evening, the body sent a resolution to William Green, AFL president, Fred Balzar, governor of Nevada, and the Las Vegas newspapers, which condemned the Big Six for their wage reduction, the deplorable conditions at the river camp, and the construction company's attempt to blame the Wobblies for the labor-management confrontation in order to excite public sentiment against the strikers. Green was requested by the council to submit the resolution to Elwood Mead, Secretary of Labor William Doak, and President Hoover. Excerpts of the resolution read:

We know that the conditions complained of by the employees of the Six Companies are the true conditions there . . . that the officials of the Six Companies make denial of these charges and endeavor to create alibis and excuses for their shortcomings and wind up telling the press and the public that it was only the dissatisfaction of a few I.W.W.'s that was the cause of the tie up. . . .

We believe that the public . . . and the department heads should be informed, if they don't know, that the Six Companies have established a wage scale below the uniform wage prevailing throughout the entire country. . . .

We feel it is a crime against humanity to ask men to work in that Hell-hole of heat they encounter at Boulder dam and do it for a mere pittance. . . .

The Las Vegas Central Labor council with its affiliated crafts, voice our protest against the conditions hereinbefore mentioned and that we appeal to that sense of fair play among men to help labor hold its place and maintain the standards which we believe are essential to good citizenship and contentment. . . .[47]

The Central Labor Council's action did not influence Walker Young. At twelve noon, August 13, the government engineer in charge of the project ordered the Big Six to hire laborers and resume work. The reduced wage scale that produced the strike remained in effect. Deputy Nevada Labor

Commissioner Leonard T. Blood opened a branch of the Las Vegas state-federal employment office at the reservation's entrance four miles north-west of Boulder City near Railroad Pass. Federal authorities then placed a large gate across the highway to prevent any unauthorized persons from entering the project area; U.S. Marshal Fulmer followed up the action by deputizing twenty reclamation engineers to guard the gate and police the area. When asked by the *Las Vegas Age* if the rumors that "semimartial" law had been established on the Boulder Canyon Project were true, Assistant U.S. Attorney Montrose obliquely remarked, "It may be called semimartial law only in that Marshal Fulmer has complete control over reservation conditions." Although the federal government had claimed to be a neutral party in this critical labor-management dispute, its actions beginning on August 11 were obviously aimed at breaking the strike.[48]

Following Superintendent Crowe's request that "old worthy" workers should be given first preference for jobs, the government employment office hired 350 former Big Six employees by 8:30 P.M., August 13. Housed at the Boulder City camp, the recently hired laborers became the day crew and resumed digging the diversion tunnels the following morning. By the afternoon of August 14, an additional 380 former employees were rehired to constitute the swing shift. In spite of over 700 workers crossing the picket line of the strikers, the strike did affect the living conditions at the project. None of the Big Six workers were housed at the river camp because cooling systems, lights, water coolers, and other simple necessities that should have been operational when the camp opened that spring were now being installed.[49]

The 200 unorganized strikers and Wobblies at Camp Stand were desperately struggling to maintain the strike on the basis that the Big Six's reduced wage scale was still in effect. "We are not beaten," the General Strike Committee announced after Walker Young's order to resume construction on the Boulder Canyon Project. "We went out on strike in protest of a wage scale based on a $4 day for muckers and as that scale is still in force we consider men returning to work as strikebreakers. The strike is still on and we intend to stick with it until it is settled."[50]

At a 3:00 P.M. meeting, August 14, in the Las Vegas Airdome theater, 200 strikers and more than 600 spectators listened to militant speakers charge that the "Hoover Dam strike [was] the focal point of the entire 'class struggle' at the present time" in the nation, and that the federal government had betrayed its neutral stand to support the Big Six. The speakers accused the government of breaking the strike because federal officials recognized there was an ongoing labor dispute when they notified the striking laborers that they had to leave the reservation. While most of the strikers who addressed the crowd still advocated using peaceful methods in conducting the strike action, some of the disgruntled workers suggested resorting to violence. One striker took the stage and declared that nonviolent action had gotten them nowhere. "Are we going out now to where these follows are going back to work as strikebreakers and take a shillelah and beat the ears off the guys?" the angry striker shouted. "Or, are we going to say 'please, mister.' "[51]

Following the speakers' addresses, a strike committee chairman and recording secretary were chosen, and then seven resolutions passed at an earlier meeting at Camp Stand were adopted by the Airdome assemblage. The resolutions advocated a dramatic policy change between the strike committee and federal officials. The government was no longer to be recognized as a third party in the labor-management dispute, but rather the agent of the Big Six. It was now obvious to the strike committee that the federal government's clearing of the reservation of strikers was actually the first step in resuming operations at the Boulder Canyon Project and that federal authorities had not made, and would not make, any attempts to encourage some form of arbitration. At the same time, immediate and intensive picketing was proposed for Las Vegas, particularly at bus stations, on the Boulder City highway near Camp Stand, at the government employment office near Railroad Pass, in Searchlight, and where the Los Angeles highway crossed the Nevada-California state line. Daily meetings were to be held in Las Vegas and aimed at recruiting unemployed workers into the ranks of the strikers. The strikers also announced that Publicity and Ways and Means committees were to be created to publicize the strike nationally and solicit financial aid from sympathetic individuals and groups. That evening the general strike committee sent Governor Fred Balzar a telegram that read:

Boulder Dam strike still on. One dollar wage still in effect for forty per cent tunnel crews. Six Companies employing strike breakers. Is the state of Nevada going to uphold Six Companies cutting wages in this time of depression? Strikers wish investigation of project.[52]

Governor Balzar promptly responded to the strikers' telegram the next day, August 15, and passed any responsibility in arbitrating the labor-management dispute back to the federal government. "State of Nevada absolutely neutral in all labor disputes," his telegram read. "Matter should properly be referred to department of labor, Washington." By that Saturday, nearly 1,100 former Big Six employees had been rehired under the reduced wage scale. Although some of the militant proposals had been initiated by the strike committee, the chances of a successful strike with no support from federal or Nevada officials, and workers flocking back to the job despite pickets, were practically nil. At a closed meeting the question of a vote to call the strike off was proposed. The strikers agreed to have a secret-ballot vote the next day.[53]

On Sunday, August 16, 1931, "Camp Despair"—formerly Camp Stand —was abandoned after the remaining die-hard strikers voted 68 to 58 to end the strike. Many of these men were Wobblies, and the resolution calling off the strike designated their organizational objectives on returning to work:

It is moved that we transfer the strike back to the job and that our demands stand the same to secure a federal investigation and that the General Strike committee be authorized to appoint or elect a committee on the job to carry on our fight to secure our demands, and we go on record that if these demands are not successful, we renew the strike.[54]

Superintendent Crowe, the following day, hoped to counter the proposed action by announcing that all former strikers known to carry "red cards . . . and bear a reputation as agitators" would not be rehired. A Wobbly optimistically responded to Crowe's statement in *Industrial Solidarity*: " 'Red cards' are on the Boulder Dam today and will continue to be there until the project is finished," proclaimed the I.W.W. member. "Maybe, Mr. Crowe, 'Red cards' may organize the Boulder Dam to strike, not as an unorganized body as was the present case, but as an unshakeable union that will not be intimidated by company arsenals or company gunmen."[55]

Wobblies continued to work on the dam until its completion on March 1, 1936—two years ahead of schedule—but the strike between August 7 and August 16, 1931, was the last significant I.W.W.-related activity on the Boulder Canyon Project. Interestingly enough, Glen E. "Bud" Bodell, former chief deputy sheriff of Clark County, was appointed a deputy U.S. marshal and police chief of Boulder City in order that "labor agitators" and "radicals" be "weeded out rapidly" from the workforce on the dam project. By the end of August, work on the open-shop job had returned to near normal. The brutal summer heat soon passed, and the river-camp workers at least had livable quarters as a result of the strike. By November 1931, most Big Six employees were housed in Boulder City, thus alleviating one of the major problems associated with labor unrest at the project. The six dormitories were equipped with combination heating and cooling systems, lavatories, and showers; the 125 family cottages contained all the basic conveniences. Besides housing, the workers were provided with a 1,300-man mess hall, a steam laundry, a garage, a clubhouse, and a company store. Boulder City's population numbered 2,500 by the end of 1931 and truly represented a well-planned model government town.[56]

Although housing conditions were vastly improved on the Boulder Canyon Project after the August labor troubles, IU No. 310 still maintained a local in Las Vegas. Frank Anderson, Fred Fuglevik, and J. S. Frast headed the small Wobbly contingent in Clark County and sponsored the national I.W.W. Construction Workers' conventions in October 1931 and 1932. Many articles criticizing the federal government, the Big Six, and working conditions on the dam project appeared in *Industrial Solidarity* until it ceased publication in December 1931 and, after *Solidarity*'s demise, in the I.W.W.'s lone national newspaper, *Industrial Worker*.[57]

Yet the Wobblies' dream of making the Boulder Canyon Project and Las Vegas an I.W.W. stronghold had suffered a mortal blow in the August strike. The last I.W.W. attempt to organize the dam workers to strike occurred two years later on August 16, 1933, in an effort to prevent the firing of all known Wobbly laborers. Eight organizers, including Frank Anderson, distributed handbills in Boulder City's Anderson mess hall demanding increased safety regulations, a six-hour day with the same pay, one dollar per day for board, a 50-percent reduction in rent, and no discrimination against I.W.W. members working on the project. The Wobblies exhorted the workers to make "a show-down with the Six Companies by remaining off shift," but the rally, as a result of the efforts of "Bud" Bodell, was an abysmal failure. The crews returned to work, and, according to Wobbly historian Fred Thompson, this was the only time in the I.W.W.'s history that it called a strike and none developed.[58]

Ironically, the Wobbly who in 1931 described the I.W.W.'s organizational drive at the Boulder Canyon Project in terms of the workers choosing between a red union card and a statue proved to be a prophet of sorts. Most dam workers never joined the I.W.W., but the men killed on the project received their monument. Entitled "They Died To Make The Desert Bloom," the memorial commemorated a sizable number of workers who died needlessly as a result of a hasty presidential decision. If President Hoover had not rushed the building of the dam in order to employ only a minute fraction of America's growing hordes of jobless, the work would not have begun in the spring and summer heat of 1931, Boulder City would have been completed on schedule, the Big Six would not have been able to exploit the laborers to the extent they did, and in the end the monument that paid tribute to the dead dam workers would have represented fewer fallen men.[59]

NOTES

1. Paul F. Brissenden, *The I.W.W.: A Study of American Syndicalism*, Columbia Studies in History, Economics and Public Law, vol. 83 (New York: Columbia University Press, 1919), p. 191; Guy Louis Rocha, "Radical Labor Struggles in the Tonopah-Goldfield Mining District, 1901-1922," *Nevada Historical Society Quarterly* 20 (Spring 1977), 3-20, *passim*. The Wobblies last sustained organizational drive appears to have been conducted in the early 1930s prior to the founding of the

Congress of Industrial Organizations (CIO). Washington State's Yakima Valley witnessed the Wobblies' unsuccessful attempt in 1933 to organize hop pickers into Agricultural Workers' Industrial Union No. 110. The I.W.W., a rapidly deteriorating labor union, after 1933 found it impossible to compete with the Communists' brand of revolution and the CIO's industrial unionism. See Cletus E. Daniel, "Wobblies on the Farm: The I.W.W. in the Yakima Valley," *Pacific Northwest Quarterly* 65 (October 1974), 166-75; James G. Newbill, "Farmers and Wobblies in the Yakima Valley, 1933," *Pacific Northwest Quarterly* 68 (April 1977), 80-87; Melvyn Dubofsky, *We Shall Be All: A History of The I.W.W.* (Chicago: Quadrangle Books, 1969), p. 478.

2. Joyce L. Kornbluh, *Rebel Voices: An I.W.W. Anthology* (Ann Arbor: University of Michigan Press, 1964), p. 2.

3. *Industrial Solidarity*, May 19, 1931, p. 1.

4. Paul L. Kleinsorge, *The Boulder Canyon Project: Historical and Economic Aspects* (Palo Alto, California: Stanford University Press, 1941), p. 300; James Robert Kluger, "Elwood Mead: Irrigation Engineer and Social Planner" (Ph.D. diss., Arizona University, 1970), pp. 201-2, 206-7, 209; "Open Shop at Boulder Dam," *The New Republic*, June 24, 1931, pp. 147-48; "Construction of Boulder Dam Begun on July 7, 1930," *New Reclamation Era* (August 1930), pp. 146-47; "Boulder Canyon Project News," *New Reclamation Era* (October 1930), p. 200; "Hoover Dam and Power Plant Contracts to be Let," *New Reclamation Era* (December 1930), p. 245. Originally there were two sites considered for Boulder City. Elwood Mead chose the present site over one three miles from the dam project because of its higher elevation (800 feet), better soil conditions, and location at the Union Pacific branch railroad terminus. Better living conditions associated with relatively cooler summer temperatures was a primary consideration in his decision.

5. Edmund Wilson, *The American Earthquake: A Documentary of the Twenties and Thirties* (Garden City, New York: Doubleday & Company, Inc., 1958), pp. 369-70; U.S. Department of the Interior, Bureau of Reclamation, *The Story of Boulder Dam*, Conservation Bulletin No. 9 (Washington, D.C.: Government Printing Office, 1941), pp. 12-17, 21-22; Kleinsorge, pp. 204-5; *The New Republic*, June 24, 1931, p. 147. The Big Six, incorporated under the laws of Delaware, included the Utah Construction (Ogden), W. A. Bechtel and Henry J. Kaiser (San Francisco), Morrison-Knudson (Boise), Pacific Bridge (Portland), J. F. Shea (Portland), and MacDonald & Kahn (San Francisco) companies. The Six Companies, Inc., building contract was the largest ever awarded by the federal government up to that time.

6. Kleinsorge, *The Boulder Canyon Project*, pp. 300-301.

7. *The Story of Boulder Dam*, pp. 26-34; *Industrial Solidarity*, March 24, 1931, p. 1; "Specifications and Plans Available For Work at Hoover Dam," *New Reclamation Era* (February 1931), p. 33; Kleinsorge, *The Boulder Canyon Project*, p. 204.

8. *Las Vegas Evening Review and Journal*, March 30, p. 1, April 9, 1931, pp. 1-2; "Boulder Canyon Project News," *New Reclamation Era* (March 1931), p. 68.

9. *Las Vegas Evening Review and Journal*, April 9, 1931, pp. 1-2.

10. Ibid., April 11, pp. 1-2, April 13, p. 1, April 20, 1931, p. 1; *Industrial Solidarity*, April 28, 1931, p. 6; Fred Thompson, *The I.W.W.: Its First Fifty Years*

(1905-1955) (Chicago: Industrial Workers of the World, 1955), pp. 158-59; U.S. Department of Commerce Bureau of the Census, *United States Census of Population: 1970*, vol. 1, *Characteristics of the Population*, pt. 30, Nevada. Las Vegas's permanent population in 1930 was 5,165 although transient job-seekers considerably boosted the town's population in the early years of the decade.

11. Thompson, *The I.W.W.*, pp. 158-59; *Industrial Solidarity*, April 28, 1931, p. 6. According to John S. Gambs, *The Decline of the I.W.W.* (New York: Columbia University Press, 1932), by September 1930 I.W.W. membership had declined to approximately seven or eight thousand members (p. 166). Estimates by Melvyn Dubofsky, *We Shall Be All*, give the Wobblies a peak membership of 100,000 just prior to World War I (p. 349).

12. *Industrial Solidarity*, June 16, 1931, p. 4; Wilson, *American Earthquake*, pp. 368, 370; "Boulder Canyon Project News," *New Reclamation Era* (July 1931), pp. 149, 151, photograph of the river camp on page 151; Kleinsorge, *The Boulder Canyon Project*, pp. 206, 222.

13. *Las Vegas Evening Review Journal*, August 4, 1931, p. 1; Wilson, *American Earthquake*, p. 370.

14. "Department of the Interior—Memorandum for the Press," March 9, 1931, p. 1; *The New Republic*, June 24, 1931, p. 147.

15. *The New Republic*, August 26, 1931, p. 48; Kluger, "Elwood Mead," p. 204.

16. *Las Vegas Evening Review and Journal*, April 25, p. 1, April 28, p. 1, May 4, p. 1, May 10, 1931, p. 1; *Industrial Solidarity*, May 19, p. 1, June 2, p. 1, June 16, p. 4, June 30, p. 1, July 7, 1931, p. 1.

17. "Well, I Quit My Job at the Dam," *The Nation*, August 26, 1931, p. 207; "A Visit to the Hoover Dam Site," *New Reclamation Era* (August 1931), pp. 172-73; *Las Vegas Evening Review Journal*, August 4, 1931, pp. 1-2. Photograph of the "Flat" (Williamsville or "Ragtown") on pages 172 and 173.

18. *Las Vegas Age*, July 11, pp. 1, 6, July 16, 1931, p. 1; *Las Vegas Evening Review Journal*, July 11, 1931, pp. 1-2; *Industrial Solidarity*, July 21, 1931, p. 1.

19. *Las Vegas Evening Review Journal*, July 13, 1931, pp. 1-2; *Industrial Solidarity*, July 21, 1931, p. 1.

20. *Las Vegas Age*, July 12, 1931, p. 1; *Las Vegas Evening Review Journal*, July 11, pp. 1-2; July 13, 1931, pp. 1-2; *Industrial Solidarity*, July 21, p. 1, July 28, 1931, pp. 1-2.

21. *Las Vegas Evening Review Journal*, July 11, 1931, pp. 1-2.

22. Ibid., July 13, pp. 1-2; July 16, 1931, p. 3; *Industrial Solidarity*, July 21, 1931, p. 1.

23. *Las Vegas Evening Review Journal*, July 16, 1931, p. 3; *Industrial Solidarity*, July 21, p. 1; July 28, 1931, pp. 1-2.

24. *Las Vegas Evening Review Journal*, July 13, 1931, pp. 1-2; *Las Vegas Age*, July 14, 1931, p. 1; *Industrial Solidarity*, July 28, 1931, pp. 1-2.

25. *Las Vegas Evening Review Journal*, July 16, 1931, p. 3; *Industrial Solidarity*, July 28, 1931, pp. 1-2.

26. *Las Vegas Age*, July 16, 1931, p. 1; *Industrial Solidarity*, July 28, 1931, pp. 1-2.

27. Ibid.; *Las Vegas Evening Review Journal*, July 11, 1931, pp. 1-2.

28. *Industrial Solidarity*, July 28, 1931, pp. 1-2. The reports for the Board of Pardons and Parole Commissioners beginning with 1919 in the *Appendix to Journals of Senate and Assembly* show no record of a criminal syndicalism conviction. Interestingly enough, the Criminal Syndicalism Law (NRS 203.117) has never been repealed. In 1967, it was amended and the penalty reduced from a maximum sentence of ten years to six years.

29. Ibid.; *Las Vegas Evening Journal*, July 16, 1931, p. 3; *Las Vegas Age*, July 17, 1931, p. 5. The Las Vegas Central Labor Council, or Central Labor Union as it was alternately known, was organized on August 3, 1929, and its members in 1931 included International Painters and Decorators Union Local No. 159; United Associations of Plumbers and Pipe Fitters Local No. 566; Common Laborers Union No. 597; Plasterers Local No. 761; Journeyman Barbers' Union Local No. 794; and Brotherhood of Carpenters and Joiners of America Local No. 1780, *Las Vegas Evening Review Journal*, September 7, 1931, p. 1; "Biennial Report of the Commissioner of Labor, 1929-1930," in *Appendix to Journals of Senate and Assembly* (Carson City, 1931), 1, 29-30;" "Biennial Report of the Commissioners of Labor, 1931-1932," in *Appendix to Journals of Senate and Assembly* (Carson City, 1933), 1, 29-30.

30. Wilson, *American Earthquake*, p. 372; *Las Vegas Evening Review Journal*, July 18, 1931, p. 1; *Industrial Solidarity*, August 11, 1931, p. 1.

31. *Industrial Solidarity*, August 11, 1931, p. 1. According to Kluger, "In 1935, four years after construction began, the Interior Department accused Six Companies of more than 70,000 violations of the eight hour day. Until then, no-one apparently seemed concerned (*or was in a position to object*) [emphasis mine] about this.

"The Six Companies sought to justify their actions by citing the exceptions to the eight hour law 'in the case of extraordinary events and conditions.' Henry J. Kaiser, President of the Six Companies, claimed the emergency of helping to relieve unemployment created by the depression and the danger of floods to the Imperial Valley as the emergencies. [Secretary of Interior] Ikes refused this reasoning and Six Companies was fined $100,000 on the $48 million contract." Kluger, "Elwood Mead," 208f.

32. *Industrial Solidarity*, August 11, 1931, p. 1; Wilson, *American Earthquake*, p. 371.

33. *Las Vegas Evening Review Journal*, August 8, 1931, p. 2; *The Nation*, August 26, 1931, pp. 207-8.

34. *Las Vegas Age*, July 14, 1931, p. 1.

35. Wilson, *American Earthquake*, pp. 372-73; *Las Vegas Evening Review Journal*, May 16, 1931, p. 1; *Industrial Solidarity*, August 18, 1931, p. 1; U.S. Department of Interior, *Annual Report of the Secretary of the Interior, for the Fiscal Year Ended June 30, 1931*, p. 21; "Williamsville" derived its name from Deputy U.S. Marshal Claude Williams, who in August was placed in charge of the federal reservation, excluding Boulder City.

36. *Industrial Solidarity*, August 18, 1931, p. 1.

37. Ibid.

38. *Las Vegas Age*, August 8, 1931, pp. 1, 6; *Las Vegas Evening Review Journal*, August 8, 1931, pp. 1-2; *New York Times*, August 9, 1931, p. 1.

39. *Las Vegas Age*, August 8, 1931, pp. 1, 6; *Las Vegas Evening Review Journal*, August 8, 1931, pp. 1-2; *Industrial Solidarity*, August 18, 1931, p. 1.

40. *Las Vegas Evening Review Journal*, August 4, pp. 1-2, August 8, 1931, p. 2.

41. *Industrial Solidarity*, August 18, 1931, p. 2.

42. *Las Vegas Age*, August 9, 1931, p. 1.

43. Ibid.; *Las Vegas Evening Review Journal*, August 10, 1931, pp. 1-2; *Industrial Solidarity*, August 18, 1931, p. 1. Both the *Las Vegas Evening Review Journal* and *Industrial Solidarity* mention the Las Vegas merchants' donations to the strikers, but neither periodical makes reference to specific businesses.

44. Wilson, *American Earthquake*, pp. 373-74; *Las Vegas Evening Review Journal*, August 10, 1931, p. 2; *Industrial Solidarity*, August 18, 1931, p. 1.

45. Wilson, *American Earthquake*, pp. 373-78; Kluger, "Elwood Mead," 204; *Las Vegas Age*, August 12, pp. 1, 6, August 13, 1931, p. 1; *Las Vegas Evening Review Journal*, August 12, 1931, pp. 1, 3.

46. Wilson, *American Earthquake*, pp. 373-78; *Las Vegas Age*, August 12, pp. 1, 6, August 13, 1931, p. 1; *Las Vegas Evening Review Journal*, August 12, 1931, pp. 1, 3.

47. *Las Vegas Age*, August 12, 1931, p. 6; *Las Vegas Evening Review Journal*, August 12, 1931, p. 3. William Green and the AFL executive council did follow through and submit the Las Vegas Central Labor Council's resolution to Secretary of Labor William Doak. Although Doak ordered E. H. Fitzgerald, Los Angeles conciliation commissioner, and Charles E. Prime, Reno federal-state public employment service director, to Las Vegas on August 20, it seems Fitzgerald and Prime either never made the trip or, if they did, were called back prior to making an investigation of conditions on the Boulder Canyon Project. Las Vegas newspapers make no mention of Fitzgerald's or Prime's arrival or any investigation. Furthermore, the department of labor in *Monthly Labor Review* reported that the "present status and terms of settlement" in regard to the project strike were "Unclassified," as opposed to "adjusted" or "pending," "Settled before commissioner's arrival," *Las Vegas Age*, August 19, p. 1, August 22, 1931, pp. 2, 6; *Las Vegas Evening Review Journal*, August 19, pp. 1-2, August 21, 1931, p. 1; *Industrial Solidarity*, September 1, 1931, p. 1; "Labor Disputes Handled by the Conciliation Service During the Month of September, 1931," *Monthly Labor Review* (November 1931), p. 118.

48. Wilson, *American Earthquake*, p. 378; *Las Vegas Age*, August 13, 1931, p. 1; *Las Vegas Evening Review Journal*, August 13, 1931, pp. 1-2; *Industrial Solidarity*, August 25, 1931, pp. 1, 3; Leonard T. Blood Papers, Special Collections, Dickinson Library, University of Nevada, Las Vegas.

49. Wilson, *American Earthquake*, p. 378; *Las Vegas Age*, August 14, 1931, pp. 1, 3; *Las Vegas Evening Review Journal*, August 13, pp. 1-2, August 14, 1931, pp. 1-2.

50. *Las Vegas Age*, August 14, 1931, pp. 1, 3; *Las Vegas Evening Review Journal*, August 14, 1931, p. 2.

51. *Las Vegas Age*, August 15, 1931, p. 1; *Las Vegas Evening Review Journal*, August 15, 1931, p. 1-2.

52. Ibid.

53. *Las Vegas Age*, August 16, 1931, p. 1; *Las Vegas Evening Review Journal*, August 17, 1931, pp. 1-2; *Industrial Solidarity*, August 25, 1931, pp. 1, 3.

54. *Las Vegas Evening Review Journal*, August 17, 1931, p. 1-2.

55. Ibid.; Wilson, *American Earthquake*, p. 378; *Las Vegas Age*, August 18, 1931, p. 1; *Industrial Solidarity*, August 25, 1931, p. 1.

56. Kleinsorge, *The Boulder Canyon Project Act*, pp. 206-7, 224-25; *Annual Report of the Secretary of the Interior, 1931*, p. 21; *Las Vegas Age*, August 23, p. 1, September 12, 1931, p. 1; *Las Vegas Evening Review Journal*, August 24, 1931, pp. 1, 5.

57. *Industrial Solidarity*, September 1, p. 1, September 22, p. 3, October 6, p. 1, October 13, pp. 1, 4, October 27, p. 1, November 3, p. 2, November 24, 1931, p. 1.

58. Thompson, *The I.W.W.*, p. 159; "Biennial Report of the Commissioner of Labor, 1933-1934," in *Appendix to Journals of Senate and Assembly* (Carson City: 1935), 1, 25; *Las Vegas Age*, August 17, 1933, pp. 1-2; *Las Vegas Evening Review Journal*, August 16, pp. 1, 3, August 17, 1933, p. 6; Paul Ralli, *Viva Vegas* (Hollywood, California: House-Warven, Publishers, 1953), pp. 239-40.

59. U.S. Department of Interior, Bureau of Reclamation, *Sculptures at Hoover Dam* (Washington, D.C.: Government Printing Office, 1968), p. 17; *Las Vegas Evening Review Journal*, April 24, Sec. 5, p. 6, April 26, p. 5, 1935. James Kluger arrived at the same general conclusion concerning culpability when he wrote that the troubles related to Boulder City and the dam project "were not so much Elwood Mead's fault as they were the result of the haste in beginning contruction to relieve unemployment and greed on the part of the Six Companies," Kluger, "Elwood Mead," 224.

PART FOUR

BIBLIOGRAPHY

SOURCES FOR THE LOCAL HISTORY OF THE I.W.W.

DIONE MILES

PRIMARY SOURCES

RESEARCH IN ARCHIVES

WASHINGTON, D.C.

The archival sources in Washington can be important to the local history of the I.W.W. Presidential papers at the *Library of Congress*,* those of Theodore Roosevelt, William Howard Taft, Woodrow Wilson, and Calvin Coolidge, occasionally reflect on the I.W.W., and some items are to be found in the papers of Newton Baker, Alfred S. Burleson, and Thomas W. Gregory. The Felix Frankfurter papers have some material on the Bisbee deportation, and the papers of Warren K. Billings are there. Most useful at the Library of Congress, however, is the vast collection of newspapers, other serials, and hard-to-find pamphlets and books.

The *Department of Labor Library* also has extensive holdings of I.W.W. newspapers as well as pamphlets. Established in 1917, this library is a rich mine of reports, studies, and documents not easily available elsewhere. There are no archival collections, but the materials on labor do cover all the I.W.W. years. State labor reports are also filed here, including those from states where the I.W.W. was active: Massachusetts, Pennsylvania, Ohio, New Jersey, Illinois, Michigan, and California. There are various commission and board reports, including documents issued in connection with specific strikes.

The National Archives include U.S. Department of Labor records (Record Group 174), among them, the President's Mediation Commission files and transcripts of hearings at Globe, Clifton, and Bisbee, Arizona. There are also the reports of the U. S. Commission on Industrial Relations, both published and unpublished. There is

*Major federal and state sources appear in italics.

a name index to the files, 1907-1942; the index alone comprises fifteen feet of cards. The records of the Conciliation Service, 1918-1919, are alphabetical. An inventory was compiled in 1964 by F. R. Holdcamper.

Immigration and Naturalization records (RG 85) would be of interest to historians dealing with specific I.W.W. members. A preliminary inventory was compiled in 1965 by Marion M. Johnson.

Federal Mediation and Conciliation Service records (RG 280) include some post-1913 correspondence and case records on lumber and copper strikes. These come in "subject" and "subject-dispute" folders, and have geographic, name, and subject indexes. There is a 1965 guide, compiled by Norwood N. Biggs.

Record Group 95, General Records of the Forest Service, contains material for historians of the Northwest, among others. The earlier guide by Harold T. Prickett was revised in 1969 by Terry W. Good.

Files of the Pardon Attorney's office (RG 204) include material on individual I.W.W. members. They include applications for executive clemency and correspondence and enclosures of various kinds. There is a special file (four feet) on political prisoners, with further records on amnesty. A guide to these was compiled by Gaiselle Kerner in 1955.

Records of Alaska (RG 126), including labor problems there, are in the Office of Territories. A guide was compiled in 1963 by Richard S. Maxwell and Evans Walker.

War Labor Board (RG 1) papers date from 1918-1919, but include some materials from the earlier National Industries Conference Board. Some of these materials (minutes of executive sessions) are at Stanford University's Hoover Library. The papers at NARS are indexed by firm, union, individual, city, and subject. A guide by Herbert Fine was compiled in 1943.

Record Group 94, General Records of the Adjutant General's Office, has some files relating to the containment of "lawlessness" where troops were called to suppress strikes or strikers.

Record Group 165, especially Military Intelligence, are among the most rewarding, since some records have been opened only recently. There is an extensive name, subject, and geographic index.

Record Group 60, the U.S. Department of Justice records, have a particular satisfaction for the I.W.W. scholar, especially the Abraham Glasser file. Related to the file, but separate, are the Federal Bureau of Investigation records (RG 65) of which the "Old German" files of the former bureau of investigation have been released. There is an index file including names, areas, and other listings.

The records of the U. S. Post Office Department (RG 28) are particularly interesting, as they contain much seized material, including papers and pamphlets denied second-class mailing privileges and, surprisingly, correspondence of interest. There are hundreds of feet of unarranged documents. A 1967 guide by F. R. Holdcamper is a revision of an earlier one. In addition, there is a useful guide to files relating to government suppression of Socialist publications, 1917-1921, by W. M. Elkins, which lists titles. This was also done in 1967.

The American Federation of Labor papers, also in Washington, at the AFL-CIO Records Department, have a small amount dealing with the AFL opposition to the I.W.W. at the local level.

ARIZONA

Arizona State University Library in Tempe has the Henry McCluskey files, which contain among other things a report of the Arizona State Council of Defense and materials relating to the Bisbee deportation. The George W. Hunt papers, relating to Bisbee and the I.W.W., are also there. This library also collects Arizona newspapers. The *Arizona Historical Society* in Tucson has papers relating to Bisbee, as well.

CALIFORNIA

The *University of California at Berkeley* has a vast collection of labor union periodicals and agricultural periodicals and reports. *Bancroft Library* papers include those of Dolbeer and Carson Co., Ira Cross, Mary Gallagher, Tom Mooney, Paul Scharrenberg, Hiram Johnson, and Simon J. Lubin.

The *Hoover Library* at Stanford University, in addition to vast holdings of radical and pacifist papers and periodicals, has material including a partial transcript of the Joe Hill trial in the Wallace Stegner papers. The Stanford University collection of Herbert C. Jones has some folders on the I.W.W.

The *San Diego Public Library* and the *A. K. Smiley (Redlands) Public Library* make a special effort to collect local periodicals, and the *Stockton Public Library* specializes in those of Northern California. The *California State Library at Fullerton* has a labor periodicals collection. The Theodore P. Gerson papers at the *Huntington Library* in San Marino have a clippings collection.

The *California State Archives* (Sacramento) include prison papers on Wheatland prisoners and the "silent defense." The *San Diego Historical Society* has a collection of I.W.W. articles, scrapbooks, and local history items.

COLORADO

The *Colorado State Archives* in Denver have the papers of James H. Peabody. There is a memorandum on the Columbine incident in the Josephine Roche papers at the *Denver Public Library*. The Western Historical Collections at the *University of Colorado Library* in Boulder have the important Western Federation of Miners papers. The *Colorado Historical Society* in Denver has local newspapers.

GEORGIA

While there was little I.W.W. activity in Georgia, the papers of Wayne Walden, at the *Southern Labor Archives* at Georgia State University in Atlanta, have some I.W.W. material.

IDAHO

The *Idaho State Historical Society* in Boise is rich in I.W.W. history. There are the Simeon G. Reed, James H. Hawley, William D. Borah, Moses Alexander, D. W. Davis, and Frank J. Smith papers, the Norman H. Willey Collection, and Congressional Delegation material on Coeur d'Alenes. A transcript of the first Haywood trial is here. This institution also is a newspaper center and has many of them on microfilm. The George F. Jewett papers are at the *University of Idaho Library* in Moscow.

ILLINOIS

The *Chicago Historical Society* has some papers of the I.W.W. as well as the Socialist party; the Mary E. McDowell papers are also there. The *Newberry Library*, besides extensive, old labor holdings, has the papers of Floyd Dell. At the *Roosevelt University Library* in Chicago there is an oral history collection including some I.W.W. recollections. The *University of Chicago Library* includes Virgil Vogel's manuscript, "Historians and the I.W.W." Local papers are collected at the *University of Illinois* in Urbana, at the *Freeport Public Library*, and at the *Chicago Historical Society*.

INDIANA

The Theodore and Eugene Debs papers are at Indiana State University's *Cunningham Memorial Library* (Terre Haute), although there is little on the I.W.W. The *Debs Library* also has some material. The *University of Indiana* in Bloomington has the journal and letters of Powers Hapgood, which include some writing on the I.W.W.

MASSACHUSETTS

The *Wellesley College Archives* have the Vida Scudder papers. She was involved in the Lawrence strike as a speaker; the actual I.W.W. material will be scarce. *Harvard University Library* has a good collection of labor periodicals. The *University of Massachusetts* in Amherst collects Massachusetts newspapers.

MICHIGAN

The *State Archives of Michigan* include (in Military Affairs, Lot ME 10) the Investigating Subcommittee proceedings on the Calumet-Hecla Copper strike involving the WFM and the I.W.W. There is further material in the Executive Office papers of Governor Woodbridge N. Ferris (Lot E1-46) about the strike.

Michigan has two archives, forty miles apart, that hold very important I.W.W. history. The *Labadie Collection*, housed in the Harlan Hatcher Library of the University of Michigan in Ann Arbor, has one of the great collections. Extensive early periodical and pamphlet collections were garnered by Agnes Inglis, late curator, who was a friend of many I.W.W. people as well as anarchists. There are extensive manuscripts. Papers of the Detroit faction, WIIU, which are not included otherwise in this listing, may also be found here. Such rare and sentimental items as Haywood's WFM pin and the original *Can-Opener* prison paper, as well as considerable I.W.W. correspondence are included. The Labadie papers also offer a large number of important unpublished papers and notes, too numerous to list here.

The *Walter P. Reuther Library* at Wayne State University in Detroit houses the Archives of Labor and Urban Affairs, and has been the official depository of the I.W.W. since 1964. The collection (ninety-one linear feet) includes extensive records dating from 1906, as well as a particularly large pamphlet collection. The complete Chicago trial (1918) transcript, a microfilm of the early Haywood trial, and many other trial papers are here. The papers and records of the various I.W.W. industrial unions and branches are included, as well as foreign administrations; material on Work Peoples College; the 1906-1911 minute book; and extensive correspondence. Also at the Reuther Library are many other I.W.W.-related collections: Alfred and Rose Anderson, Oscar Ameringer, John Beffel, Sam Dolgoff, Minneapolis Branch, Ben Legere, Edward Falkowski, George Lutzai, John Oneka, John Panzner. Matilda Robbins (Rabinowitz), Frank Cedarvall, Nicolaas Steelink, Nemmy Sparks, Andrew Wiener, Mary Heaton Vorse, and others. Manuscripts include Ben Williams's "Saga of the One Big Union," and writings of Hagburt "Herb" Edwards, Minnie Corder, and Covington Hall. The Covington Hall manuscript, "Labor Struggles in the Deep South," is the first carbon, with margin notes. The *Tulane University Library* has the second carbon; the original is still missing. There are detailed guides to most of the Reuther Library Collections.

MINNESOTA

The *Minnesota Historical Society* in St. Paul has the Albert G. Wagner papers and the important Workers Socialist Publishing Company (Duluth) Collection. There are also papers of E. G. Hall, Robley Cramer, Marian Le Seuer, John Lind, and E. W. Latchem. For opposition to the I.W.W., see the Joseph A. Burnquist papers.

MONTANA

Important hearings of the Montana Council of Defense are at the *Montana Historical Society* in Helena. The state archives are housed there. A small amount of correspondence on lumbering may be found in the C. H. McLeod papers at the *University of Montana Library* in Missoula, but there is little else in the state on the I.W.W.

NEBRASKA AND NEVADA

Nebraska State Historical Society in Lincoln has I.W.W. material in the State Council of Defense papers, Series 3. Very good photographs of Goldfield are in the collections of the *Nevada Historical Society*, Reno.

NEW JERSEY

Princeton University has the American Civil Liberties Union papers at the *Firestone Library*. Alex Baskin wrote a guide for these papers in 1971. There is material dating from 1917 on I.W.W. trials and other problems. Some of the papers are in duplicate at the New York Public Library.

NEW YORK

Oral history collections both at Columbia University and the *Tamiment Library of New York University* include I.W.W. recollections. Tamiment also has extensive holdings of I.W.W. newspapers, pamphlets, documents, and manuscripts. Secondary research materials at the *New York Public Library* are excellent, and they also have scrapbooks of the Commission on Industrial Relations. The Frank P. Walsh papers are there. Cornell University in Ithaca has the Paul F. Brissenden Collection, including five boxes of miscellaneous items and correspondence from 1920–1930. *The State Library in Albany* has the Clayton R. Lusk papers, with material on the state investigations. Papers of Elizabeth Gurley Flynn are at the *Library of the Institute of Marxist Studies* (New York City), although some of her papers are at the *Wisconsin State Historical Society* in Madison.

NORTH CAROLINA

The Socialist Party of America papers at *Duke University* in Durham have material of especial relevance for I.W.W. historians.

OREGON

A collection entitled "US Attorney for Oregon" at the *Oregon Historical Society Library* in Portland is listed as having some material on the I.W.W.; it also has the papers of Leo H. Faust, and a number of taped I.W.W. interviews. The University of Oregon in Eugene, and the *Baker County Public Library* in Baker, have newspaper holdings. Also at the University of Oregon are records of the Loyal Legion of Loggers and Lumbermen, including minutes and convention papers.

TEXAS

Papers on the Southern Lumber Operators Association in the Joseph Kurth collection, and the Forest History collections, are at the *Stephen F. Austin State University Library* in Nacogdoches. The collection of lumberman John Henry Kirby is at the *University of Houston Library*.

UTAH

The Utah State Federation of Labor papers are in the Western Americana collections at the *University of Utah* in Salt Lake City.

WASHINGTON

Washington State University in Pullman has collections on Pacific Northwest agriculture as well as lumber. In 1978 Paul J. Green and Siegfried A. Vogt compiled an excellent bibliography on I.W.W. material especially as relating to the Pacific Northwest. One of the outstanding features of the WSU Library is the extensive indexing of various city newspapers, including Centralia. This is in addition to the WPA index of Northwest newspapers, 1901-1920.

The papers of Ralph Chaplin are held at the *Washington State Historical Society* in Tacoma. There also are the Thomas Bogard, P. Speek, Ottilie Markholt, Harold Slater, Ben Weatherwax, Redmond S. Brennan, and Patrick F. Gill papers.

The *University of Washington* in Seattle has many collections relating to the I.W.W. They include collections of lawyer Mark Litchman, Broussais Conan Beck, Anna Louise Strong, Will C. Ruegnitz, Edwin W. Hopkinson, and an I.W.W. Collection of approximately four linear feet. The Merrill Ring Company and Puget

Mill Company papers and the Kinnear Papers are there also. The Industrial Espionage papers, 1920, can be found in the university library.

Many county libraries are interested and productive collectors. The *Centralia Timberland Library* has the local newspapers from the I.W.W. years.

WISCONSIN

Due to the interest of Richard Ely and John R. Commons, Wisconsin took an early lead in the collection of labor books, documents, and papers. Daniel DeLeon and Elizabeth Gurley Flynn papers can be found at the *State Historical Society* in Madison. The Hixon and Company Collection has correspondence on the I.W.W. in the lumber industry. Unpublished reports of the U.S. Commission on Industrial Relations can be seen here.

Canadian materials are outside the scope of this description, but it is only reasonable to add that some I.W.W. materials are included in the Thunder Bay, Ontario regional collections, at Confederation College; at New Westminster, Alberta; at the Labor Library in Ottawa; in the Public Archives of Canada; and at the University of British Columbia at Vancouver.

DOCUMENTS

U.S. Commission on Industrial Relations. *Final Report and Testimony*, 11 vols. Document 415, 64th Cong., 1st sess. Washington, D.C.: G.P.O., 1916.

> This is an important source for local history, covering the whole country with reports of field investigations. Original, including unpublished reports, may be found in the U.S. Department of Labor Records (RG 174) at the National Archives; also deposited at the State Historical Society of Wisconsin in Madison. Testimony of many I.W.W. leaders is included.

Report of the President's Mediation Commission to the President of the United States. Washington, D.C.: G.P.O., 1918.
> These reports include information on Bisbee, Arizona, and unrest in the lumber industry.

Oliver E. Baker. *Seed Time and Harvest.* U. S. Department of Agriculture Bulletin No. 183. Washington, D.C.: G.P.O., March 1922.

D. D. Lescohier. *Conditions Affecting the Demand for Harvest Labor in the Wheat Belt.* U.S. Department of Agriculture Bulletin No. 1230. Washington, D.C.: G.P.O., 1924.

Daniel Harrington. *Lessons from the Granite Mountain Shaft Fire, Butte.* U.S. Department of the Interior, Bureau of Mines Bulletin No. 188. Washington, D.C.: G.P.O., 1922.

_____. *Underground Ventilation at Butte.* U.S. Department of the Interior, Bureau of Mines Bulletin No. 204. Washington, D.C.: G.P.O., 1923.

U.S. Department of the Navy, Office of Naval Intelligence. "Investigation of the Marine Transport Workers and the Alleged Threatened Combination Between Them and the Bolsheviki and Sinn Feiner." Mimeographed Report,

Washington, D.C., December 23, 1918. National Archives Record Group 174.

War Department. *History of the Spruce Production Division*. Portland, Oregon, 1920.

Reuben Oppenheimer. *The Enforcement of the Deportation Laws of the United States: Report to the National Commission on Law Observance and Enforcement*. Washington, D.C.: G.P.O., 1931.

U.S. Federal Writers' Project. "Toilers of the World" (1936).

U.S. Federal Writers' Project. "Industrial Workers of the World in California Agriculture" (1936?).

Works Progress Administration Writers' Project, State of Montana. *Copper Camp Stories of the World's Greatest Mining Town, Butte, Montana*. New York: Hasting House Publishers, 1943.

SENATE DOCUMENTS

U.S. Congress, Senate. *Labor Troubles in Idaho*. 56th Cong., 1st sess. Senate Document No. 42.

_____. *Federal Aid in Domestic Disturbances, 1787-1923*, by Frederick T. Wilson. 57th Cong., 2d sess. Senate Document No. 209.

_____. *Coeur d'Alene Mining Troubles*. 56th Cong., 1st sess. Senate Document No. 24.

_____. *Coeur d'Alene Mining Troubles*. 56th Cong., 1st sess. Senate Document No. 25.

_____. *Coeur d'Alene Mining Troubles*. 56th Cong., 1st sess. Senate Document No. 142.

_____. *Statement of the Western Federation of Miners*. 58th Cong., 2d sess. Senate Document No. 86.

_____. *Transmission Through the Mails of Anarchistic Publications*. 60th Cong., 1st sess. Senate Document No. 426, Ser. No. 5265.

_____. *Report on the Strike of the Textile Workers in Lawrence, Mass., in 1912*, by C. P. Neill and Fred Coxton. 62d Cong., 2d sess. Senate Document No. 870.

_____. *Conditions in the Paint Creek District, West Virginia. Hearings Before a Subcommittee of the Committee on Education and Labor*. 63d Cong., 1st sess., pursuant to Senate Res. 37, a Resolution Authorizing the Appointment of a Committee to Make an Investigation of Conditions in the Paint Creek District.

_____. Committee on the Judiciary. *Hearings Before a Subcommittee on Bolshevik Propaganda*. 65th Cong., 3d sess., and thereafter. February 11 to March 10, 1919.

_____. *Committee on Education and Labor Report. Investigation of Strike in Steel Industry*. 66th Cong., 1st sess.

_____. Subcommittee on the Judiciary. *Hearing, Charges of Illegal Practices of the Department of Justice*. 66th Cong., 1st sess.

_____. *Investigation Activities of the Department of Justice, 1919*. 66th Cong., 1st sess. Document No. 153, Ser. No. 7607.

_____. Judge Advocate General's Department, Army. *Federal Aid in Domestic Disturbances, 1903-1922*; prepared by Office of Judge Advocate General.

67th Cong., 2d sess. Supplemental to Senate Document No. 209, 57th Cong., 2d sess., *Federal Aid in Domestic Disturbances, 1787-1903*, prepared by Frederick T. Wilson, Adjutant General's Office. Reprinted as part of this document.

———. *Conditions in the Coal Fields of Harlan and Bell Counties, Kentucky.* Hearings on Senate Resolution No. 178, Senate Subcommittee on Manufacture. 72d Cong., 1st sess.

HOUSE DOCUMENTS

U.S. Congress, House. *Coeur d'Alene Labor Troubles.* 56th Cong., 1st sess. House Report No. 1949.

———. *Papers Relative to the Labor Troubles at Goldfield, Nevada. Message from the President of the U.S., Transmitting Report of Special Commission on Labor Troubles at Goldfield, Nev. and Papers Relating Thereto.* 60th Cong., 1st sess. House Exec. Document No. 607.

———. *Peonage in Western Pennsylvania, Hearings before the Committee on Labor of the House of Representatives.* 62d Cong., 1st sess.

———. *The Strike at Lawrence, Massachusetts.* 62d Cong., 2d sess. House Document No. 671.

———. *Miners' Strike in the Bituminous Coal Field in Westmoreland County, Pa. in 1910-1911*, by Walter B. Palmer. 62d Cong., 2d sess. House Document No. 847.

———. *Industrial Disputes in Colorado and Michigan. Hearings on House Res. 290 and 313, Dec. 10 and 17, 1913, Before the House Committee on Rules.* Washington, D.C.: Supt. of Documents, 1913.

———. *I.W.W. Deportation Cases. Hearings Before the Subcommittee of the House Committee on Immigration and Naturalization.* 66th Cong., 2d sess., April 27-30, 1920.

———. *Amnesty for Political Prisoners. Hearings Before the Committee on the Judiciary, House of Representatives.* 67th Cong., 2d sess. March 16, 1922.

STATE DOCUMENTS

California. Commissioner to Investigate Disturbances in San Diego. *Report of Harris Weinstock, Commissioner to Investigate the Recent Disturbances in the City of San Diego.* Sacramento: Supt. of State Printing, 1912.

———. Commission of Immigration and Housing. *Annual Report, 1913.* Sacramento: State Printers. (Further reports by year.)

Colorado. *Industrial Disputes: the Northern Coal Fields Strike.* Biennial Report of the Bureau of Labor Statistics, 1911-1912. Denver: 1913.

Commonwealth of Massachusetts. *13th Annual Report on Strikes and Lockouts, 1912.* Part 3 of *42d Annual Report on the Statistics of Labor, 1912.* Boston: Massachusetts Bureau of Statistics, 1913. See similar reports for other years.

———. *Annual Report of the State Board of Conciliation and Arbitration for the Year Ending December 31, 1912.* See other annual reports.

———. Bureau of Statistics. *Labor Bibliography, July 15, 1913.* Boston: State Printers, 1913. See bibliographies for several years.

Lawrence, Massachusetts. *Annual Report of the Director of the Department of Public Health and Charities for the Year 1912.*

Minnesota. House of Representatives. Committee of Labor and Labor Legislation, Hearings. "Labor Troubles in Northern Minnesota, Jan. 30, 1917." In John Lind Papers, Minnesota Historical Society.

Montana. "Testimony of Hearings Held at the State Capitol, Helena, Montana, May 31, June 1, June 2, 1918, by Montana Council of Defense." Reporter's typed manuscript at Montana Historical Library, Helena.

Nebraska. *Industrial Survey of the Wage Earners; Labor Unions; Occupational Diseases; Industrial Accidents; Cost of Living; General Labor Conditions of Nebraska.* Bulletin No 25, BLIS, November 1912.

New Jersey. Bureau of Statistics of Labor and Industry of New Jersey. *Annual Report*, for 1911, 1912, 1913, 1914. Camden: S. Chev and Sons.

New York. Legislature. Joint Legislative Committee Investigating Seditious Activities. *Revolutionary Radicalism: Its History, Purposes and Tactics.* 4 vols. Albany, 1920.

New York. *Industrial Relations in New York. Bulletin of the New York Department of Labor*, vol. 14, March, June, September, and December 1912.

Ohio. 80th General Assembly. Appendix of "Reports of Committee Investigating Akron Rubber Industries." *Journal*, 1913.

Washington. State Council of Defense. *Report of the State Council of Defense to the Governor of Washington Covering Its Activities During the War, June 16, 1917, to January 9, 1919.* Olympia, 1919.

West Virginia. West Virginia Mining Investigation Commission Report. Appendix to *Regular Biennial Message of Governor Glasscock to the Legislature for the Period October 1, 1910, to September 30, 1912.*

I.W.W. PUBLICATIONS

Books, newspapers, magazines, pamphlets, and leaflets have been published by the Industrial Workers of the World in great number since the proceedings of the first convention in June 1905. Those proceedings were published for them by the New York Labor News Company in that year.

Proceedings and convention minutes are very widely available, at least on microfilm. Fourth convention minutes were not taken, but reports of the convention can be found in *Industrial Union Bulletin* for October 10, 24, November 7, and December 12, 1908; and in February 20, 27, and March 6, 1909. The Reuther Library and some other repositories have all the proceedings except the fourth.

Executive Board Minutes from between 1911 and 1924 are rare due to government seizures, but scattered copies can be found in trial evidence, in microfilmed files of the Federal Bureau of Investigation, and in various libraries. From 1923 to date, such records are quite complete in the I.W.W. files, and *Executive Board Bulletins* are complete from 1930. Some of the office records seized in the 1918 raids (163 (sheets) were found tucked into the Chicago Trial transcript belonging to the I.W.W. defense, and these are now at the Reuther Library. They are sparse but include some bulletins from 1913 to 1917, and other odds and ends, such as convention notes and calls, reports, and some correspondence.

There are financial statements in the Minute Book (*Minutes of the General Executive Board of the Industrial Workers of the World*, 1906-1908, 1910-1911), and others may be found in periodicals, in the seized materials mentioned, and occasionally in microfilmed U.S. Justice Department Bureau of Investigation Files (RG 65). Financial Records are relatively complete from 1919 to date. After 1956 they are included as part of the *General Office Bulletin*. The bulletins themselves, which in fact contain much historical information, date from 1921, with good regularity. In 1929 the name was changed to *General Organization Bulletin*.

Thanks to increased microfilming, many of the I.W.W. papers are now widely available in libraries or on library loan. The following is a partial list of serial publications of the I.W.W., with dates given only roughly since they can be determined more exactly at any library. As they are an important source for local history, they should be listed here.

Daily Bulletin (Chicago)

This daily sheet was, from February 2 to March 23, 1918, titled *Jail Bulletin*. It was *Daily Bulletin* from April 2 to 17, and became *Trial Bulletin* from April 19 to August 10, 1918. These bulletins were published by the I.W.W. during the Chicago trial so that members need not rely on public newspaper coverage, considered biased, for news of the trial and, no doubt, to increase contributions to the defense fund.

Defense News Bulletin (See *Industrial Solidarity*)

Fellow Worker (New York)

1920
This is to be found at the U.S. Department of Labor Library. It was superseded by *Industrial Unionist*.

Junior Wobbly and *Junior Recruit*

Mostly mimeographed children's magazines, dating in the 1930s.

Industrial Pioneer (Chicago)

1921-1922, 1923-1926

Industrial Solidarity (Chicago)

This has many varying titles:
1909-1917 as *Solidarity*
1917-1918 as *Defense News Bulletin*
1918-1920 as *New Solidarity*
1920-1931 as *Solidarity*.
After September 1921, it merged into *Industrial Worker*.
Industrial Solidarity can be seen at many places, as it was microfilmed. In addition to the Reuther Library, various holdings can be found at the University of California, Library of Congress, University of Chicago, University of Illinois, Harvard, Johns Hopkins, Minnesota Historical Society, Hamilton College

(New York), New York Public Library, Columbia University, State Historical Society of Wisconsin, and the University of Washington.

Industrial Union Bulletin (Chicago)

1907-1909

Industrial Unionist (Portland, Oregon)

Published by Emergency Program branches, from 1925 to 1926.

Industrial Worker (Spokane, Washington)

1909-1913

Industrial Worker (Seattle)

1916-1918
These issues are at the University of California at Berkeley, U.S. Department of Labor Library, Library of Congress, University of Illinois, Massachusetts Institute of Technology, Harvard University, Minnesota Historical Society, New York Public Library, State Historical Society of Wisconsin, University of Wisconsin, and Wayne State University's Reuther Library.

Industrial Worker (Chicago)

First series, 1916-1918
New series, 1919 to the present
These issues are at the U.S. Department of Labor Library, Massachusetts Institute of Technology, Harvard University, Minnesota Historical Society, New York Public Library, Reuther Library at Wayne State University, and the University of Washington.

New Solidarity (See *Industrial Solidarity*)

One Big Union Advocate (New York)

This magazine was published by the One Big Union Club in New York from 1939 to 1940.

One Big Union Monthly (Chicago)

1919-1921, 1937-1938

Rebel Worker (New York)

1918-1919
Volume 1 entitled *Labor Defender*
Has been microfilmed and can be seen widely, with originals at Stanford University's Hoover Library, U.S. Department of Labor Library, Library of Congress, and State Historical Society of Wisconsin.

Solidarity (New Castle, Pennsylvania; see *Industrial Solidarity*)

Voice of the People (New Orleans and Portland, Oregon)

1912-1914

This is on microfilm and at various places; originals are at the U.S. Department of Labor Library and State Historical Society of Wisconsin.

Workers Defense (Chicago, GDC)

1931-1932, superseded *Defense News Bulletin*
Also on microfilm, it can be seen at Stanford University's Hoover Library, University of Illinois, New York Public Library, Vassar College, Duke University, and the Reuther Library at Wayne State University.

I.W.W. PAMPHLETS

Abbreviations

BIR — Bureau of Industrial Research
CDC— California District Committee, sometimes California Defense Committee
CPC — Centralia Publicity Committee
GDC— General Defense Committee

Adress of the Defendant Arturo M. Giovannitti to the Jury. I.W.W. 12 pp.
　　　—Lawrence strike

After Liberalism Had Failed, George P. West. Chicago: GDC, 1923, reprint leaflet. 1 p.
　　　—Criminal syndicalism; longshoremen's strike

Agriculture: The Mother of Industry. AWIU No. 110, I.W.W. 4 pp.

Agriculture: The World's Basic Industry and Its Workers. Chicago: BIR, I.W.W. 64 pp.

American Legion and the Centralia Case. Chicago: GDC, 1924. 4 pp.

And in the United States Liberty Lies Crushed. Chicago: GDC. 4 pp.
　　　—I.W.W. Trials

Are You Inconvenienced by a Strike on the SP Line? Mountain View, California: I.W.W., 1972. 2 pp.

Are You Ready? Buffalo: I.W.W., 1935(?). 1 p.
　　　—Westinghouse-Markel, MMWIU No. 440.

Are You Ready to Defend Your Rights? The Rights Guaranteed to You by the Constitution. Seattle: I.W.W. 4 pp.
　　　—Political prisoners

Associated Industries of Cleveland, Ohio vs. the Union of Their Slaves. Bulletin, GDC, 1935. Distributed as pamphlet. 4 pp.

Attention Apple Knockr's! Watsonville, California: I.W.W. 1 p.

Attention Coal Miners! CMWIU No. 220, I.W.W., 1929. 3 pp.
　　　—Illinois miners

Attention! Direct Mail Workers! New York: I.W.W. 1 p.

Auto, Steel, Metal and Machinery Workers, Shall it be No Unionism or New Unionism? Chicago: I.W.W., c. 1930. 4 pp.

Auto Workers! Motor Industry Profits a Half Billion Dollars! Detroit, I.W.W. 2 pp.

Auto Workers: This Is the I.W.W. Way Out. Detroit: I.W.W., 1933. 4 pp.

Be It Resolved: That the Mine Workers of Butte Are Entitled to an Increase in Wages of $1.00 a Day. Butte: 1927, 1 p.

Bindle Stiff. I.W.W., 4 pp.

Brothers and Sisters of the ILU, We're with You. Honolulu: IU No. 450, I.W.W. 2 pp.

Bulletin No. 2. Marine Workers in Philadelphia Appeal to Their Fellow-Workers in Other Ports for Support. Philadelphia: Publicity Committee, MTWIU No. 510, I.W.W. 1 p.
    —General strike; longshoremen's strike

Bulletin No. 5. Appeal to the Seamen. Philadelphia: Publicity Committee, MTWIU No. 510, I.W.W. 1 p.

California the Beautiful and Damned. Chicago: GDC, I.W.W. 1 p.

California, Be on Guard! San Francisco: California District Defense Committee. 4 pp.

California in Chains. California Branch, GDC. 4 pp.

California Oil World Teaches Violence and Tries to Cause a Reign of Terror, James Elliott and Claude Irwin. San Francisco: I.W.W. 1 p.

Call to Action—to All Agricultural Workers! AWIU No. 110, I.W.W. 2 pp.

Centralia Case. Friends of Ray Becker. 2 pp.

Centralia Case. Speeches by Elmer Smith and Capt. Edward P. Coll. Centralia, Washington: CPC. 15 pp.

Centralia Case (by an American Legionnaire), signed by Edward Patrick Coll. Chicago: GDC, I.W.W. 4 pp.

Centralia Case—A Chronological Digest. Chicago: GDC, I.W.W. 4 pp.

Centralia Conspiracy, Ralph Chaplin. Chicago: GDC. 82 pp.

Cigar Makers—Draw Up Your Own Code. Detroit: I.W.W. 1 p.

Cigar Makers Meeting. Detroit: I.W.W. 4 pp.

Coal Miners! Butte: CMIU No. 220. 2 pp.

Coal Miners Awaken! Butte: CMIU No. 220. 4 pp.

Coal Mines and Coal Miners, the Story of a Great Industry and the Men Who Work in it. Chicago: I.W.W. 112 pp.

Colored Workers of America: Why You Should Join the I.W.W. Chicago: I.W.W. 4 pp.

Comparisons Are Odious to Labor Skates and Grafters. Aberdeen, Washington: LWIU No. 120, I.W.W. 2 pp.

Copper Kings Have Spoken: Workers, What is Your Reply? Salt Lake City: Haywood and Perry. 1 p.

Courage, Confidence and Loyalty to the Cause. Philadelphia: MTWIU No. 510. 1 p.

Crime of Centralia, W. F. Dunn. Butte: the author. 16 pp.

Dare to Be Different. Chicago: AWIU No. 110, I.W.W. 4 pp.
    —Migratory workers

Dollars and Steel Against Humanity: Iron Ore Miners Strike. Cleveland: Solidarity Publishing Co. 16 pp.
    —Mesaba miners

Do You Know These Salient Facts About Humboldt County? San Francisco: California Branch, GDC, I.W.W. 1 p.

Do You Know These Truths About Washington? Seattle: Washington Branch, GDC. 1 p.

East Coast and Gulf Seamen—Don't Join the ISU. New York: GOC, MTWIU No. 510, I.W.W. 2 pp.

Eight Men Buried Alive. Chicago: GDC, I.W.W., 1924. 32 pp.
    —Centralia

Eight Men Buried Alive! Six Centralia Jurors Confess. I.W.W. 4 pp.

Eleven Blind Leaders, or "Practical Socialism" and "Revolutionary Tactics" from an I.W.W. Standpoint, Ben H. Williams. New Castle, Pennsylvania: I.W.W. Publishing Bureau, 1909. 29 pp.

Elmer Smith Pleads for Liberty of Centralia Men. Centralia, Washington: CPC. 4 pp.

Employees of Cedar Valley Coffee House Are on Strike. San Francisco: I.W.W. 1 p.

An Enormous Contrast and the Reason. Chicago: LWIU No. 120. 4 pp.

Ettor and Giovannitti Before the Jury at Salem, Massachusetts. Chicago: I.W.W. 80 pp.

Ettor and Giovannitti Before the Jury at Salem, Massachusetts, November 23, 1912. Chicago: I.W.W. 84 pp.

Evidence and Cross-Examination of J. T. (Red) Doran in the Case of the U.S.A. vs. William D. Haywood, et al. Chicago: I.W.W. 151 pp.

Evolution of American Agriculture, Abner E. Woodruff, with introduction by Wm. D. Haywood. Chicago: AWIU No. 400, 1919. 77 pp.

Exposed by the Marine Transport Workers Industrial Union No. 510 of the I.W.W. Chicago: I.W.W., 1923. 28 pp.

Fair Trial?, Frank Walkin. I.W.W. 16 pp.
    —Centralia

Fellow Workers. Oklahoma City, Oklahoma: OWIU No. 230. 4 pp.

A Few Reasons Why Packard Employees Should Join. Detroit: I.W.W., 1933. 4 pp.

Four Fighting Years: A Short History of the Marine Workers Industrial Union. New York: I.W.W., 1934.

Following the Trail of the I.W.W.; a First-hand Investigation into Labor Troubles in the West; a Trip into the Copper and Lumber Camps of the Inland Empire With the Views of Men on the Job, Robert Bruere. New York: New York Evening Post, 1918.

Fruit Pickers Attention: What Are We Going to Do? Sunnyvale, California: AWIU No. 110, I.W.W. 1 p.

Fruit Workers Attention! Chicago: I.W.W. 2 pp.
  —Yakima, Washington

Great Conspiracy. Seattle: John Grady. 4 pp.
  —NW lumber strikes

Harvest Time is Honey Time. AWIU No. 110, I.W.W. 2 pp.

Harvest Workers Attention! Minneapolis: AWIU No. 110, I.W.W. 4 pp.

Has the Constitution of the United States Been 'Recalled' in Paterson N.J.?
  Paterson: I.W.W. 4 pp.

Hi-Jacks, Boot-Leggers, Holdups, Gamblers, Etc., in the Harvest Fields: Warning
  to You. I.W.W. 2 pp.

"Hip" Rip. Chicago: I.W.W. 2 pp.

Historical Catechism of American Unionism. Chicago: I.W.W. 96 pp.

History of "400", signed by E. Workman. New York: OBU Club, 1939. 24 pp.

Hoof and Mouth Disease Spreads: Beware of California Products. Chicago: GDC,
  1924. 2 pp.

Hungry Babies! Hungry Mothers! Hungry Men! Five Months on Strike at
  Paterson. I.W.W., 1913. 1 p.

Immediate Attention, to Labor Men and Taxpayers of San Francisco. San
  Francisco: CDC. 1 p.

Is Freedom Dead?, Harrison George, Chicago: I.W.W., 1918. 24 pp.

I.W.W. in the Lumber Industry, James Rowan. Seattle: I.W.W. 64 pp.

The I.W.W.: Its History, Structure and Methods, Vincent St. John. Chicago:
  I.W.W. 47 pp.

I.W.W. Statement. San Pedro: I.W.W. Publicity Committee, 1924. 4 pp.

Judicial Murder. Seattle: Washington Branch, GDC. 4 pp.

Justice and the I.W.W., Paul F. Brissenden. Chicago: GDC, 1918. 32 pp.

Justice for the Negro—How He Can Get It. Chicago: I.W.W. 4 pp.

Lake Seamen Join Now, Wake Up. MTWIU No. 510, I.W.W. 1 p.

Legion Officer and Overseas Captain Demands Release of Centralia Victims.
  Centralia: CPC, 1928. 4 pp.

Loggers and Millmen! IU No. 120, I.W.W. 2 pp.

Los Angeles Garment Workers. Los Angeles: I.W.W. 2 pp.

Lumber Industry and Its Workers. Chicago: I.W.W. 96 pp.

Lumber Workers of Columbia River. LWIU No. 120, I.W.W. 4 pp.

Lumber Workers Organize! Chicago: LWIU NO. 120, I.W.W. 4 pp.

Lumberworkers You Need Organization. I.W.W. Post 1927.
  —Six-hour day demand; thirteen addresses given, after 1927.

Martyrs of Texas. Oakland, California: Defense Committee. 4 pp.

Masters of the West. Hill Defense Fund. 4 pp.

Medieval California, Land of Orange Groves and Jails. Chicago: GDC, I.W.W.
  8 pp.

Members of the Draper Shop Branch of the I.W.W. Who Have Joined the United States Army, Navy, or Coast Guard. I.W.W. 1 p.

Message from the City Jail of Centralia, Washington. Seattle: Equity Printing. 4 pp.

Message from the Sacramento County Jail. I.W.W. The Ten Defenders. 4 pp.

Metal Mine Workers! Butte: I.W.W. 4 pp.

Miners, Attention! Butte: 1927-1928. 1 p.

Miners of Illinois, signed by Forrest Edwards. Chicago: I.W.W. 2 pp.

Mob Scalds Children. San Pedro: Relief Committee. 4 pp.

My Findings on the Centralia Case, Elizabeth Attridge. Centralia: CPC, 1929. 4 pp.

New Idea: Why Union Men Are Persecuted in California. San Francisco: California Branch, GDC. 4 pp.

No Surrender. Casper, California: Education Department of Fishing Workers IU, I.W.W. 1 p.

Oil Workers! Oklahoma City, Oklahoma: OWIU No. 230, I.W.W. 4 pp.

One Big Industrial Union in the Textile Industry. Chicago: TWIU No. 410, I.W.W. 24 pp.

One Big Union in the Textile Industry, Ewald Koettgen. Cleveland: I.W.W. Publishing Bureau. 15 pp.

Open the Iron Gates in Idaho! Chicago: GDC. 2 pp.

Open Letter to Briggs Employees. Detroit: I.W.W., 1933. 4 pp.

Open Letter from the I.W.W. to the State's Attorneys of California. San Francisco: California Branch, GDC. 15 pp.

Open Letter to Mssrs. Nelson and Hill of Humboldt County, California, Tom Doyle. I.W.W. 14 pp.

Pageant of the Paterson Strike. New York: Success Press. 32 pp.

Persecution of Union Men in California. Los Angeles: California Branch, GDC, I.W.W. 6 pp.

Philadelphia Controversy. Philadelphia Branch, MTWIU No. 510, I.W.W. 35 pp.

Remedy for California's Misery. Chicago: I.W.W., 1924. 4 pp.

Request I.W.W. Delegates to Visit Gandy Gangs. Tacoma: I.W.W. 4 pp.

Sabotage, Elizabeth Gurley Flynn. Cleveland: I.W.W. Publishing Bureau, 1915. 31 pp.

Sabotage: Its History, Philosophy and Function. Chicago: I.W.W., 1913. 32 pp.

Sacramento 'Cutor Breaks Law to Make Large Reputation. San Francisco: GDC, I.W.W. 4 pp.

San Pedro Calls! Los Angeles: I.W.W. 4 pp.

Shall Our Brothers Be Murdered? Chicago: I.W.W., 1906. 1 p.

Shall Freedom Die? 166 Union Men in Jail For Labor, By One of Them. Chicago: I.W.W., 1917. 23 pp.

Shame of California. San Francisco: California Branch, GDC. 4 pp.

Shame of Centralia: A Travesty on Justice. Seattle: CPC. 4 pp.

Shame That is Kentucky's, E. J. Costello. Chicago: GDC. 28 pp.

Silent Defenders: Courts and Capitalism in California, Harvey Duff. Chicago:
       I.W.W. 112 pp.

Silent Defense. Chicago: I.W.W. 47 pp.

Speech of Wm. D. Haywood on the Case of Ettor and Giovannitti. Lawrence,
       Massachusetts: Ettor-Giovannitti Defense Committee. 16 pp.

Speeches by Elmer Smith, Captain Edward P. Coll. Centralia: CPC, 1929. 16 pp.

Story of the Sea—Marine Transport Workers' Hand Book. Chicago: I.W.W. 80 pp.

Strike! Blueberry Pickers, Michigan: AWIU No. 110, I.W.W. 1 p.

Strike at the Bond Plant. Buffalo: I.W.W. 1 p.

Strike at Hetchy Hetchy and UC Camps. GCWIU No. 310, I.W.W., 1922. 1 p.

Strike: Nation Cut Off. Strike Committee, IU No. 310, I.W.W. 1 p.

Strike! Strike! Proclamation. New York: MTWIU No. 510, I.W.W. 1 p.

Suppressed Evidence in the Centralia Case. Chicago: GDC. 4 pp.

Testimony of William D. Haywood Before the Industrial Relations Commission.
       Chicago: I.W.W. Publishing Bureau, 1913. 71 pp.

That "Victory" of the Coal Miners, Analyzed. Chicago: I.W.W. 15 pp.
              —Butte

These Are the Facts! The Truth About the Attempted Mob Outrage in Centralia.
       Chicago: I.W.W. 14 pp.

Three New Witnesses of Centralia Tragedy. Chicago: GDC. 4 pp.

To All Building Workers in Los Angeles and Vicinity. Los Angeles: BCWIU No.
       330, I.W.W. 4 pp.

To All Marine Transport Workers. Chicago, MTWIU No. 510, I.W.W. 1 p.

To All Wage Earners and Friends of Labor, signed, Relief Committee, by P. W.
       Kirschbaum. Paterson: I.W.W., 1913.

To Harvest Workers: Attention! Chicago: AWIU No. 110. 4 pp.

'To the Beasts'—in California as in Ancient Rome. San Francisco: GDC, 1924.
       30 pp.

To the Citizens of Sacramento County. San Francisco: California Branch, GDC.
       4 pp.

To the Iron Workers. Chicago: BCWIU No. 330. 2 pp.

To the Lumber Workers of British Columbia. Canada: I.W.W. 4 pp.

To the Lumber Workers of Michigan, Wisconsin and Minnesota. Chicago: LWIU
       No. 120, I.W.W. 4 pp.

To Organized Labor of Butte. San Francisco: California Branch, GDC. 2 pp.

To the People of Bishop. Bishop, California: MMIU No. 210, I.W.W. 1 p.

To the Public From the Striking Charwomen. I.W.W. 1 p.

To the Silk Workers of Paterson. Paterson: I.W.W. Local No. 152, 1912. 1 p.

To the Workers in the Lumbering Industry. Chicago: I.W.W. 2 pp.

To the Workers Who Clothe the World. Chicago: I.W.W. 4 pp.

To the Workers Who Feed the World. Chicago: WMIU No. 460, I.W.W. 8 pp.

Tourists Beware of California! San Francisco: California Branch, GDC. 1 p.

Trail to Truth. San Pedro: San Pedro Publicity Committee. 9 pp.

Truth About the I. W. W., by Harold Callender. Chicago: I.W.W. 16 pp.

UAW Pay Cut—GM. Cleveland: I.W.W. 2 pp.
> —Auto workers

Uncle Sam: Jailor, Winthrop D. Lane. Chicago: I.W.W. 40 pp.

Unemployed Soldiers Listen! Chicago: I.W.W. 2 pp.

A Union for all Railroad Workers. Chicago: I.W.W. 32 pp.

A Union for Farm Wage Workers. Chicago: I.W.W. 4 pp.

Union Scabs and Others. Oscar Ameringer. New Castle, Pennsylvania: I.W.W. Publishing Bureau, 1912. 2 pp.

Vegetable and Fruit Workers! Chicago: AWIU No. 110. 2 pp.

Warning to Seamen and Longshoremen. Chicago: MTWIU No. 510, I.W.W. 1 p.

Was it Murder? The Truth About Centralia, Walker C. Smith. Seattle: Northwest District Defense Committee, 1922. 48 pp.

Washington's Gory History, Page by Page. Seattle: Washington Branch, GDC. 2 pp.

Washington's Judicial Mockery. Seattle: Centralia Release Committee, 1929. 4 pp.

Washington's Legal Mockery. Seattle: GDC. 4 pp.

We Never Forget! Organize and Act!, William D. Haywood. Chicago: I.W.W. 4 pp.

What Do You Think of This? Chicago: GDC, I.W.W. 4 pp.
> —Tulsa lynchings

What Lumber Workers Want. Chicago: LWIU No. 120, I.W.W. 4 pp.

What's Your Answer? Do You Sleep as Well as Chessie in Your Bunk Car? I.W.W. 1 p.
> —Gandy drive

Who Has Paterson by the Throat? Paterson: Local No. 1521, 1913. 1 p.

Who Is Guilty of Conspiracy? San Francisco: California Branch, GDC. 4 pp.

Why Eleven Members of the I. W. W., Imprisoned at Leavenworth, Refused Conditional Pardon. Philadelphia: H. F. Kane for the prisoners, 1923. 2 pp.

Why Mill Workers Must Organize. LWIU No. 120, I.W.W. 2 pp.

Why We're Picketing the Three Penny. Chicago: I.W.W. 1 p.

Will It Be Freedom for us or Death on the Gallows? Spokane: Metaline Miners Defense Committee. 4 pp.

With Drops of Blood, William D. Haywood. I.W.W., 1919(?). 4 pp.

A Word to That Miner. Chicago: I.W.W. 4 pp.

Workers of the Coal Mines. Butte and Chicago: I.W.W. 4 pp.

Workers Will You Stand for More Bloodshed? I.W.W., 1907. 4 pp.

World Wide Strike in the Marine Industry: Strike! Seattle: MTWIU No. 510. 1 p.

A Year's Persecution of Industrial Unionists in California Under the Syndicalism Law. San Francisco: I.W.W. 4 pp.

You Ought to Know. Centralia: CPC. 4 pp.

NON-I.W.W. PAMPHLETS

Abbreviations

ACLU— American Civil Liberties Union
NCLB— National Civil Liberties Board
GEB   — General Executive Board

Amnesty for Political Prisoners. New York: ACLU, 1920.

Anarchy in Colorado, Who Is to Blame?, H. E. Bartholomew. Colorado: Bartholomew Publishing Co., 1905.

Butte Troubles, 1917, Address Before Chamber of Commerce at Missoula, Montana, Wednesday, August 29, 1917, L. O. Evans. Butte, Montana: 1917.

Centralia Case: A Joint Report on the Armistice Day Tragedy at Centralia, Washington, November 11, 1919. Issued by the Department of Research and Education of the Federal Council of Churches of Christ in America, the Social Action Department of the National Catholic Welfare Conference, and the Social Justice Commission of the Central Conference of American Rabbis, 1930.

Centralia—Tragedy and Trial, Ben Hur Lampman. Tacoma and Centralia: American Legion, 1920.

The Church and Industrial Warfare: A Report on the Labor Troubles in Colorado and Michigan, Henry A. Atkinson. Federal Council of Churches of Christ in America, 1914.

Civil Liberty Since the Armistice. New York: ACLU, 1920.

Class Struggle in Idaho, J. Harreman. New York: Labor Publishing Association, 1904.

Copper Country Commercial Strike Investigation, Chicago: M. A. Donohue and Co., 1913.

Criminal Record of the Western Federation of Miners—Coeur d'Alene to Cripple Creek—1894-1904. Colorado Springs: Colorado Mine Operators Association, 1904.

Deceit of the I.W.W. A Year's Record of the Activity of the Industrial Workers of the World in the Cloth Hat and Cap Trade. New York: GEB of United Cloth Hat and Cap Makers of North America, 1906.

Direct Action and Sabotage, William E. Trautmann. Pittsburgh: Socialist News Co., 1912.

Facts as to the Moyer and Other Decisions of the Supreme Court of Colorado,

H. L. Vamey. Denver: Republican State Central Committee of Colorado, 1906.

The Fight for Free Speech. New York: ACLU, 1921.

Governor Peabody to the Voters—the Colorado Situation discussed and Misstatements Refuted, J. H. Peabody. Denver, Colorado.

Haywood Case, C. F. Koelsch. Boise: Idaho Mining Association, 1946.

Haywood Trial: Closing Arguments of W. E. Borah. Boise, Idaho: Statesmen Shop.

History of Activities of Seattle Labor Movement and the Conspiracy of Employers to Destroy It; and Attempted Suppression of Labor's Daily Newspaper, the Seattle Union Record. Seattle, 1919.

History versus Histerics: An Open Letter to the Vigilantes and the I.W.W. Sage of La Jolla, 1912. 7 pp.

Hysteria or Common Sense. New York: ACLU, 1919.

Industrial Communism—the I.W.W. Butte: The Bulletin Print, 1919.

Industrial Workers: A Clear and Forcible Expose of the Crimes and Policies of the I.W.W. Chicago: Bureau American.

Introductory Chapter to the History of the Trials of Moyer, Haywood and Pettibone, F. Wood. Caldwell, Idaho: Caxton Printers, 1931.

The Issues in the Centralia Murder Trial. New York: ACLU, 1920.

I.W.W., Joseph Mereto. Chicago: Iconoclast Publishing Company, 1919.

I.W.W., W. V. Woehlke. Cleveland: National Metal Trades Association, 1912.

The I.W.W. an Auxiliary of the German Espionage System: History of I.W.W. Wartime Activities, Showing How the I.W.W. Program of Sabotage Inspired the Kaiser's Agents in America, T. Everett Harré. New York: 1918.

The "Knights of Liberty" Mob and the I.W.W. Prisoners at Tulsa, Oklahoma (November 9, 1917). New York: ACLU, 1918.

Labor Scrap Book. Chicago: C. H. Kerr and Company, 1918. 31 pp.

Leadville, Colorado—the Most Wonderful Mining Camp in the West, J. Loomis. Colorado Springs: Gazette Publishing Company.

Memoirs of a Silk Striker; an Exposure of the Principles and Tactics of the I.W.W., J. H. Stieger. Privately printed, 1914.

Memorandum Regarding the Persecution of the Radical Labor Movement in the United States. New York: NCLB, 1919.

The Menace of the I.W.W., J. W. Batdorf. New York: Anti-Socialist Press, 1917.

Mob Violence in the United States. New York: ACLU, 1923.

Ol' Rags an' Bottles. New York: NCLB, 1919.
    —Sacramento trial

On the Nature and Uses of Sabotage, Thorstein Veblen. New York: Dial, 1919.

On to Sacramento. Southern California Councils for Constitutional Rights, 1936.

Persecution of the I.W.W. New York: ACLU, 1921.

Plotting to Convict Wheatland Hop Pickers. Oakland, California: International Press, 1914.

Political Prisoners in Federal Military Prisons. New York: NCLB, 1918.

Political Socialism: Capturing the Government, B. E. Nilsson. Portland, Oregon: The Author.

Reign of Terror in an American City. Lawrence, Mass.: Lawrence Citizens Association, 1912.

Report Upon the Illegal Practices of the United States Department of Justice. Washington, D.C.: National Popular Government League, 1920.

Rule or Ruin Policy of the Industrial Workers. Official Statement of the Capmakers' Union on a Matter of Vital Importance to the American Labor Movement. New York: GEB of the United Cloth Hat and Cap Makers of North America, n.d.

San Diego's Free Speech Controversy. San Francisco: San Francisco Labor Council, 1912.

Seattle General Strike: An Account of What Happened in Seattle . . . February 6 to 11, 1919. Seattle: *Seattle Union Record* (1919), Seattle General Strike Committee.

Some Factors Bearing on the Wage Question in the Clifton-Morenci-Metcalfe District, N. Carmichael. Clifton, Arizona: 1917.

Story of a New Labor Union, Jno. Kenneth Turner. Portland Mill Workers Industrial Union Leaflet No. 16, 1906-1907.

Strike Investigation by the Committee of the Copper Country Commercial Club of Michigan, 1913. Chicago: N. A. Donohue and Co., 1913.
          —Report of conditions, wages, welfare, etc.

Struggle of the Marine Workers, N. Sparks. New York: International Pamphlets, 1930.

Truth About Butte, George R. Tompkins. Butte: Century Printing, 1917.

Truth About the I. W. W. New York: ACLU, 1922.

The Truth About the I. W. W. New York: NCLB, 1918.

The Truth About the I. W. W. Prisoners, Harrison George. New York: ACLU, 1922.

Twenty-four Cartoons of Mr. Block, Ernest Riebe. Minneapolis: Block Supply Company, 1912(?). 27 pp.

Union-smashing in Sacramento, the Truth About the Criminal Syndicalism Trial, Herbert Solow. New York: National Sacramento Appeal Committee, 1935.

Veritas. Denver: Smith Brooks Press for the Republican Party, 1906.

War on the Colorado Miners. New York: ACLU, 1928.

War-time Prosecutions and Violence Involving the Rights of Free Speech, Free Press and Peaceful Assemblage from April 1, 1917, to May 1, 1918. New York: NCLB, 1918.

Were the Lawrence Strike Funds Honestly Managed? New England Civic Federation Bulletin No. 14. Boston: New England Civic Federation 1913.

Why Two Governors Freed Political Prisoners. New York: ACLU, 1923.

DOCTORAL DISSERTATIONS

Adams, Graham. "Age of Industrial Violence: Social Conflict in America as Revealed by the U.S. Commission on Industrial Relations." Columbia University, 1963.

Allen, Winfred G., Jr. "Spokesman for the 'Disspossessed'; a Content Analysis of the Public Addresses of Eugene Debs, Daniel De Leon and William Haywood." University of California, Los Angeles, 1977.

Altenbaugh, Richard J. "Forming the Structure of a New Society within the Shell of the Old: A Study of Three Labor Colleges and Their Contributions to the American Labor Movement." University of Pittsburgh, 1980.

Applen, Allen G. "Migratory Harvest Labor in the Midwestern Wheat Belt, 1870-1940. Kansas State University, 1974.

Barnes, Donald M. "The Ideology of the Industrial Workers of the World, 1905-1921." Washington State University, 1962.

Bates, James L. "Senator Walsh of Montana, 1918-1924: A Liberal Under Pressure." University of North Carolina, 1952.

Bedford, Henry F. "Socialism and Workers in Massachusetts, 1886-1912." University of Massachusetts, Amherst, 1966.

Brinley, John E. "The Western Federation of Miners." University of Utah, 1972.

Brooks, Robert R. "The United Textile Workers of America." Yale University, 1935.

Brown, Myland. "The I.W.W. and the Negro Worker." Ball State University, 1969.

Brown, Roland C. "Hard-rock Miners of the Great Basin and Rocky Mountain West, 1860-1920." University of Illinois, Urbana-Champaign, 1975.

Burki, Mary Ann. "Paul Scharrenberg: White Shirt Sailor." University of Rochester, 1971.

Byrkit, James W. "Life and Labor in Arizona, 1901-1921: with Particular Reference to the Deportations of 1917." Claremont Graduate School, Claremont, California, 1972.

Calvert, Jerry W. "A Changing Radical Political Organization: The Wobblies Today." Washington State University, Pullman, 1972.

Close, J. A. "Some Phases of the History of the Anaconda Copper Mining Company." University of Minnesota, 1946.

Coben, Stanley. "The Political Career of A. Mitchell Palmer." Columbia University, 1961.

Cole, Donald B. "Lawrence, Massachusetts: Immigrant City, 1845-1912." Harvard University, 1957.

Cole, Terry W. "Labor's Radical Alternative: the Rhetoric of the Industrial Workers of the World." University of Oregon, 1974.

Conlin, Joseph R. "The Wobblies: a Study of the Industrial Workers of the World Before World War I." University of Wisconsin, Madison, 1966.

Cox, John H. "Organizations of the Lumber Industry in the Pacific Northwest to 1917." University of California, Berkeley, 1937.

Daniel, Cletus E. "Labor Radicalism in Pacific Coast Agriculture." University of Washington, 1972.

Dowell, Eldridge F. "A History of the Enactment of Criminal Syndicalism Legislation in the United States." Johns Hopkins University, 1933.

Engberg, George B. "Labor in the Lake States Lumber Industry, 1830-1930." University of Minnesota, 1950.

Fenton, Edwin. "Immigrants and Unions: a Case Study: Italians and American Labor, 1870-1920." Harvard University, 1958.

Finney, John D., Jr. "A Study of Negro Labor During and After World War I." Georgetown University, 1957.

Francis, Robert C. "A History of Labor on the San Francisco Waterfront." University of California, 1934.

Frost, Richard H. "The Mooney Case." University of California, Berkeley, 1961.

Fuller, Levi V. "The Supply of Agricultural Labor as a Factor in the Evolution of Farm Organization in California." University of California, Berkeley, 1939.

Gaboury, William J. "Dissension in the Rockies: a History of Idaho Populism." University of Idaho, 1966.

Garber, Morris W. "The Silk Industry of Paterson, New Jersey, 1840-1913: Technology and the Origins, Development and Changes in an Industry." Rutgers University, 1968.

Gedicks, Al. "Working Class Radicalism Among Finnish Immigrants in Minnesota and Michigan." University of Wisconsin, 1979.

Green, James R. "Socialism and the Southwestern Class Struggle, 1898-1918: a Study of Radical Movements in Oklahoma, Texas, Louisiana and Arkansas." Yale University, 1972.

Glengarelly, William A. "Resistance Spokesmen: Opponents of the Red Scare, 1919-1921." Boston University, 1972.

Greenberg, Irving. "Theodore Roosevelt and Labor: 1900-1918." Harvard University, 1960.

Gronquist, Ray E. "The Ideology of the Industrial Workers of the World as Represented in the Discursive Acts of William D. Haywood." Washington State University, 1975.

Grover, David H. "Debaters and Dynamiters: the Rhetoric of the Haywood Trial." University of Oregon, 1962.

Grubbs, Frank L. "The Struggle for the Mind of American Labor, 1917-1919." University of Virginia, 1963.

Gunns, Albert F. "Civil Liberties and Crisis: the Status of Civil Liberties in the Pacific Northwest, 1917-1940." University of Washington, 1971.

Gutfeld, Arnon. "Years of Hysteria: Montana, 1917-1921: A Study of Local Intolerance." University of California, Los Angeles, 1971.

Helmes, Winfred O. "The People's Governor, John A. Johnson: a Political Biography." University of Minnesota, 1948.

Hoglund, Arthur W. "Paradise Rebuilt: Finnish Immigrants and Their America, 1880-1920." University of Wisconsin, 1957.

Jaffe, Julian F. "Anti-Radical Crusade in New York, 1914-1924: a Case Study of the Red Scare." New York University, 1971.

Jamieson, Stuart M. "Labor Unionism in American Agriculture." University of California, Berkeley, 1943.

Jensen, Joan M. "The American Protective League, 1917-1919." University of California, Los Angeles, 1962.

Jones, Dallas Lee. "The Wilson Administration and Organized Labor, 1912-1919." Cornell University, 1954.

Kluger, James R. "Elwood Mead: Irrigation Engineer and Social Planner." University of Arizona, 1970.

Knight, Robert E. L. "A History of Industrial Relations in the San Francisco Bay Area, 1900-1918." University of California, Berkeley, 1958.

Krivy, Leonard P. "American Organized Labor and the First World War, 1917-1918: a History of Labor Problems and the Development of a Government War Labor Program." New York University, 1965.

Mabon, David White. "The West Coast Waterfront and Sympathy Strikes of 1934." University of California, Berkeley, 1966.

Maroney, James C. "Organized Labor in Texas, 1900-1929." University of Houston, 1975.

Makarewicz, Joseph T. "The Impact of World War I on Pennsylvania Politics, with Emphasis on the Election of 1920." University of Pittsburgh, 1972.

Mason, Alpheus T. "Organized Labor and the Law, with Special Reference to the Sherman and Clayton Acts." Princeton University, 1923.

McClurg, Donald J. "Labor Organization in the Coal Mines of Colorado, 1878-1933." University of California, 1959.

McCormack, Andrew Ross. "The Origins and Extent of Western Labour Radicalism, 1896-1919." University of Western Ontario, 1973.

McEnroe, Thomas. "I.W.W. Theories, Organization Problems and Appeals as Revealed in the Industrial Worker." University of Minnesota, 1960.

McGovern, George S. "The Colorado Coal Strike, 1913-1914." Northwestern University, 1953.

McKee, Donald D. "The Intellectual and Historical Influence Shaping the Political Theory of Daniel DeLeon." Columbia University, 1955.

Meany, Edmond S. "The History of the Lumber Industry in the Pacific Northwest

Meehan, (Sister) Maria E. "Frank P. Walsh and the American Labor Movement, 1864-1939." New York University, 1962.

Miller, Richard C. "Otis and His *Times*: the Career of Harrison Gray Otis of Los Angeles." University of California, Berkeley, 1961.

Murray, Robert K. "The Great Red Scare of 1919-1920." Ohio State University, 1950.

Myers, Howard B. "The Policing of Labor Disputes in Chicago." University of Chicago, 1929.

Nash, Michael H. "Conflict and Accommodation: Some Aspects of the Political Behavior of America's Coal Miners and Steel Workers, 1890-1920." University of New York, Binghamton, 1975.

Nichols, Claude W., Jr. "Brotherhood in the Woods: A Twenty Year Attempt at 'Industrial Cooperation.' " University of Oregon, 1959.

Olson, Richard E. "Some Economic Aspects of Agricultural Development in Nebraska, 1854-1920." University of Nebraska, 1965.

Pawar, Sheelwant B. "An Environmental Study of the Development of the Utah Labor Movement, 1860-1935." University of Utah, 1968.

Pinola, Rudolph. "Labor and Politics on the Iron Range of Northern Minnesota." University of Wisconsin. 1957.

Powell, Allen K. "A History of Labor Union Activity in the Eastern Utah Coal Fields, 1900-1934." University of Utah, 1976.

Prago, Albert. "The Organization of the Unemployed and the Role of the Radicals, 1929-1935." Union Graduate School, Ohio, 1976.

Preston, William. "The Ideology and Techniques of Repression: Government and the Radicals, 1903-1933." University of Wisconsin, 1957.

Ragan, Fred D. "The *New Republic*: Red Hysteria and Civil Liberties." University of Georgia, 1965.

Randall, John H. "The Problem of Group Responsibility to Society: An Interpretation of the History of American Labor." Columbia University, 1922.

Robinson, Leland W. "Social Movement Organizations in Decline: a Case Study of the I.W.W." Northwestern University, 1974.

Scheinberg, Stephen J. "The Development of Corporation Labor Policy, 1900-1940." University of Wisconsin, 1966.

Schwantes, Carlos A. "Left-Wing Unionism in the Pacific Northwest: A Comparative History of Organized Labor and Socialist Politics in Washington and British Columbia, 1885-1917." University of Michigan, 1976.

Shaffer, Ralph E. "Radicalism in California, 1869-1929." University of California, Berkeley, 1962.

Smith, Robert W. "The Idaho Antecedents of the Western Federation of Miners, 1890 to 1893." University of California, Berkeley, 1938.

Sperry, James R. "Organized Labor and Its Fight Against Military and Industrial Conscription, 1917-1945." University of Arizona, 1969.

Stevenson, Billie Jean Hackley. "The Ideology of American Anarchism, 1880-1910." University of Iowa, 1972.

Stokes, George A. "Lumbering in Southwest Louisiana: a Study of the Industry." Louisiana State University, 1954.

Syrjamaki, John. "The Development of Mesabi Communities." Yale University, 1940.

Tobie, Harvey E. "Oregon Labor Disputes, 1919-1923: A Study of Representative Controversies and Current Thought." University of Oregon, 1936.

Toole, Kenneth R. "A History of the Anaconda Mining Company: A Study in the Relationships Between a State and Its People and a Corporation, 1880-1950." University of California, 1955.

Tyler, Robert L. "Rebels of the Woods and Fields: a Study of the I.W.W. in the Pacific Northwest." University of Oregon, 1953.

Villere, Maurice F. "The Theme of Alienation in the Popular Twentieth Century American Industrial and Organizational Novel." University of Illinois, Urbana-Champaign, 1971.

Whitten, Woodrow C. "Criminal Syndicalism and the Law in California, 1919-1927." University of California, Berkeley, 1946.

Wood, Samuel E. "The California State Commission of Immigration and Housing: A Study of Administrative Organization and the Growth of Function." University of California, Berkeley, 1942.

Wortman, Roy T. "The I.W.W. in Ohio, 1905-1950." University of Ohio, 1972.

Wyman, Walker D., Jr. "The Underground Miner, 1860-1910: Labor and Industrial Change in the Northern Rockies." University of Utah, 1972.

Youngdale, James. "Populism in a New Perspective: an analysis of Political Radicalism in the Upper Midwest." University of Minnesota, 1972.

MASTER'S ESSAYS AND THESES

Allison, Theodore F. "History of the Northwest Mining Unions Through 1920." State College of Washington, 1943.

Bernhardt, Debra, "We Knew Different: the Michigan Timber Workers Strike of 1937." Wayne State University, 1977.

Biagi, Robert. "Rip in the Silk: the 1912 and 1913 Paterson Textile Strikes." Wayne State University, 1971.

Burns, John J. "The I.W.W. in Illinois During World War I." Western Illinois University, 1972.

Buechel, Henry T. "Labor Relations in the West Coast Lumber Industry." State College of Washington, 1936.

Bush, Charles C. "The Green Corn Rebellion." University of Oklahoma, 1932.

Clark, Douglas M. "Wheatland Hop Fields Riot." Ohio State University, 1963.

Comstock, A. P. "History of the Industrial Workers of the World in the United States." Columbia University, 1913.

Conlin, J. H. "The Industrial Workers of the World and the Lawrence Strike." Dartmouth, 1948.

Cook, D. G. "Western Radicalism and the Winnipeg Strike." McMaster University, 1921.

Cox, Annie M. "History of Bisbee, 1877 to 1937." University of Arizona, 1938.

Crow, John E. "Ideology and Organization: a Case Study of the Industrial Workers of the World." University of Chicago, 1958.

Denn, Harold B. "The History of the Silk Workers in Paterson, New Jersey, with Special Emphasis on Strikes, 1910-1920." New York University, 1947.

Delli Quadri, Carmen L. "Labor Relations on the Mesabi Range." University of Colorado, 1944.

De Shazo, Peter. "The Industrial Workers of the World in Chile." University of Wisconsin, 1973.

Diehl, Robert W. "San Diego Free Speech Fight." University of San Diego, 1977.

Eckberg, Robert C. "The Free Speech Fight of the Industrial Workers of the World, Spokane, Washington, 1909-1910." Washington State University, 1967.

Evanko, J. "The Anaconda Copper Mining Company: Its Influence in Montana." University of Colorado, 1939.

Evans, Robert E. "Montana's Role in The Enactment of Legislation Designed to Suppress the I.W.W." University of Minnesota, 1964.

Faigin, Henry. "Industrial Workers of the World in Detroit and Michigan from the Period of Beginnings Through the World War." Wayne State University, 1937.

Fast, Stanley P. "The AWO and the Harvest Stiff in the Mid-Western Wheat Belt, 1915-1920." Mankato State University, 1974.

Fowler, James H. "Extralegal Suppression of Civil Liberties in Oklahoma During the First World War, and its Causes." Oklahoma State University, 1974.

Griesel, George H. "Study of the Personnel of the I.W.W. Movement." University of Nebraska, 1920.

Gutfeld, Arnon. "The Butte Labor Strikes and Company Retaliation During World War I." University of Montana, 1967.

Halonen, Arne. "The Role of Finnish Americans in the Political Labor Movement." University of Minnesota, 1945.

Harris, Abram L., Jr. "The Negro Worker in Pittsburgh." University of Pittsburgh, 1924.

Herrin, Robert. "Great Lumber Strikes in Northern Idaho." Northern Illinois University, 1967.

Hull, Robert E. "I.W.W. Activity in Everett, Washington, from May, 1916 to June, 1971." Washington State University, 1938.

Jensen, Vernon H. "Labor Relations in the Douglas Fir Industry." University of California, 1939.

Johnson, Clarence H. "Origins, Population, Locations, Occupations and Activities of the Swedes in Detroit." Wayne State University, 1940.

Jokinen, Walfrid. "The Finns of Minnesota." Louisiana State University, 1953.

Katz, Louis. "Free Speech and the I.W.W." Wayne State University, 1973.

Kimber, Catherine. "History of Cripple Creek, Colorado, 1891-1971." University of Colorado, n.d.

Landis, Paul H. "Three Iron Mining Towns: A Study in Cultural Change." University of Michigan, 1930.

Lawson, Harry O. "The Colorado Coal Strike of 1927-1928." University of Colorado, 1950.

Levine, Irving J. "The Lawrence Strike." Columbia University, 1936.

Lynch, Patrick. "Pennsylvania Anthracite—a Forgotten I.W.W. Venture, 1906-1916." Bloomsburg State University, 1974.

Macpherson, James L. "Butte Miners Union: an Analysis of Its Development and Economic Bargaining Position." Montana State University, 1949.

McCord, Charles. "A Brief Survey of the Brotherhood of Timber Workers." University of Texas, 1959.

McWhiney, H. Grady. "The Socialist Vote in Louisiana, 1912: an Historical Interpretation of Radical Sources." Louisiana State University, 1951.

Mooney, Martin C. "The Industrial Workers of the World and the Immigrants of Paterson and Passaic, N.J., 1907-1913." Seton Hall University, 1969.

Morland, Robert. "Political Prairie Fire: the Non-Partisan League, 1915-1922." University of Minnesota, 1955.

Nettleton, Allan L. "Persuasive Techniques Utilized in the I.W.W. Free Speech Fight in Everett, Washington, 1916." Washington State University, 1968.

Newman, Philip C. "The I.W.W. in New Jersey." Columbia University, 1940.

Perrin, Robert A., Jr. "Two Decades of Turbulence: a Study of the Great Lumber Strikes in Northern Idaho, 1916-1936." University of Idaho, 1961.

Pittler, Alexander. "The Hill District of Pittsburgh—a Study in Succession." University of Pittsburgh, 1930.

Pope, Virginia C. "The Green Corn Rebellion: a Case Study of Newspaper Censorship." University of Oklahoma, Stillwater, 1940.

Sain, Wilma Gray. "A History of the Miami Area, Arizona." University of Arizona, 1944.

Samuels, Elliot. "Red Scare in Ontario: the Reaction of the Ontario Press to the Internal and External Threat of Bolshevism, 1917-1919." Queens University, 1971.

Schleef, Margaret L. "Rival Unionism in the Lumber Industry." University of California, Berkeley, 1950.

Schmidt, Dorothy B. "Sedition and Criminal Syndicalism in the State of Washington, 1917-1919." Washington State College, 1940.

Scorup, D. A. "A History of Organized Labor in Utah." University of Utah, 1935.

Scruggs, Joseph C. "Labor Problems in the Fruit Industry of the Yakima Valley." University of Washington, 1937.

Sideman, Michael S. "The Agricultural Labor Market and Organizing Activities of the I.W.W., 1910-1935." University of Illinois, 1965.

Smill, Eva. "The Stogy Industry on the Hill in Pittsburgh, Pa." Carnegie Institute, 1920.

Smith, Norma. "The Rise and Fall of the Butte Miners' Union, 1878-1914." Montana State College, 1961.

Smith, Sharon C. "Intellectuals and the Industrial Workers of the World, 1905-1920." University of Wisconsin, 1956.

Souers, Ralph E. "The Industrial Workers of the World." University of Chicago, 1913.

Tierney, Ruth. "The Decline of the Silk Industry in Paterson, N.J." Cornell University, 1938.

Van Tine, Warren R. "Ben H. Williams: Wobbly Editor." Northern Illinois University, 1967.

Wakefield, Richard R. "A Study of Seasoned Farm Labor in Yakima County, Washington." Washington State College, 1937.

Weintraub, Hyman. "The I.W.W. in California, 1905-1931." University of California, Los Angeles, 1947.

White, Laura. "Rise of the Industrial Workers of the World in Goldfield, Nevada." University of Nebraska, 1912.

Wilkinson, Charles A. "Anti-German Reaction and Suppression of Dissent in Illinois During World War I." Western Illinois University, 1969.

Wilson, Ione E. "I.W.W. in California, with Special Reference to Migratory Labor, 1910-1913." University of California, 1941.

Youngman, W. S. "The Anaconda Copper Mining Company and Some Phases of its Influence in the Politics of Montana, 1880-1929." Harvard University, 1929.

ARTICLES

"Acquittal of the I.W.W. Leaders." *Literary Digest* 45 (December 7, 1912), pp. 1049-50.
    —Aftermath of Lawrence strike

"Acquittal of William D. Haywood." *Arena* 38 (September 1907), pp. 332-33.

Adamic, Louis. "Assassin of Wilson." *American Mercury* 21 (October 1930), pp. 138-46.
    —Jack Kips, Seattle, September 13, 1919—the folded-arms ploy

Adams, John D. "Clod or Brother." *Survey* 27 (March 30, 1912), pp. 2014-15.
    —Lawrence strike

"Aftermath of a Strike." *Outlook* 100 (June 1, 1912), pp. 237-38.
    —About Lawrence strike

"Aftermath of the Paterson Strike." *Outlook* 105 (November 29, 1913), p. 679.

"Agricultural Workers." *International Socialist Review* 18 (November-December 1917), p. 307.
    —California migrants

Ainsworth, C. L. Letter to Editor on I.W.W. *Survey* 39 (November 10, 1917), p. 151.
    —Dreadful I.W.W. pamphlets on scabbing insult women and preachers

"Alarums and Excursions." *Freeman* 8 (January 9, 1924), pp. 412-14.
    —Palmer raids

"Alaska Labor Union, 1916." *International Socialist Review* 17 (March 1917), pp. 601-2.

Alaskan Miner. "Shall We Unite?" *International Socialist Review* 12 (June 1912), pp. 843-44.

"Alexander Scott Freed." *International Socialist Review* 14 (June 1914), p. 763.
    —Paterson strike

Allen, Edgar F. "Aftermath of Industrial War at Ipswich, Massachusetts." *Survey* 32 (May 23, 1914), pp. 216-17.

"Americanization." *Outlook* 112 (March 1, 1916), pp. 482-84.
    —East Youngstown events

"Among the Persons Convicted." *New Republic* 36 (October 17, 1923), pp. 190-91.
    —Sacramento and Wichita prisoners still in prison—"Coolidge quibbles"

Andrews, Clarence A. "Big Annie and the 1913 Michigan Copper Strike." *Michigan History* 57 (Spring 1973), pp. 53-68.
    —Annie Clemenc and good yarn about the strike, with good photos

"Armistice Day Parade." *Nation* 109 (November 29, 1919), p. 673.
    —Centralia—a "godsend to the Republicans"

Ashleigh, Charles. "Defense Fires Opening Guns." *International Socialist Review* 17 (May 1917), pp. 673-74.
    —Everett aftermath

_____. "Everett, November Fifth." Poem. *International Socialist Review* 17 (February 1917), p. 479.

_____. "Lumber Trust and Its Victims." *International Socialist Review* 17 (March 1917), pp. 536-38.

"Automobile Industry." (By L. A.) *International Socialist Review* 13 (September 1912), 255-58.
    —Problems looming in Detroit

Bakeman, Robert A. "Little Falls—a Capitalist City Stripped of its Veneer." *New Review* 1 (February 8, 1913), pp. 167-74.

"Barbarous Spokane." *Independent* 68 (February 10, 1910), p. 330.
    —Crimes and cruelties against free speech—"doubtless there was roughness but the authorities did right."

"The Battle at Bayonne." *International Socialist Review* 16 (September 1915), pp. 138-41.
    —New Jersey oil workers' strike

Bauer, Kaspar. "Bauer Replies." *International Socialist Review* 14 (September 1913), pp. 188-89.
    —Free speech fight, San Diego

Baxandall, Rosalyn Froud. "Elizabeth Gurley Flynn: The Early Years." *Radical America* 8 (January-February 1975), pp. 97-115.
    —Gurley Flynn at the big strikes

Bayard, Charles J. "The 1927-1928 Colorado Coal Strike." *Pacific Historical Review* 32 (August 1963), pp. 235-50.
    —I.W.W. role in more than usual detail

Beck, William. "Law and Order During the 1913 Copper Strike." *Michigan History* 54 (Winter 1970), pp. 257-92.

Beffel, John N. "Fear in the Jury Box." *Liberator* 3 (April 1920), p. 13.
    —Centralia

Bell, George L. "Wheatland Hop Fields' Riot." *Outlook* 107 (May 16, 1914), pp. 118-23.

Belknap, Michael R. "The Mechanics of Repression: J. Edgar Hoover, the Bureau of Investigation and the Radicals, 1912-1925." *Crime and Social Justice* 7 (Spring-Summer, 1978) pp. 49-58.

"Ben Fletcher, Class and Political Amnesty." *Messenger* 3 (July 1921), p. 213.
    —The Philadelphia waterfront leader gets notice

"Benjamin J. Legere." (By J. E.) *New Review* 1 (July 1913), pp. 656-57.
    —Legere and the Little Falls strike

Bercowich, Henry. "Capitalist Dynamiters." *International Socialist Review* 14 (July 1913), p. 40.
    —Lawrence strike problems

Bercuson, David J. "The One Big Union in Washington." *Pacific Northwest Quarterly* 69 (July 1978), pp. 127-34.
    —Canadian OBU's influence and comparison with I.W.W.

Berkman, Alexander. "Tannenbaum Before Pilate." *Mother Earth* 9 (April 1914), pp. 45-49.
    —New York City's unemployed

Berner, Richard C. Rev. of *Mill Town* (by Clark). *Labor History* 12 (Summer 1971), pp. 461-63.

Betton, Neil. "Riot, Revolution, Repression in the Iron Range Strike of 1916." *Minnesota History* 41 (Summer 1968), pp. 82-94.
    —Was it "relatively peaceful?"—cartoons and photos

_____. "Strike on the Mesabi—1907." *Minnesota History* 40 (Fall 1967), pp. 340-47.
    —WFM strike—again relatively peaceful—good photos

"Big Annie." *International Socialist Review* 14 (December 1913), p. 342.
    —Annie Clemenc in Calumet, Michigan

"Bisbee Deportations." *Survey* 38 (July 21, 1917), p. 353.
    —Stamp out the spirit of violence

"The Bisbee Deportations Illegal." *Survey* 39 (December 8, 1917), pp. 291-92.

Biscay, J. S. "The Ispwich Strike." *International Socialist Review* 14 (August 1913), pp. 90-92.

_____. "Liberty or the Penitentiary? A Plot to Railroad Innocent Strikers of Little Falls Now on Trial." *International Socialist Review* 13 (April 1913), pp. 750-54.
    —Photos and story

_____. "Two Jurors Disappeared." *International Socialist Review* 13 (May 1913), p. 822.
    —Little Falls strike

Blaisdell, Lowell L. "Was it Revolution or Filibustering? The Mystery of the Flores Magon Revolt in Baja California." *Pacific Historical Review* 23 (May 1954), pp. 147-64.

"Bloodshed at Everett." *Literary Digest* 53 (November 25, 1916), p. 1395.

"Bloodshed in Labor-Wars." *Literary Digest* 51 (August 7, 1915), pp. 237-38.
    —Bayonne, New Jersey, wars, with photos

"Blood Spilling in Colorado." *Literary Digest* 95 (December 3, 1927), pp. 5-7.

"Bloody Colorado." *Nation* 125 (November 6, 1927), p. 534.
    —"It is the old old bloody story—perilously like 1914."

Boaz, R. P. "The Loyal Legion of Loggers and Lumbermen." *Atlantic Monthly* 127 (February 1921), pp. 221-26.
    —Lumber companies liked the legion

Bohn, Frank. "The Strike of the New York Hotel and Restaurant Workers." *International Socialist Review* 13 (February 1913), pp. 620-21.

"A Bolsheviki Crew Visit Seattle." *Survey* 39 (January 26, 1918), p. 465.

Boose, Arthur. "The Lumber Jack." *International Socialist Review* 16 (January 1916), pp. 414-16.

Booth, E. T. "Wild West." *Atlantic Monthly* 126 (December 1920), pp. 785-88.
    —Working with men whose single hope . . . lay in the program of the I.W.W.

Botting, David C., Jr. "Bloody Sunday." *Pacific Northwest Quarterly* 49 (October 1958), pp. 162-72.
    —Everett massacre

Bowden, Witt. "Two Alternatives in the Settlement of the Colorado Coal Strike." *Survey* 31 (December 20, 1913), pp. 320-22.
    —Good photo of Mother Jones, Colorado background without much I.W.W.

Boyd, Frederick Sumner. "General Strike in the Silk Industry," *Pageant of the Paterson Strike* (New York: Success Press, 1913), pp. 3-8.

Brewster, Edwin T. "Free Speech in Lawrence." *Survey* 27 (March 30, 1912), pp. 2015-16.
    —Lawrence strike aspects

Brewster, Giles T. "West Coast Phase of the Maritime Strike of 1921." *Pacific Historical Review* 19 (November 1950), pp. 385-96.

Brinley, John E., Jr. "Radicalism and the Western Federation of Miners." *Intermountain Economic Review* 3 (Spring, 1972), pp. 51-58.

Brissenden, Paul. "Butte Miners and the Rustling Card." *American Economic Review* 10 (December 1920), pp. 755-75.
　　—Montana problems

Brown, Giles T. "West Coast Phase of the Maritime Strike of 1921." *Pacific Historical Review* 19 (November 1950), pp. 385-96.
　　—On one hand their influence was absent. But "Members of the Seamen's Union are constantly compelled to work, eat, sleep, with travelling agents of the I.W.W."

Broyles, Glen J. "The Spokane Free Speech Fight, 1909-1910: a Study in I.W.W. Tactics." *Labor History* 19 (Spring 1978), pp. 238-52.

Bruere, Robert W. "Copper Camp Patriotism." *Nation* 106 (February 21, 1918), pp. 202-3.
　　—More on Bisbee

_____. "Copper Camp Patriotism: An Interpretation." *Nation* 106 (February 28, 1918), pp. 235-36.
　　—And more on Bisbee and patriotism

Burbank, Garin. "Agrarian Radicals and Their Opponents: Political Conflict in Southern Oklahoma, 1910-1924." *Journal of American History* 58 (June 1971), pp. 5-23.

Burki, Mary Ann Mason. "The California Progressives: Labor's Point of View." *Labor History* 17 (Winter 1976), pp. 24-37.
　　—California liberal milieu, mostly in years of Hiram Johnson; liberal background for Mooney, Billings, but little on I.W.W.

Busick, Charles O. "California Justice." *Nation* 121 (August 12, 1925), p. 182.
　　—Sacramento—a judge who gets down off the bench and serves as witness for the prosecution

"Butte Lynching: Industrial Workers of the World." *Outlook* 116 (August 15, 1917), p. 572.

Byers, J. C., Jr. "Harlan County—Act of God?" *Nation* 134 (June 15, 1932), pp. 672-74.
　　—I.W.W. in Evarts, Kentucky

Byrkit, James W. "The I.W.W. in Wartime Arizona." *Journal of Arizona History* 18 (Summer 1977), pp. 149-70.
　　—Bisbee, etc.

_____. "Reply to Pamela Mayhall on Bisbee." *American West* 9 (November 1972), p. 48.

"California Injunction Against the I.W.W. Sustained on the Ground that this Organization is a Public Nuisance." *Law and Labor* 6 (September 1924), pp. 240-43.
　　—In re Wood, Superior Court, California, June 20, 1924.

"California Labor Tragedy." *Literary Digest* 48 (May 23, 1914), pp. 1239-40.
 —Wheatland riot
"California's Anti-Red Law Upheld." *Literary Digest* 93 (May 28, 1927), pp. 9-10.
 —Syndicalism laws discussed
"Call to Justice." *Messenger* 4 (June 1922), p. 432.
Callender, Harold. "New Unionism in Seattle." *Forward* 3 (May 1919), pp. 72-75.
_____. "The Truth About the I.W.W." *International Socialist Review* 17 (January
 1918), pp. 332-42.
 —Butte, Bisbee, and the Lumber Country
"Calument—Investigation." *Life & Labor* 4 (March 1914), pp. 74-77.
"Canada's Labor War." *Literary Digest* 61 (June 14, 1919), pp. 18-19.
 —Affecting the Northwest
Carstens, C. C. "The Children's Exodus from Lawrence." *Survey* 28 (April 6,
 1912), pp. 70-71.
Carter, C. F. "West Virginia Coal Insurrection." *North American* 198 (October
 1913), pp. 457-69.
 —Paint and Cabin Creek from the other side
"Case of the Hop Pickers." *International Socialist Review* 14 (April 1914), pp.
 620-21.
"Catholic View of the Copper Miners' Strike in Upper Michigan." *Survey* 31
 (January 31, 1914), pp. 521-22.
"Centralia." *New Republic* 22 (April 14, 1920), pp. 217-20.
 —Montesano trial; points of concentration
"Centralia Before the Court." (By E. M.) *Survey* 44 (April 3, 1920), pp. 13-15.
"Centralia Case Again." *New Republic* 62 (May 14, 1930), pp. 340-41.
"Centralia Prisoners." *New Republic* 61 (January 15, 1930), p. 226. See also
 New Republic 64 (September 17, 1930), p. 128.
 —Letters, and Upton Sinclair shares some correspondence
"Centralia Tragedy." *Outlook* 156 (October 22, 1930), p. 287.
Chafee, Zechariah, Jr. "California Justice." *New Republic* 36 (September 19,
 1923), pp. 97-100.
 —Man can be punished merely for saying something; breaking up the
 I.W.W. in California
Chaplin, Ralph. "Violence in West Virginia." *International Socialist Review* 13
 (April 1913), pp. 729-36.
 —From one who was there; with poem and photos
Cheney, Charles B. "Labor Crisis and a Governor; An Averted Strike on the
 Mesaba Range." *Outlook* 89 (May 2, 1908), pp. 24-30.
"Chicago: Hobo Capital of America." (By G. S.) *Survey* 50 (June 1, 1923), pp.
 287-90, 303-5.
Child, R. W. "Industrial Revolt at Lawrence." *Collier's* 48 (March 9, 1912), pp.
 13-15.
 —Good cartoons and account of Lawrence

_____. "Who's Violent?" *Collier's* 49 (June 29, 1912), pp. 12-13, 22.
    —Photos and narration on Lawrence strike

"Children as Exhibits." *Independent* 72 (February 22, 1912), p. 427.
    —"Something not very fitting" about the Lawrence strike

"Children of a Strike." *Survey* 27 (February 24, 1912), p. 1791.
    —Photos of the Lawrence strikers' children in New York

Christenson, Otto. "Invading Miners' Homes." *International Socialist Review* 17
    (September 1916), pp. 161-62.
    —Mesabi strike in Minnesota

"Churches Raided by the Jobless." *Literary Digest* 48 (March 14, 1914), pp. 556-57.
    —New York city's unemployed go to church; cartoons and photos

"The Churches, the City and the 'Army of the Unemployed' in New York." *Survey*
    31 (March 28, 1914), pp. 792-95.
    —Frank Tannenbaum's army

Clark, Earl. "Wages in Cotton Mills at Home and Abroad." *Survey* 27 (March 23,
    1912), pp. 1957-58.
    —In reference to the New England strikes

Clark, H. F. "What I Learned from a Strike." *Survey* 31 (November 22, 1913), p.
    207.
    —New England strikes

Clark, Norman. "Everett, 1916 and After." *Pacific Northwest Quarterly* 57 (April
    1966), pp. 57-64.

Clay, Samuel H. "The Man Who Heads the Spruce Drive." *Review of Reviews* 57
    (June 1918), pp. 633-35.
    —Story of Disque and his ploys

Cleland, Hugh G. "The Effects of Radical Groups on the Labor Movement."
    Pennsylvania History 26 (April 1959), 119-32.
    —Pressed Steel Car strike (1909): "There were more I.W.W. Locals in
    Pennsylvania than in any other state,"—they anticipated the CIO.

Cole, Donald B. "Lawrence, Massachusetts: Model Town to Immigrant City, 1845-
    1912." *Historical Collections of the Essex Institute* 92 (October 1956), pp.
    349-75.

Cole, John N. "The Issue at Lawrence." *Outlook* 100 (February 24, 1912), pp.
    405-6.

Coleman, B. S. "I.W.W. and the Law—the Result of Everett's Bloody Sunday."
    Sunset 39 (July 1917), pp. 35, 68-70.
    —Story of an acquittal; photos

"Colonel Disque and the I.W.W." *New Republic* 14 (April 6, 1918), pp. 284-85.
    —What are Disque's reasons in seeking to commandeer property?
    Northwest lumber problems

"Colorado Coal Battle." *Outlook* 147 (December 7, 1927), p. 422.

"Colored and White Workers Solving the Race Problem for Philadelphia."
    Messenger 3 (July 1921), pp. 214-15.
    —Local 8 of the Marine Transport Workers

"Commission on Industrial Relations." *Public* 17 (September 11, 1914), pp. 878-79.
  —Learning about Wheatland

"Conciliation Versus Strikes." *Outlook* 88 (January 4, 1908), pp. 8-9.
  —Goldfield and the WFM

"Conditions at Lawrence." *Outlook* 100 (March 16, 1912), p. 566.

"Congress Asked to Look Into 'Bloody Sunday.' " *Survey* 37 (February 10, 1917), p. 553.
  —More on Everett, Washington

Conlin, Joseph R. Rev. of *Colorado's War on Militant Unionism* (by Suggs). *Labor History* 15 (Summer 1973), pp. 448-51.

_____. "The Haywood Case: An Enduring Riddle." *Pacific Northwest Quarterly* 59 (January 1968), pp. 23-32.

"Conspiracy & Street Speaking." *International Socialist Review* 14 (July 1913), p. 42.
  —San Diego free speech fight

"Constitution and the Police." *Survey* 29 (October 26, 1912), pp. 93-94.
  —Little Falls strike

"The Conviction of Alexander Scott." *International Socialist Review* 14 (July 1913), pp. 10-11.
  —Paterson strike aftermath

Cook, Bernard A. "Covington Hall and Radical Rural Unionization in Louisiana." *Lousiana History* 18 (Spring 1977), pp. 227-38.

Cook, Philip. "Red Scare in Denver." *Colorado Magazine* 43 (Fall 1966), pp. 309-26.
  —Excellent cartoons accompany the story

Cooper, Charles. "Stogy Makers and the I.W.W. in Pittsburgh." *Survey* 31 (November 28, 1913), p. 214.

"Copper-Mine Owners' Side." *Outlook* 106 (February 21, 1914), pp. 397-400.
  —Michigan strike unfair?

"Copper Mine Strike." *American Industries* 14 (November 1913), pp. 7-8.
  —Michigan

"Copper-Miners' Strike." *Outlook* 106 (February 7, 1914), pp. 294-95.
  —Calumet-Hecla

"The Copper Settlement in Arizona." *Survey* 39 (November 3, 1917), pp. 128, 130.

"Copper Strike." *International Socialist Review* 14 (November 1913), pp. 269-71.
  —Michigan's Calumet-Hecla strike, with photos

"Copper Strike Investigation." *American Industries* 14 (March 1914), pp. 9-10.
  —Michigan

Corbin, David A. "Betrayal in the West Virginia Coal Fields: Eugene V. Debs and The Socialist Party of America, 1912-1914." *Journal of American History* 64 (March, 1978), pp. 987-1009.

_____. "The Socialist and Labor Star; Strike and Suppression in West Virginia, 1912-1913." *West Virginia History* 34 (January 1973), pp. 168-86.
  —Chaplin's role described

Corcoran, (Sister) Theresa. "Vida Scudder and the Lawrence Textile Strike."
    Essex Institute Historical Collections 115 (July 1979), pp. 183-95.

"Cossack Regime in San Diego." *Mother Earth* 7 (June 1912), pp. 97-107.
    —Whole issue given to San Diego experiences

Cothren, Marion B. "When Strike-Breakers Strike." *Survey* 36 (August 26, 1916),
    pp. 535-36.
    —Mesabi strike in Minnesota

"Counting the Copper Strike's Cost." *Literary Digest* 48 (April 25, 1914), pp.
    973-74.
    —Calumet-Hecla strike

"Country-wide Free Speech Fight." *Mother Earth* 7 (April 1912), pp. 46-49.

Creel, George. "Feudal Towns of Texas." *Harper's Weekly* 60 (January 23, 1915),
    p. 76.

Currie, B. W. "How the West Dealt with One Labor Union." *Harper's Weekly*
    51 (June 22, 1907), pp. 908-10.

Daniel, Cletus E. "In Defense of the Wheatland Wobblies: A Critical Analysis of the
    I.W.W. in California." *Labor History* 19 (Fall 1978), pp. 485-509.

————. "Radicals on the Farm in California." *Agricultural History* 49 (October
    1975), pp. 629-46.

————. "Wobblies on the Farm: the I.W.W. in the Yakima Valley." *Pacific
    Northwest Quarterly* 65 (October 1974), pp. 166-75.

Davis, L. E. "Strike-riot in Pennsylvania." *Independent* 67 (September 2, 1909),
    pp. 533-537.
    —McKees Rocks—a veritable battle; described, however, without
    mentioning I.W.W.

Davis, W. T. "Southern Colorado Coal Strike." *Outlook* 106 (January 3, 1914),
    pp. 24-26.
    —Viewpoint of a trooper-soldier, gives background, of a sort

————. "Strike War in Colorado." *Outlook* 107 (May 9, 1914), pp. 67-73.

Dawson, Frank. "St. Mary's Fighting Mayor." *International Socialist Review*
    13 (June 1913), pp. 874-76.
    —Ohio mayor's tribulations

Debs, Eugene V. "Murder in the First Degree." *International Socialist Review* 17
    (October 1916), pp. 203-5.
    —Comments on the Mesabi crimes

"Decision on the Application of the Kansas Criminal Syndicalism Act." *Congressional Digest* 6 (June 1927), p. 212.
    —Kansas CS Act decision

"Defenders of the Despised." Letter. *Nation* 110 (February 14, 1920), p. 202.
    —Letter on Centralia.

"Defense Fires Opening Guns—Everett Brutality Revealed in Court." *International
    Socialist Review* 17 (May 1917), pp. 673-74.

"Defining Vagrancy." *Survey* 42 (September 13, 1919), pp. 850-51.
    —Vagrancy in Kansas

de Ford, Miriam Allen. "Injury to All; Criminal Syndicalism Law of California." *Overland* 82 (December 1924), pp. 536-37, 575-76.

_____. "Vacation at San Quentin." *World's Work* 26 (August 1913), pp. 402-20.

_____. "Vacation at San Quentin." *Nation* 117 (August 1, 1923), pp. 114-15.
—Conditions of the Sacramento prisoners, none of whom had committed a crime

_____. "Wheatland—1921." *Liberator* 4 (September 1921), p. 24.
—Poem on Wheatland

Deland, L. F. "The Lawrence Strike: A Study." *Atlantic Monthly* 109 (May 1912), pp. 694-705.

Dennett, Tyler. "The Mining Strike in Minnesota—The Other Side." *Outlook* 113 (August 30, 1916), pp. 1046-48.

Devine, E. T. "Social Forces." *Survey* 28 (April 6, 1912), pp. 1-2.
—Lawrence strike forces

_____. "Winnipeg and Seattle." *Survey* 43 (October 4, 1919), pp. 5-8.

"Dividing War Profits With Copper Miners." *Survey* 34 (June 12, 1915), p. 239.
—Calumet-Hecla pays a few back

"Does the I.W.W. Spell Social Revolution?" *Current Literature* 52 (April 1912), pp. 380-84.
—On Lawrence strike; good photos

Doran, J. T. "Murder in Centralia." *Liberator* 3 (February 1920), pp. 16-18.

Doree, E. F. "Gathering the Grain." *International Socialist Review* 15 (June 1915), pp. 740-43.
—Midwest agricultural workers

_____. "Ham-stringing the Philadelphia Sugar Hogs." *International Socialist Review* 17 (April 1917), pp. 615-17.
—Sugar wars, I.W.W. No. 497, and the longshoremen

Dosch, Arno. "What the I.W.W. Is." *World's Work* 26 (August 1913), pp. 406-20.
—After Lawrence and Paterson, a description with many photos; about the I.W.W.'s "ability to organize discontent"

"A Double Labor War." *Outlook* 104 (May 3, 1913), p. 11.
—Paterson, the AFL, and the I.W.W.

Downing, Mortimer. "The Case of the Hop Pickers." *International Socialist Review* 14 (October 1913), pp. 210-13.

"Dramatizing the Paterson Strike." *Survey* 30 (May 31, 1913), p. 316.

Dubofsky, Melvyn. "James H. Hawley and the Origins of the Haywood Case, 1892-1899." *Pacific Northwest Quarterly* 58 (January 1967), pp. 23-32.

_____. "The Origins of Western Working Class Radicalism, 1890-1905." *Labor History* 7 (Spring 1966), pp. 131-54.

_____. "Radicalism of the Dispossessed: William D. Haywood and the I.W.W." In Alfred F. Young, ed., *Dissent: Explorations in the History of American Radicalism* (De Kalb: Northern Illinois University Press, 1968), pp. 175-213.

_____. Revs. of *Seattle General Strike*, R. L. Friedheim, and *Revolution in Seattle*, Harvey O'Connor. *Labor History* 6 (Fall 1965), pp. 264-66.

Du Bois, W. E. B. "I.W.W." *Crisis* 18 (June 1919), p. 60.
    —"We do not believe the I.W.W. methods are advisable"; Ben Fletcher

Duchez, Louis. "Class War in New Castle." *International Socialist Review* 10 (April 1910), pp. 876-77.

_____. "The Passive Resistance Strike." *International Socialist Review* 10 (November 1909), pp. 409-12.
    —Pressed Steel Car Co., McKees Rocks strike—the "working class of America has entered a new period."

_____. "Victory at McKees Rocks." *International Socialist Review* 10 (October 1909), pp. 289-300. See also November 1909, pp. 410-11.

"Dynamite in the Lawrence Strike." *Literary Digest* 45 (September 14, 1912), p. 407.
    —William Wood and a dynamite plot

Eastman, Phineas. "The Southern Negro and the One Big Union." *International Socialist Review* 13 (June 1913), pp. 890-91.

Ebner, Michael H. "I Never Died; the Case of Joe Hill v. the Historians." *Labor History* 12 (Winter 1971), pp. 139-43.

_____. "The Passaic Strike of 1912 and the Two I.W.W.'s." *Labor History* 11 (Fall 1970), pp. 452-66.

Edwards, George. "Free Speech in San Diego." *Mother Earth* 10 (July 1915), pp. 182-85.
    —At last, free speech

Eldridge, Maurice E. "Preston and Smith." *International Socialist Review* 10 (April 1910), pp. 894-98.
    —Nevada problems

Eldridge, P. W. "The Wheatland Hop Riot and the Ford and Suhr Case." *Industrial and Labor Relations Forum* 10 (May 1974), pp. 165-95.

"Elizabeth Flynn's Contest with Paterson." *Survey* 35 (December 11, 1915), p. 283.

Elliott, Russell R. "Labor Troubles in the Mining Camp at Goldfield, Nevada, 1906-1908." *Pacific Historical Review* 19 (November 1950), pp. 369-84.

"Embargo on the Strike Children." *Survey* 27 (March 2, 1912), p. 1822.
    —Lawrence strike children displeased some people.

"End of a Great Strike at McKees Rocks." *Outlook* 93 (September 18, 1909), p. 84.

"End of the Mesaba Range Strike." *Survey* 37 (January 6, 1917), pp. 411-12.

"End of the Paterson Strike." *Outlook* 104 (August 9, 1913), p. 780.

"End of the Strike at Lawrence." *American Review of Reviews* 45 (April 1012), p. 402.

"Enemy Within Our Midst." *Gateway* 29 (December 1917), pp. 13-16.

Engdahl, J. Louis. "William D. Haywood—'Undesirable Citizen.' " *Communist* 7 (July 1928), pp. 434-441.

Englemann, Larry D. "We Were the Poor People—The Hormel Strike of 1933." *Labor History* 15 (Fall 1974), pp. 483-510.
    —A little on the Omaha I.W.W.

"Episcopal View of the Calumet Copper Miners Strike." *Survey* 32 (August 15, 1914), pp. 502-4.

"Ethics of a General Strike." *Independent* 68 (March 17, 1910), pp. 588-89.
   —The Philadelphia attempt: "It is not strange that it finds but partial approval—of a general strike almost none at all." (I.W.W. not mentioned, although there)

Ettor, Joseph J. "I.W.W. versus A.F.L." *New Review* 2 (May 1914), pp. 275-85.
   —Lawrence and Paterson philosophy

Ettor, Joseph, and Giovannitti, Arturo. "Appeal from Lawrence." *Mother Earth* 7 (May 1912), pp. 92-94.

"Ettor in Jail: Strike Goes On." *Survey* 27 (February 10, 1912), p. 1726.

"Exoneration of William M. Wood." *Outlook* 104 (June 21, 1913), pp. 351-52.
   —Lawrence dynamite plot

Fair, Agnes T. Telegram from agitator. *International Socialist Review* 10 (December 1909), p. 558.
   Northwest organizing

"Fall of the American Bastille." *Wilshire's Magazine* 17 (May 1913), p. 1.
   —Some I.W.W.'s escaped the sentence

"The Fall of Kansas City." *Agitator* 2 (December 1, 1911), p. 1.
   —Free speech fight described

"The Farmer and the War." *New Republic* 13 (November 3, 1917), pp. 8-9.

"Federal Commission to Study Calumet and Colorado." *Survey* 31 (January 24, 1914), p. 486.

"Federal Investigation of Strike Region." *Survey* 31 (February 7, 1914), p. 541.
   —Colorado and Michigan

Fenton, Edwin. "Italians and the Labor Movement." *Pennsylvania History* 26 (April 1959), pp. 133-48.
   —The organized I.W.W. barbers never made it

Fickle, James E. "The Louisiana-Texas Lumber War of 1911-1912." *Louisiana History* 16 (Winter 1975), pp. 59-85.

Fishbein, Meyer. "The President's Mediation Commission and the Arizona Copper Strike, 1917." *Southwestern Social Science Quarterly* 30 (December 1949), pp. 175-82.

Fitch, J. A. "Arson and Citizenship; East Youngstown and the Aliens Who Set it On Fire." *Survey* 35 (January 22, 1916), pp. 477-80.
   —Some I.W.W. mention

_____. "Baiting the I.W.W." *Survey* 33 (March 6, 1915), pp. 634-35.
   —Oregon unpleasantness

_____. "Colorado Strike." *Survey* 31 (December 20, 1913), pp. 333-34.

_____. "The I.W.W.: An Outlaw Organization." *Survey* 30 (June 7, 1913), pp. 355-62.
   —Hitting many localities: Lawrence, Paterson, San Diego, Akron

_____. "Lawrence—a Strike for Wages or for Bolshevism?" *Survey* 42 (April 5, 1919), pp. 42-46.

Fitch, John A., et al. "Probing the Causes of Unrest." *Survey* 32, 33, 34, and 35.
    Parts 1-8: John A. Fitch, April 18, 1914, to July 11, 1914. Part 9: C. Merri-
    man, August 8, 1914. Parts 10-21: John A. Fitch, August 29, 1914, to
    February 27, 1915. Part 22: C. W. Holman, April 17, 1915. Part 23: O.
    McFeely, May 8, 1915. Parts 24-25: G. R. Taylor, May 22, 1915, and May 29,
    1915. Part 26: John A. Fitch, June 5, 1915. See also "Review of Reports" by
    John A. Fitch, *Survey* 35, Part 1: December 18, 1915, pp. 317-33. Part 2:
    January 1, 1916, pp. 395-402. Part 3: January 8, 1916, pp. 432-34.

"Flare-up Among Pittsburgh Steel Workers." *Survey* 28 (July 6, 1912), pp. 487-88.

Fletcher, Ben. "Negro and Organized Labor." *Messenger* 5 (July 1923), pp. 759-60.
    —Philadelphia dockside experience

_____. "Philadelphia Waterfront's Unionism." *Messenger* 5 (June 1923), pp.
    740-41.

Flynn, Elizabeth G. "Contract Slavery in Paterson Silk Mills," *Pageant of the
    Paterson Strike* (New York: Success Press, 1913), pp. 29-31.

_____. "Figures and Facts," *Pageant of the Paterson Strike* (New York: Success
    Press, 1913), p. 15.

_____. "Free Speech Fight at Spokane." *International Socialist Review* 10
    (December 1909), pp. 483-89.

_____. "Latest News from Spokane." *International Socialist Review* 10 (March
    1910), pp. 828-34.

_____. "One Boss Less: the Minersville Strike." *International Socialist Review* 12
    (July 1911), p. 8.
    —Pottsville, Tremont, and Mahoney City, Pennsylvania

_____. "Shall This Man Serve Ten Years in Sing Sing?" *International Socialist
    Review* 11 (May 1911), pp. 685-88.
    —New York, the Buccafori defense

_____. "The Shame of Spokane." *International Socialist Review* 10 (January 101),
    pp. 610-19.

_____. "The Weavers." Letter. *Survey* 35 (February 26, 1916), p. 648.
    —Letter on Lawrence, Massachusetts

Flynt, Wayne. "Florida Labor and Political Radicalism, 1919-1920." *Labor History*
    9 (Winter 1968), pp. 73-90.

Foner, Philip. "United States of America vs. Wm. D. Haywood et al.: The I.W.W.
    Indictment." *Labor History* 11 (Fall 1970), pp. 500-530.

Ford, Grace. "For Life." *International Socialist Review* 15 (December 1914), pp.
    342-43.
    —Wheatland aftermath

"Ford and Suhr." *International Socialist Review* 15 (October 1914), p. 256.
    —Wheatland convictions

Ford, James. "The Cooperative Franco-Belge of Lawrence." *Survey* 28 (April 6,
    1912), pp. 68-70.

Forster, C. H. "Despised and Rejected of Men: Hoboes of the Pacific Coast."
    Survey 33 (March 20, 1915), pp. 671-72.

Fosdick, Harry E. "After the Strike—in Lawrence." *Outlook* 101 (January 15, 1912), pp. 340-46.

"Foster Homes Investigated." *Survey* 27 (February 24, 1912), pp. 1791-92.
—Fuss over the Lawrence strike children

Foster, James C. "AFL, I.W.W. and Nome, 1905-1908." *Alaska Journal* 4 (No. 2, 1974), pp. 130-41.

_____. "The Treadwell Strikes, 1907 and 1908." *Alaska Journal* 6 (No. 1, 1976), pp. 2-11.

_____. "The Western Federation Comes to Alaska." *Pacific Northwest Quarterly* 66 (October 1975), pp. 161-73.

Foster, Warren D. "New Bedford Textile Strike." *Survey* 28 (August 24, 1912), pp. 658-59.

Foster, William Z. "The Miners' Revolt in Butte." *Mother Earth* 9 (September 1914), pp. 216-20.

Fowler, James H. "Tar and Feather Patriotism: The Suppression of Dissent in Oklahoma During World War One." *Chronicles of Oklahoma* 56 (Winter 1978-79), pp. 409-30.

Fox, Jay. "Organizing the Woodsmen." *Syndicalist* 3 (March 1, 1913), p. 2.
—Results of the I.W.W. efforts were meager

_____. "The Paterson Strike—Its Lesson." *Syndicalist* 3 (September 1-15, 1913), p. 54.
—"You can't teach anything from a soap-box."

"The Free Speech Fight." *Agitator* 1 (December 15, 1910), p. 1.
—Fresno free speech fight, and a "sturdy little band of I.W.W. rebels"

"Free Speech Fight in Kansas City." *International Socialist Review* 14 1914), p. 510.

"Free Speech in Paterson." *Outlook* 111 (November 24, 1915), pp. 692-93.

"Freedom of Press at Issue in Paterson." *Survey* 30 (June 14, 1913), p. 368.

Friedheim, Robert. "The Seattle General Strike of 1919." *Pacific Northwest Quarterly* 52 (July 1961), pp. 81-98.

"From the Railroad Workers." *International Socialist Review* 14 (May 1914), pp. 687-88.
—St. Clair, Pennsylvania

Gaffield, Chad. "Big Business, the Working-Class, and Socialism in Schenectady." *Labor History* 19 (Summer 1978), pp. 350-72.
—Schenectady I.W.W. somewhat overlooked

Gedicks, Al. "Ethnicity, Class Solidarity, and Labor Radicalism among Finnish Immigrants in the Michigan Copper Country." *Politics and Society* 7 (No. 2, 1977), pp. 127-56.

"General Strike of Lumber Workers." *International Socialist Review* 18 (August 1917), p. 113.
—Western lumberjacks, a threat

Genini, Ronald. "Industrial Workers of the World and their Fresno Free Speech Fight, 1910-1911." *California Historical Quarterly* 53 (1974), pp. 100-114.
—Good cartoons and a story of the fight

"Genteel Tradition." Rev. of *Dwelling Place of Light*, W. Churchill, novel on Lawrence strike. *New Republic* 12 (October 13, 1917), pp. 306-7.

"George Andreytchine." *International Socialist Review* 17 (September 1916), p. 170.
      —Minnesota deportations

George, Harrison. "The Cow-Boy." *International Socialist Review* 15 (May 1915), pp. 663-65.

_____. "Hitting the Trail in the Lumber Camps." *International Socialist Review* 17 (February 1917), pp. 454-57.

_____. "The Mesaba Iron Range." *International Socialist Review* 17 (December 1916), pp. 328-32.

_____. "Victory on the Mesaba Range." *International Socialist Review* 17 (January 1917), pp. 429-31.

Gerhard, Peter. "The Socialist Invasion of Baja, California, 1911." *Pacific Historical Review* 15 (September 1946), pp. 295-304.

"Getting Into Business." *American Industries* 13 (July 1913), p. 9.
      —Financial side of Paterson pageant

Gill, Robert S. "The Four L's in Lumber." *Survey* 44 (May 1, 1920), pp. 165-70.

Gilmore, Inez Haynes. "Marysville Strike." *Harper's Weekly* 58 (April 4, 1914), pp. 18-20.
      —Wheatland

Glazer, Sidney. "The Michigan Labor Movement." *Michigan History* 29 (January-March 1945), pp. 73-82.
      —Includes a little about the Studebaker strike of 1913

Goldman, Emma. "The Outrage of San Diego." *Mother Earth* 7 (June 1912), pp. 115-22.
      —Personal account of the trouble

_____. "Power of the Ideal." *Mother Earth* 7 (June 1912), pp. 125-31.
      —San Diego fight

Gompers, Samuel. "Lawrence Dynamite Conspiracy." *American Federationist* 19 (October 1912), pp. 815-23.

_____. "Lawrence Strike." *American Federationist* 19 (April 1912), pp. 281-93.

_____. "Upton Sinclair's Mental Marksmanship." *American Federationist* 21 (April 1914), pp. 293-302.
      —Mr. Sinclair should join the true reformers

Good, J. E. "Akron and the I.W.W." *Collier's* 51 (June 21, 1913), p. 31.

Goodyear, De Mont. "The Lawrence Textile Strike." *Independent* 72 (February 8, 1912), pp. 299-300.
      —Eyewitness account—the scene, the generals, the causes

Gordon, F. G. R. "A Labor Man's Story of the Paterson Strike. Aftermath of the I.W.W. Reign of Violence, Intimidation and Graft." *National Civic Federation Review* 2 (December 1, 1913), pp. 16, 17.
      —As in Paterson, so in Lawrence, Hopedale, Ipswich, McKees Rocks and wherever

Graham, John. "Upton Sinclair and the Ludlow Massacre." *Colorado Quarterly* 21 (Summer 1972), pp. 55-67.
    —I.W.W. had protested the outrages

Grant, Luke. "The Idaho Murder Trial." *Outlook* 85 (April 6, 1907), pp. 805-11.

Grant, Percy S. "Brains Versus Bayonets." *North American* 196 (August 1912), pp. 183-93.
    —Lawrence strikers versus the guards

Green, B. A. "Portland's Mayor-Made Revolution." *Nation* 115 (December 6, 1922), pp. 605-6.
    —How a strike was turned into a revolution

_____. "Sedition Run Riot." Letter. *Nation* 116 (April 25, 1923), p. 495.
    —States lumber workers' demands; Oregon defender of I.W.W.; sole charge: being I.W.W.

Green, James R. "Brotherhood of Timberworkers, 1910-1913: A Radical Response to Industrial Capitalism in the Southern USA." *Past and Present* 60 (August 1973), pp. 161-200.

Green, W. R. "I.W.W. Organization." *Congressional Record* 56 (May 9, 1918), pp. 6799-6800.

Griffin, C. R. "The Short Log Country." *International Socialist Review* 17 (January 1917), pp. 422-23.

Grob, Gerald N. Rev. of *Bread and Roses Too*, Joseph Conlin. *Journal of American History* 57 (December 1970), pp. 733-34.

Grover, David H. "Borah and the Haywood Trial." *Pacific Historical Review* 32 (February 1963), pp. 65-77.

Gunns, Albert F. "Ray Becker, the Last Centralia Prisoner." *Pacific Northwest Quarterly* 59 (April 1968), pp. 88-99.

Gutfeld, Arnon. "The Murder of Frank Little: Radical Labor Agitation in Butte, Montana, 1917." *Labor History* 10 (Spring 1969), pp. 177-92.

_____. "The Speculator Disaster in 1917: Labor Resurgence at Butte, Montana." *Arizona and the West* 11 (Spring 1969), pp. 27-38.

Hader, John J. "Honk Honk Hobo." *Survey* 60 (August 1, 1928), pp. 453-55.
    —Hoboes in a Chicago milieu

Hall, Covington. "Negroes Against Whites." *International Socialist Review* 13 (October 1912), pp. 349-50.

_____. "Revolt of the Southern Timber Workers." *International Socialist Review* 13 (July 1912), pp. 51-52.

_____. "The Southern Lumber War." *Coming Nation* (June 22, 1912), p. 2.

_____. "The Victory of the Lumber Jacks." *International Socialist Review* 13 (December 1912), pp. 470-71.

_____. "With the Southern Timber Workers." *International Socialist Review* 13 (May 1913), pp. 805-6.

Halverson, Guy, and Ames, William E. "The Butte 'Bulletin': Beginnings of a Labor Daily." *Journalism Quarterly* 46 (Summer 1969), pp. 260-66.

Ham, W. T. "*Seattle Union Record* Suppressed for Condoning the Centralia
    Outrage." Letter. *New Republic* 21 (December 17, 1919), pp. 78-79.

Hanson, Nils. H. "Among the Harvesters." *International Socialist Review* 16
    (August 1915), pp. 75-78.

_____. "Texas Justice! 99 Years!" *International Socialist Review* 16
    (January 1916), pp. 476-78.

_____."Threshing Wheat." *International Socialist Review* 16 (December 1915), pp.
    344-47.

Hanson, Ole. "Fighting the Reds in Their Home Town." *World's Work* 39
    (December 1919 to March 1920): "Why and How I Became Mayor of
    Seattle," December 1919, pp. 123-26; "Smashing the Soviet in Seattle,"
    January 1920, pp. 302-7; "Seattle's Red Revolution," February 1920, pp.
    401-8; "The Victory Over Seattle Reds," March 1920, pp. 484-87.

Hard, William. "After the Strike." *New Republic* 21 (January 28, 1920), pp. 259-62.
    —Catholic priests, the I.W.W., and the steel strike in Pennsylvania

_____. "Moments in the Steel Strike—Mr. Brown is Talking About the I.W.W."
    New Republic 21 (December 3, 1919), p. 23.
        —AFL organizer says, "I.W.W. don't have to eat. He don't have to
        sleep, he leaks through a brick wall."

Haug, Charles J. "The Industrial Workers of the World in North Dakota, 1913-
    1917." *North Dakota Quarterly* 39 (Winter 1971), pp. 85-102.

Hayes, John. "Scabs Again." *International Socialist Review* 14 (May 1914), p. 688.
    —St. Louis Bag and Trunk Workers

Haynes, John E. "Revolt of the Timberbeasts: I.W.W. strike in Minnesota."
    Minnesota History 42 (Spring 1971), pp. 160-74.
        —Their organization was destroyed by suppression.

Hays, Arthur G. "The Right to Get Shot." *Nation* 134 (June 1, 1932), p. 619.
        —UMW forced out—I.W.W. entered—I.W.W. was suppressed—NMU
        came in

Haywood, William D. "An Appeal for Industrial Solidarity." *International
    Socialist Review* 14 (March 1914), pp. 544-46.

_____. "The Battle at Butte." *International Socialist Review* 15 (October 1914),
    pp. 223-26.

_____. "Butte Better." *International Socialist Review* 15 (February 1915), pp.
    473-75.
        —Recovering from the spasm of martial law

_____. "On the Paterson Picket Line." *International Socialist Review* 13 (June
    1913), pp. 847-51.

_____. "On the Picket Line at Little Falls, New York." *International Socialist
    Review* 13 (January 1913), pp. 519-23.

_____. " 'Reasonable' Crime." *International Socialist Review* 12 (August 1911),
    pp. 84-85.
        —Minnesota struggle

_____. "Revolt at Butte." *International Socialist Review* 15 (August 1914), pp.
    89-96.

_____. "The Rip in the Silk Industry." *International Socialist Review* 13 (May 1913), pp. 783-88.
  —Paterson, New Jersey

_____. "Smoothing Out the Wrinkles in Silk," *Pageant of the Paterson Strike* (New York: Success Press, 1913), pp. 22-27.

_____. "Timber Workers and Timber Wolves." *International Socialist Review* 13 (August 1912), pp. 105-10.

_____. "When the Kiddies Came Home." *International Socialist Review* 12 (May 1912), pp. 716-17.
  —Lawrence strike aftermath

_____. "With the Copper Miners of Michigan." *International Socialist Review* 11 (August 1910), pp. 65-68.

"Haywood at Uniontown, Pa." *International Socialist Review* 13 (October 1912), p. 374.

"Haywood's Battle in Paterson." *Literary Digest* 46 (May 10, 1913), pp. 1043-44.

Heaton, James P. "The Legal Aftermath of the Lawrence Strike." *Survey* 28 (July 6, 1912), pp. 503-10. See also December 7, 1912, pp. 301-4.

_____. "The Salem Trial." *Survey* 29 (December 7, 1912), pp. 301-4.
  —After Lawrence

Hedrick, P. C. "The I.W.W. and Mayor Hanson." *Unpartizan Review* 12 (July 1919), pp. 35-45.
  —Spokane's police chief, former friend of Bat Masterson and Wyatt Earp, applies learned techniques on I.W.W.

Henry, W. G. "Bingham Canyon." *International Socialist Review* 13 (October 1912), pp. 341-43.
  —Organizing the copper miners

Heslewood, Fred. "Barbarous Spokane." *International Socialist Review* 10 (February 1910), pp. 705-13.

Hibschman, Harry. "The I.W.W. Menace Self-Revealed." *Current History* 16 (August 1912), pp. 761-68.
  —Attorney for the legion discusses Centralia

Hill, Mary A. "The Free Speech Fight at San Diego." *Survey* 28 (May 4, 1912), pp. 192-94.

Hillier, Alfred J. "Albert Johnson, Congressman." *Pacific Northwest Quarterly* 36 (July 1945), pp. 193-211.
  —I.W.W. affects a political career

"Hoarse." *New Yorker* 22, part 3 (October 26, 1946), p. 25.
  —E. G. Flynn recollections

Hobby, Daniel T., ed. "We Have Got Results: A Document on the Organization of Domestics in the Progressive Era." *Labor History* 17 (Winter 1976), pp. 103-8.
  —I.W.W. woman organizer; letters on organizing domestics, Colorado, 1917

Hodges, Leroy. "Immigrant Life in the Ore Region of Northern Minnesota." *Survey* 28 (September 7, 1912), pp. 703-9.

Hofteling, Catherine. "Arbuckle and the I.W.W." *Nation* 116 (February 14, 1923), pp. 170-71.
　　—Sacramento syndicalist prisoners; didn't get the publicity Arbuckle did; cites terrible conditions

＿＿＿. "Sunkist Prisoners." *Nation* 113 (September 21, 1921), p. 316.
　　—No I.W.W. to blame for these fires, riots

Hogaboom, W. "Trouble Between the Western Federation of Miners and Goldfield Mine Operators Association." *Overland* 41 (February 1908), pp. 111-19.

Hokanson, Nels. "Swedes and the I.W.W." *Swedish Pioneer Historical Quarterly* 23 (January 1972), pp. 25-35.

Holbrook, Stewart H. "Last of the Wobblies." *American Mercury* 62 (April 1946), pp. 462-68.
　　—Supposedly it's A. Boose

Holmes, John Haynes. "Tannenbaum in the Large." *Survey* 32 (April 25, 1914), pp. 94-96.
　　—New York City unemployed

Hopkins, Ernest J. "San Diego Fight." *Coming Nation* (May 4, 1912), pp. 7-9.

"The Hop-Pickers' Strike." *Life and Labor* 4 (May 1914), pp. 151-52.

Hough, Merrill. "Leadville and the Western Federation of Miners." *Colorado Magazine* 49 (Winter, 1972), pp. 19-34.

"How Does the Public?" *New Republic* 13 (January 5, 1918), p. 262.
　　—They didn't like the president's commission report on Bisbee

"How the Capitalists Solve the Problem of the Unemployed." *International Socialist Review* 14 (May 1914), pp. 648-50.
　　—California capitalists

Howard, Joseph K. "Butte Remembers Big Bill Haywood." *Nation* 141 (October 30, 1935), pp. 514-515.

"Illinois and Illinoisians, 1876-1876—Woman Suffrage." *Journal of the Illinois State Historical Society* 69 (November 1976), pp. 269-70.

Illinois Manufacturers' Association. "I.W. of W. at Work in Illinois." *International Socialist Review* 14 (September 1913), p. 76.
　　—Letter of warning on I.W.W.

"In the Copper Country." *American Industries* 14 (February 1913), p. 10.
　　—Michigan miners exploited by unions

"Industrial Action News." *International Socialist Review* 17 (June 1917), pp. 727-28.
　　—Tom Tracy trial and conviction news from the Northwest

"Industrial Unionism or Destruction—The Industrial Railroad Workers." *International Socialist Review* 14 (June 1914), pp. 761-63.
　　—Pennsylvania workers

"Industrial War at McKees Rocks." *Outlook* 93 (September 4, 1909), pp. 1-3.

"Industrial Workers Who Wont Work." *Literary Digest* 55 (July 28, 1917), pp. 20-21.
　　—Bisbee and western strikes

Ingham, John M. "A Strike in the Progressive Era: McKees Rocks, 1909." *Pennsylvania Magazine of History and Biography* 90 (July 1966), p. 353-77.

"Issue in Colorado." *Independent* 78 (May 11, 1914), pp. 248-49.

Ivey, Paul W. "Economic Significance of the Calumet Strike Situation." *Review of Reviews* 49 (April 1914), pp. 445-46.

"I.W.W. and the Shingle Weavers." *International Socialist Review* 14 (April 1914), p. 620.

"The I.W.W. Closes the Saloons." *Nation* 116 (May 23, 1923), p. 588.
—Seattle strike—was anything more "deliciously comic?"

"I.W.W. Pageant." *Outlook* 104 (June 21, 1913), pp. 352-53.

"I.W.W. Scare in Salt Lake City—Conviction of Joseph Hillstrom for Murder." *Sunset* 35 (November 1915), pp. 854-55.
—Threats against officials?

"I.W.W. vs. AFL at Butte." *New Review* 2 (September 1914), pp. 550.
—Montana controversy

"Jack Whyte Dead." *International Socialist Review* 15 (March 1915), p. 571.
—News from Nevada

Jewell, Gary. "The History of the I.W.W. in Canada." *Our Generation* 11 (Summer, 1976), pp. 35-45.

Johnson, Aili K. "Finnish Labor Songs from Northern Michigan." *Michigan History* 31 (September 1947), pp. 331-43.
—Reminiscence of lumbering I.W.W.'s, I.W.W. songs from the Finnish, translated

Johnson, Michael L. "The I.W.W. and Wilsonian Democracy." *Science and Society* 28 (Summer 1964), pp. 257-74.
—The initial attitude of Wilson's administration was reversed

"Judicious Estimate of the Centralia Case." *Christian Century* 47 (October 24, 1930), pp. 1299-1300.
—Federal Council of Churches report considered

"Juries Uphold Free Speech." *Public* 17 (November 6, 1914), p. 1069.
—Becky Edelson not convicted in Tarrytown

Kanarek, Harold K. "Pennsylvania Anthracite Strike of 1922." *Pennsylvania Magazine of History and Biography* 99 (April 1975), pp. 207-55.
—I.W.W. had little appeal

"Keep Your Eyes on Everett!" *International Socialist Review* 17 (April 1917), pp. 608-9.

Keister, Jack. "Why the Socialists Won at Butte." *International Socialist Review* 11 (June 1911), p. 733.

Keller, Helen. Letter on Little Falls to John Macy. *International Socialist Review* 13 (January 1913), p. 518.

Kellogg, Paul U. "The McKees Rocks Strike." *Survey* 22 (August 7, 1909), pp. 656-65.

———. "McKees Rocks Strike." *Review of Reviews* 40 (September 1909), pp. 353-55.

"Killed on the Way to Spokane!" *International Socialist Review* 10 (December 1909), pp. 557-58.
> —The death of poet James Kelly Cole

Kinnear, Peter. "Rubber Workers Rebel." *International Socialist Review* (March 1013), p. 654.
> —Akron, Ohio, rebellion

Kinkead, W. L. "Paterson Silk Strike." *Survey* 30 (May 31, 1913), pp. 315-16.

Kirk, E. E., and McKee, Harry M. "Propaganda in Jails and Prisons." *International Socialist Review* 14 (October 1913), pp. 250-51.
> —After the free speech fight, the jail

Kizer, B. H. "Elizabeth Gurley Flynn." *Pacific Northwest Quarterly* 57 (July 1966), pp. 110-12.

Kolb, Harold H. "Industrial Millstone." *Idaho Yesterdays* 16 (Summer, 1972), pp. 29-32.

Koettgen, Ewald. "Making Silk." *International Socialist Review* 14 (March 1914), pp. 551-55.

_____. "No Grievances at All!" *Pageant of the Paterson Strike* (New York: Success Press, 1913), pp. 9-11.

Koppes, Clayton R. "The Industrial Workers of the World and County-jail Reform in Kansas, 1915-20." *Kansas Historical Quarterly* 41 (Spring 1975), pp. 63-86.

_____. "The Kansas Trial of the I.W.W, 1917-1919." *Labor History* 16 (Summer 1975), pp. 338-58.

"Labor Camps in California." *Monthly Labor Review* 11 (October 1920), pp. 222-24.

"Labor and the Law." *Nation* 96 (May 22, 1913), pp. 515-16.
> —"Law abiding citizens must assert themselves"—Quinlan's conviction after Paterson

"Labor Fight at Everett." *Outlook* 114 (November 1915), pp. 583-84.

"A Labor Law That Caused a Strike." *Literary Digest* 44 (January 27, 1912), pp. 148-49.
> —Lawrence strike

"Labor Notes: After Youngstown—What." *International Socialist Review* 16 (April 1916), pp. 621-22.

"Labor Troubles at Home." *Independent* 72 (March 14, 1912), pp. 544-45.
> —Investigating what happened at Lawrence

"Labor Unrest in the Southwest." *Survey* 38 (August 11, 1917), pp. 428-29.

"Labor War." *Public* 17 (February 27, 1914), p. 204.
> —Calumet-Hecla beatings

"Labor War." *Public* 17 (March 20, 1914), pp. 276-77.
> —Moyer's deportations from Michigan; Tannenbaum's indictment in New York

"Labor War." *Public* 17 (April 17, 1914), pp. 372-73.
> —I.W.W. riot at Rutgers Square, New York protested by Lincoln Steffens

Lane, Winthrop D. "Presumption of Innocence in Kansas." *Liberator* 3 (January 1920), p. 39.

_____. "Strike at Fort Leavenworth." *Survey* 41 (February 15, 1919), pp. 687-93.

_____. "Uncle Sam: Jailor." *Survey* 42 (September 6, 1919), pp. 806-812, 834.
    —Kansas trials and troubles

Larrowe, Charles P. "Maritime Strike of 1934." *Labor History* 11 (Fall 1970), pp. 403-51.

Lauck, W. J. "The Lawrence Strike; a Review." *Outlook* 100 (March 9, 1912), pp. 531-36.

_____. "Lesson From Lawrence." *North American Review* 195 (May 1912), pp. 665-72.

_____. "The Significance of the Situation at Lawrence." *Survey* 27 (February 17, 1912), pp. 1772-74.

Laut, Agnes C. "Revolution Yawns!" *Technical World* 18 (September 1912), pp. 134-44.
    —Canadian Pacific Railroad and I.W.W. in the Pacific Northwest; unusual photos

"Lawrence and Indianapolis." *Independent* 72 (February 1, 1912), pp. 220-21.
    —Quoting an Ettor speech

"Lawrence and the Industrial Workers of the World." *Survey* 28 (April 6, 1912), pp. 79-80.

"Lawrence Demonstration Strike." *Survey* 29 (October 12, 1912), p. 53.

"The Lawrence Labor Victory." *Literary Digest* 44 (March 23, 1912), pp. 575-76.

"The Lawrence Leaders." *Agitator* 2 (October 1, 1912), p. 1.
    —Ettor and Giovannitti praised, but the real leader was the man who refused his lowered paycheck

"Lawrence Once More in the Foreground." *Survey* 28 (September 7, 1912), pp. 693-94.

"The Lawrence Settlement." *Survey* 27 (March 23, 1912), pp. 1949-50.

"The Lawrence Strike." *Independent* 72 (February 8, 1912), pp. 280-81.
    —Days of rioting and death

"The Lawrence Strike." *Shoe Workers' Journal* 13 (February 1912), pp. 12-14.
    —"They are Industrial Wreckers not Industrial Workers."

"The Lawrence Strike." *Agitator* 2 (February 15, 1912), p. 1. See also March 15, 1912, p. 1.

"The Lawrence Strike." *Life & Labor* 2 (April 1922), p. 124.

"The Lawrence Strike—a Poll of the Press." *Outlook* 100 (February 17, 1912), pp. 356-58.

"The Lawrence Strike Children." *Literary Digest* 44 (March 9, 1912), pp. 471-72.

"Lawrence Strike From Various Angles—A Symposium." *Survey* 28 (April 6, 1912), pp. 65-80.

"Lawrence Strikers." *Independent* 72 (February 22, 1912), p. 382.
    —Parades, children

Legere, Benjamin J. "The Red Flag in the Auburn Prison." *International Socialist Review* 15 (December 1914), pp. 337-341.

"Legere Sentenced to One Year." *International Socialist Review* 14 (July 1913), p. 41.
    —Little Falls strike

Lepschutz, Celia. "Pittsburgh Traitors." *International Socialist Review* 13 (May 1913), p. 821.
    —Oliver Iron and Steelworkers

Le Sueur, Arthur. "Legal Side Lights on Murder." *International Socialist Review* 17 (November 1916), pp. 298-300.
    —Mesaba strike

Le Sueur, Meridel. "Notes on North Country Folkways." *Minnesota History* 25 (September 1944), pp. 215-23.
    —Based on, but not always giving credit to, I.W.W. folkways

"Letter from a Butte Miner." *International Socialist Review* 15 (October 1914), pp. 227-28.

"Letter to the President, from Local 8." *Messenger* 4 (March 1922), p. 377.
    —Philadelphia longshoremen

Leupp, Constance D. "The Lawrence Strike Hearings." *Survey* 27 (March 23, 1912), pp. 1953-54.

Le Warne, Charles P. "The Aberdeen, Washington, Free Speech Fight of 1911-1912." *Pacific Northwest Quarterly* 66 (January 1975), pp. 1-12.

———. "The Bolsheviks Land in Seattle: the Shilka Incident of 1917." *Arizona and the West* 20 (Summer 1978), pp. 107-22.

———. "On the Wobbly Train to Fresno." *Labor History* 14 (Spring 1973), pp. 264-89.
    —Long letter, a report by E. M. Clyde

Lewis, Austin. "The Drift in California." *International Socialist Review* 12 (November 1911), pp. 272-74.
    —Organizing unskilled workers

Lewis, Austin. "Movements of Migratory Unskilled Labor in California." *New Review* 2 (August 1914), pp. 458-65.
    —Fresno, Wheatland

———. "The New Labor Movement of the West." *Class Struggle* 1 (September-October 1917), pp. 1-10.

Lewis, Tom J. Telegram about Spokane. *International Socialist Review* 10 (December 1909), p. 558.

"Lexington Explosion—Repudiation of Our Dead Comrades by the I.W.W." *Mother Earth* 9 (July 1914), pp. 132-33.

Lindquist, John H. "Jerome Deportation of 1917." *Arizona and the West* 11 (Autumn 1969), pp. 233-46.
    —From *Pacific Northwest Quarterly*

———. and Fraser, James. "A Sociological Interpretation of the Bisbee Deportation." *Pacific Historical Review* 37 (November 1968), pp. 401-22.

"Little Falls Strike Settled." *Review of Reviews* 47 (February 1913), p. 148.
  —Good portrait of Haywood

Lively, D. O. "Agricultural Labor Problems During the Past Season." *Monthly Bulletin* of California State Commission of Horticulture (January-February 1918), pp. 70-73.

"Local 8 of I.W.W. on Firing Line." *Messenger* 4 (February 1922), pp. 355-56.
  —Philadelphia longshoremen

Lockhart, J. W. "The I.W.W. Raid at Centralia." *Current History* 17 (October 1922), pp. 55-57.

"Lockout in Kansas City." *Syndicalist* 3 (August 1-15), 1913), p. 52.
  —No free speech during the lockout

Lovejoy, Owen R. "Right of Free Speech in Lawrence." *Survey* 27 (March 9, 1912), pp. 1904-5. See also *Survey* 28 (April 6, 1912), pp. 76-77.

Lovin, Hugh T. "Moses Alexander and the Idaho Lumber Strike of 1917—The Wartime Ordeal of a Progressive." *Pacific Northwest Quarterly* 66 (July 1975), pp. 115-22.

_____. "Red Scare in Idaho, 1916-1918." *Idaho Yesterdays* 17 (Fall 1973), pp. 2-13.
  —I.W.W. threatened "trouble"

"Lumber Strike." *International Socialist Review* 18 (November-December, 1917), pp. 308-9.

"Lynch-law and Treason; Lynching of Frank Little in Butte." *Literary Digest* 55 (August 18, 1917), pp. 12-13.

MacDonald, J. A. "A New Chapter in Industrial Revolution." *International Socialist Review* 16 (December 1915), pp. 347-49.
  —Organizing midwest agricultural workers

_____. "From Butte to Bisbee." *International Socialist Review* 18 (August 1917), pp. 69-71.

MacDonald, William. "Seattle Strike and Afterwards." *Nation* 108 (March 29, 1919), pp. 469-70.
  —I.W.W. not included in this discussion, although there

_____. "Where Labor Points the Way." *Nation* 108 (April 5, 1919), pp. 499-501.
  —Government's response not adequate

Macfarlane, P. C. "Issues at Calumet." *Collier's* 52 (February 7, 1914), pp. 5-6, 22-25.

MacPhee, Donald A. "The Centralia Incident and the Pamphleteers." *Pacific Northwest Quarterly* 62 (July 1971), pp. 110-16.

Madison, Charles A. "Out of Labor's Past: the Insurgent I.W.W." *Labor and Nation* 5 (July 1949), pp. 35-38.
  —"Idealistic, reckless, revolutionary, intransigent"

Magnusson, Leifur. "Agricultural Camp Housing." *Monthly Labor Review* 6 (May 1918), pp. 277-87.
  —Wheatland aftermath

"The Man That Was Hung." *International Socialist Review* 18 (September 1917), pp. 135-38.
  —Frank Little's murder

Mannheimer, Leo. "Darkest New Jersey—How the Paterson Strike Looks to One in the Thick of the Conflict." *Independent* 74 (May 29, 1913), pp. 1190-92.
  —"For the past 3 months I have come into constant contact with the strikers and employers . . ."

Marcus, I. M. "Benjamin Fletcher: Black Labor Leader." *Negro History Bulletin* 35 (October 1972), pp. 138-40.

Marcy, Leslie H. "Calumet." *International Socialist Review* 14 (February 1914), pp. 453-61.

_____. "The Eleven Hundred Exiled Copper Miners." *International Socialist Review* 18 (September 1917), pp. 160-62.
  —Bisbee deportation

_____. "800 Per Cent and the Akron Strike." *International Socialist Review* 13 (April 1913), pp. 711-24.

_____. "The Iron Heel on the Mesabi Range." *International Socialist Review* 17 (August 1916), pp. 74-80.

_____. "More 'Law and Order.' " *International Socialist Review* 17 (November 1916), pp. 269-70.
  —Pennsylvania order

_____. "On the Strike Field—the Fight in the Mountains." *International Socialist Review* 13 (March 1913), pp. 647-49.
  —West Virginia strike

_____, and Boyd, Frederick S. "One Big Union Wins." *International Socialist Review* 12 (April 1912), pp. 613-30.

Marcy, Mary. "The Battle for Bread in Lawrence." *International Socialist Review* 12 (March 1912), pp. 533-43.

_____. "A Month of Lawlessness." *International Socialist Review* 18 (September 1917), pp. 154-57.
  —Frank Little lynching

Margolis, Jacob. "The Streets of Pittsburgh." *International Socialist Review* 13 (October 1912), pp. 313-20.
  —Pittsburgh free speech fight

Martin, John. "Industrial Revolt at Lawrence." *Independent* 72 (March 7, 1912), pp. 491-95.
  —" . . . Perhaps a legal minimum wage would avoid this trouble"; photos and bayonets

_____. "News from the Lumber Workers' Strike." *International Socialist Review* 18 (September 1917), pp. 144-48.

Mason, Gregory. "Industrial War in Paterson." *Outlook* 104 (June 7, 1913), pp. 283-87.

"Mass Action—Where We Stand." Editorial. *International Socialist Review* 17 (December 1916), pp. 367-69.
  —Socialist view on I.W.W., direct action, etc.

"Mass and Craft Unions." *Survey* 27 (February 1912), pp. 1792-94.
　　—Lawrence controversy

Mayhall, Pamela. "Bisbee's Response to Civil Disorder—a Matter of Circumstance." *American West* 9 (May 1972), pp. 22-31. Reply by J. W. Byrkit, *American West* 9 (November 1972), p. 48.

"Mayor Ole Hanson, Who Sat Tight at Seattle." *Literary Digest* 60 (March 8, 1919), pp. 47-50.

McClelland, John M., Jr. "Terror on Tower Avenue." *Pacific Northwest Quarterly* 57 (April 1966), pp. 65-72.
　　—Everett massacre

McClurg, Donald J. "The Colorado Coal Strike of 1927—Tactical Leadership of the I.W.W." *Labor History* 4 (Winter 1963), pp. 68-92.

McCormick, Kyle. "The National Guard of West Virginia During the Strike Period of 1912-1913." *West Virginia History* 22 (October 1960), pp. 34-35.

McDonald, P. B. "Michigan Copper-Miners." *Outlook* 106 (February 7, 1914), pp. 297-98.

McGurty, Edward J. "The Copper Miners' Strike." *International Socialist Review* 14 (September 1913), pp. 150-53.
　　—Calumet-Hecla

McKee, Harry M., and Kirk, E. E. "Review Vindicated." *International Socialist Review* 14 (October 1913), p. 231.
　　—San Diego free speech fight

"McKees Rocks Strikers Win." *Survey* 22 (September 11, 1909), p. 795.

McMahon, Theresa S. "Centralia and the I.W.W." *Survey* 43 (November 29, 1919), pp. 173-74.

McWhiney, Grady. "Louisiana Socialists in the Early Twentieth Century: A Study of Rustic Radicalism." *Journal of Southern History* 20 (August 1954), pp. 315-36.

"Meaning of the Western Strikes." *Literary Digest* 60 (March 1, 1919), pp. 14-15.

"Membership Criminal in California." *Nation* 114 (April 19, 1922), p. 456.

"Membership in the I.W.W. a Criminal Offense Under California Statute." *Monthly Labor Review* 16 (February 1923), pp. 471-73.

"Men Whom We are Deporting." *American Review of Reviews* 61 (February 1920), pp. 123-30.

Merz, Charles. "The Issue in Butte." *New Republic* 12 (September 22, 1917), pp. 215-17.
　　—A courageous attempt to put control of industry on a more democratic basis

_____. "Tying Up Western Lumber." *New Republic* 12 (September 29, 1917), pp. 242-44.

Meyer, E. F. "Six Killed, Twenty Wounded; a Case Study of Industrial Conflict." *Survey* 59 (February 15, 1928), pp. 644-46.
　　—Colorado mayhem

Meyers, Rex C. "Vigilante Numbers: a Re-Examination." *Montana, Magazine of Western History* 24 (Autumn 1974), pp. 67-70.
    —3-7-77 mystery

Michaelis, G. V. S. "Westinghouse Strike." *Survey* 32 (August 1, 1914), pp. 463-65.
    —Pittsburgh problems

"Michigan Copper Miners' Strike; Fight of Western Federation of Miners to Unionize Famous Calumet and Hecla and Other Peninsula Properties." *American Employer* 2 (November 1913), pp. 227-30.

"Michigan Copper Strike." *Literary Digest* 47 (December 6, 1913), pp. 1097-98.

"Michigan Copper Strike." *Outlook* 106 (January 31, 1914), pp. 237-39.

"Michigan Press on the Copper War." *Literary Digest* 48 (January 10, 1914), pp. 47-49.

"A Militia Man's Experiences." *Survey* 28 (April 6, 1912), pp. 76-77.
    —Lawrence strike memory

_____. "Strike in Seattle." *Survey* 41 (March 8, 1919), pp. 821-23.

"A Mill Overseer's View." *Survey* 28 (April 6, 1912), pp. 75-76.
    —Lawrence viewpoint

Miller, Charles H. "Our Great Neglected Wobbly." *Michigan Quarterly Review* 6 (Winter 1967), pp. 57-61.

Miller, Grace, "The I.W.W. Free Speech Fight: San Diego 1912." *South California Historical Society Quarterly* 54 (Fall 1972), pp. 211-38.

"Millions Made on the Mesaba." *International Socialist Review* 17 (October 1916), p. 230.

Mills, Edward L. "The Centralia Report." *Christian Century* 47 (November 26, 1930), p. 1461.

_____. "Churches' Plea Wins Parole." *Christian Century* 48 (July 29, 1931), p. 980.
    —Quest of paroling the Centralia prisoners

"Miners Strike." *Life & Labor* 3 (November 1913), pp. 346-47.
    —Calumet-Hecla

"Miners' Strike at Goldfield." *Outlook* 87 (December 21, 1907), pp. 833-39.

"Mining War in Colorado." *Outlook* 107 (May 9, 1914), p. 49.

"Minnesota' Striking Iron Miners." *Literary Digest* 53 (September 23, 1916), pp. 732-33.
    —"A bitter contest stirred up entirely by outside agitators."

Minor, Robert. "In the Anthracite Hills." *International Socialist Review* 16 (April 1916), pp. 589-94.
    —Pennsylvania

"Miss Scudder's Misreported Speech." *Outlook* 100 (April 20, 1912), pp. 846-47.
    —Lawrence strike recollection

Mittleman, Edward B. "Gyppo System." *Journal of Political Economy* 31 (December 1923), pp. 840-51.
    —System of remuneration that gave us a word, from the Northwest

_____. "Loyal Legion of Loggers and Lumberman." *Journal of Political Economy* 31 (June 1923), pp. 313-41.

Monaco, F. "San Francisco Shoe Workers Strike." *International Socialist Review* 13 (May 1913), pp. 818-19.

"Montesano—is the I.W.W. on Trial?" *Survey* 43 (March 13, 1920), pp. 734-35.

Montgomery, James. "The Lawrence Strike and the Literacy Test." *New Review* 1 (March 22, 1913), pp. 376-81.

Morgan, George T., Jr. "The Gospel of Wealth Goes South: John Henry Kirby and Labor's Struggle for Self-Determination, 1901-1916." *Southwestern Historical Quarterly* 75 (October 1971), pp. 186-97.

_____. "No Compromise—No Recognition: John Kirby, the Southern Lumber Operators' Association and Unionism in the Piney Woods 1906-1916." *Labor History* 10 (Spring 1969), pp. 193-204.

Morgan, J. Edward. "The Unemployed in San Francisco." *New Review* 2 (April 1914), pp. 193-99.
   —The march to the governor's house.

Morris, James O., and Foner, Philip. "Philip Foner and the Writing of the Joe Hill Case: An Exchange." *Labor History* 12 (Winter, 1971), pp. 81-114.

Morton, Jack. "Trial of the Timber Workers." *International Socialist Review* 13 (November 1912), p. 407.

"Mr. D'Olier's Warning to the American Legion." *New Republic* 21 (December 31, 1919), p. 129.

Mr. Kent on the I.W.W." *Public* 21 (July 13, 1918), pp. 878-79.
   —Reasons to help the defense

Mueller, J. R. "Food in the Lumber Camps." *Journal of Home Economics* 13 (June 1921), pp. 241-45.
   —"They all work 8 hours a day but the I.W.W., and they don't want to work at all."

"Municipal Plans for the Unemployed." *Survey* 31 (February 21, 1914), pp. 633-35.
   —Kansas City and St. Louis

"Murder is Murder." *Outlook* 109 (January 27, 1915), p. 151.
   —In a fertilizer works in New Jersey

Muray, Keith. "Issues and Personalities of Pacific Northwest Politics." *Pacific Northwest Quarterly* 41 (July 1950), pp. 213-33.

Murray, Robert K. Revs. of *Rebels of the Woods*, Robert Tyler. *Journal of American History* 55 (December 1968), pp. 674-75.

_____. "Centralia: An Unfinished American Tragedy." *Northwest Review* 6 (Spring 1963), pp. 7-18.

_____. "Communism and the Great Steel Strike of 1919." *Mississippi Valley Historical Review* 38 (December 1951), pp. 445-66.
   —Giving I.W.W its small place in the strike

Nearing, Scott. "On the Trail of the Pittsburgh Stogies." *Independent* 65 (July 1908), pp. 22-24.
   —Children at work

"A Needless Labor War." *Outlook* 100 (January 27, 1912), pp. 151-52.
   —If Lawrence was needless

Nef, W. T. "Job Control in the Harvest Fields." *International Socialist Review* 17 (September 1916), pp. 141-43.

———. "The Militant Harvest Workers." *International Socialist Review* 17 (October 1916), pp. 229-30.

"A New and Better Wheatland." *Outlook* 111 (October 15, 1915), pp. 348-49.

"A New Element in Strikes." *World's Work* 24 (May 1912), pp. 13-14.
   —Lawrence, the example

"New Jersey Needs the Recall." *Public* 17 (June 16, 1914), p. 605.
   —Quinlan sentence

"A New Jersey Weaver, a Budget and a Gospel of Revolution." *Survey* 28 (May 18, 1912), pp. 289-91.
   —Paterson weaver

"New Jersey's Journalistic Perils." *Literary Digest* 46 (June 21, 1913), pp. 1366-67.
   —Alexander Scott indictment

"The New Labor Movement." *Literary Digest* 44 (April 6, 1912), pp. 677-78.
   —Movement in the textile mills of New Jersey and Massachusetts

"New Philosophy of the Labor Movement." *Nation* 94 (March 28, 1912), pp. 304-6.
   —Syndicalism was brought by the Lawrence strike

"The New Wild West." *Liberator* 3 (January 1920), pp. 21-23.
   —Centralia

"New York a Prey to Strikes." *Outlook* 103 (January 18, 1913), pp. 102-3.

Newbill, James G. "Farmers and Wobblies in the Yakima Valley, 1933." *Pacific Northwest Quarterly* 68 (April 1977), pp. 80-87.

Newman, Philip. "The First I.W.W. Invasion of New Jersey." *New Jersey Historical Society Proceedings* 58 (October 1940), pp. 268-83.

"News from Lawrence." *Independent* 72 (March 7, 1912), pp. 484-85.
   —Various complications in the strike

Nochlin, Linda. "The Paterson Strike Pageant of 1913." *Art in America* 62 (May-June 1974), pp. 64-68.

North, Cedric. "Brotherhood of Man and the Wobblies." *North American* 227 (April 1929), pp. 487-92.
   —South Dakota and the bums

"O For Mark Twain!" *Nation* 112 (June 29, 1921), p. 905.
   —Ed Garman got seven more months in prison for organizing a branch of I.W.W. in prison, Northumberland, Pennsylvania

Oates, J. "Globe-Miami District." *International Socialist Review* 18 (August 1917), pp. 72-74.
   —Bisbee; the demands of the workers are listed

O'Brian, John L. "Uncle Sam's Spy Policies: Safeguarding American Liberty During the War." *Forum* 61 (April 1919), pp. 407-16.

O'Connor, Harvey. Rev. of *I.W.W.—First Fifty Years*, F. W. Thompson. *Nation* 183 (August 25, 1956), p. 165.

"Of a Similar Character." *Nation* 110 (January 3, 1920), p. 843.
—Editorial opinion on Spokane vs. I.W.W.

"Ol' Rags an' Bottles." *Nation* 108 (January 25, 1919), pp. 114-16.
—Sacramento indictments

Older, C. "Last Day of the Paint Creek Court Martial." *Independent* 74 (May 15, 1913), pp. 1085-88.
—For the Mother Jones buffs

"One Hundred American Labor Leaders Sent to Prison." *Public* 21 (August 24, 1918), pp. 1068-69.

"On Numerous Occasions." *New Republic* 39 (July 9, 1924), pp. 169-70.
—San Pedro, a "holy war to make the world safe for private property?"

"Open Shop at Boulder Dam." *New Republic* 47 (June 24, 1931), pp. 147-48.
—The Big dam as aggravation and open shop

Orth, S. P. "Battle Line of Labor—II, the Warfare." *World's Work* 25 (December 1912), pp. 197-205.

O'Sullivan, Mary K. "Labor War at Lawrence." *Survey* 28 (April 6, 1912), pp. 72-74.

Ovington, Mary White. "The Status of the Negro in the United States." *New Review* 1 (September 1913), pp. 744-49.
—Philadelphia and southern timberworkers set an example

"Pageant as a Form of Propaganda." *Current Opinion* 55 (July 1913), p. 32.

"Pageant of the Paterson Strike." *Survey* 30 (June 28, 1913), p. 428.

Palmer, Frank L. "Solidarity in Colorado." *Nation* 126 (February 1, 1928), pp. 118-20.
—Did the I.W.W. cause the strike?

Palmer, Fred. "War in Colorado." *Nation* 125 (December 7, 1927), pp. 623-24.
—Constant newspaper campaign to connect I.W.W with violence.

Palmer, Lewis E. "A Strike for Four Loaves of Bread at Lawrence." *Survey* 27 (February 3, 1912), pp. 1690-97.

"Panic and Death—The Copper Strike in Michigan." *Outlook* 106 (January 3, 1914), p. 6.

Pankratz, Herbert. "The Suppression of Alleged Disloyalty in Kansas During World War I." *Kansas Historical Quarterly* 42 (Autumn 1976), pp. 277-307.

Papanikolas, Helen Z. "Life and Labor Among the Immigrants of Bingham Canyon." *Utah Historical Quarterly* 33 (1965), pp. 289-315.
—Early Wobblies, then WFM

Parker, Carleton H. "The California Casual and His Revolt." *Quarterly Journal of Economics* 30 (November 1915), pp. 110-26.
—Migrant laborers are the finished products of their environment.

_____. "The I.W.W." *Atlantic Monthly* 120 (November 1917), pp. 651-62.
—Classic summary

"Paterson Convictions Again Set Aside." *Survey* 31 (November 22, 1913), pp. 191-92.

"Paterson Strike." *Independent* 74 (May 29, 1913), p. 1172.
    —Disapproves the I.W.W. principles, but praises the leaders

"Paterson Strike." *International Socialist Review* 14 (September 1913), pp. 177-78.

"Paterson Strike Leaders in Jersey Prison." *Survey* 34 (April 3, 1915), p. 3.
    —F. Sumner Boyd's appeal

"Paterson Strike Pageant." *Independent* 74 (June 19, 1913), pp. 1406-7.
    —Unusual photo of pageant being enacted

"Paterson—West Virginia—California." *New Review* 1 (June 1913), pp. 545-47.

"Paterson's Authorities." *New Republic* 4 (September 18, 1915), p. 164.
    —*N.Y. Times* says authorities are justified in suppressing free speech if they are spouters, routers, vultures, or rattlesnakes.

Pawar, Sheelwant B. "The Structure and Nature of Labor Unions in Utah, and Historical Perspective, 1890-1920." *Utah Historical Quarterly 35* (Summer 1967), pp. 236-55.
    —Also about L. J. Trujillo, organizer of Building Employees' IU No. 262.

Payne, C. E. "Captain Coll—Legionnaire." *Nation* 129 (July 10, 1929), pp. 38-39.
    —Centralia still a burning issue; story of one legionnaire defender who had to move away

————. "The Spring Drive of the Lumber Jacks." *International Socialist Review* 17 (June 1917), pp. 729-30.

Perry, Grover H. "Metal Miners Blast." *International Socialist Review* 17 (June 1917), pp. 730-31.
    —Arizona

————. "Transport Workers Join I.W.W." *International Socialist Review* 13 (May 1913), p. 812.

Peterson, Richard H. "Conflict and Consensus: Labor Relations in Western Mining." *Journal of the West* 12 (1973), pp. 1-17.

Pfeffer, C. Whit. "From Bohunks to Finns." *Survey* 36 (April 1, 1916), pp. 8-14.
    —Mesaba range

"Philadelphia's Sugar Strike." *Survey* 37 (March 17, 1917), p. 696.

"Pickers Pinching Apples." *Outlook* 116 (August 29, 1917), pp. 639-40.
    —Washington farmers have trouble

"Pittsburgh's Morning After." (By R. H. S.) *Everybody's* 23 (October 1910), pp. 570-71.

"The Pity of It." *Independent* 74 (June 12, 1913), p. 1317.
    —"We are weary of this mob madness."

"Poet of the I.W.W." *Outlook* 104 (July 5, 1913), pp. 504-6.
    —Giovannitti at Lawrence

"Poor Mr. Dooley." *Nation* 108 (January 25, 1919), p. 126.
    —Mr. Dooley quoted at the Sacramento trial

"Possible Paterson." *Outlook* 104 (June 14, 1913), pp. 318-21.

Pratt, W. M. "The Lawrence Revolution." *New England Magazine* 44 (March 1912), pp. 7-16.

"President's Commission at Bisbee." *New Republic* 13 (December 8, 1917), pp. 140-41.

Price, W. D. "Greasy Olivers of Pittsburgh." *Technical World* 20 (September 1913), pp. 8-19.
    —Conditions at the Oliver Mill

Priddy, Al. "Controlling the Passions of Men in Lawrence." *Outlook* 102 (October 19, 1912), pp. 343-45.

"Prison Life of Ettor and Giovannitti." *Literary Digest* 45 (September 14, 1912), pp. 441-43.

"Prisoners of War." *Sunset* 39 (September 1917), p. 6.
    —Bisbee deportees

"Private War at the Mount Hope Mine." *Outlook* 104 (May 10, 1913), pp. 44-45.
    —New Jersey

"Private War in Colorado." *Outlook* 107 (May 9, 1914), pp. 61-62.

"Probing the Causes of Unrest." *Survey* 32 (April 18-25; May 30-June 27; July 11; August 8, 29; October 3; December 12, 1914), pp. 71, 92-93, 230-31, 252, 303-4, 320-21, 339-40, 397-99, 483-85, 538-39, 558-60, 593-94, 609-10, 632-33, and continued in *Survey* 33 and 34.

"Proposed Truce in Colorado." *Outlook* 108 (September 30, 1914), p. 237.

"Public Which Has a Short Memory—New Light on the Centralia Trial in 1919." *Nation* 114 (June 7, 1922), p. 662.
    —Juror affidavits of no avail

Quinlan, Patrick. "Glorious Paterson." *International Socialist Review* 14 (December 1913), pp. 355-57.

_____. "The Paterson Strike and After." *New Review* 2 (January 1914), pp. 26-33.

Rader, Benjamin G. "The Montana Lumber Strike of 1917." *Pacific Historical Review* 36 (May 1967), pp. 189-207.

"The Railroad Boys." *International Socialist Review* 15 (July 1914), p. 62.
    —Pennsylvania railroad workers

"R. D. Ginther, Working Man Artist and Historian of Skid Row." *California Historical Quarterly* 54 (Fall 1975), pp. 263-71.
    —Wobbly self-taught artist who painted skid-row scenes

Reading, A. B. "California Syndicalist Act, Strong or Wobbly?" *Overland* 83 (March 1925), pp. 117-18.

"The Real Question." *Outlook* 100 (February 24, 1912), pp. 385-86.
    —Lawrence strike

"Rebellion in Colorado." *Nation* 126 (January 11, 1928), p. 33.
    —I.W.W. an outlaw organization—make the strike unlawful—"I won't let the Wobblies meet under my nose," one militia commander said

"A Red Brigade—How the I.W.W. of Columbus Ohio Collected $40 for the Little Falls Strikers." *International Socialist Review* 13 (February 1913), pp. 599-600.

Reed, John. "War in Paterson." *International Socialist Review* 14 (July 1913), pp. 43-48.

Reed, Mary. "San Pedro." *Nation* 119 (July 9, 1924), pp. 45-46.

Reed, Merl. "I.W.W. and Individual Freedom in Western Louisiana, 1913." *Louisiana History* 10 (Winter 1969), pp. 61-69.

_____. "Lumberjacks and Longshoremen: The I.W.W. in Louisiana." *Labor History* 13 (Winter 1972), pp. 41-59.

Reitman, Ben L. "Impressions of the Chicago Convention." *Mother Earth* 8 (October 1913), pp. 239-42.
          —I marvelled at the big things they have done."

_____. "The Respectable Mob." *Mother Earth* 7 (June 1912), pp. 109-114.
          —San Diego firsthand account

"Religious Press on the I.W.W. Invaders." *Literary Digest* 48 (April 4, 1914), p. 760.
          —Reaction to Tannenbaum's church invasion

"Report of the President's Mediation Commission, Condemning Deportations from Warren District of Arizona." *Monthly Labor Review* 6 (January 1918), pp. 13-17.

Reuss, Carl F. "The Farm Labor Problem in Washington, 1917-1918." *Pacific Northwest Quarterly* 34 (October 1943), pp. 339-52.

"Review of the Michigan Copper Strike." *American Industries* 14 (April 1914), pp. 13-14.
          —A view from the other side

Rhea, M. "Revolt in Butte." *New Review* 2 (September 1914), pp. 538-42.
          —Inferentially, the I.W.W. was involved.

Rice, M. M. "Bloody Monday Again in Colorado." *Independent* 119 (December 31, 1927), pp. 655-56.
          —"A caravan . . . lead by Adam Bell of the I.W.W. . . . advanced toward the mine."

"Rioting at McKees Rocks." *Survey* 22 (August 28, 1909), p. 719.

Rocha, Guy Louis. "The I.W.W. and the Boulder Canyon Project: The Final Death Throes of American Syndicalism." *Nevada Historical Quarterly* 21 (Spring 1978), pp. 3-24.
          —Last significant organizational activities

_____. "Radical Labor Struggles in the Tonapah-Goldfield Mining District, 1901-1922." *Nevada Historical Society Quarterly* 20 (Spring 1977), pp. 2-45.

Rogers, Bruce. "Mutiny of the Lumber Army." *Coming Nation* (May 11, 1912), pp. 5-6.

_____. "The War of Gray's Harbor." *International Socialist Review* 12 (May 1912), pp. 750-53.

Rose, Gerald A. "The Westwood Lumber Strike." *Labor History* 13 (Spring 1972), pp. 171-99.

Rowell, Wilbur E. "The Lawrence Strike." *Survey* 27 (March 23, 1912), pp. 1958-60.

Ruetten, Richard. "Anaconda Journalism: The End of an Era." *Journalism Quarterly* 37 (Winter 1960), pp. 3-12, 104.

Russell, Phillips. "Acquittal of Ettor and Giovannitti." *International Socialist Review* 13 (January 1913), pp. 556-57.

_____. "The Arrest for Haywood and Lessig." *International Socialist Review* 13 (May 1913), pp. 789-92.

_____. "Arrest of Haywood and Lessig," *Pageant of the Paterson Strike* (New York: Success Press, 1913), pp. 11-14.

_____. "The Class Struggle on the Pacific Coast (An Interview with O. A. Tveitmoe)." *International Socialist Review* 13 (September 1912), pp. 236-38.

_____. "The Dynamite Job at Lawrence." *International Socialist Review* 13 (October 1912), pp. 308-11.

_____. "The Fourteen in Jail." *International Socialist Review* 13 (February 1913), pp. 598-99.
    —Little Falls strike

_____. "Living on Determination in Paterson." *International Socialist Review* 14 (August 1913), pp. 100-101.

_____. "The Second Battle of Lawrence." *International Socialist Review* 13 (November 1912), pp. 417-23.

_____. "The Strike at Little Falls." *International Socialist Review* 13 (December 1912), pp. 455-60.

_____. "Strike Tactics." *New Review* 1 (March 29, 1913), pp. 405-9.
    —Lawrence and Little Falls

_____. "To Frank Little." Poem. *International Socialist Review* 18 (September 1917), pp. 132-33.

_____. "What is a Riot Anyhow?" *New Review* 1 (February 1, 1913), pp. 145-47.
    —Little Falls, New York

_____. "The World's Greatest Labor Play: The Paterson Strike Pageant." *International Socialist Review* 14 (July 1913), pp. 6-9.

Russell, Phillips, et al. "On the Strike Field." *International Socialist Review* 13 (March 1913), pp. 647-54.
    —News from West Virginia, New York, etc.

"Russianism in the Little Falls Strike." *Syndicalist* 3 (January 1, 1913), p. 2.
    —A plea for help

Ryan, John A. "Good and Bad Labor Unions." *Survey* 31 (January 10, 1914), p. 451.
    —In Philadelphia

_____. "The Unemployed and the Churches: A Reply." *Survey* 32 (June 27, 1914), pp. 342-43.
    —New York's problem

"The Salem Trial of the Lawrence Case." *Outlook* 102 (December 7, 1912), pp. 739-40.

Sander, H. F. "Butte—the Heart of the Copper Industry." *Overland* 48 (November 1906), pp. 367-84.

"San Diego *Union*'s Challenge." *Nation* 115 (November 22, 1922), p. 539.
    —Testimony of unreliable person (Townsend) at San Diego trial

"San Diego's Free Speech Troubles." *Literary Digest* 44 (June 1, 1912), p. 1146.

"San Diego's Only Hope." *Wilshire's Magazine* 16 (June-July, 1912), p. 3.

"Sanitation in Hop Fields." *Life and Labor* 4 (October 1914), p. 318.

Sanville, Florence L. "Silk Workers in Pennsylvania and New Jersey." *Survey* 28 (May 18, 1912), pp. 307-12.

Sawyer, Rev. Roland D. "The Socialist Situation in Massachusetts." *New Review* 1 (January 25, 1913), pp. 117-18.
_____. "What Threatens Ettor and Giovannitti." *International Socialist Review* 13 (August 1912), pp. 114-15.

Scharrenberg, Paul. "Sanitary Conditions in Labor Camps." *American Federationist* 25 (October 1918), pp. 891-93.
    —I.W.W. shouldn't get credit for the improvements

Scott, Alexander. "What the Reds Are Doing in Paterson." *International Socialist Review* 13 (June 1913), pp. 852-56.

"Scott Indicted Again." *International Socialist Review* 14 (August 1913), pp. 101-2.
    —Paterson aftermath

Scudder, Vida. "For Justice Sake." Address delivered at Lawrence. *Survey* 28 (April 6, 1912), pp. 77-79.

"Seattle General Strike, 1919: Can We Do Better Next Time?" *Progressive Labor* 9 (July 1973), pp. 32-44.

"Seattle's Red Flag Incident." *Literary Digest* 47 (August 2, 1913), pp. 160-61.
    —Raid by sailors

Selavan, Ida C. "Jewish Wage Earners in Pittsburgh, 1890-1930." *American Jewish Historical Quarterly* 65 (March 1976), p. 274.
    —Small but some mention of I.W.W.

"Shame of Texas." *International Socialist Review* 16 (December 1915), p. 383.
    —Charles Cline's arrest

Shanks, Rosalie. "The I.W.W. Free Speech Movement, San Diego, 1912." *Journal of San Diego History* 19 (No. 1, 1973), pp. 25-33.

Shannon, David A. "The Socialist Party Before the First World War: An Analysis." *Mississippi Valley Historical Review* 38 (September 1951), pp. 279-88.
    —A note on the I.W.W. and Socialist party

"Sheriff Kinkead's Busy Day." *Literary Digest* 51 (August 7, 1915), pp. 256-61.
    —Bayonne, New Jersey

Shields, Arthur. "For the Silent Defenders." *Liberator* 5 (September 1922), pp. 22-23.

Shippey, Hartwell, S. "The Shame of San Diego." *International Socialist Review* 12 (May 1912), pp. 718-23.

Short, Wallace M. "How One Town Learned a Lesson in Free Speech." *Survey* 35 (October 30, 1915), pp. 106-8.
  —Sioux City, South Dakota

Sims, Robert C. "Idaho's Criminal Syndicalism Act: One State's Response to Radical Labor." *Labor History* 15-4, (Fall 1974), pp. 511-27.

Sirola, George. "Finnish Working Peoples' College." *International Socialist Review* 14 (August 1913), pp. 102-4.

"Situation as Seen By a Manufacturer." *Survey* 28 (April 6, 1912), p. 75.
  —Textile problems from another viewpoint

"The Situation at Goldfield." *Outlook* 88 (January 11, 1908), pp. 57-58.

"Situation in Lawrence." *Outlook* 102 (October 12, 1912), pp. 286-87.

"Slaughter at Roosevelt." *Outlook* 109 (February 3, 1915), pp. 241-42.
  —New Jersey

Smith, Rufus. "Some Phases of the McKees Rocks Strike." *Survey* 23 (October 2, 1909), pp. 38-45.

Smith, Walker C. "Remember the Fifth of November." *International Socialist Review* 17 (January 1917), pp. 396-99.
  —Everett, Washington, that day

_____. "The Voyage of the Verona." *International Socialist Review* 17 (December 1916), pp. 340-46.
  —Includes photos

Synder, Robert E. "Women, Wobblies, and Workers' Rights: The 1912 Textile Strike in Little Falls, New York." *New York History* 60 (January 1979), pp. 29-57.

"So-called American Wage-Earners and the Strike at Lawrence." *Review of Reviews* 45 (June 1912), pp. 746-47.

"Social War in New Jersey." *Current Opinions* 55 (August 1913), pp. 80-81.

Sofschalk, Donald G. "Organized Labor and the Iron Ore Miners of Minnesota, 1907-1936." *Labor History* 12 (Spring 1971), pp. 214-42.

"Solidarity Wins in Fresno." *International Socialist Review* 11 (April 1911), pp. 634-36.

Spero, S. D., and Aronoff, J. B. "War in the Kentucky Mountains." *American Mercury* 25 (February 1932), pp. 226-33.
  —Harlan—"about 500-some joined the I.W.W."

"Spruce and the I.W.W." *New Republic* 14 (February 23, 1918), pp. 99-100.
  —I.W.W. mobilized as firefighters but problems in Spruce

Stanwood, Edward B. "The Marysville Case." *Harper's Weekly* 58 (June 20, 1914), p. 23.

"State Investigation of the Little Falls Strike." *Survey* 29 (January 4, 1913), p. 414.

Stephens, D. "Fair Play for the I.W.W.—a Reply to H. Hibschman." *Current History* 17 (October 1922), p. 58.
  —Revised view of Centralia

Sterling, Jean. "The Silent Defense in Sacramento." *The Liberator* 1 (February 1919), pp. 15-17.

Stewart, Oliver D. "West Virginia Coal Strike." *American Employer* 2 (November 1913), pp. 195-202; (December 1913), pp. 259-69.
  —Paint Creek, Cabin Creek, and other areas

St. John, Vincent. "The Fight for Free Speech at San Diego." *International Socialist Review* 12 (April 1912), p. 649.

"The Strike at the Woolen Mills." *Independent* 72 (February 29, 1912), pp. 433-34.
  —Pauper labor from Europe

"Strike Failures a Joy to the I.W.W. Leaders." *Current Opinion* 68 (June 1920), pp. 835-36.

"Strike at the Copper Miners." *Life & Labor* 3 (December 1913), pp. 375-77.

"Strike of the Jersey Silk Weavers." *Survey* 30 (May 31, 1913), p. 300.

"Strike of the Jersey Silk Workers." *Survey* 30 (April 19, 1913), pp. 81-82.

"Strike of the Jersey Silk Workers—Reply." *Survey* 30 (May 31, 1913), p. 316.

"Strike that Oiled its Own Troubled Waters; Seattle Strike." *Literary Digest* 61 (April 12, 1919), pp. 90-92.

"Strike Riot in Pennsylvania." *Independent* 67 (September 2, 1909), pp. 533-37.
  —Pressed steel car, McKees Rocks; what is the psychological situation?

"Strikes and Rumors of Strikes." *Outlook* 110 (August 4, 1915), pp. 776-77.
  —New Jersey rumors

"Strikes by Proclamation." *Agitator* 2 (October 1, 1912), p. 1.
  —Pittsburgh I.W.W. proclaimed, but will they respond?

Strong, Anna Louise. "Centralia: An Unfinished Story." *Nation* 110 (April 17, 1920), pp. 508-10.

———. "Everett's Bloody Sunday." *Survey* 37 (January 27, 1917), pp. 475-76.

———. "Newspaper Confiscated—and Returned." *Nation* 109 (December 13, 1919), pp. 738-40.
  —On Centralia

———. "The Verdict at Everett." *Survey* 38 (May 19, 1917), p. 161.

"Struggles of Textile Workers Depicted by Labor Cartoonists." *Textile Labor* 34 (February 1913), p. 5.
  —Paterson and Lawrence cartoons

Suhr, Matilda. "A Mother's Appeal." *International Socialist Review* 15 (January 1915), pp. 416-17.

Sullivan, William A. "The 1913 Revolt of the Michigan Copper Miners." *Michigan History* 43 (September 1959), pp. 294-314.

Sumner, Mary B. "Arturo Giovannitti." *Survey* 29 (November 2, 1912), pp. 163-66.
  —Lawrence lyrics

———. "Broad Silk Weavers of Paterson." *Survey* 27 (March 16, 1912), pp. 1932-35.

Taft, Clinton J. "California Justice." Answer. *New Republic* 40 (October 29, 1924), p. 228.
  —Professor Leo Gallagher jailed for holding an I.W.W. songbook in his hands

Taft, Philip. "The Bisbee Deportation." *Labor History* 13 (Winter 1972), pp. 3-40.

_____. "The I.W.W. in the Grain Belt." *Labor History* 1 (Winter 1960), pp. 53-67.

_____. "The I.W.W. and the West." *American Quarterly* 12 (Summer, 1960), pp. 175-187.

_____. "Mayor Short and the I.W.W. Agricultural Workers." *Labor History* 7 (Spring 1966), pp. 173-77.

_____. "Strife in the Maritime Industry." *Political Science Quarterly* 54 (June 1939), pp. 216-36.
   —He has not forgotten his I.W.W. background.

"Tannenbaum Case to be Appealed." *Public* 17 (August 21, 1914), pp. 806-7.

Tarpey, M. F. "Some Possibilities of the Development of New Labor During the War." *Monthly Bulletin* of California State Commission of Horticulture (January-February 1918), pp. 74-79.

"The Task of Local 8—The Marine Transport Workers of Philadelphia." Messenger 3 (October 1921), pp. 262-63.

Taussig, F. W. "Copper Strike and Copper Dividends." *Survey* 31 (February 14, 1914), pp. 612-13.

Taylor, G. R. "The Clash in the Copper Country—The First Big Strike in Fifty Years in the Industrial Backwoods of Upper Michigan." *Survey* 31 (November 1, 1913), pp. 127-35; 145-49.

_____. "Moyer's Story of Why He Left the Copper Country." *Survey* 31 (January 10, 1914), pp. 433-35.

_____. "Shifting Blame for the Shooting in New Jersey." *Survey* 33 (January 30, 1915), pp. 457-48.

Thomas, A. E. "Goldfield—the New Eldorado." *Putnam's* 1 (March 1907), pp. 658-72.

Thomas, Horace E. "Bone and Sinew for Our Aircraft." *Scientific American* 118 (June 22, 1918), pp. 564-65, 577-79.
   —The I.W.W. was told politely to go

"Thugs Rule in Aberdeen." *Agitator* 2 (December 15, 1911), p. 1.
   —Lumber kings drive industrial workers into the swamps—why?

"To The Old Question." *Nation* 109 (September 13, 1919), p. 359.
   —On Wichita

Tobin, Eugene M. "Direct Action and Conscience: The 1913 Paterson Strike as Example of the Relationship Between Labor Radicals and Liberals." *Labor History* 20 (Winter 1979), pp. 73-88.

"Tribute to Jack Whyte." (By R. E. R.) *Mother Earth* 10 (April 1915), pp. 90-91.
   —San Diego hero

Tucker, Irwin. "The Church and the I.W.W." *Churchman* 108 (August 30, 1913), pp. 278, 290.
   —After Paterson, new ideas

Tugwell, Rexford G. "The Casual of the Woods." *Survey* 44 (July 3, 1920), pp. 472-74.

"Tulsa, November 9th." *Liberator* 1 (April 1918), pp. 15-17.
      —Deported from Tulsa

Turner, G. K. "The Actors and Victims in the Tragedies." *McClure's Magazine*
    29 (September 1907), pp. 524-29.
      —More on Haywood-Moyer-Pettibone

"Two Church Views of the Colorado Strike." *Literary Digest* 95 (December 17,
    1927), pp. 31-32.

"Two Reports on the Little Falls Strike." *Survey* 29 (March 29, 1913), p. 899.

"Two Ways to Speak of the Trial of the I.W.W." *Nation* 110 (March 27, 1920),
    pp. 385-86.
      —Montesano (Centralia)

Tyler, Robert L. "The Everett Free Speech Fight." *Pacific Historical Review* 23
    (February 1954), pp. 19-30.
      —Climaxed the decade

————. "I.W.W. in the Pacific N.W.; Rebels of the Woods." *Oregon Historical
    Society Quarterly* 55 (March 1954), pp. 3-44.

————. "The I.W.W. and the West." *American Quarterly* 12 (Summer 1960),
    pp. 175-87.

————. "The United States Government as Union Organizer: the Loyal Legion of
    Loggers and Lumbermen." *Mississippi Valley Historical Review* 47
    December 1960), pp. 434-51.

————. "Violence at Centralia, 1919." *Pacific Northwest Quarterly* 45 (October
    1954), pp. 116-24.

"Under the Big Tops—by a Ballahoo Wobbly." *International Socialist Review* 17
    (February 1917), pp. 486-88.

"Unionizing the Negro Workers." *Messenger* 2 (October 1919), pp. 8-9.

"Unjustifiable Strike at Akron." *American Industries* 13 (April 1913), p. 13.

Vanderveer, G. F. "Winning Out in Idaho." *International Socialist Review* 18
    (January 1918), p. 344.

Van Valen, Nelson. "Bolsheviki and the Orange Growers." *Pacific Historical
    Review* 22 (February 1953), pp. 39-50.
      —The Wobblies were the "American arm" of the Bolsheviki

Van Valkenburgh, W. S. "The Murder of Joseph Hillstrom." *Mother Earth* 10
    (December 1915), pp. 326-28.
      —More dangerous dead than alive

Varney, H. L. "Battle for the Lakes." *International Socialist Review* 17 (June 1917),
    pp. 731-32.

Veblen, Thorstein. "Using the I.W.W. to Harvest Grain—an unpublished paper on
    the I.W.W." *Journal of Political Economy* 40 (December 1932), pp. 796-807.
      —Memo to Hoover, 1918; appendix has April 1918 letter of Maurice
      Bresna, HWO

Venn, George W. "The Wobblies and Montana's Garden City." *Montana* 21
    (October 1971), pp. 18-30.

"The Victory at Lawrence." *International Socialist Review* 12 (April 1912), p. 679.

Vincent, Fred W. "Getting Out Airplane Spruce." *Scientific American* 119 (November 30, 1918), pp. 438-39.
> —The army lumbermen

_____. "Wing-bones of Victory." *Sunset* 30 (June 1918), pp. 30-69.
> —The western lumber story—the I.W.W.'s fault

"Violence and Democracy." *Outlook* 100 (February 17, 1912), pp. 352-53.
> —Lawrence

Vogler, Theodore K. "Centralia's Prisoners Stay Behind Bars." *Christian Century* 46 (April 4, 1929), pp. 450-51.
> —Parole board

Vorse, Mary H. "The Mining Strike in Minnesota—from the Miners' Point of View." *Outlook* 113 (August 30, 1916), pp. 1036, 1045-46.

_____. "The Police and the Unemployed." *New Review* 2 (September 1914), pp. 530-38.
> —Calvary Baptist unemployed

_____. "The Trouble at Lawrence." *Harper's Weekly* 56 (March 16, 1912), p.10.

Wagaman, David G. "The Industrial Workers of the World in Nebraska." *Nebraska History* 56 (Fall 1975), pp. 295-337.

Wahmann, Russell. "Railroading in the Verde Valley, 1894-1951." *Journal of Arizona History* 12 (Autumn 1971), pp. 153-66.
> —The railroads that carried the deportees

Walker, John H. "Revolt of the Copper Miners." *Syndicalist* 3 (September 1-15, 1913), p. 55.
> —News from Calumet, Michigan

Wallace, Andrew. "Colonel McClintock and the 1917 Copper Strike." *Arizoniana* 3 (Spring 1962), pp. 24-26.
> —Letters from the McClintock Collection

"War in Colorado." *Outlook* 107 (May 2, 1914), pp. 6-7.

Warrick, Sherry. "Radical Labor in Oklahoma: the Working Class Union." *Chronicles of Oklahoma* 52 (Summer 1974), pp. 180-95.
> —Help from the I.W.W.

Watne, Joel. "Public Opinion Toward Non-Conformists and Aliens During 1917." *North Dakota History* 34 (Winter 1967), pp. 6-29.

Watson, Fred. "Still on Strike: Recollections of a Bisbee Deportee." *Journal of Arizona History* 18 (Summer 1977), pp. 171-84.

Wax, Anthony. "Calumet and Hecla Copper Mines: An Episode in the Economic Development of Michigan." *Michigan History* 16 (Spring 1932), pp. 218-24.
> —Incredible praise for a "benevolent meritorious company"

Weed, Inis. "Reasons Why the Copper Miners Struck." *Outlook* 106 (January 31, 1914), pp. 247-51.
> —Michigan strike

Weintraub, Hyman. Rev. of *Rebels of the Woods*, Roberty Tyler. *Pacific Historical Review* 37 (November 1968), pp. 482-83.

Weisberger, Bernard A. "Here Come the Wobblies!" *American Heritage* 18 (June 1967), pp. 31-35, 87-93.

West, G. P. "After Liberalism Had Failed, the Imprisonment of the Striking Longshoremen in Los Angeles." *Nation* 116 (May 30, 1923), p. 629.
　　　—"Complete tie-up under I.W.W. auspices"; more on 400 striking longshoremen; San Pedro

＿＿＿＿. "The Mesaba Range Strike." *New Republic* 8 (September 2, 1916), pp. 108-9.

＿＿＿＿. "Mesabi Strike." *International Socialist Review* 17 (September 1916), pp. 158-61.

Wetzel, Kurt. "The Defeat of Bill Dunne; an episode in the Montana Red Scare." *Pacific Northwest Quarterly* 64 (1973), pp. 12-20.

Weyl, Walter. "It Is Time to Know." *Survey* 28 (April 6, 1912), pp. 65-67.
　　　—About Lawrence strike

＿＿＿＿. "The Lesson of Lawrence—It Is Time to Know." *Life & Labor* 2 (July 1912), pp. 196-97.

＿＿＿＿. "The Strikers at Lawrence." *Outlook* 100 (February 10, 1912), pp. 309-12.

"What Is Hostility to Government?" *Outlook* 104 (June 21, 1913), p. 351.
　　　—Alexander Scott and Paterson

"What Is the Matter with Minnesota?" *Nation* 85 (August 1, 1907), pp. 92-93.
　　　—Don't want strike? Others may insist on working man being honest and earning wages.

"Wheatland Boys." *International Socialist Review* 14 (January 1914), pp. 442-43.

"Wheatland Boys." *International Socialist Review* 14 (March 1914), p. 522.

"Wheatland Riot and What Lay Back of It." *Survey* 31 (March 21, 1914), pp. 768-70.

Wheeler, Robert J. "The Allentown Silk Dyers Strike." *International Socialist Review* 13 (May 1913), pp. 820-21.

Whitaker, Robert. "Centralia and the Churches." *Christian Century* 47 (December 3, 1930), pp. 1478-80.
　　　—Ripple effect in California; "Cowed spirit of people who are ordinarily good and kind, when official outrage and legal blundering is directed against economic heresy."

White, Earl Bruce. "Might Is Right: Unionism and Goldfield, Nevada, 1904 to 1908." *Journal of the West* 16 (July 1977), pp. 75-84.

Whitten, Woodrow C. "The Wheatland Episode." *Pacific Historical Review* 17 (February 1948), pp. 37-42.

"Why Negroes Should Join the I.W.W." *Messenger* 2 (July 1919), p. 8.

Wilson, Marjorie H. "Governor Hunt, the 'Beast' and the Miners." *Journal of Arizona History* 15 (Summer 1974), pp. 119-38.
　　　—Trying to keep the trouble down; with photos

Wing, M. T. C. "Flag at McKees Rocks." *Survey* 23 (October 2, 1909), pp. 45-46.
　　　—Marching with an American flag, then a flareback

Winstead, Ralph. "Enter a Logger: An I.W.W. Reply to the Four L's." *Survey* 44 (July 3, 1920), pp. 474-77.

"Winstead's 'Enter A Logger' Reply." *Survey* 44 (August 16, 1920), p. 640.

Wiprud, Theodore. "Butte: a Troubled Labor Paradise." *Montana* 21 (October 1971), pp. 31-38.
——National guard corporal's story of the Wobbly suppression

Withington, Anne. "The Lawrence Strike." *Life & Labor* 2 (March 1912), pp. 73-77.

"Wobblies in the Northwest." *Nation* 145 (November 13, 1937), p. 543.
——Description of Idaho short-log strike of I.W.W.—June 1936—Potlatch—asked for troops; letter by R. M. K.

Woehlke, Walter V. "Bolshevikis of the West." *Sunset* 40 (January 1918), pp. 14-16, 70-72.

——. "The I.W.W. and the Golden Rule—Why Everett Used the Club and Gun on the Red Apostles of Direct Action." *Sunset* 38 (February 1917), pp. 16-18, 62-65.
——Shingle-weavers' story and Everett

——. "Porterhouse Heaven and the Hobo." *Technical World* 21 (August 1914), pp. 808-18, 938.
——Hoboes of the West; Ford and Suhr

——. "Red Rebels Declare War." *Sunset* 39 (September 1917), pp. 20-21.
——"Professional revolutionaries are using the national emergency to cripple the capitalists"—Yakima and elsewhere out west

——. "Revolution in America; Seattle Crushes the First Soviet Uprising." *Sunset* 42 (April 1919), pp. 13-16, 64.
——Photos; "the strong wine of power went to their heads—nobody lost who placed his coin on America to win."

Wolff, W. A. "The Northwestern Front." *Collier's Weekly* 61 (April 20, 1918), pp. 10-11, 31-32.
——Colonel Disque as answer to I.W.W.

Woods, R. A. "The Breadth and Depth of the Lawrence Outcome." *Survey* 28 (April 6, 1912), pp. 67-68.

——. "The Clod Stirs." *Survey* 27 (March 16, 1912), pp. 1929-32.

"Work of the I.W.W. in Paterson." *Literary Digest* 47 (August 9, 1913), pp. 197-198.

Wortman, Roy. "The Resurgence of the I.W.W. in Cleveland: A Neglected Aspect of Labor History." *Northwest Ohio Quarterly* 47 (Winter 1974-75), pp. 20-29.

Wortman, Roy, ed. "An I.W.W. Document on the 1919 Rossford Strike." *Northwest Ohio Quarterly* 43 (Summer 1971), pp. 20-29.
——Strike at the Ford Plate Glass Company—last effort until the 1930s

"Youngstown and Americanization." *Outlook* 112 (January 26, 1916), p. 168.

"Youngstown: The Riot." *Outlook* 112 (January 19, 1916), pp. 121-23.

Zieger, Robert H. Rev. of *Bread and Roses Too*, Joseph Conlin. *Labor History*
      11 (Fall 1970), pp. 564-69.
_____. "Robin Hood in the Silk City: the I.W.W. and the Paterson Silk Strike of
      1913." *New Jersey History* (*Proceedings of the New Jersey Historical
      Society* 84 (July 1966), pp. 182-95.

BOOKS

Adamic, Louis. *Dynamite: The Story of Class Violence in America*. Gloucester,
      Massachusetts: P. Smith, 1960 (c. 1931).
Adams, Graham, Jr. *Age of Industrial Violence, 1910-1915; the Activities and
      Findings of the United States Commission on Industrial Relations*. New
      York: Columbia University Press, 1966.
Albrecht, Arthur E. *International Seamen's Union of America*. Bulletin of
      United States Bureau of Labor Statistics, No. 342. Washington, D.C.:
      G.P.O., 1913.
Allen, Ruth. *East Texas Lumber Workers; an Economic and Social Picture, 1870-
      1950*. Austin: University of Texas Press, 1961.
Ameringer, Oscar. *If You Don't Weaken: The Autobiography of Oscar
      Ameringer*. New York: H. Holt and Co., 1940.
Anderson, Nels. *The Hobo: The Sociology of the Homeless*. Chicago: University
      of Chicago Press, 1923.
Baratz, Morton S. *The Union and the Coal Industry*. New Haven: Yale University
      Press, 1955.
Bardwell, George E., and Seligson, Harry. *Organized Labor and Political Action
      in Colorado, 1900-1960*. Denver: College of Business Administration,
      University of Denver, 1959,
Barger, H., and Schurr, S. H. *The Mining Industries, 1899-1939*. New York:
      Bureau of Economic Research, 1944.
Barnett, George E., and McCabe, David A. *Mediation, Investigation and
      Arbitration in Industrial Disputes*. New York: Appleton and Company, 1916.
Beal, Fred. *Proletarian Journey: New England, Gastonia, Moscow*. New York:
      Hillman-Curl, 1937.
Beal, Merrill D., and Wells, Merle. *History of Idaho*. New York: Lewis Historical
      Publishing Co., 1959.
Bean, Walton. *Boss Ruef's San Francisco: The Story of the Union Labor Party,
      Big Business, and the Graft Prosecution*. Berkeley: University of California
      Press, 1952.
Bedford, Henry F. *Socialism and the Workers in Massachusetts, 1889-1912*.
      Amherst: University of Massachusetts Press, 1966.
Bercuson, David J. *Confrontation at Winnipeg: Labour, Industrial Relations
      and the General Strike*. Montreal: McGill-Queen's University Press, 1974.
Beshoar, Barron B. *Out of the Depths*. Denver: the Denver Trades and Labor
      Assembly, 1942.

Bing, Alexander M. *War-time Strikes and Their Adjustment*. New York: E. P. Dutton and Company, 1921.

Binns, Archie. *Sea in the Forest*. Garden City, New York: Doubleday & Co., 1953.

_____. *Northwest Gateway, the Story of the Port of Seattle*. Garden City, New York: Doubleday, Doran & Co., 1941.

Blaisdell, Lowell L. *The Desert Revolution, Baja California, 1911*. Madison: University of Wisconsin Press, 1962.

Blegen, Theodore C. *Minnesota: A History of the State*. Minneapolis: University of Minneapolis Press, 1963.

Bloor, Ella Reeve. *We Are Many*. New York: International Press, 1940.

Botkin, B. A., ed. *Treasury of Western Folklore*, rev. ed. New York: Crown, 1975 (1951).

Boyer, Richard O., and Morais, Herbert M. *Labor's Untold Story*. New York: Cameron Associates, 1955.

Brissenden, Paul F. *The I.W.W.: A Study of American Syndicalism*. Columbia University Studies in History, Economics and Public Law, No. 193. New York: Columbia University Press, 1919.

_____. *Launching of the Industrial Workers of the World*. University of California Publications in Economics, vol. 4, no. 1. Berkeley: University of California Press, 1913.

Brody, David. *Labor in Crisis: The Steel Strike of 1919*. Philadelphia: Lippincott, 1965.

Brooks, John G. *American Syndicalism: The I.W.W.* New York: Da Capo Press, 1970 (1913).

Brooks, Thomas R. *Toil and Trouble: A History of American Labor*, 2d ed. New York: Delacorte Press, 1971.

Budish, Jacob M., and Soule, George. *New Unionism in the Clothing Industry*. New York: Harcourt, Brace and Howe, 1920.

Burns, William J. *The Masked War: The Story of a Peril that Threatened the United States, by a Man Who Uncovered the Dynamite Conspirators and Sent Them to Jail*. New York: George H. Doran, 1913.

Byington, Margaret F. *Homestead: The Households of a Mill Town*. Pittsburgh Survey, vol. 4. New York: Charities Publication Committee, 1910.

Cahn, William. *Mill Town*. New York: Cameron & Kahn, 1954.

Cannon, James P. *Notebook of an Agitator*. New York: Pioneer Publishers, 1958.

Caughey, John W. *Their Majesties, the Mob*. Chicago: University of Chicago Press, 1960.

Chaffee, Zechariah, Jr. *Freedom of Speech*. New York: Harcourt, Brace and Howe, 1920.

_____. *Free Speech in the United States*. Cambridge: Harvard University Press, 1941.

Chaplin, Ralph. *Wobbly: The Rough and Tumble Story of an American Radical*. Chicago: University of Chicago Press, 1948.

Chrislock, Carl H. *The Progressive Era in Minnesota, 1899-1918*. St. Paul: Minnesota Historical Society, 1971.

Claghorn, Kate H. *the Immigrant's Day in Court*. New York: Harper & Bros., 1923.

Clark, Norman H. *Mill Town: A Social History of Everett, Washington, from its Earliest Beginnings on the Shores of Puget Sound to the Tragic and Infamous Event Known as the Everett Massacre*. Seattle: University of Washington Press, 1970.

Coben, Stanely. *A. Mitchell Palmer: Politician*. New York: Columbia University Press, 1963.

Cohen, Julius H. *Law and Order in Industry: Five Years' Experience*. New York: Macmillan, 1916.

Cole, Donald B. *Immigrant City: Lawrence, Massachusetts, 1845-1921*. Chapel Hill: University of North Carolina Press, 1963.

Coleman, McAlister. *Men and Coal*. New York: Farrar and Rinehart, 1943.

Collier, John. *The First Fifty Years of the Southern Pine Association, 1915-1965*. New Orleans: Southern Pine Association, 1965.

Colquhoun, James. *The Early History of the Clifton-Morenci District*. London: William Clowes & Sons, 1935.

Commons, John R. *Labor and Administration*. New York: A. M. Kelley, Bookseller, 1964 (1913).

Conlin, Joseph R. *Big Bill Haywood and the Radical Labor Movement*. Syracuse: Syracuse University Press, 1969.

_____. *Bread and Roses Too: Studies of the Wobblies*. Westport, Connecticut: Greenwood Publishing Corp., 1969.

Cross, Ira B. *A History of the Labor Movement in California*. Publications in Economics, vol. 14. Berkeley: University of California Press, 1935.

Darrow, Clarence S. *The Story of My Life*. New York: C. Scribner's Sons, 1932.

Debs, Eugene V. *Eugene V. Debs Speaks*. Edited by Jean Y. Tussey. New York: Pathfinder Press, 1970.

De Caux, Len. *Labor Radical; from the Wobblies to the CIO*. Boston: Beacon Press, 1970.

_____. *The Living Spirit of the Wobblies*. New York: International Publishers, 1978.

Delaney, Ed, and Rice, M. T. *The Bloodstained Trail: A History of Militant Labor in the United States*. Seattle: Industrial Worker, 1927.

Dell, Floyd. *Homecoming: An Autobiography*. New York: Farrar and Rinehart, 1933.

Dowell, Eldridge F. *A History of Criminal Syndicalism Legislation in the United States*. Baltimore: Johns Hopkins Press, 1939.

Dreiser, Thoedore, et al. *Harlan Miners Speak: Report of Terrorism in the Kentucky Coal Fields*. New York: Harcourt, Brace, 1932.

Dubofsky, Melvyn. *Industrialism and the American Worker, 1865-1920*. New York: Crowell, 1975.

_____. *We Shall Be All: A History of the Industrial Workers of the World.* Chicago: Quadrangle Books, 1969.

Dunn, Robert W., ed. *The Palmer Raids.* New York: International Publishers, 1948.

Dunne, William F. *The Great San Francisco General Strike: The Story of the West Coast Strike, the Bay Counties General Strike, and the Maritime Workers' Strike.* New York: Workers Library, 1934.

Eaves, Lucile. *A History of California Labor Legislation, With an Introductory Sketch of the San Francisco Labor Movement.* Publications in Economics, vol. 2. Berkeley: University of California Press, 1910.

Ebert, Justus. *The Trial of a New Society, Being a Review of the Celebrated Ettor-Giovannitti-Caruso Case, Beginning with the Lawrence Textile Strike.* Cleveland: I.W.W. Publishing Bureau, 1913.

Elliott, Russell R. *Nevada's Twentieth-Century Mining Booms: Tonopah, Goldfield, Ely.* Reno: University of Nevada Press, 1966.

_____. *Radical Labor in the Nevada Mining Booms, 1900-1920.* Carson City, Nevada: State Printing Office, 1961.

Faulk, Odie B. *Land of Many Frontiers: A History of the American Southwest.* New York: Oxford University Press, 1968.

Flynn, Elizabeth Gurley. *The Rebel Girl: An Autobiography, My First Life, 1906-1926.* New York: International Publishers, 1973.

_____. *Debs, Haywood, Ruthenberg.* New York: Workers Library Publishers, 1939.

_____. *I Speak My Own Piece: Autobiography of "The Rebel Girl."* New York: Masses and Mainstream, 1955.

Foner, Philip S. *The Bolshevik Revolution: Its Impact on American Radicals Liberals and Labor: A Documentary Study.* New York: International Publishers, 1967.

_____. *The Case of Joe Hill.* New York: International Publishers, 1965.

_____. *History of the Labor Movement in the United States: From the Founding of the American Federation of Labor to the Emergence of American Imperialism*, vol. 4. New York: International Publishers, 1965.

_____. *Organized Labor and the Black Worker, 1619-1973.* New York: Praeger Publishers, 1974.

Foster, William Z. *Pages from a Worker's Life.* New York: International Publishers, 1939.

_____. *From Bryan to Stalin.* New York: International Publishers, 1937.

_____. *The Great Steel Strike and Its Lessons.* New York: B. W. Huebach, 1920.

Freeman, Harry. *A Brief History of Butte, Montana.* Chicago: Henry O. Shepard Co., 1900.

Friedheim, Robert. *The Seattle General Strike.* Seattle: University of Washington, 1964.

Fritz, Percy S. *Colorado: The Centennial State.* New York: Prentice-Hall, Inc., 1941.

Frost, Richard. *The Mooney Case.* Stanford: Stanford University Press, 1968.

Fuchs, Lawrence H. *Hawaii Pono. A Social History*. New York: Harcourt, Brace and World, Inc., 1961.

Fuller, George W. *A History of the Pacific Northwest*. New York: Alfred A. Knopf, 1931.

Gambs, John S. *The Decline of the I. W. W.* Columbia University Studies in History, Economics and Public Law, No. 361. New York: Columbia University Press, 1932.

Gandy, L. C. *The Tabors; a Footnote of Western History*. New York: Press of the Pioneers, Inc., 1934.

Gates, William B. Jr. *Michigan Copper and Boston Dollars, an Economic History of the Michigan Copper Mining Industry*. Cambridge: Harvard University Press, 1951.

Gentry, Curt. *Frame-Up; The Incredible Case of Tom Mooney and Warren Billings*. New York: Norton, 1967.

Ginger, Ray. *The Bending Cross: A Biography of Eugene V. Debs*. New Brunswick: Rutgers University Press, 1949.

Gitlow, Benjamin. *I Confess, the Truth About American Communism*. New York: E. P. Dutton, 1940.

Glasscock, C. B. *Gold in Them Hills; the Story of the West's Last Wild Mining Days*. Indianapolis: Bobbs-Merrill Co., 1932.

_____. *The War of the Copper Kings: Builders of Butte and Wolves of Wall Street*. Indianapolis: Bobbs-Merrill Co., 1935.

Glock, Margaret. *Collective Bargaining in the Pacific Northwest Lumber Industry*. Institute of Industrial Relations. Berkeley: University of California Press, 1955.

Goldman, Emma. *Living My Life*, vol. 1. New York: A. Knopf, 1931.

Goldman, Eric. *Rendezvous With Destiny: A History of Modern American Reform*. New York: A. Knopf, 1952.

Greaves, C. D. *The Life and Times of James Connolly*. London: Lawrence and Wishart, 1961.

Grover, David H. *Debaters and Dynamiters: The Story of the Haywood Trial*. Corvallis: Oregon State University Press, 1964.

Hanson, Ole. *Americanism versus Bolshevism*. New York: Doubleday, Page & Co., 1920.

Hapgood, Hutchins. *A Victorian in the Modern World*. New York: Harcourt, Brace & Co., 1939.

Hapgood, Norman, ed. *Professional Patriots*. New York: A. and C. Boni, 1927.

Hardy, George. *Those Stormy Years. Memories of the Fight for Freedom on Five Continents*. London: Laurence and Wishart, 1956.

Hawley, J. H. *History of Idaho, the Gem of the Mountains*. Chicago: S. J. Clarke Publishing Co., 1920.

Hawley, Lowell S., and Potts, Ralph B. *Council for the Damned: A Biography of George Francis Vanderveer*. Philadelphia: Lippincott, 1953.

Haywood, William D. *Bill Haywood's Book: The Autobiography of William D. Haywood.* New York: International Publishers, 1958 (1929).

Hicks, Granville, *John Reed: The Making of a Revolutionary.* New York: MacMillan, 1936.

Hidy, Ralph W., Hill, Frank E., and Nevins, Allan. *Timber and Men: The Weyerhaeuser Story.* New York: Macmillan, 1963.

Higham, John. *Strangers in the Land: Patterns of American Nativism, 1860-1925.* New York: Atheneum, 1968 (1955).

Hillstrom, Joseph. *The Letters of Joe Hill.* Comp. and ed. by Philip S. Foner. New York: Oak Publications, 1965.

Hofstadter, Richard. *The Age of Reform; from Bryan to F.D.R.* New York: A. Knopf, 1955.

Hoglund, A. William. *Finnish Immigrants in America, 1880-1920.* Madison: University of Wisconsin Press, 1960.

Holbrook, Stewart H. *Holy Old Mackinaw: A Natural History of the American Lumberjack.* New York: Macmillan, 1939.

_____. *The Rocky Mountain Revolution.* New York: Henry Holt, 1956.

Hough, Emerson. *The Web.* Chicago: Reilly & Lee Co., 1919.

Howard, Sidney C. *The Labor Spy.* New York: Republic Publishing Co., 1924.

Howbert, I. *Memories of a Lifetime in the Pike's Peak Region.* New York: G. P. Putnam Sons, 1925.

Howd, Cloice R. *Industrial Relations in the West Coast Lumber Industry.* Bulletin of the United States Bureau of Labor Statistics, No. 349. Washington, D.C.: G.P.O., 1924.

Hulse, James W. *The Nevada Adventure: A History.* Reno: University of Nevada Press, 1969.

Hunter, Robert. *Violence and the Labor Movement.* New York: Macmillan Co., 1919.

Hyman, Harold. *Soldiers and Spruce: Origins of the Loyal Legion of Loggers and Lumbermen.* Los Angeles: University of California Press, 1963.

Interchurch World Movement of North America, Commission of Inquiry. *Report on the Steel Strike of 1919.* New York: Putnam, 1923.

Jaffe, Julian F. *Crusade Against Radicalism: New York During the Red Scare, 1914-1924.* Port Washington, New York: Kennikat Press, 1972.

Jamieson, Stuart. *Labor Unionism in American Agriculture.* Washington, D.C.: G.P.O., 1945.

Jensen, Joan. *Price of Vigilance.* Chicago: Rand McNally, 1968.

Jensen, Vernon H. *Heritage of Conflict: Labor Relations in the Nonferrous Metals Industry up to 1930.* Ithaca: Cornell University Press, 1950.

_____. *Lumber and Labor.* New York: Arno Press, 1971 (1945).

Johnson, Claudius. *Borah of Idaho.* New York: Longmans Green and Co., 1936.

Johnson, Olive M. *Daniel De Leon, American Socialist Pathfinder.* New York: New York Labor News Company, 1935 (1923).

Jones, Alden H. *From Jamestown to Coffin Rock; a History of Weyerhaeuser Operations in Southwest Washington.* Tacoma: Weyerhaeuser Co., 1974.

Jones, Mary Harris. *Autobiography of Mother Jones.* 3d ed., with intro. and bibl. by Fred Thompson. Chicago: Charles H. Kerr, 1975 (1925).

Karni, Michael G., ed. *The Finnish Experience in the Western Great Lakes Region: New Perspectives.* Institute for Migration, Turku, Finland, in cooperation with the Immigration History Research Center. Minneapolis: University of Minnesota Press, 1975.

Keller, Helen. *Helen Keller: Her Socialist Years; Writings and Speeches.* Edited by P. S. Foner. New York: International Publishers, 1967.

Kleinsorge, Paul L. *Boulder Canyon Project: Historical and Economic Aspects.* Stanford: Stanford University Press, 1941.

Kluger, James R. *The Clifton—Morenci Strike Labor Difficulty in Arizona 1915-1916.* Tucson: University of Arizona Press, 1970.

Knight, Harold V. *Working in Colorado: A Brief History of the Colorado Labor Movement.* Boulder: Center for Labor Education and Research, University of Colorado, 1971.

Knight, Robert E. L. *Industrial Relations in the San Francisco Bay Area, 1900-1918.* Berkeley: University of California Press, 1960.

Koelsch, Charles F. *The Haywood Case.* Boise: Idaho Mining Association, 1946.

Kornbluh, Joyce L., ed. *Rebel Voices: An I.W.W. Anthology.* Ann Arbor: University of Michigan Press, 1964.

Lane, Roger, and Turner, John J., Jr. *Riot, Rout, and Tumult. Readings in American Social and Political Violence.* Continuing American History. Westport, Connecticut: Greenwood Press, 1977.

Lane, Winthrop D. *Civil War in West Virginia: A Story of the Industrial Conflict in the Coal Mines.* New York: Arno Press, 1976 (1921).

Langdon, Emma F. *The Cripple Creek Strike: A History of Industrial Wars in Colorado, 1903-4-5.* Denver: Great Western, 1905.

_____. *Labor's Greatest Conflict: The Formation of the Western Federation of Miners—a Brief Account of the Rise of the United Mine Workers of America.* Denver: Great Western, 1908.

Larkin, Emmet. *James Larkin, Irish Labour Leader, 1876-1947.* Cambridge: MIT Press, 1965.

Lasswell, Mary. *John Henry Kirby, Prince of the Pines.* Austin: Encino Press, 1967.

Lens, Sidney. *The Labor Wars: From the Molly Maguires to the Sit-downs.* Garden City, New York: Doubleday, 1973.

Levin, Murray B. *Political Hysteria in America: The Democratic Capacity for Repression.* New York: Basic Books, 1971.

Lovestone, Jay. *The Government: Strikebreaker.* New York: Workers Party of America, 1923.

Lowenthal, Leo, and Guterman, Norbert. *Prophets of Deceit: A Study of the Techniques of the American Agitator.* New York: Harper and Brothers, 1950.

Lucia, Ellis. *Head Rig: Story of the West Coast Lumber Industry*. Portland: Overland West Press, 1965.

Luhan, Mable Dodge. *Movers and Shakers*. New York: Harcourt, Brace, 1936.

Marot, Helen. *American Labor Unions*. New York: Holt, 1914.

Mason, Alpheus T. *Organized Labor and the Law*. Durham, North Carolina: Duke University Press, 1925.

McNaught, Kenneth, and Bercuson, David J. *The Winnipeg Strike, 1919*. Don Mills, Ontario: Longman, 1974.

McWilliams, Carey. *Factories in the Field: The Story of Migratory Farm Labor in California*. Boston: 1939.

Morgan, Murray. *Skid Road: An Informal Portrait of Seattle*. New York: Viking Press, 1951.

Morlan, Robert L. *Political Prairie Fire: The Nonpartisan League*. Minneapolis: University of Minnesota Press, 1955.

Murdoch, Angus. *Boom Copper*. New York: Macmillan Co., 1943.

Murray, Robert K. *Great Red Scare: A Study in National Hysteria*. Minneapolis: University of Minneapolis Press, 1955.

National Industrial Conference Board. *Strikes in American Industry in War Time*. Research Report No. 3. Washington, D.C.: National Industrial Conference Board, 1918.

O'Connor, Harvey. *Revolution in Seattle*. New York: Monthly Review Press, 1964.

O'Connor, Richard, and Walker, Dale L. *The Lost Revolutionary: A Biography of John Reed*. New York: Harcourt, Brace and World, 1967.

Orchard, Harry. (Albert E. Horsley) *The Confessions and Autobiography of Harry Orchard*. New York: S. S. McClure Co., 1907.

Orth, Samuel P. *The Armies of Labor*. New Haven: Yale University Press, 1919.

Panunzio, Constantine M. *The Deportation Cases of 1919-1920*. New York: Commission on the Church and Social Service, 1921.

Parker, Carleton H. *The Casual Laborer and Other Essays*. New York: Russell and Russell, 1967 (1920).

Peterson, H. C., and Fite, Gilbert C. *Opponents of War 1917-1918*. Madison: University of Wisconsin Press, 1957.

Post, Louis Freeland. *The Deportations Delirium of Nineteen twenty: A Personal Narrative of an Historic Official Experience*. Intro. by Moorfield Storey. Chicago: C. H. Kerr and Co., 1923.

Potts, Ralph B. *Seattle Heritage*. Seattle: Superior Publishing Co., 1955.

Preston, William. *Aliens and Dissenters: Federal Suppression of Radicals, 1903-1933*. Cambridge: Harvard University Press, 1963.

Rastall, Benjamin M. *The Labor History of the Cripple Creek District*. University of Wisconsin Bulletin No. 198. Madison: University of Wisconsin Press, 1908.

Reeve, Carl, and Reeve, Ann B. *James Conolly and the United States—the Road to the 1916 Irish Rebellion*. Atlantic Highlands, New Jersey: Humanities Press, 1978.

Renshaw, Patrick. *The Wobblies: The Story of Syndicalism in the United States.* Garden City, New York: Doubleday, 1967.

Richmond, Alexander. *Native Daughter: The Story of Anita Whitney.* San Francisco: Anita Whitney 75th Anniversary Committee, 1942.

Rubin, Lester. *The Negro in the Longshore Industry.* Report No. 29. Philadelphia: University of Pennsylvania Press, 1974.

Rubin, Lester, Swift, William S., and Northrup, Herbert R. *Negro Employment in the Maritime Industries: A Study of Racial Policies in the Shipbuilding, Longshore and Offshore Maritime Industries.* Philadelphia: Industrial Research Unit, the Wharton School, 1974.

Sanders, H. F. *A History of Montana.* Chicago and New York: Lewis Publishing Co., 1930.

_____. *Left Wing Unionism, A Study of Radical Policies and Tactics.* New York: Russell & Russell, 1967 (1926).

Savage, Marion Dutton. *Industrial Unionism in America.* New York: Ronald Press, 1922.

Schonbach, Morris. *Radicals and Visionaries: A History of Dissent in New Jersey.* Princeton: Van Nostrand, 1964.

Schroeder, Theodore. *Free Speech for Radicals.* Riverside, Connecticut: Hillacre Bookhouse, 1916.

The Seattle General Strike: An Account of What Happened in Seattle and Especially in the Seattle Labor Movement During the General Strike February 6 to 11, 1919. Seattle: Seattle Union Record Publishing Co., 1919.

Selekman, Ben M., and van Kleeck, Mary. *Employee's Representation in the Coal Mines.* New York: Russell Sage Foundation, 1924.

Selekman, Sylvia K. *Rebellion in Labor Unions.* New York: Boni and Liveright, 1924.

Smelser, David P. *Unemployment and American Trade Unions.* Johns Hopkins University Studies in the Social Sciences. 37th series. Baltimore: Johns Hopkins University Press, 1919.

Smith, Gibbs M. *Joe Hill.* Salt Lake City: The University of Utah Press, 1969.

Smith, Walker C. *The Everett Massacre: A History of the Class Struggle in the Lumber Industry.* Chicago: I.W.W., 1917; New York: Da Capo, 1971.

Smolen, Joseph S. *Organized Labor in Minnesota: A Brief History.* St. Paul: Minnesota AFL-CIO Federation of Labor, 1965.

Spero, Sterling D., and Harris, Abram L. *The Black Worker: The Negro and the Labor Movement.* New York: Columbia University Press, 1931.

Sprague, Marshall. *Money Mountain: The Story of Cripple Creek Gold.* Boston: Little, Brown, 1953.

Steffens, J. Lincoln. *The Autobiography of Lincoln Steffens.* New York: Harcourt, Brace, 1931.

Steiger, John H. *The Memoirs of a Silk Striker, an exposure of the principles and tactics of the I. W. W.* Paterson, New Jersey: Privately printed, 1914.

Steuben, John. *Labor in Wartime*. New York: International Publishers, 1940.

Stimson, Grace H. *The Rise of the Labor Movement in Los Angeles, 1870-1914*. Berkeley: University of California Press, 1955.

Stone, Irving. *Clarence Darrow for the Defense*. Garden City, New York: Doubleday, Doran and Co., 1941.

Stone, W. F. *History of Colorado*. 5 vols. Chicago: J. S. Clarke, 1918-1919.

Strong, Anna Louise. *I Changed Worlds; the Remaking of an American*. Garden City, New York: Garden City Publishing Co., 1937.

Suggs, George G., Jr. *Colorado's War on Militant Unionism: James H. Peabody and the Western Federation of Miners*. Detroit: Wayne State University Press, 1972.

Symes, Lillian, and Travers, Clement. *Rebel America: The Story of Social Revolt in the United States*. New York: Harper, 1934.

Taylor, Paul S. *The Sailors Union of the Pacific*. New York: The Ronald Press, 1923.

Thompson, Fred. *The I.W.W. Its First Seventy Years, 1905-1975*. Chicago: Industrial Workers of the World, 1977.

Three Views of the Armistice Day Tragedy at Centralia, Washington, November 11, 1919; The Centralia Conspiracy, by Ralph Chaplin; Centralia: Tragedy and Trial by Ben Hur Lampman; The Centralia Case: a Joint Report. New York: Da Capo Press, 1971.

Todes, Charlotte. *Lumber and Labor*. New York: International Publishers, 1931.

Toplin, Robert B. *Unchallenged Violence: An American Ordeal*. Westport, Connecticut: Greenwood Press, 1975.

Tridon, André. *The New Unionism*. New York: B. W. Huebsch, 1913.

Trotsky, Leon. *My Life*. New York: Charles Scribner's Sons, 1930.

Troy, Leo. *Organized Labor in New Jersey*. Princeton: D. Van Nostrand, 1965.

Tyler, Robert L. *Rebels of the Woods: The I.W.W. in the Pacific Northwest*. Eugene: University of Oregon Press, 1967.

Urofsky, Melvin. *Big Steel and the Wilson Administration: A Study in Business and Government Relations*. Columbus: Ohio State University Press, 1969.

Van Tine, Warren R. *The Making of the Labor Bureaucrat: Union Leadership in the United States, 1870-1926*. Amherst: University of Massachusetts Press, 1973.

Veblen, Thorstein. *Essays in Our Changing Order*. Edited by L. Ardzrooni. New York: Viking Press, 1934.

Vorse, Mary Heaton. *Footnote to Folly*. New York: Farrar and Rinehart, 1935.

_____. *Labor's New Millions*. New York: Modern Age Books, 1938.

Walker, Charles R. *American City: A Rank-and-File History*. New York: Farrar and Rinehart, 1937; New York: Arno Press, 1971.

_____. *Steeltown, an Industrial Case History of the Conflict Between Progress and Security*. New York: Harper, 1950.

Warner, Hoyt L. *Progressivism in Ohio, 1897-1917*. Columbus: Ohio State
University Press, 1964.

Warner, Sam Bass. *The Private City: Philadelphia in Three Periods of Its Growth*.
Philadelphia: University of Pennsylvania Press, 1968.

Weinberg, Arthur M., ed. *Attorney for the Damned*. New York: Simon and
Schuster, 1957.

Weinstein, James. *The Decline of Socialism in America, 1912-1925*. New York:
Monthly Review Press, 1967.

_____. *Amibiguous Legacy: The Left in American Politics*. New York: New
Viewpoints, 1975.

Werstein, Irving. *Pie in the Sky: An American Struggle, the Wobblies and Their
Time*. New York: Delacorte Press, 1969.

Willison, George F. *Here They Dug Gold, the Story of the Colorado Gold Rush*.
New York: A. L. Burt Co., 1931; London: Eyre and Spottiswoode, 1950.

Winther, Oscar Osburn. *The Great Northwest: A History*. New York: A. A. Knopf,
1947.

Wood, Clement, et al. *Don't Tread on Me: A Study of Aggressive Legal Tactics
For Labor*. New York: Vanguard Press, 1928.

Woodward, C. Vann. *Origins of the New South, 1877-1913*. Baton Rouge:
Louisiana State University Press, 1951.

Wright, James E. *The Politics of Populism: Dissent in Colorado*. New Haven:
Yale University Press, 1974.

Yellen, Samuel. *American Labor Struggles*. New York: Monad Press, 1974.
(1936, 1956, 1969).

Yellowitz, Irwin. *Labor and the Progressive Movement in New York State,
1897-1916*. Ithaca: Cornell University Press, 1965.

INDEX

CONTRIBUTORS

Joseph R. Conlin, the editor of this volume, has written over a dozen articles on the subject of the I.W.W. and related topics as well as *Big Bill Haywood and the Radical Union Movement* (1969); *Bread and Roses Too: Essays on the Wobblies* (1969); and *The American Radical Press* (1974). He has lectured extensively on American social history in the United States, England, and Italy.

James E. Fickle is a well-known authority on labor and economic history, particularly in reference to the forest products industry of the southern states. He is the author of *The New South and the New Competition* (1979) and is presently associate professor of history at Memphis State University.

Patrick M. Lynch is a tenth-grade world cultures teacher in the North Allegheny School District in Pittsburgh. His M.A. thesis at Bloomsburg State College, Pennsylvania (1975), centered on I.W.W. activities in the Pennsylvania anthracite fields. He is a doctoral candidate at the University of Pittsburgh, continuing his studies of the I.W.W. in the Pittsburgh region, and is actively involved in curriculum development in the Pittsburgh schools.

Ronald L. McMahan is director of the Western Coal Mining Project of the University of Colorado, Institute of Behavioral Science. He is currently completing production of a public broadcast series on the life of the western coal miner and has previously produced "Coal Mining as a Way of Life," "Black Lung," and "Coal Miners Look at Strip Mining," video productions. He recently published "Understanding Impact: Visual Media and Reflexive Research" in Roy S. Dickins and Carol Hill, *Cultural Resources* (1978).

Dione Miles is the reference archivist at the Archives of Labor and Urban Affairs, Walter P. Reuther Library, Wayne State University, Detroit. She received her M.S.L.S. degree from Wayne State University and processed and arranged the extensive I.W.W. papers there, writing the *Guide and Index* to the collection. She is presently compiling a complete bibliography of the I.W.W. to be published in honor of the union's seventy-fifth anniversary.

James Newbill is a member of the history department of Yakima Valley College, Washington, where he teaches American and European history. He has been awarded two Fulbright fellowships, the William Robertson Coe fellowship at Stanford University, and a research grant from the National Endowment for the Humanities. With the latter, Mr. Newbill began his work in labor history and published "Farmers and Wobblies in the Yakima Valley, 1933" in the *Pacific Northwest Quarterly* (April 1977). His essay in this volume is an expansion on that article. Mr. Newbill is coeditor of *The American Spectrum* (1971).

James D. Osborne received his Ph.D. from the University of Warwick in England for his work on the social history of the industry and working class of Paterson, New Jersey. Another part of this research was published as "Italian Immigrants and the Working Class in Paterson: The Strike of 1913 in Ethnic Perspective" in Paul A. Stellhorn, ed., *New Jersey's Ethnic Heritage*. A study of discontent among British soldiers in World War I (with David Englander) appeared in *The Historical Journal* (1978).

Guy Louis Rocha is curator of manuscripts at the Nevada Historical Society, Reno. He received his B.A. from Syracuse University and his M.A. from San Diego State University. Mr. Rocha is currently completing his doctorate at the University of Nevada. Among his research interests is the history of organized labor in Nevada, and he is the author of "Radical Labor Struggles in the Tonopah-Goldfield Mining Districts, 1901-1922," *Nevada Historical Society Quarterly* (Spring 1977). He has written numerous other articles for Nevada newspapers and county historical society journals and an earlier version of his essay in this volume appeared in the *Nevada Historical Society Quarterly* (Spring 1978).

Robert E. Snyder studied at Union College and received his Ph.D. from Syracuse University where he is presently a teaching associate. His articles have received several awards: "Huey Long and the Cotton Holiday Plan" was awarded the General L. Kemper Williams Prize in 1974 for the best article-length manuscript on southern history by an unpublished author; the Louisiana Historical Society selected "Huey Long and the Presidential Election of 1936" for the Robert Brown Award for the best article in *Louisiana History* in 1975; the Mississippi Historical Society awarded the Willie D. Halsell Prize for the best article in *The Journal of Mississippi History* in 1978 to "The Cotton Holiday Movement in Mississippi." Other essays by Mr. Snyder have appeared in *Southern Studies* and his contribution to *At the Point of Production* appeared in *New York History* (1979).

David G. Wagaman is senior executive management analyst for postsecondary education in the Governor's Budget Office in Lincoln, Nebraska. His major areas of research have been the history of labor and collective bargaining in the public sector.

"The Evolution of Some Legal-Economic Aspects of Collective Bargaining by Public Employees in Nebraska since 1919" was published in *Nebraska History* (1977). Dr. Wagaman received the James A. Sellers Award for excellence in research in 1976 from the Nebraska State Historical Society and, in 1977, an award for excellence in research by a graduate student from the College of Business Administration. An earlier, less extensive version of the present article appeared in *Nebraska History* (1975).

Earl Bruce White is associate professor of history at Sterling College, Kansas. He has been studying the I.W.W. with particular emphasis on the early years with the Western Federation and has published a number of articles on the subject: "Archives of the Western Federation of Miners and the International Union of Mine, Mill, and Smelter Workers and the Latin American Historian," *The Americas* (1975); "A Note on the Archives of the Western Federation of Miners" (1976); "Might is Right: Unionism and Goldfield, Nevada, 1904-1908," *Journal of the West* (1977).

Roy Wortman is assistant professor of history at Kenyon College, Gambier, Ohio. He received his Ph.D. from Ohio State University and has published articles on the Wobblies in *Northwest Ohio Quarterly* and *Historical Musings*. An essay on "Denver's Anti-Chinese Riot, 1880" appeared in *Anti-Chinese Violence in North America* (1979). He is currently researching the history of the Ohio Farmers Union and is producing a videotape history of Ohio's citizen-soldiers.